Social and Psychological Factors in Stress

With contributions by:

Irwin Altman
Thomas E. Drabek
J. Eugene Haas
J. Richard Hackman
William W. Haythorn
Robert L. Kahn
Richard Lazarus
David Mechanic
S. B. Sells
Ivan D. Steiner
Karl E. Weick
Joseph Weitz

Social and Psychological Factors in Stress

JOSEPH E. McGRATH
Editor
University of Illinois

HOLT, RINEHART AND WINSTON, INC.

New York · Chicago · San Francisco · Atlanta
Dallas · Montreal · Toronto · London · Sydney

Preface

This book is mainly the product of a three-day conference on social and psychological factors in stress, sponsored by the Behavioral Science Division, Air Force Office of Scientific Research (under grants AF 1161–66 and AF 1161–67) and held under the auspices of the Psychology Department of the University of Illinois at Urbana, in April 1967. The purpose of the conference was to identify crucial issues in the area of social-psychological stress and to seek potential research approaches to those issues.

The conference participants were the following:

Irwin Altman, University of Utah (formerly Naval Medical Research Institute, Bethesda, Maryland)

Thomas E. Drabek, University of Denver, Denver, Colorado

J. Eugene Haas, University of Colorado, Boulder, Colorado

J. Richard Hackman, Yale University, New Haven, Connecticut

William W. Haythorn, Florida State University (formerly Naval Medical Research Institute, Bethesda, Maryland)

Robert L. Kahn, University of Michigan, Ann Arbor, Michigan

Richard Lazarus, University of California, Berkeley, California

David Mechanic, University of Wisconsin, Madison, Wisconsin

S. B. Sells, Texas Christian University, Fort Worth, Texas

Ivan D. Steiner, University of Illinois, Urbana, Illinois

Karl E. Weick, University of Minnesota, Minneapolis, Minnesota

Joseph Weitz, New York University, New York, New York

In addition, four observers attended the conference: Dr. Glen Finch and Dr. Herman Sander, both of the Air Force Office of Scientific Research; Dr. Rudolph Berkhouse, Army Research Office; and Dr. Jane McReynolds, Office of Aerospace Research.

The participants prepared and distributed their papers in advance of the conference. At the conference, each participant led a discussion of issues and problems relevant to his own area of emphasis within the stress problem.

The participant papers appear as Chapters 6–16 of this volume. The first four chapters are presentations of ideas covered in our deliberations during conference sessions. They are *not* verbatim presentations of that conference discussion, nor do they retain chronology or source of ideas. Rather, they are chapters about stress research, built by the editor on the basis of the conference discussion.

Thus, we have tried to order the conference discussion into a series of coherent pieces about stress research, not about the conference. Although the first four chapters of this volume bear my name as chapter author, I make no claim for personal origin of the *ideas* in those chapters. The ideas belong to the conference participants, usually to more than one of them. At the same time, I must bear full responsibility for the clarity and accuracy of expression of those ideas, for their interconnections, and for the plausibility of the assertions made about them.

Let it also be clear that the conference did not deal with everything relevant to stress and dealt with some things only tangentially. Where crucial to the discourse, I have handled such omissions by adding my own conceptions to round out presentation of the topic.

By the same token, it should be noted that not everything that was said in the conference discussion is reflected in those chapters. Some parts of any conversation are "non-task-relevant"; some are personal or humorous asides; some are redundant; and some are task-relevant but banal. Others are relevant and important in the particular context in which they occurred, but lose this point when the topic is set in a broader context. Finally, some important points in the discussion are paraphrases of what has been said—usually more clearly—in the participants' papers.

It is my hope that the "conference" chapters (1–4) be, first of all, coherent and useful discussions of important issues about stress. Second, they are designed to tie together the separate (and sovereign) participant papers. If the first of these aims is successful, the second may or may not follow from it. If the first is not achieved, the second cannot be.

Nevertheless, the volume should have a certain degree of coherence. The papers themselves, even though separate, are by no means totally unrelated. In many cases they share a common frame of reference and deal with common issues. This relatedness is highlighted by the sequencing of chapters within the book, while the conference chapters represent a broad organizing context within which such connections ought to be more visible.

This book would have been impossible, literally, without the efforts and encouragement of two sets of people. One set are the representatives of the Behavioral Sciences Division, Air Force Office of Scientific Research. Drs. Charles Hutchinson, Herman Sander, and Glen Finch, all of AFOSR, have guided and encouraged our work throughout, and I am most grateful for their support.

The other set are, of course, the conference participants. Without their fabulous cooperation and effort there would have been no conference, no book. But more than that: without their intellectual stimulation at the conference, I would have missed one of the most enriching experiences of my professional life. My profound thanks.

A special note of appreciation is due Professor Richard Lazarus. It was agreed prior to the conference that he would participate but would not prepare a paper for the conference, for reasons of administrative overload. Hence, there is no chapter authored by him. His contributions to the conference discussion, however, were exceptional. While credit is given in several footnotes throughout, he deserves at least this additional note of appreciation for his contributions.

Acknowledgment of, and gratitude for, contributions of many other persons and agencies are also in order. The several invited observers who attended and enriched the conference: Dr. Jane McReynolds, Office of Aerospace Research; Dr. Rudolph Berkhouse. Army Research Office; as well as Drs. Finch and Sander of AFOSR. Several agencies of the University of Illinois gave valuable support: the Psychology Department under whose auspices the project was conducted; the Hott Memorial Center where the conference was held; and the University of Illinois radio station, WILL, whose personnel recorded the entire conference as unobtrusively as possible.

A large number of graduate students helped develop my review and analysis of a sample of the stress literature (Chapter 5) and aided in conducting the conference. In alphabetical order they include Margaret

Blackburn, Dr. J. R. Hackman, Judy Hackman, Sue Kaess, Ron Kent, Gerald Oncken, Dr. Neil Vidmar, and Sue Weidemann.

Dr. Mort Appley, University of Massachusetts, and Dr. Richard Trumbull, Office of Naval Research, were especially helpful in this work. Their conference on stress, held at York University in 1966, and the resulting book (*Psychological Stress*) provided a groundwork of findings and issues upon which our conference could build. Its pages are cited in many places in this volume and might have been cited in many other instances as well. Moreover, Dr. Trumbull generously gave me access to the galley proofs of that book months before it would have been available in print, in order to facilitate our project and conference efforts. Dr. Appley subsequently provided an extremely helpful review of the manuscript of the first five chapters of this volume. I am very grateful for their help.

A special word of appreciation to Professor Ivan Steiner, who, in addition to his role as conference participant, has joined me as co-investigator for the research program of which the conference was part.

Urbana, Illinois   Joseph E. McGrath
January 1970

Contents

Social and
Psychological
Factors in Stress

CHAPTER

1

introduction

This is a book about research on human stress. It is in large part the product of a conference on social and psychological factors in human stress, sponsored by the Air Force Office of Scientific Research and held at the University of Illinois, Urbana, in April 1967. We will begin with brief comments about stress research, about the nature of the conference, and about the nature and purpose of this book.

THE TOPIC: HUMAN STRESS

Why study "stress"? And why hold a conference about it, or publish a book about that conference?

There are many reasons, and rationalizations, for behavioral scientists to concern themselves with the wide range of phenomena which have been given the label "stress." The least worthy of these is that stress happens to be an "in" term in A.D. 1967–1968. Weybrew (see Appley & Trumbull, 1967, p. 327) refers to "public image" research, and Appley (1964) refers to the "bandwagon effect," in describing the recent proliferation of research on both physiological and psychological aspects of

1

stress. Cofer and Appley (1964) note that the term stress "has all but preempted a field previously shared by a number of other concepts [p. 441]," which include conflict, frustration, anxiety, and so forth. They comment further: "It is as though, when the word stress came into vogue, each investigator, who had been working with a concept he felt was closely related, substituted the word stress for it and continued in his same line of investigation [p. 449]." In part, then, much research is being done on stress these days *because* much research on stress is being done.

This condition is not unique to stress research, by any means. The same kind of "bandwagon effect" has increased the volume of research on many other concepts, in their time. Nor is it necessarily an undesirable thing. What is a "popular" area of research, at a given time, is not at all a random matter. There is often a theoretic and methodological history leading up to the point at which a research topic blossoms; and there is usually a contemporaneous *zeitgeist* containing forces conducive to that blossoming.

In the case of stress, the historic forces have to do with the convergences and potential integration of a number of areas of research and theory: Selye's (1956) theoretic work on nonspecific stress and the arousal syndrome; Helson's (1948) adaptation level theory; extensive work on sensory deprivation (for example, Ruff, Levy, & Thaler, 1959; Solomon, Leiberman, Mendelson, & Wexler, 1957; Solomon, Kubzansky, Leiberman, Mendelson, Trumbull, & Wexler, 1961; Wexler, Mendelson, Leiberman, & Solomon, 1958); advances in psychopharmacology and in the study of electrical and chemical functions of the brain; findings regarding developmental effects of impoverished environments (for example, Davis, McCourt, Courtney, & Solomon, 1961; Cohen, 1958); voluminous research on social conflict, conformity, dissonance (for example, Allen, 1965; Brehm & Cohen, 1962); and other areas. Excellent brief histories of the stress concept are presented in Cofer and Appley (1964, p. 441) and in Appley and Trumbull (1967, p. 2).

The contemporary forces—the *zeitgeist*—are both conceptual and practical. On the conceptual side, the stress concept seems to hold much promise as an integrating concept through which we can make some fundamental connections among the neighboring but isolated fields of physiology, psychology, sociology, medicine, and so forth. On the practical side, the study of stress seems, on the face of it, to be directly applicable to some of the most pressing problems of the social order, and to offer a route to understanding, if not eliminating, these problems.

Many of the practical problems to which stress research seems relevant, for instance combat and other hazardous occupations, have long been with us. Others are relatively new and are the products of rapid social change. We now must concern ourselves with stress effects on man in space and under the sea; with situations involving long-run social isolation, and others involving crowding and lack of privacy; with tasks involving extremely high demands and novel situations, and others involving repetition, drudgery, and boredom; with work and social situations involving highly constrained interpersonal and role relations (authoritarian patterns), and with others involving unstructured, ambiguous, and conflicting role demands. All of these situations represent very real problems pertinent to our everyday lives as well as to the work of "system planners" of advanced military and technological endeavors; all of them involve conditions which have been the focus of stress research.

To state the potential relevance of stress research to these practical problems is not to say that results of this research, to date, contain solutions to those problems. In spite of the voluminous research on stress in recent years, the study of stress, especially of the social and psychological aspects of human stress, is still in a fairly primitive state. We have no solid basis to suppose, for example, that, in the range of situations cited above as relevant to stress research, we are dealing with the same or even closely related phenomena. There may be many kinds of stress, rather than one. Furthermore, our techniques for measuring stress and its effects are as yet crude, far less advanced, for example, than our ability to measure intelligence, or attitudes, or perceptual skills.

There is a still further and more fundamental reason why stress research is not, in its present state, directly applicable to the solution of operational problems. It is probably true that practical concerns (such as, "How can we best select and train men for the first manned lunar expeditions?") provide the impetus for support of much current research on stress. It does not follow, however, that the best strategy for investigation of stress, or even for the solution of these specific problems, is to conduct applied research which tries to answer those truly enormous questions directly "in a single bound." Indeed, the stress research literature (as well as that of other areas of the behavioral sciences) is liberally strewn with studies which, in trying to solve specific but complex operational problems, have failed either to solve these problems or to contribute to our understanding of the basic processes involved in them.

An alternative strategy—the "longer way round" of systematic basic research—is often the quicker as well as the more fruitful route to scientific knowledge which is both sound and applicable to real-life problems. A great deal of the research on human stress follows this basic research strategy, and this volume is about a portion of the stress research field as it is. Thus, while the reader should keep in mind the pervasiveness of stress phenomena to which stress research findings may ultimately be applicable, he must be warned that application to, and solution of, such real-life problems are *not* the focus of this book. Rather, its purpose is to explore a number of the conceptual, substantive, and methodological issues which are crucial to stress research, and which are therefore preconditions to advancing our knowledge of human stress and its effects.

THE FOCUS: SOCIAL-PSYCHOLOGICAL STRESS

As the title implies, the conference on which this book is based was focused on key issues and approaches in the study of human stress, with particular emphasis on the contribution of social and psychological factors to such stress. The decision to focus upon social-psychological aspects, rather than upon physical and physiological aspects of stress, was based on several interrelated considerations.

First of all, the conference was held shortly after the publication of an excellent integrative volume (Appley & Trumbull, 1967) which was based upon an earlier stress conference held at York University, May 1965. The Appley and Trumbull book, and the York conference upon which it was based, had as one of its purposes "to provide an opportunity to examine side-by-side some of the physical, physiological, social and cultural aspects of stress [Appley & Trumbull, 1967, p. 12]." Indeed, the York conference devoted equal time—one full day, with consideration of four papers—to physiological, psychological, and social factors, respectively. This broad focus and allocation of time produced an excellent review of significant issues in stress research, and an integration of them over a broad spectrum, from neurophysiological to social and cultural areas. At the same time, as these authors note, this necessarily limited the depth and breadth of treatment which could be given to each of these areas within the confines of a single conference and book.

Furthermore, it seemed apparent, both from the stress literature in general and from the coverage of different areas in the Appley and Trumbull volume, that there had been far more research and theory devoted to physical-physiological-psychophysiological factors than to social and psychological factors. Without in any way devaluing studies of physical and physiological factors in stress and the importance of continued research in these areas, it seemed that very important sources of stress (for example, role conflict, interpersonal disagreements, sociocultural impoverishment) and important stress effects (hostility, alienation, disruption of interpersonal relationships) were not being given the attention which their importance merited.[1]

Therefore, the conference on which this book is based (the Illinois

---

[1] Along with these judgments, and perhaps underlying them, was the fact that the conference organizer and editor of this volume is himself a social psychologist, attuned by training and practice to see "importance" and "past neglect" with regard to the variables of his own area of study.

conference) was designed to extend and complement the York conference and other related integrative efforts such as those of Sells (1961), Weitz (1966), and Lazarus (1966). The plan was to limit the scope of the conference to a relatively narrow portion of the total spectrum of stress research—namely, to consideration of social-psychological factors—and thereby to permit a more concentrated treatment of this narrower focal area.

It was also intended that results of the York conference, and of other recent integrative efforts dealing with social-psychological stress, could serve as a base upon which to build. Thus the Illinois conference could go forward from the integrative question, "Where do we stand?" toward the programmatic question, "What are the needs for future research?"

The distinction between physical and physiological factors on the one hand, and social-psychological concerns on the other, is not nearly as clear-cut as the preceding paragraphs imply. Many stress research problems deal with relations between "physical" stressors conditions and social-psychological consequences (for example, see the papers of Haythorn, Chapter 11 of this book; Altman, Chapter 12; Haas & Drabek, Chapter 15). Many others deal with relations between social-psychological conditions and physiological consequences (see Kahn, Chapter 14; Steiner, Chapter 10). Furthermore, as Kahn, Haythorn, Altman, and others have noted, there are intimate relationships between physical and social conditions as antecedents of stress, as well as among physiological, psychological, and social interactional responses to stress. Any distinction of the sort proposed here is necessarily arbitrary and will be a "bad fit" for some particular issues and studies.

On the other hand, there is much tradition and some firm theoretical conceptualizations that offer precedents for the kind of limiting focus here intended by the term social-psychological stress. Cofer and Appley (1964, p. 441), for example, distinguish between *systemic stress*, referring primarily to physiological and psychobiological concerns, and *psychological stress*, which implies a psychological state of the organism inducing perception of threat. Appley and Trumbull (1967, p. 2) propose the same distinction. Our focus here is upon the latter rather than the former.

Lazarus (1966) has distinguished between three levels of analysis within the field of stress: sociological, psychological, and physiological. These refer not so much to classes of variables measured as to the focus of the investigator's interest and interpretation. As Lazarus points out, "social or personality psychologists frequently employ physiological indicators of stress reaction, but their interest is usually not in the physiological mechanisms. The physiological measure is not an end in itself but is rather a sign of a certain psychological state [p. 27] . . . ." He further points out that one or another of these levels might apply as a function of the investigator's focus regardless of whether the initial source of the reaction was a physical, societal, or individual event.

The intended focus of this book will include both sociological and psychological levels, as Lazarus characterizes them. Thus, concern with isolation and with arrangements of objects and space in Haythorn's (see Chapter 11) and in Altman's (see Chapter 12) analyses is included because in these analyses the central focus is interpersonal compatibility and conflict. We are also concerned with the physiological measure, GSR, in Steiner's work (see Chapter 10) and with indices of physical illness in Kahn's work (see Chapter 14) because the basic interpretive focus of their analyses deals with effects resulting from interpersonal disagreement, role conflict, and ambiguity. At the same time, the focus of this book does *not* include analyses of effects of purely physical variables (for instance, temperature and physiological processes); nor does it include analyses of neurophysiological mechanisms under stress, whatever the origin of the stress. The reader should note that the term "stress" as used in this book should always be interpreted to mean social-psychological stress, even when the adjective "social-psychological" has been omitted.

THE CONFERENCE

Toward the aims noted previously, of building upon and extending recent integrative efforts regarding social and psychological factors in stress, a two-part research effort was undertaken. The major part involved the conference.

Each of a dozen behavioral scientists (psychologists, sociologists, and social psychologists), with background and interests in one or another aspect of the social-psychological stress problem, was asked to prepare a paper on his own relevant conceptual and empirical work and on the issues and concepts stemming from that work. These papers were distributed prior to the conference. They were not "given" at the conference, but rather represented a shared text of ideas for our discussions. (These papers constitute Chapters 6 through 16 of this volume.) The conference itself consisted of three days of intensive discussion of the issues and concepts, pertinent to research on social-psychological stress, which arose from the participants' papers and other relevant stress literature.

In keeping with the intent to build upon and extend recent integrative work in the stress area, five of the twelve invited participants[2] (Altman, Haythorn, Lazarus, Mechanic, & Sells) had also participated

---

[2] The twelve conference participants are listed on the title page. In addition to these men the conference also included the editor and several observers listed on pages v–vi.

in the York conference. This overlap helped insure continuity, while the other seven participants (Drabek, Haas, Hackman, Kahn, Steiner, Weick, & Weitz) provided new perspectives and insights.

The particular focal topics of the conference, and thus of this book, flowed largely from the areas of knowledge and interest of the participants. Specifically, the topics which were discussed in the papers and in the conference, and the theoretical, methodological, and empirical ideas which were promulgated, were limited by the limits of our collective repertoires. There are doubtless many crucial findings, hypotheses, and issues which were never touched upon. But many of the issues with which we did concern ourselves, and which are explored in this book, seem important and even crucial ones; and these explorations may make a useful contribution to our knowledge of human stress.

Prior to the conference the editor directed a second research effort, designed to review, systematically abstract, and integrate a substantial sample of research literature bearing on social-psychological stress. By this effort, we hoped to gain a better picture of the range and comprehensiveness of research bearing on the focal topic; to determine the kinds of methodologies employed, and especially, the methods used for measuring "stress" and its social-psychological consequences; and to extract whatever basic themes—empirical generalizations—seemed to be warranted by the findings of the research review. A report of this effort was also distributed as an input to the conference. A portion of the material appears as Chapter 5 of this book.

PLAN OF THE BOOK

This book contains three chapters (2–4) written by the editor based on material discussed during the conference; one chapter (5) reviewing a portion of the stress research literature; and eleven chapters (6–16) which are the papers prepared by the conference participants for the conference; and a brief final chapter (17) by the editor, which reiterates some of the major issues for future research.

The chapters on the conference (2–4) are not verbatim presentations of conference discussions; they make no attempt to retain chronology or origin of ideas. They are simply chapters *about stress research*, very broad in concept, based upon the ideas discussed in the conference.

The conference discussion ranged far and wide within the general context of social-psychological stress. Over-all, three broad categories emerged. First, much discussion had to do with the conceptual or theoretical side of the problem: matters of definition, frame of reference, and relatedness of concepts. These aspects of the discussion seemed to yield a broad, but by no means unanimous, consensus on a general framework and paradigm for conceptual formulation of social-psychological stress. This consensus, and some of the conceptual issues which it raises, is the subject of Chapter 2.

Second, much of the discussion dealt with particular substantive issues. The substantive portion of the conference discussion seemed to be centered around three areas of concern: temporal factors, setting factors, and the dynamics of the coping process. These three areas and some of the research issues to which they give rise are the subject of Chapter 3.

The third area with which much conference discussion was concerned is that of methodology. Here, issues of research strategy, design, measurement, and ethics were prominent. Such methodological issues are the subject of Chapter 4.

Chapter 5 presents results of a review of some 200 stress research studies. It attempts to classify the wide variety of behavior settings and conditions within which stress research has been conducted; to review and compare methods used for the measurement of stress and its effects; and to extract some general themes which seem to have gained empirical support.

The same three categories used to organize material from the conference discussion—conceptual, substantive, and methodological—provided the basis for sequencing the participant papers (Chapter 6–16). Many of the papers do not fit neatly into one of the three categories because they deal with issues pertaining to two or even all three of these categories. In such cases, papers were located in the sequence so as to reflect whatever emphasis (conceptual, substantive, or methodological) seemed to the editor to predominate. Generally, Chapters 6–9 (by Kahn, Mechanic, Weitz, and Sells, respectively) seemed to emphasize conceptual issues; Chapter 10–15 (by Steiner, Haythorn, Altman, Hackman, Kahn, and Haas & Drabek, respectively) seemed predominantly substantive; and Chapter 16 (Weick) emphasized methodological issues.

References

Allen, V. L. Situational factors in conformity. In L. Berkowitz (Ed.), *Advances in experimental social psychology*. Vol. 2. New York: Academic Press, 1965.

Appley, M. H. On the concept of psychological stress. Paper presented at the Psychology Colloquium, State University of New York, Buffalo, December 1964.

Appley, M. H., & Trumbull, R. *Psychological stress*. New York: Appleton, 1967.

Brehm, J. W., & Cohen, A. R. *Exploration in cognitive dissonance*. New York: Wiley, 1962.

Cofer, C. N., & Appley, M. H. *Motivation: Theory and research*. New York: Wiley, 1964.

Cohen, W. Some perceptual and physiological aspects of uniform visual stimulation. Progress Report No. 1, 1958, Research and Development Division, Office of the Surgeon General, Department of the Army.

Davis, J. M., McCourt, W. F., Courtney, J., & Solomon, P. Sensory deprivation: The role of social isolation. *Archives of General Psychiatry*, 1961, **5**, 84–90.

Helson, H. Adaptation level as a basis for a quantitative theory of frames of reference. *Psychological Review*, 1948, **55**, 297–313.

Lazarus, R. S. *Psychological stress and the coping process.* New York: McGraw-Hill, 1966.

Ruff, G., Levy, E., & Thaler, V. Studies in isolation and confinement. *Aerospace Medicine*, 1959, **30**, 599–604.

Sells, S. B. Military small group performance under isolation and stress—An annotated bibliography. III. Environmental stress and behavior ecology. Technical Report No. 61-21, Project 8243-11, October 1961, Department of Psychology, Texas Christian University.

Selye, H. *The stress of life.* New York: McGraw-Hill, 1956.

Solomon, P., Kubzansky, P., Leiberman, P., Mendelson, J., Trumbull, R., & Wexler, D. (Eds.) *Sensory deprivation: A symposium.* Cambridge: Harvard University Press, 1961.

Solomon, P., Leiberman, P., Mendelson, J., & Wexler, D. Sensory deprivation: A review. *American Journal of Psychiatry*, 1957, **114**, 357–363.

Weitz, J. Stress. Research paper, P-251 (IDA/HQ 66-4672), April 1966, Institute for Defense Analyses (IDA), Research and Engineering Support Division.

Wexler, D., Mendelson, J., Leiberman, P., & Solomon, P. Sensory deprivation: A technique for studying the psychiatric aspects of stress. *American Medical Association Archives of Neurological Psychiatry*, 1958, **79**, 225–233.

2

a conceptual formulation for research on stress

Joseph E. McGrath

What is stress? Even a cursory review of the research literature makes it clear that stress has been defined in many ways, which partially overlap but by no means converge on a common definition. (See, for example, Appley & Trumbull, 1967; Weitz, 1966; Weitz, Chapter 8 of this volume.) Some of these definitions are reviewed in subsequent pages of this chapter.

The behavioral phenomena to which stress refers range wide indeed: from what are sometimes called "life stresses" such as loss of a limb, slum existence, prison life; to intense periods of hazard and physical danger such as combat, parachute-jumping, polar expeditions, and periods of disaster; to unusual conditions of stimulation leading to bizarre experiences, such as effects of drugs and of sensory deprivation; to situations marked by adverse social-psychological conditions such as interpersonal conflict, failure, and rejection. These phenomena differ widely, both in the situational conditions that presumably give rise to them and in the covert and overt response patterns of the organisms that experience them.

Given all this diversity, of phenomenal referent and of definition, how can one best proceed to analyze, to integrate, to "come to grips with" the problem? There are legitimate differences in strategy, in this as in any research area, based on differences in conceptions of stress, in aims and in judgment about the current status of theory and evidence.[1] One strategy is to abandon the concept, or rather the term. Another is to define the concept rigidly, thus "ruling out" by definitional fiat much that has been labeled stress in the past. A third is to accept the concept as a general rubric, or focal concept, with heuristic value as a basis for "connecting" seemingly diverse areas, but at the same time to recognize that it is *not* a rigorous scientific concept with hypothetic-deductive power. All of these are imperfect strategies entailing risks. This volume takes the third position.

One consequence of adoption of this strategy is that we shift our focus from the question "What is stress?" to the question "What is stress research?" In other words, we shift from an attempt to determine what *the* phenomenon of stress is to a consideration of what kinds of phenomena have been referred to and investigated under this label and how those phenomena are related to one another.

Another consequence of this approach is that we are not now faced with the need for a choice among mutually exclusive alternate definitions of stress (for example, in terms of response pattern versus in terms of stimulus conditions). Instead, each of the classes of stress definition becomes one strand, or aspect, within the total fabric of the "stress research problem."

The main task of this second chapter, therefore, is an attempt to lay out a broad-based frame of reference, or conceptual structure, for considering the total stress research problem. Given that structural framework, we can then use it to generate one paradigm (*not* the only paradigm) of the dynamics of operation of stress. In both of these endeavors, one guiding principle is comprehensiveness. The framework and paradigm should take into account, as much as possible, all of the widely advocated definitions of stress and all of the phenomena to which that term has been applied. Before attempting to build the framework and paradigm, therefore, we will consider briefly some of the major classes of stress definitions, to thus identify some of the elements which our framework must encompass.

---

[1] Such differences in conceptual strategy were evident in the conference. The position taken here reflects the dominant, but by no means unanimous, view of that group.

SOME ELEMENTS OF A DEFINITION OF STRESS

In the course of the history of stress research, a variety of specific definitions of stress have been offered. (See Weitz, 1966; Appley & Trumbull, 1967). A number of these are discussed here, not so much as definitions of stress per se, but rather as conceptual elements with which any adequate treatment of the stress concept must reckon.

Response-Based Definitions of Stress

Perhaps the most basic element of a stress definition involves the specification of a class or classes of response which will be taken as evidence that the organism is, or recently has been, under stress. Selye's definition, which gave much of the early momentum to the stress research area, was essentially such a response definition. His notion of a general adaptation syndrome essentially was a particular pattern of physiological responses of the organism. Occurrences of the response syndrome *defined* the prior or simultaneous occurrence of stress.

As a total definition of stress, the "response-class" approach has at least three weaknesses. First, if *any* (objective and subjective) situation that results in a particular response pattern is to be considered a "stress inducing situation," then we may find all sorts of conditions—passion, exercise, surprise—included under the stress umbrella which, on other grounds, we might not wish to consider as "stressful" situations.

This suggests the second weakness in a "response-class" definition. The *same response pattern* may arise from different stimulus situations, because it can be produced through entirely different intraindividual processes (physiological or psychological). For example, blood pressure and heart rate will both increase with heavy exercise, and they will both increase when the individual is frightened or threatened. But the *meanings*—particularly the *psychological meanings*—of these two states of affairs are entirely different.

The third weakness of the response-pattern definition of stress arises because all symptoms in the syndrome do not always go together. The work of Lacey (in Appley & Trumbull, 1967, pp. 14–37) for example, suggests that we ought not to be overly optimistic about the inter-correlation of the specific physiological indices which have been included in the general adaptation syndrome. And there is considerable evidence of the same kind of variable relationship among psychological and behavioral indices of stress, and between them and physiological measures. (See for example, Mandler, Mandler, Kremen, & Sholiton, 1961; Holtzman & Bitterman, 1956.) (Lazarus makes a strong argument which is summarized under response patterning in Chapter 4, for giving special attention to subjects displaying such discrepant response patterns as a potential source of new theoretical insights.)

One special kind of response-based definition has received considerable attention, namely, stress as performance degradation. To define stress as performance degradation poses several problems. First, it is at best only a starting place, because very quickly one raises the question of why—in terms of intraindividual or interindividual processes—some situations lead to performance degradation while others do not, or why even the same ones do not for other people. Presumably stressful situations lead to nondegradation or even enhancement of performance for some individuals and/or on some occasions. Moreover, all performance degradation does not arise from "stress"; sometimes performance is degraded for reasons of skill, motivation, and the like. Indeed (as Kahn points out in Chapter 6), performance degradation may be risky even as a starting point, for it tends to get the investigator committed to particular performance criteria. Thereafter, he is likely to reckon as degradation *any* shift of performance, even an adaptive or functional shift, which represents a reorientation by the individual and which thereby yields a decrease on the *particular* criteria he has selected for measurement.

Situation-Based Definitions of Stress

Frequently stress involves the presence of certain classes of situations, or situations involving certain classes of stimulus properties. Situational definitions of stress have a special appeal because they seem to solve or avoid the weaknesses of the response-class definition. But they in turn incur several other problems.

There is the question of specifying just what kinds of situations, and what properties of them, make for stress. There is the further question— one which has plagued stress theory and research—of individual differences in response to the *same*, presumably stressful, situation. If the *presence* of stress is to be defined solely on the basis of properties of the stimulus or situation without reference to the individual who is undergoing the presumed stress, then we will have to accept a broad range of reactions as outcomes or effects of "stress" situations: performance enhancement as well as degradation, for example, and "no reaction" as well as strong physiological or psychological reaction. Furthermore, a situation-based definition, with individual differences in responses, requires a means for calibrating stimulus or situational properties in order to establish, quantitatively, the degree of stress of different situations. Without such a calibration, it will be very difficult to develop a situation-based definition of stress that *unifies* a range of types of situations, other than arbitrarily. The tendency will be to develop separate stress theories for each of a whole collection of relatively distinct classes of situations or stimulus conditions.

Stress as an Organism-Environment Transaction

Much of the preceding discussion implies that a useful stress definition must include some reference to intraindividual (or intraorganizational) processes. One specification for this is the "instigation to flight or fight" (see Haythorn, Chapter 11). Another is the perception of "threat" (Lazarus, 1966). Both of these imply that the intraindividual processes involved are a special class of emotions (Weitz, Chapter 8; see also Arnold, in Appley & Trumbull, 1967, pp. 123–150).

But stress is not just an individual emotional state. It is a particular kind of reaction of an organism to environmental events. The occurrence of environmental change, which leads to the perception of threat, is a starting place for building a transactional definition of stress, but *any* change in the environment does not lead to threat. Indeed, many of the reactions we might want to consider stress reactions sometimes arise from continued interaction with an "objectively" unchanging environment. On the other hand, some stress literature (for example, Haas & Drabek, Chapter 15) implies that the study of stress is most concerned with *extreme* states of the environment. This, of course, reopens some of the earlier questions of calibration, or at least of specification of boundaries of classes of potentially stressful situations.

The Engineering Analogy: A Transactional Definition

It is interesting to compare the social-psychological use of the term stress with the engineer's use of it. In engineering, stress is the application of an external force, while the "strain" which it produces must be reckoned in terms of the substance to which it is applied. Hence, the stress-strain effect is a relationship between an entity and its environment. Furthermore, environmental stress can cause a bridge to fall at a point in time when there is no *apparent change* in the application of external force because stress can be continual or cumulative through time. Although the term has been borrowed from the field of engineering, there are several aspects in which the engineering use of stress differs from the social-psychological use. First, the engineer has the great advantage of being able to *calibrate* the stressing forces with which he deals, so that his conceptualization can transcend the particularities of the stimulus situation. Furthermore, he quantifies his measure of the impact of environment (force) in terms *commensurate with* his measure of stress effects (Kahn, in Chapter 6, argues for development of commensurate measures in the study of social-psychological stress). Finally, although the engineer has to reckon with the "internal conditions" of the object to which force is applied, he does not have to reckon with the added complexity that the effect of the force can be altered by the *perceptions* (of threat) of the object of the force.

Discussion of these several classes of definition of stress, and the weaknesses which they entail, serves two functions in what follows. First, it points up the diversity of meanings which have adhered to the stress concept, and reinforces the need for an organizing framework for conceptualization of stress. Second, the definitions represent important considerations which must somehow be taken into account in any organizing framework which tries to present a comprehensive conceptualization of the stress area.

A FRAME OF REFERENCES FOR STRESS RESEARCH

We turn now from the always-vexing question of concept definition ("What *is* stress?") to what appears, at least, to be a question more fruitful for our purposes, namely: "What is stress research?" We will deal with this question prescriptively rather than descriptively (leaving the latter to discussion in Chapter 5). The following series of propositions collectively provide a conceptual structure of the problem area:[2]

1. The *focal organism* (or "actor") for stress research can reasonably be at any of the various system levels—individual humans, groups, or large functional organizations.[3] Such a focal organism, at whatever level, is embedded in a broader physical-social system and always functions within it.

2. The stress problem involves a series of at least four classes of events, or panels of factors, or stages. (See Kahn, Chapter 6.) The first of these takes place in the environment—the physical-social system in which the focal organism (the individual, group or organization whose reaction to stress is to be studied) is embedded. This class of events can be called *demand*, (or load, or input, or "stressor," or press, or environmental force). Second, there is the *reception* (recognition, cognitive appraisal, perception, acceptance) of that "objective" demand by the focal organism (at some conscious or unconscious level when an individual is the focal organism; by some portion or functional part when an organization is the focal organism). This class of events can be labeled

---

[2] These propositions reflect the convergence of frames of reference among the conference participants.

[3] The focal unit for the study of stress can also be at suborganism levels—cells, organs, etc. In the present context, where the focus is on social and psychological aspects of human stress, such suborganism levels are less relevant.

subjective demand (or "strain," or "personal definition"). Third, there is the focal organism's *response(s)* to the subjective demand—at physiological, psychological, behavioral, and social-interactive levels. Fourth, there are the *consequences* of response, both for the focal organism and for the larger system or environment in which it is embedded.

3. Properties or attributes of the focal organism come into play at several "locations" in this four-stage paradigm. First, they affect the reception of environmental demand. Different focal organisms, at whatever level, are differentially sensitive to, or capable of accurate coding of, environmental events, and may place different interpretations on the same event (because of past experience and/or internal conditions of the organism). Lazarus' (1966) term, "cognitive appraisal," represents this "coding" or "interpreting" function. Second, various attributes of the organism—the response repertoire, skills, capabilities and preferences of the organism, momentary conditions of the organism, and effects of prior responses all may influence the response to the subjectively defined situation. (Lazarus' term "secondary appraisal" applies here.) Third, attributes of the focal organism may affect—or alter the import of—the consequences of responses, both because different organisms (individuals or organizations) will have different criteria for evaluating outcomes, and because the effects of outcomes on the focal organism will depend on that organism's current condition.

4. Wherever in this series of events the individual researcher may choose to apply the word stress, if indeed he uses that term at all, the legitimate business of stress research is the tracing out of these *sequences* of events which take place between environment (embedding system) and focal organism. Some may prefer to apply the word stress to the demand originating in the embedding system. Others may wish to reserve the word stress for certain psychological translations of those environmental events (subjective demand, perceived threat). Still others may wish to use the term stress to refer to reactions of certain kinds (as in Selye's GAS), or to specific consequences of those reactions (for example, performance degradation). Whatever these terminological preferences may be, the stress research problem should be seen as involving the *linkages* among these classes of events. In principle, every programmatic stress research effort should be concerned with this whole series of events and their linkages, although specific stress research studies may well wish to limit concern to portions of this total span.

5. Stress, then, involves some *relationship* between focal organism and environment. Stress not only involves a "state" of the focal organism and a "state" of the environment, but also involves a relationship between the two.

6. Implicit in much of the foregoing discussion is the notion that productive stress research should conceptualize man as an active, adapta-

tive, coping organism, rather than as merely a passive or reactive organism.

7. There is the further implication that the sequence of events in the stress problem, that is, objective demand—subjective demand—response—consequences, takes place through time. A proper study of that sequence of events must give appropriate attention to the temporal dimension. Furthermore, "feedback loops" are needed to reflect the "flow" of events, and these four stages are to be considered as a cyclic process through time. (The temporal aspects of the stress problem are discussed further in Chapter 3. For an enlightening discussion of the complexity of processes involved, and of feedback among those processes, see Appley & Trumbull, 1967, especially pp. 169–173.)

These seven propositions form a broad pattern or frame of reference for conceptualizing the stress research area, within which we can consider the nature of stress and the dynamics of its occurrence. The next section is an attempt to specify *one* conceptual paradigm for stress, and to review the various limitations and qualifications of its propositions.

THE NATURE OF STRESS: A CONCEPTUAL PARADIGM

Let us begin with a general formulation of the nature of that relationship between focal organism and environment which we call stress. Stress occurs when there is substantial *imbalance* between environmental demand and the response capability of the focal organism. This formulation needs a number of crucial qualifications before it can serve as a useful paradigm for stress research.

One important qualification is represented in Lazarus' (1966) concept of cognitive appraisal and psychological stress or threat. In this view, an environmental demand can produce (psychological or perceived) stress only if the focal organism *anticipates* that he will not be able to cope with it, or cope with it adequately, or cope with it without endangering other goals. In this view, stress exists not in an imbalance between objective demand and the organism's response capability, but in an imbalance between *perceived* or subjective demand and *perceived* response capability. One is not threatened by demands which he does not "receive," or by demands which he perceives himself to be capable of handling without undue expenditure of resources (whether or not that judgment is in fact correct). One is threatened by the anticipation that he will not be able to handle perceived demands adequately (whether those perceived demands are or are not "real," and whether the anticipated inability to handle them does in fact occur). This view makes the cognitive appraisal of a demand-capability imbalance the necessary and sufficient condition for "threat" or "psychological stress."

(See Lazarus, 1966, for a detailed presentation of this position; see also, Cofer & Appley, 1964, pp. 457–461 for discussion of related points).

Another qualification of the general formulation—stress as imbalance of demand and response capability—is that stress or threat only occurs when the consequences of failure to meet the demand are important; or rather, when they are perceived by the organism to be important. (See Sells, Chapter 9, for a discussion of this view.) Thus, when environmental demands are such that the focal organism can ignore them, or fulfill them inadequately, without serious consequences to himself, those demands will not generate threat for that organism however accurately he may perceive them and however much they may exceed his response capabilities. Threat or psychological stress, then, implies the anticipation of adverse consequences arising from failure to meet demands. Presumably, the organism can alter the state of stress (deliberately or otherwise) by: (1) avoiding the consequences; (2) fulfilling the demands (at a "tolerable" cost); or (3) altering perception of demands, of capabilities, and/or consequences.

Two further and important qualifications of the formulation have to do with the nature of demand or "load." Most formulations of the stress problem imply that the stressful imbalance in the organism-environment relation consists of an *overload*—that is, too much demand, or demand of a kind that is beyond the organism's capabilities. But there is now a substantial body of literature—on sensory isolation and restriction, stimulus impoverishment, social isolation, and confinement—which suggests that stress-like effects may result from an environment that places *too little* demand on (or at least provides too little or too uninteresting a pattern of stimulation for) the focal organism. (See Cofer & Appley, 1964, pp. 441–465, for a discussion of "excess" and "deficit" stimulation.) Whether or not effects of such overload and underload should be conceptualized as the same or different phenomena is a moot question; but both kinds of imbalances must be reckoned with in any broad, programmatic consideration of stress research.

The nature of the imbalance, either overload or underload, also raises questions of quantitative versus qualitative load, and of differential load on different "parts" of the focal organism. A threat-producing overload might be an environmental demand of a kind or intensity which the organism could not handle under any circumstances. Or it might be of a kind and intensity which he could ordinarily handle but at a rate exceeding his capability; or at a rate he could normally handle but which is too much when added to other concurrent demands; or a load which he could ordinarily handle but which is beyond his momentary capability because of a temporary depletion of his normal resources. These notions raise interesting and important questions, regarding short-term and long-term overload and temporal factors in general, and regarding fluctuations in organism capability (with or without changes in the environment) as an origin of stress.

Along with sheer quantitative or qualitative overload, there is the possibility of overload on some but not all portions of the focal organism. In an organization, some functional parts may be suffering serious overload—hence potential stress—while at the same time other parts are undergoing normal load or even underload. This possibility also applies to the individual; some, but not all, of his capabilities are likely to be overloaded in any given demand situation.

When we turn to the underload situation, the matter seems even more complex. There may be insufficient "input," in the quantitative sense. There may be input of a quality which represents insufficient variation (or novelty, or complexity, or heterogeneity). There may be underload for certain functional parts but normal or even overload for others. And there is the clear suggestion, in both the individual sensory restriction literature (for example, Brownfield, 1965) and the "organization-under-stress" literature (for example, Haas & Drabek, Chapter 15) that an *under*stimulated organism may *seek* increased demand or even generate its own input.

All of this discussion of underload is based on certain premises yet unstated. First (as Kahn points out in Chapter 6), the "steady state" for human organizations or individuals—unlike machines—is not a "zero-load" condition. Rather, it is a condition of load roughly in balance with capability. Furthermore, unused capabilities tend to atrophy or otherwise deteriorate. Thus, substantial underload may be a condition of stress as serious as—though not necessarily of the same kinds as—substantial overload. There is the strong suggestion, too, in the literature on stimulus impoverishment, that human beings may have something akin to a basic need for adequate amounts and varieties of stimulation, and that their basic intellectual capabilities may be impaired (atrophied) by sustained periods of understimulation.

The whole consideration of underload also brings up a distinction, familiar in the general systems literature. Much, perhaps all, stimulation impinging on humans carries two kinds of commodities: energy and information. The importance of these two components varies greatly from one stimulus situation to another. But even those where the physical energy exchange is most predominant (for instance, extreme temperatures) have an information component (for example, "I may be frozen to death") which may be important; and even those exchanges which are predominantly informational are accomplished via some physical energy medium. With this in mind, it is likely that the apparent need for stimulation of human organisms has more to do with the informational than with the energic aspects of that stimulation. And the reported tendency for individuals under extreme and prolonged sensory deprivation to hallucinate also seems to be a case of self-generated "information" (patterned and interpretable images) rather than energy in its more physical sense. (The latter statement is not intended to deny electrical or chemical activities of the neural system under these circumstances.)

Let us return now to the general formulation that stress has to do with a (perceived) substantial imbalance between demand and response capability, under conditions where failure to meet demand has important (perceived) consequences. Ought we then to suppose that stress from underload requires an analogous condition of (perceived) lack of demand for extant capabilities with (perceived) important consequences (perhaps the threat of atrophy, or the thwarting of a "need for stimulation") if additional demand is not "generated" to fulfill those capabilities? This seems a rather unorthodox view, but may be less so than it at first appears. Much of Freudian theory, for example, has to do with the organism's struggle to find adequate outlets (demands) for expression of his internal drives (capabilities)—even in an environment hell-bent on preventing expression of those needs—and the forms of negative consequences for the organism when he fails in his efforts to "use up" these capabilities. Of course, in the Freudian view, perception in the sense of conscious awareness is not required, nor even likely. Nor is conscious awareness necessary to "appraisal" as formulated by Lazarus, Arnold, and others. (See Appley & Trumbull, 1967, pp. 124–127; 146; 168–172.)

But far-fetched, Freudian, or otherwise, this conceptualization of the underload side of the stress problem requires the strong assumption that the focal organism (individual or organization) has an *inherent need to use* extant capabilities, and that constraint on (or lack of opportunity for) doing so has undesirable potential consequences.

These questions of underload, and the general formulation of stress as a gross imbalance, in either direction, between demand and capability, raise a still further question of the dual relation of organism and environment as origins of a "stressful" situation. An overload—more demand than the organism can handle—may arise either because of an increase (or accumulation) of environmental demand, or because of a decrease of organism capability. Similarly, an underload—less demand than the organism can tolerate while fulfilling his capacities—can arise either through a marked decrease in demand (as in restricted or impoverished environments) or through an increase in the organism's capabilities or resources. Thus, instead of talking about stress as overload or underload, we might just as reasonably talk about it as overcapability or undercapability.

This way of conceptualizing the problem leads, again, to a rather unorthodox description of the organism-environment relationship. It is probably easy for most of us to see that a major loss in capability may put an individual or an organization in a situation where unchanged (and previously normal) environmental demands now constitute a serious potential threat. It may be harder to justify, as potentially threatening, the obverse situation wherein an individual or organization has greatly increased capabilities in an environment which continues to place the same (previously sufficient) demand. This case may not be so readily recognized as a situation of potential stress because organisms (individuals and organizations) may cope with it rather easily by generating tasks and other demands to use up that increased capability. (This raises the interesting problem of what Altman calls "preventive coping," which will be discussed in Chapter 3.) Such overcapability conditions certainly seem a part of some societal-level problems (for example, unemployment, the tensions resulting from rising expectations) and may well constitute an unlabeled source of stress in many individuals.

The four-stage sequence of events viewed as the stress research problem, and the conceptualization of stress as a (perceived) substantial imbalance (in either direction) between demand and response capability with resulting adverse consequences, together provide a broad and potentially useful conceptual formulation to guide research on social and psychological aspects of stress. Parts of this paradigm are reflected in many of the papers of Chapters 6 through 16; but each of those papers is concerned with an "indepth" treatment of certain aspects, and not others, within the overall paradigm.

With this conceptual formulation as a background, we will now turn in the chapters to follow to consideration of some of the substantive and methodological issues which were focused upon during the stress conference.

References

Appley, M. H., & Trumbull, R. *Psychological stress.* New York: Appleton, 1967.

Brownfield, C. A. *Isolation: Clinical and experimental approaches.* New York: Random House, 1965.

Cofer, C. N., & Appley, M. H. *Motivation: Theory and research.* New York: Wiley, 1964.

Holtzman, W. H., & Bitterman, M. E. Factorial study of adjustment to stress. *Journal of Abnormal and Social Psychology,* 1956, **52,** 179–185.

Lazarus, R. S. *Psychological stress and the coping process.* New York: McGraw-Hill, 1966.

Mandler, G., Mandler, J., Kremen, I., & Sholiton, R. D. The response to threat: Relations among verbal and physiological indices. *Psychology Monographs—General and Applied,* 1961, **75** (9, Whole No. 513).

Weitz, J. Stress. Research paper, P-251 (IDA/HQ 66-4672), April 1966, Institute for Defense Analyses (IDA), Research and Engineering Support Division.

3

major substantive issues: time, setting, and the coping process

Joseph E. McGrath

This chapter is a discussion of three major sets of substantive issues which were the focus of much of the conference discussion.[1] The first has to do with a whole complex of time-related factors which are part of, and which affect, stress. The second is concerned with aspects of the settings in which stress takes place—tasks, situations, environments—as they influence stress and its consequences. The third has to do with the processes by which organisms respond to stress, the anticipation of it, and its consequences. These three inter-

---

[1] This chapter, and the next are attempts to formulate some critical issues pertaining to social-psychological stress as they emerged from conference discussion. They are not an attempt to cover all issues in the field. The editor found it useful to tie in the discussion with *some* of the stress literature in order to round out consideration of certain topics. However, no attempt was made to cover all relevant literature bearing on these issues. Some additional breadth is given in the material presented in Chapter 5, which reviews methods and findings of some 200 stress research studies.

related themes, which are treated in successive sections, pose crucial conceptual issues and represent critical foci for future theory and research in the stress area.

SOME TEMPORAL FACTORS IN THE STRESS PROBLEM

Temporal factors are crucial, and manifold, in research on human stress. Practically every participant paper raises some temporal questions. Temporal factors are involved in both methodological and substantive issues. They relate to stressor conditions, the experience of stress, coping behavior and consequences. And there are temporal considerations at both macrolevels (for example, questions of longitudinal studies versus studies at a single point in time) and microlevels (questions about interval between signal and stress, about duration of demands, and the like). Yet, very little consideration has been given to such temporal factors in theory or in research on human stress. Time may be one of the most important, and most neglected, parameters of the problem (see Appley & Trumbull, 1967, p. 410). This section represents an attempt to identify a number of the many ways in which temporal factors enter and influence the stress sequence, and to indicate what these factors imply for future stress research.

Stress as Anticipation

In the first place, in the conceptual paradigm presented in the previous chapter, stress as a *psychological* condition has an inherent temporal aspect. Stress is defined as the *anticipation* of inability to respond adequately (or at a reasonable cost) to perceived demand, accompanied by anticipation of negative consequences for inadequate response. (See Lazarus, 1966, for a similar formulation.) This formulation implies a temporal context as a precondition for the occurrence of stress.

Duration of Stress Conditions

The stress-inducing conditions (in the objective environment) may be of relatively long or short duration. Weitz (1966) cites the need for study of the special case where short-run demands are imposed upon an organism already fully loaded with more long-run demands. Furthermore (as Haas & Drabek, Chapter 15, note), either short- or long-run demands may carry requirements for a response which meets some temporal criterion. The latter can take any of four forms: (1) completion of response *by* a certain time (speed); (2) production of the appropriate response *at* a certain time (timely action); (3) response to satisfy a unit-per-time rate) requirement; or (4) response to satisfy a cumulative quantity-per-time (volume) requirement.

Perceived Duration of Stress Conditions

The duration of demand also has a subjective or anticipatory aspect. Tolerance for, or adequate response to, a particular stressor condition may be quite different if the organism anticipates that the condition will have a short, or a long, or an indeterminate duration. Literature on the effects of certain life stresses suggests that an immutable physical handicap (like loss of a limb) may produce stress of a different kind or degree than even rather severe enduring stressor conditions (like the stress of extended exposure to combat) which are perceived to have some *finite* duration.

Activity at Time of Stress

Weick (in Chapter 16) points out that the occurrence of a potentially stress-inducing condition is always a temporally localized event within an ongoing organism-behavior-environment context; and that its meaning, as well as responses to it, depend in part on *what had been ongoing.* Thus, not only the temporal "stream" involving the stress-inducing events and reactions to them, but also the temporally simultaneous surrounding context, must be taken into account in understanding the occurrence, effects, and consequences of stress.

Cyclical Response Capabilities

There are also short-term (momentary) and long-term aspects which affect shifts in organism capability. These include such processes as satiation, adaptation, learning, extinction, fatigue, rest, mood shifts, and cyclical physiological and psychological processes (see Appley & Trumbull, 1967, p. 17). These must be reckoned with in considering the stress effects of any given demand-capability imbalance, at any given point in time.

The cyclic or phasic aspects of response capabilities, along with the temporal features of demand, suggest that we must consider the whole problem of demand and response within a dynamic, temporal context. In planning the design of complex man-machine systems, part of this problem is often dealt with under the label of "work-rest cycles." But our concern here is much broader than just formalized work-role situations. So perhaps a term such as *temporal pattern of demand and response* is more appropriate.

Time and Coping

Temporal factors also seem to be crucial in the organism's adaptation to stress. Coping activity takes place as a process through time. One crucial time relationship within that process has to do with the interval between; (1) the onset of cues leading to the anticipation of forthcoming stressful circumstances, and (2) the actual onset of those circumstances. The work of Lazarus and associates (Nomikos, Opton, Averill, & Lazarus, 1968) suggests that even rather small differences in that interval may affect the adequacy of coping and that the relationship may well be nonmonotonic. Another important temporal relation within the coping process is the interval between demand-response and the (anticipated) onset of consequences (good or bad) ensuing from the response (as well as the uncertainty about those consequences). An example here might be the lack of perceived stress that apparently occurs for cigarette smokers when warned of dire, but far-distant consequences. (See the work of Janis and his colleagues, 1958, for an excellent program of research dealing with some of these temporal factors in coping.)

Anticipatory and Preventive Coping

Moreover, some kinds of coping behaviors appear to occur *before*, rather than after, potentially stress-inducing demand. One form involves planned changes in capability, by an organization or an individual, which will permit rapid but usually temporary marshaling of additional resources not normally available. Haas and Drabek (Chapter 15) consider this temporal aspect for organizations. Military reserves are an illustration of such *anticipatory* plans for increased response capability at the organization level. Habits, defense preferences, or preferred interpersonal strategies (see Steiner, Chapter 10) might represent examples of similar anticipatory coping at the level of the individual.

In an even broader perspective, temporal factors are involved in what might be called *preventive coping*—actions by individuals or organizations which so structure the situation, and the organism's relation to it, that potentially stress-inducing conditions are prevented from occurring. Altman (Chapter 12) treats this aspect in his discussion of use of self-markers and environmental props in managing interpersonal relationships. The anticipatory coping processes, noted in the previous paragraph, involve anticipatory planning of *response* to certain demands, when and if they occur; preventive coping, on the other hand, involves anticipatory avoidance or prevention of the stress-inducing demand. In a very general sense, all planning by persons or organizations, is a kind of anticipatory or preventive coping.

Need for Time-Oriented Studies

All of these temporal considerations are implicit in one of the basic propositions in our working frame of reference: that man stands in an active, dynamic relation to his environment, rather than in a passive, reactive one (see also, Mechanic, Chapter 7). Consideration of temporal factors implies two strong *dicta* for the strategy of future stress research. First, there is an urgent need for studies that encompass relatively long segments of the focal organism's life. In contrast, most past stress studies (field and laboratory studies alike) have concentrated on cross-sectional relationships and on studies of stress over relatively short segments of time.

Second, regardless of the time duration involved in the over-all study, which we might call the macrotemporal consideration, future stress research should give much more attention than has been the case to the various microtemporal factors here discussed. The very nature of stress as here conceived implies a continuously changing, dynamic interplay between organism and environment. Furthermore, even in studies of relatively short-term stress, follow-up or post study measurements often are useful in identifying time-related compensatory effects. Basowitz et al. (1954), for example, found an interesting difference between experienced and inexperienced paratroopers as to the *time* (relative to jump time) at which they experienced maximum anxiety. The study of such processes requires a dynamic rather than a static focus even in studies of short-term stress.

ENVIRONMENT, TASK, AND SITUATION IN STRESS RESEARCH

Concepts such as environment, task, setting, stimulus, situation, abound in the research literature on human stress, as in the many other behavioral science fields. Yet there is very little in the way of systematic treatment of these concepts. There is certainly not a theory of environments—or tasks, or situations—in the sense that these are personality theories and group theories, even though we all endorse the Lewinian formulation that behavior is a function of organism *and* environment. One step toward systematizing consideration of environmental factors in stress is to lay out some of the major distinctions or facets of the topic, in short to present a logical structure or framework, for considering environment-related concepts.

Environmental factors can be considered at various levels, of which two will be distinguished for the purpose of this discussion: (1) the broad, total environment or macrosetting; and (2) the narrower, time-place-thing milieu which is the microsetting or immediate context of behavior.[2] Within each of these levels, we can consider substantively different aspects of environment. Some environmental factors and their inputs have to do with inputs of physical energy. Other aspects of environments are sociocultural, and their inputs have to do with information and values. Still other aspects of environment are combinations of these, which will be designated here as technological or task aspects, and which represent applications of means and goals to materials.

Moreover, for any aspect, and at either level, environmental factors can function in any of three ways to affect behavior: (1) environmental forces can compel or require certain classes of response behavior, a *demand* function; (2) environmental characteristics can preclude certain classes of behavior, a *constraint* function; and (3) environmental properties can permit, but not compel, certain classes of behavior, a *potentiality* function which serves to broaden the alternatives in the behavior repertoire of the focal organism.[3]

The distinction between macro- and microlevels is often a useful one, although it cannot always be made with precision. One key weakness of stress research done in laboratory settings is that it often emphasizes behavior occurring within experimentally contrived microsettings under conditions where the effects of macrosetting are attenuated to the vanishing point. Conversely, one of the weaknesses apparent in many field studies of human stress is a tendency to treat the entire interdependent system of variables which compose a macrosetting as a single, unanalyzed independent variable (for example, a remote versus a less remote airbase) without consideration of microsettings within that macrosetting.

The distinction between physical and social aspects is, likewise, not always clear cut. Some aspects of settings are combinations of physical and sociocultural factors. Moreover, many concrete conditions generate both physical and sociocultural consequences simultaneously. A good example might be the physically restrictive aspects of spatial crowding and the accompanying sociopsychologically restrictive aspects of lack of privacy. It is very difficult to study these two effects separately; although in principle the two can be separated, experimentally, they almost always occur together in real-life settings.

The Physical and Sociocultural Aspects of Environment

Actually, there has been very little research on physical environment in relation to sociopsychological stress. (There has been considerable

---

[2] During the conference, Sells pointed out this distinction, adding a third category, focal stimuli. What the focal stimuli are depends on the investigator's purpose and conceptualization. Hence, that third category is not appropriate here.

[3] Haythorn described these three functions of environmental factors during the conference discussion.

research, of course, on physical variables in relation to physical and physiological stress. Much of this is reviewed in Trumbull, 1965.) Sells (Findikyan, Duke, & Sells, 1966; Sells, 1962;) has perhaps done more than anyone else to bring such physical environmental variables to the attention of behavioral scientists in the stress area. But apparently there has been only a limited amount of empirical research in response to such urgings.

Perhaps one reason for the lack of concern of behavioral scientists for properties of the physical environment in the context of stress research has to do with basic assumptions about the nature of psychological stress. If it is true that psychological stress inevitably has an intraorganismic and psychological component (for example, anticipation of inability to cope), then physical conditions of the environment will affect psychological stress only after somehow being translated into sociopsychological terms. If so, then (or so the rationale we are here supposing might argue) it is better to study these more proximal sociopsychological variables as they affect psychological stress than to work with the more distal physical variables from which they originate. Moreover, it is sometimes argued, (for example, McGrath & Altman, 1966) that the business of the behavioral sciences is to be concerned with sociopsychological variables, and that physical variables as such are therefore "none of our business."

The premise that physical environmental variables as such *do not have* sociopsychological stress effects, apart from the intraorganismic translations of them in anticipations or threats, is exemplified by studies which argue that it is not the cold but *fear* of the cold that "kills" in the arctic setting. Perhaps this is true under special conditions, where considerable technology has been brought to the arctic; but that statement is certainly not true under other conditions. Perhaps the more correct statement might be that *fear* of the cold *as well as* the cold itself can produce undesirable effects on humans in arctic settings.

If the premise of anticipation is accepted, then it is not unreasonable to assume that effects of physical environmental variables are translated through social-psychological processes. But this is not the same thing as saying that those physical-environmental variables have *no other* effects pertinent to research on psychological stress. It may well be, for example, that fear of cold produces direct psychological stress, while cold itself alters the functioning of the organism (for example, alters his performance capabilities) and thus indirectly increases psychological stress. (See Trumbull, 1965, and Sells, 1966, for evidence of direct effects of cold and other physical-environmental variables on human social-psychological functioning. See also, Weick, Chapter 16, for several interesting experimental uses of temperature manipulation.)

Barker and his associates (for example, Barker & Wright, 1955;

Barker & Gump, 1964) have built a very convincing case for the importance of physical aspects of the setting as determinants of behavior in general. Hall (1963) and Sommer (1959) have explored the use of space; Haythorn (Chapter 11), Altman (Chapter 12), and others have begun building a body of knowledge about effects of the physical environment on behavior under the stresses of isolation and confinement.

For some years, role theories and students of role behavior (see Biddle & Thomas, 1966; Katz & Kahn, 1966; Kahn et al., 1964) have investigated effects of sociocultural aspects of the microsetting. Indeed, much of the emphasis of the entire field of small-group research has been on these effects. More recently, Kahn and his associates (see Kahn et al., 1964; and Chapter 14) have begun to investigate these effects within the context of studies of social-psychological stress.

But these efforts are just beginnings. One of the clear needs for future research on social-psychological stress is an emphasis on investigation of the effects of both physical and sociocultural factors, especially at the level of the microsetting or situation. This assertion is based on both theoretical and practical grounds. The theoretical reasons have to do with a judgment as to the importance of such factors (that is, the proportion of variance which they control). The practical reasons derive from a judgment that environments in general, and microsettings in particular, often are much more amenable to deliberate change (in the interests of reducing stress or offsetting its undesirable effects) than are human properties or behavior repertoires.

Task and Task Performance in Stress Research

One strong emphasis within stress research has been on the use of task performance measures as indices of presence or degree of stress— usually with the presumption that the greater the stress the more performance decrement. This emphasis is mentioned by Kahn (Chapter 6), Weitz (Chapter 8), and by Hackman (Chapter 13) and in the discussion of definition in Chapter 2. In the latter discussion, certain criticisms of the use of performance decrement as a criterion of stress were raised. Here, some other problems in the use and interpretation of task performance measures are considered.

Tasks, and the performance of tasks, may have any of several different functional roles within the stress research sequence. (See Hackman, Chapter 13, for further discussion of the function of tasks in stress research.) First of all, a task itself may contain the (potentially) stress-inducing demands. It may do so because of its inherent qualitative difficulty or complexity. Or, a task may be stressful because it represents quantitative levels of demand which approach the organism's capacity;

for example by speeded input, by increased volume of input, by requiring quick or precise response timing, or by being of such nature and duration as to be repetitive and boring. Or, a task may induce stress because failure on it would involve ego threat.

Alternatively, a task may simply be the organism's ongoing behavior context at a time when some nontask stress condition (for example, cold, or electric shock, or noise) is imposed upon the organism. Perhaps a classic example of this is a pilot or bombardier who does his job while flak bursts around the plane.

Still a third way in which a task may play a part in the stress sequence is when performance of the task will avoid, reduce, or overcome the effects of some otherwise stress-producing condition. In this use, the task itself was not part of the organism's behavior context prior to the onset of some stress condition; nor is the referent task itself stress-inducing; rather, the referent task is one by which the focal organism attempts to cope with stress from some other source (for example, he builds a shelter *because* it gets cold).

These three task functions may be distinguished, respectively, as: (1) performance of a stressful task; (2) performance of a task under stressful conditions; and (3) performance of a task to cope with stress.

We would expect measures based on performance of stressful tasks to show performance degradation by definition. If they do not, then the investigator has failed, somehow, in constructing or identifying tasks which are indeed stressful (or else the stress appears after a delay, or in some aspect of performance not measured). The dependent variable outcome—level of task performance—is primarily a check on the adequacy of specification of the independent variable (difficulty, or complexity, or degree of stress *in* the task).

It is not at all clear, though, that we should expect, uniformly, a degradation of performance on system-intrinsic tasks under conditions where a nontask based stressor is present. First of all, our conceptualization (see Chapter 2) and certain evidence (see U-shaped function in Chapter 5) would lead us to expect performance enhancement as task demand increases from very low to moderate levels. Furthermore learning, adaptation, and individual differences effects (see Chapter 5) would lead us to expect performance degradation to vary over time, between individuals, and over levels of experience on the task.

There is also a suggestion in the stress research literature that performance of a task, which is meaningful in the setting, may help reduce psychological stress. Having a task to perform may serve to shift the organism's attention away from the anticipated stress-inducing circumstances. If so, then the crucial question in such studies may not be, "How does stress affect task performance?" but rather, "How does task performance affect stress?" The question may be rephrased to ask: "Are task requirements and stress-reduction requirements consistent or con-flicting?"

The latter may hold, also, for performance of tasks to cope with stress. If successful task performance removes the stressing condition, or its effects then there would seem to be, *by definition*, a built-in negative correlation between performance effectiveness and degree of stress. On the other hand, the stress may lead to increased motivation to perform the coping task, hence to a *positive* relation between level of stress and task performance effectiveness. But increased stress, especially at high levels of intensity may also be disruptive to performance of coping tasks, hence tend to correlate negatively with task performance effectiveness.

In any case, the central point here is that stress research must take into account not only the substantive nature of the tasks involved, but also the functional place of such tasks in the stress situation. Furthermore, the direction of relationship (positive, negative, or zero), as well as its causal direction (that is, level of task performance affects level of stress, level of stress affects level of performance, both, or neither) depends on just which function the task is serving. In performance of stressful tasks, the direction *has to be* negative, and its direction has to be from level of stress in the task to level of task performance, by definition. In performance of tasks to cope with stress, the direction of relation would presumably be negative, although perhaps partly suppressed by the positive motivational effects of stress, but the causal direction would be the opposite: level of task performance affects level of stress. In perform-ance of tasks under stressful conditions, the direction could be negative or positive (or zero), and there seems just as much reason to expect task performance to affect stress by distraction as to expect stress to affect ongoing task performance by disruption.

There is a fourth way in which tasks have been used in stress re-search, a way which is an artifact of the research situation itself. Some-times a performance task is introduced into an otherwise presumably stressful situation in order to obtain a measure of performance effective-ness under these stressing conditions. For example, a pilot is asked to perform a pursuit-rotor task immediately after completion of a stressful mission, in order to obtain an index of stress, or of performance decre-ment under stress. This use will be called performance of a task to measure stress. It differs from the second function of tasks, discussed above, in that the focal organism has no reason of his own for perform-ing the task independent of the experimental demands (Orne, 1962) of the research situation. The outcome of that performance may well have limited consequences for him—certainly not the kinds of consequences ensuing from performance of tasks intrinsic to the setting. Indeed, the imposition of a task may function in a way which *alters* the property intended to be measured. A task imposed during the stress may provide a relief from the stressful situation, by "taking his mind off it." A task imposed immediately after a stress situation may serve as a tacit signal that the threat is over (see Weick, Chapter 16); or it may even show an artifactual performance enhancement because of poststress euphoria.

It is easy to "put down" this kind of methodology, of course, but much harder to devise good alternatives. Many kinds of measures besides those based on psychomotor tasks also are vulnerable to such reactive effects, as Webb et al. (1966) have discussed so convincingly. Potential reactive effects of self-report measures such as questionnaires and rating scales are obvious. It is perhaps not so obvious that physiological measures, derived from poststress sampling of body products or functions, also may be altered by the measurement process itself. Having my blood pressure taken after a dangerous situation may just as well be a tacit signal of end-of-stress and may be just as sensitive to poststress euphoria as being faced with a questionnaire or a pursuit-rotor task.

But measure we must, if we are to do stress research, and those measures ought to include indices of effects of stress on the organism and on his performance capabilities. Imposing a poststress motor performance task may be no more and no less obtrusive (reactive) than use of questionnaires or physiological measures. Stress researchers would do well to consider some of the broader range of techniques for unobtrusive measures suggested by Webb et al. (1966). Meanwhile, it is important that results of task performance (and other) measures be understood and interpreted in the light of their potentially reactive effects, as well as in the light of their functional role within the stress situation.

Both Hackman (Chapter 13) and Weitz (Chapter 8) treat some of these problems and raise a number of other task-related questions. Hackman goes on to provide a definition for the task concept and a tentative model of the task process as it relates to stress research.

Note particularly, the similarities in the frameworks presented by: (1) Kahn (Chapter 14), dealing primarily with the sociocultural side of settings; (2) Altman (Chapter 12), dealing mainly with the physical aspects of microsettings; and (3) Hackman (Chapter 13), dealing with the task process. For example, Kahn distinguishes between objective demand and received demand; Altman distinguishes situation and personal definition of situation; Hackman deals with objective task and subjective task. Note, also, that each of these implies a translation of environmental input from its physical and sociocultural form into intraorganismic processes of a psychological nature. Thus, each of them embodies the anticipation premise as a necessary condition for stress and its effects. Such convergences tempt one to predict that a unifying theory, or at least a unifying metatheory, is not too far beyond the reach of the present state of the stress field.

STRESS AND THE COPING PROCESS

A third major substantive area, in which a concentration of research effort is needed, has to do with the processes by which man copes with stress. The coping process is here broadly conceived as an array of covert and overt behavior patterns by which the organism can actively prevent, alleviate, or respond to stress-inducing circumstances.[4]

The issue of coping is involved in much of what has already been said. Our broad conception of coping, as above, implies man as an active organism. It also implies some of the temporal dimensions discussed earlier in this chapter, and the anticipation premise as well. Much stress research has attempted to map stressor to stress, or stressor to consequences, without exploring the coping processes by which the organism deals with the impact of the stress. Such research is, of course, useful in developing our knowledge of the stress sequence. But it is not sufficient. Studies which directly focus on the coping process—to investigate the varieties of coping techniques, the circumstances under which they are or can be utilized, and the range of consequences of their use—are both few in number and vital in their contribution to our knowledge of human stress. More effort on studies of the coping process is a clear and critical need for future stress research.

This chapter will not attempt to list a catalogue of coping techniques. Some partial listings are available, such as Anna Freud's discussion of defense mechanisms (Freud, 1946; Blum, 1953) and Lazarus' (1966) thorough treatment of the coping process. What will be attempted here, rather, is a consideration of some of the basic issues within the topic of coping.

It may be useful to begin by making certain logical distinctions to classify and structure the topic. The first distinction to be made is a temporal one. Coping behavior may take place before, during, or after the occurrence of a stress-inducing condition. Secondly, at whatever stage, coping behavior may be directed toward preventing or removing the stressor condition, or toward preventing or undoing the consequences of that stress.

It is tempting to make a third categorization of coping techniques in terms of healthy-unhealthy, or effective-ineffective. Such normative distinctions, however, turn out to be more complicated than a mere dichotomy. Among ineffective outcomes are those which simply do not

---

[4] The term "coping" has been made current and systematized by Richard Lazarus (for example, 1966). The many contributions of Professor Lazarus to the conference are gratefully acknowledged. His contributions were especially helpful in formulating this section and the section on problems in design and measurement in Chapter 4.

accomplish the removal of the stressor or of its consequences; those which work in the short run but not in the longer run; and those which work but do so at a cost—in damage to the organism or his aims, or in other secondary consequences. Besides, such normative distinctions also involve value premises. (See Chapter 4 for a discussion of the problem of implicit values in stress.)

A fourth characteristic of coping behavior is the extent to which the organism uses multiple coping techniques, simultaneously or in succession, rather than just a single coping method.

Preventive and Anticipatory Coping

Some behavior can be interpreted as coping with stress before the fact (onset of stress). One set of such behaviors has to do with ways in which the organism uses objects in and properties of the microsetting to initiate, maintain, prevent, or otherwise manage interpersonal interaction. Altman (Chapter 12) calls these environmental props. For example, Haythorn (Chapter 11) in related work shows differential use of geographic territoriality (systematic place and object preferences), and of social interaction and withdrawal, for pairs of subjects who are or are not isolated and who are and are not compatible in terms of personality characteristics. One implication of these findings is that a tacit but systematic division of "ownership" of space and functional objects (chairs, beds), and systematic shifts in amount and type of verbal communication, represent alternative ways for isolated and potentially incompatible pairs to regulate their interpersonal relationship so as to *prevent* occurrence of conflict.

Steiner's work (see Chapter 10) presents another interesting form of coping before the fact. He found that subjects who showed systematic preference for any one of several alternative techniques for resolution of interpersonal disagreement experienced less psychological stress (as evidenced by GSR readings) than subjects who alternated among the alternative techniques for resolution. Furthermore, differences (in GSR level) begin to appear after the *possibility* of interpersonal disagreement has become apparent but before any actual disagreement has occurred. These results suggest that some individuals "carry with them" preferred coping techniques for handling interpersonal stress situations, that thus being forearmed they are less affected by incipient or actual interpersonal stress than others who do not carry such preferred coping modes. In terms of our discussion in Chapter 2, these subjects are confident of having adequate response capabilities to handle the impending demand; hence, they do not anticipate an inability to respond, and they thereby do not experience psychological stress. (See Appley & Trumbull, 1967, pp. 170–172, for discussion of related points.)

Both of these examples are mixtures of coping before and during stress. Perhaps an example of pure coping before-the-fact would be the construction of emergency plans for organizations involved in public protection and safety.[5] These are often techniques for temporary increase of capabilities (for example, two of three shifts of personnel, rather than one, are kept on duty) *if* and when an emergency occurs. The idea of military reserve—a readily available substantial increase in resources to be used *if* and when needed—is another example of preventive or before-the-fact coping.

Note, though, that military reserves, emergency plans, and even built-in preferences for resolution of interpersonal disagreements are all techniques for coping with a set of otherwise stress-inducing conditions given that they do occur. These might well be called anticipatory coping —preparations for preventing or reducing the undesired consequences of a stressor condition. There is another form of behavior, more reasonably called preventive coping, which has the effect of preventing the stress-inducing condition from occurring. This is exemplified in the findings on territoriality behavior of isolated groups (see Haythorn, Chapter 11; Altman, Chapter 12), if we interpret the systematic division of ownership of objects and areas as a technique for minimizing interpersonal contact, hence minimizing the probability of occurrence of interpersonal conflict.[6]

The coping techniques for resolving interpersonal disagreement which Steiner (Chapter 10) has studied differ in regard to whether they serve to avoid the stressor or to mitigate its consequences. One of them—under-recall of amount of disagreement—seems to be a technique for preventing stress by denying the occurrence of what would be a stress-inducing condition (disagreement). The other three—conforming, rejection, and devaluation of issue—all seem to be techniques for preventing stress not by preventing the stress-inducing condition of disagreement, but by preventing the occurrence of the normal consequences (dissonance) of such disagreement. The two distinctions emphasized in this discussion— coping before or after onset of stress and coping by preventing (or removing) its consequences—may well be useful ones for clarifying the coping concept in future stress research. It seems likely that these different classes of coping techniques are differentially available and effective under different stress situations, and that they have different degrees and kinds of secondary effects on the focal organism and on the setting.

---

[5] Haas and Drabek, whose work on community disasters is discussed in Chapter 15, provided this example during the conference.

[6] In this interpretation, territoriality behavior serves to *avoid* stressful circumstances. It is also reasonable, however, to interpret those same territoriality findings as a reduction of interpersonal contact *in response to* interpersonal conflict, in which case they would represent *escape* rather than avoidance.

Coping as a Process in Time

Lazarus and his associates (see Lazarus, 1968) have initiated research to try to determine some of the temporal aspects of psychological stress. For example, immediately repeated exposure of psychologically disturbing material does not reduce the threat-impact (GSR response), but repeat exposure after a substantial time lapse (a week) does show such reduction. Partial results of studies in which the interval between the warning of impending stressor (shock) and its onset is systematically varied, suggesting that coping is a process that *requires time for its accomplishment*.

It is likely, however, that amount of time for coping (that is, between warning and onset of stress) has a nonmonotonic relationship with coping effectiveness. Results of disaster studies seem to indicate that warnings are ineffective if too early or too late. Moreover, the failure of some attitude and behavior-change programs to induce behavior change (for example, warnings of the effects of cigarette smoking, warnings of effects of neglect of dental care) seem in part the result of the temporal distance of the threatened consequences.

Such long temporal intervals may have even more complex effects in the coping process. Mechanic (1962, and Chapter 7 in this volume) has found that an individual's interpretation of the nature of a situation, and of his relation to it, is likely to change profoundly over long time intervals (months). Partly on this basis, he questions the value of retrospective self-report measures and argues for longitudinal studies encompassing large temporal segments of the focal organism's life. Mechanic's findings also tend to support the central point of this subsection: that coping is a process which takes place through time in a nonlinear manner, that its effects alter the meaning of the situation and therefore alter the levels and kinds of stresses involved at various stages of the process.

Selye and others have postulated several phases in the stress process. There may or may not be a uniform sequence of phases involved in coping with stress; we certainly need to find this out but we do not now know. If there is such a uniform sequence of phases, there may or may not be consistency over individuals or over situations in the absolute temporal durations needed for completion of each phase. But the issue of time to do the work of coping (see Janis, 1958) is a crucial one which needs more research attention.

Flexibility of Coping

Lazarus and his associates (see Lazarus, 1968) have also initiated studies of the degree to which individuals can alter their reactions to stress (upon instruction or in response to manipulated conditions). They pose such questions as: Can individuals (or some individuals) deliberately "tune out" psychologically disturbing material so that it fails to induce stress for them (for example, GSR response), and on other occasions deliberately "tune in" so that such materials elicit high stress (GSR response)? If there are individual differences in the ability to thus turn on or turn off stress, then it would seem that those with greater flexibility or versatility are in some sense more adaptive or effective copers. Individuals with only one level of sensitivity—whether that level is high, low, or moderate sensitivity—would seem more likely to find themselves in situations where their particular level of sensitivity is nonadaptive or even maladaptive. There are certainly situations of real and serious threat where *not* being stressed (that is, not reacting psychologically and physiologically) has undesirable consequences for the organism. Similarly, there are surely situations where feeling threatened hinders rather than facilitates the organism's adaptation. If some individuals can alter their degree of sensitivity to stressors, and perhaps utilize a spectrum of methods for coping with stress, those individuals may have a strategic advantage in coping.

Steiner's results (Chapter 10), however, give a somewhat different view of the problem. He finds that those who tend to use *any* one single coping method for resolving interpersonal disagreements experience less stress (GSR) than those who tend to use multiple methods. His results do not indicate that one coping alternative is better than another, although, because of the limitations of his samples, this remains an open question. Rather, Steiner's results indicate that *any* coping procedure used consistently is more effective—that is, reduces level of GSR response more—than alternating use of more than one coping method. This would seem to indicate that the person with a broad repertoire of coping alternatives, which he applies with flexibility, is in a less strategic position (for preventing or reducing stress) than the person with a single, fixed coping pattern.

These two lines of reasoning are hard to reconcile although they are not directly contradictory. The flexibility discussed in relation to Lazarus' studies has to do with deliberate variation in *perception* of threat in a given situation. The flexibility discussed in relation to Steiner's findings has to do with (probably unwittingly) consistency in response to a threatening situation. It may be that the former kind of flexibility, in perception of threat, is useful in controlling degree of felt stress, while the latter kind of flexibility, in response to an extant threat, really reflects a lack of adequate resources for coping with the threat. It is also possible, and perhaps likely, that felt stress would be extreme for Steiner's subjects if their preferred coping pattern were denied them (for example, by experimental means). They might then be unable to cope as well as the more flexible responders because they have relied so heavily in the past on the one coping technique that is now blocked.

But the whole question of the extent to which individuals can, and do, modify their openness to situations and to the stresses which those situations involve, remains largely unexplored and has major implications for human stress. Similarly, we still have quite limited knowledge of the degree of versatility which individuals have in their modes of coping; the degree to which such versatility varies among individuals and over situations; and the consequences, good and bad, which versatile coping patterns bring about. These, too, are crucial questions deserving a concentration of future research effort.

CONCLUDING COMMENTS

It would be unfortunate if the format of this chapter left the impression that either the editor or the conference participants find the topics of the chapter's three sections to be *the* three crucial problems, or even the three most crucial problems, in stress research. That impression is not intended. Actually, the topics of the chapter sections (time, settings, and the coping process) are not research problems as such. They are labels for related clusters of problems. The chapter organization is intended to provide focal concepts to help identify major substantive themes and issues within stress research, and to relate them to one another. The emphasis has been on those major substantive issues which seem (1) to have been understudied and (2) to be conceptually and heuristically crucial issues for advancing the present state of knowledge about human stress.

We feel, also, that these focal issues are ripe for attack—provided that certain methodological issues can be handled adequately. Some of these methodological issues are technical problems (for example, measures of stress) which should yield to concerted research efforts. Others are true dilemmas (such as, choice of research setting) which cannot be solved in general, only resolved for specific purposes and by explicit compromises. Still other methodological issues border on and are interdependent with conceptual, value, and ethical considerations. These are not resolvable at all, except in the form of choices by individual researchers regarding how, when, where, and why they choose to do research in the stress area. Such methodological issues, many of which are interwoven with the substantive issues here raised, are the topic of the next chapter.

References

Appley, M. H., & Trumbull, R. *Psychological stress.* New York: Appleton, 1967.

Barker, R. G., & Gump, P. *Big school, small school.* Stanford, Calif.: Stanford University Press, 1964.

Barker, R. G., & Wright, H. F. *Midwest and its children.* New York: Harper & Row, 1955.

Basowitz, H., Korchin, S. J., & Grinker, R. R. Anxiety in a life stress. *Journal of Psychology,* 1954, 38, 503–510.

Biddle, B. J., & Thomas, E. J. (Eds.) *Role theory: Concepts and research.* New York: Wiley, 1966.

Blum, G. S. *Psychoanalytic theories of personality.* New York: McGraw-Hill, 1953.

Findikyan, N., Duke, M., & Sells, S. B. Thermal stress—cold. Technical Report No. 8, July 1966, Institute of Behavioral Research, Contract Nonr 3436(00), Office of Naval Research.

Freud, Anna. *The ego and the mechanisms of defense.* New York: International Universities Press, 1946.

Hall, E. T. A system for the notation of proxemic behavior. *American Anthropology,* 1963, 65, 1003–1025.

Janis, I. L. *Psychological stress.* New York: Wiley, 1958.

Kahn, R. L., Wolfe, D. M., Snoek, J. D., & Rosenthal, R. A. *Organizational stress. Studies in role conflict and ambiguity.* New York: Wiley, 1964.

Katz, D., & Kahn, R. L. *The social psychology of organizations.* New York: Wiley, 1966.

Lazarus, R. S. *Psychological stress and the coping process.* New York: McGraw-Hill, 1966.

Lazarus, R. S. Emotion and adaptation: Conceptual and empirical relations. Paper presented at Nebraska Symposium, on motivation, University of Nebraska, Lawrence, Nebraska, April 11–12, 1968.

McGrath, J. E., & Altman, I. *Small group research: A synthesis and critique of the field.* New York: Holt, Rinehart and Winston, 1966.

Mechanic, D. *Students under stress: A study in the social psychology of adaptation.* New York: The Free Press, 1962.

Nomikos, M. S., Opton, E., Averill, J., & Lazarus, R. S. Surprise versus suspense in the production of stress reaction. *Journal of Personality and Social Psychology,* 1968, 8, 204–208.

Orne, M. T. On the social psychology of the psychological experiments: With particular reference to demand characteristics and their implication. *American Psychology,* 1962, 17, 776–783.

Sells, S. B. (Ed.) Dimensions of stimulus situations which account for behavior variance. Technical Report No. 5, April 1962, Group Psychology Branch, Contract Nonr 3436(00), Office of Naval Research.

Sommer, R. Studies in personal space. *Sociometry,* 1959, 22, 99–110.

Trumbull, R. Environmental modification for human performance. ONR Report ACR-105, July 1965, Office of Naval Research.

Webb, E. J., Campbell, D. T., Schwartz, R. D., & Sechrest, L. *Unobtrusive measures: Nonreactive research in the social sciences.* Skokie, Ill.: Rand McNally, 1966.

Weitz, J. Stress. IDA/HQ 66-4672, April 1966, Institute for Defense Analysis.

CHAPTER

4

major methodological issues

Joseph E. McGrath

One cannot look far into the stress research literature without being struck by some of the methodological problems which beset the field. Such problems exist, to be sure, throughout the behavioral sciences; but many of these appear in stress research in ways that pose special difficulties. This situation arises in part out of the traditions of stress research. Certain trends in methods have developed in the past, and certain issues have been handled (or bypassed) in certain ways in the past. Stress research shows a kind of methodological pluralism that tends to occur in most interdisciplinary fields. This is an advantage up to a point, but becomes a hindrance if it leads to separate, non-overlapping bodies of knowledge.

Most researchers are acutely aware of the dependence of theory on methodology. A science of subatomic particles had to await development of tools capable of detecting such particles and their effects. It is less obvious, but perhaps no less crucial, that development of methodology

41

in a field is also dependent upon the state of theory—or at least of meta-theory—in that field. There would have been no basis for development of projective techniques, for example, before Freudian theory proposed the operation of unconscious forces. Methodology in stress research currently suffers from this problem; stress theory has for the most part not been good enough to direct the development of adequate methods for its validation.

This is not the whole story, to be sure. Good methodological tools are hard to come by; and work to develop methods seems less glamorous, more pedestrian, than conducting substantive studies. Consequently, there has thus far been limited investment of resources to develop methods for research on stress. Then, too, there are some aspects of stress research which pose especially difficult methodological problems. A few of them have already been suggested: the pervasiveness of individual differences; the central place of anticipation, or cognitive appraisal, in psychological stress; the myriad of temporal factors involved. Above all, both practical and ethical limitations greatly restrict the investigation of some of the most interesting stress phenomena.

So the presence of serious methodological problems in the stress area is neither surprising nor deplorable. Still, these problems need to be identified; and, if possible, approaches to them need to be presented, for it is highly unlikely that we will make major substantive advances until we have made some large gains in our methods for investigation of stress.

The methodological problems dealt with here are mainly those which received considerable attention during the conference. Additional discussions of methodological issues appear in Chapter 5; in Weick, Chapter 16; and in Appley and Trumbull, 1967, pp. 400–412.

PROBLEMS OF STRATEGY: THE SPECTRUM OF METHODS

There are a number of general strategies, or types of settings, for behavioral science research: sample surveys, field studies, field experiments, simulations, laboratory experiments. Many behavioral scientists specialize by using one broad strategy, one type of setting, and seldom or never do research using the other strategies. Such specialization is very marked in stress research. The dominant strategies are field studies and laboratory experiments; there are a few sample surveys and a small but growing number of experimental simulations. Such specialization is not surprising. Good research requires training and adequate resources. We cannot all be well trained in all types of research. Nor does every investigator have available the resources necessary to carry out all types of research. Some of us have, or can tap the services of, a survey organization. Others have laboratory facilities. Still others have access to real-life situations and organizations.

Nor is this specialization an adverse comment on the perverseness of stress researchers. The issue is not: Why doesn't investigator X do research by various methods? Why should he? Rather, the issue is: What happens to an area of study if all or nearly all researchers in it use one and only one research strategy? One answer to this question is that researchers develop subfields, clustered around each strategy. Methods diverge, results diverge, theories diverge. Ultimately, researchers in these different subfields lose effective communication with each other; and another fractionation has taken place in science, which is supposed to unify, not fractionate, our knowledge.

In this section, we will examine the consequences of use of various research strategies in the study of stress and consider some approaches to reduce the negative effects of these consequences.

Field Studies and Laboratory Experiments

The strategic advantages and weaknesses of both field studies and laboratory experiments have been discussed in detail elsewhere[1] and will not be dealt with here except where their application to stress research presents special problems. In general, field studies tend to maximize realism, at a cost in precision and often at a cost in internal validity. Laboratory studies tend to maximize precision, at a cost in realism and often at a cost in external validity. These two strategies, and other available strategies (for example, experimental simulation, computer simulations, sample surveys) represent alternative ways of trying to gain information about real-world events. Each strategy serves some aims of research well and serves other equally desirable aims poorly.

The strategy of laboratory experimentation has two especially crucial problems when applied to stress research. The first is the sharp limitation on kinds and levels of intensity of stressor conditions which can be manipulated in the laboratory because of practical as well as ethical considerations. The second, related to the conceptualization of stress as anticipation of threat, is the question of whether there can be perceived threat of any substantial degree within a contrived situation which is only an interlude in the subject's life. The latter is a question of the motivations—not how much, but what kinds—which lead to and channel subject behavior in the laboratory.

The field-study strategy does not pose any particular problems as

---

[1] See for example, Festinger & Katz, 1953; McGrath, 1964; Lindzey, 1954; Weick, 1965; Appley & Trumbull, 1967.

applied to stress research, beyond those intrinsic to that strategy. But the fact is that many field studies in the stress literature are badly done, from a methodological point of view. Some of these involve fundamental design errors, for example, studies of a single, stressed group, with neither control nor baseline comparisons, from which *comparative* conclusions (for example, statements about *shifts* in attitude) are extracted. (Campbell & Stanley, 1963, refer to such designs as pre-experimental one-shot designs.) Other field studies involve design weaknesses which are understandable results of practical limits on resources. Good field studies are hard to do!

For whatever reasons they occur, however, the upshot of design limitations in many field studies of stress is that the investigator gathers rich and complex data but gains very little systematic information about stress from them. That is to say, such design weaknesses make many field studies highly vulnerable to internal invalidity: the investigator cannot make valid inferences about the relationships he sought to study. The laboratory experiment, in contrast, is likely to have considerable internal validity but to be highly vulnerable to external invalidity; that is, its results permit valid inferences about the specific cases in the study, but these inferences cannot be generalized to other more realistic stress situations. The usefulness of a study depends on *both* internal and external validity.

Experimental Simulation

The experimental-simulation strategy, which appears to combine some of the desirable features of field studies and laboratory experiments, seems a likely candidate as a strategy for stress research. Experimental simulations are those studies which attempt to create a dynamic simulation of a concrete class of behavior settings. They differ from field studies in that the setting is experimentally contrived, hence amenable to better control and measurement. They differ from laboratory experiments in that there is a deliberate attempt to recreate or simulate some concrete class of real-life situations, rather than to deal with an abstract or generic class of behavior situations. (An experimental simulation is like a greenhouse; a laboratory experiment is like a test tube.)

Experimental simulations have been used in many fields[2]: dynamic flight simulators, automobile-driving simulators, simulations of military systems, management games, international relations games, and the like. This strategy has been applied in the stress field by Haas and Drabek (see Chapter 15) to study police communications systems during simu-

---

[2] For a discussion of simulation, and a number of excellent examples, see Guetzkow, 1962.

lated disasters. Haythorn and his co-workers (see Chapter 11) have used a modified simulation strategy to study effects of isolation and confinement.

In principle, simulation seems a promising strategy for stress research. If properly devised, it can achieve greater precision (but less realism) than field studies, and greater realism (but less precision) than laboratory experiments. But in practice, the simulation strategy has at least three serious potential weaknesses.

The first of these is the problem of fidelity of simulation. This has two facets. One is the question of whether the simulated system acts as the real system would for the same situation. The other is the question of whether the organisms being studied act, while in the simulate, as they would act in the real system. The former—system fidelity—is a matter of degree; it can usually be increased, at a cost in resources and complexity. The latter—behavior fidelity—again involves the question of subject motivation and is especially crucial in stress research. The trainee *knows* that if he crashes a flight simulator he will not die, and no degree of system fidelity will change that cognitive condition. One must question here, as with the laboratory experiment, whether certain kinds of stress involving cognitive appraisal by the focal organism can ever really be generated within a simulation.

A second problem for simulation is costs. There is a built-in positive relationship between system fidelity and cost. And, unlike computer simulations where there is a large initial cost but a very low cost per additional case, the cost per case of an experimental simulation does not diminish substantially with additional runs. Also, again in contrast to computer simulation, experimental simulations are usually run in real time, or at least consume appreciable time per case. Furthermore, there is a rapid increase in cost as the investigator attempts to increase the richness of data collection (see Weick, Chapter 16). Over-all, experimental simulation of reasonably high fidelity, with reasonably rich data yield, using reasonable numbers of replications, may be by far the most costly of the several available research strategies.

The third problem of simulation, closely related to the cost problem, is the problem of *seduction*. It is relatively easy (or, at least, frequent) for an investigator to become so involved with *development* of a simulation, and with establishing and increasing its system fidelity, that he loses sight of the research goals which led him to build the simulate in the first place. To build and successfully run a simulation often requires solution of an enormous number of conceptual and technical problems. In the process, the investigator becomes an expert in the simulation and in the real system which is being simulated. He sees numerous applications of his tool and ways to extend and improve it. Frequently he begins to behave like the man who buys an expensive computer and must then keep finding uses for it. And frequently, a well-designed simulation cries out for training, rather than research, applications; and the investigator —now a system manager—shifts his goals. It is noteworthy that many experimental simulations in behavioral science have had more extensive use as training, rather than research, devices.

Approaches to the Problem of Specialization

It is clear that we cannot and should not *require* investigators to use multiple strategies, or to form alliances with other investigators for parallel studies of the same problem by different strategies. It is also clear that the latter, parallel efforts, ought to be encouraged whether they be joined administratively or not. Lazarus (in the conference discussion) emphasized the need for building bridges between the laboratory and the field. Weick (Chapter 16) suggests some areas where this may be fruitful. The isolation studies of Haythorn, Altman, and their associates (see Chapters 11 and 12), the organization-stress studies of Kahn and his co-workers (see Chapter 14), and the field and simulation studies of disasters by Haas and Drabek and co-workers (see Chapter 15), represent outstanding examples of multiple-strategy programs on stress. We need more of them.

Perhaps we also need, in the stress area, a somewhat different approach. We can probably safely assume that, for the near future at least, most programs of studies of stress will continue to use one particular strategy. If so, then it might be wise to invest some resources, now, in an effort to make the information contained in diverse studies as valuable and cumulative as possible. Perhaps we should try to invent schema by which the empirical information from field, laboratory, simulation, and other studies can be translated, converted, rationalized, or in some way related, so that *all* research on stress can yield related and mutually supportive evidence.

This is admittedly a vague concept, vaguely stated. There are some examples in related areas, though, which might serve as partial models for such integration: Collins and Guetzkow's (1964) and McGrath and Altman's (1966) treatments in the small group area; Hovland's (1965) classic paper comparing field and laboratory findings on attitude change; Bronfenbrenner's (1958) integration of divergent findings on social class and child-rearing practices. None of these is a perfect model for what is needed in the stress area; but each represents a useful approach to integration of evidence from disparate sources. At worst, such integrations yield a hodge-podge catalogue of results; but at best, they can yield a comprehensive metatheory, a useful synthesis of present evidence, and a conceptual framework for relating subsequent findings to past evidence. The diversity of both concepts and strategies in the stress area would suggest that it is a problem area in which such integrative schema could be of great value.

But choice of strategy is not the only methodological issue in stress research, and it may not even be the most crucial. We turn now to consideration of some other vital issues of design and measurement in stress research.

SOME ISSUES IN DESIGN AND MEASUREMENT

The Methods-Variance Issue

The information in any set of observations is in part a function of the techniques used to obtain those observations. For example: results of measures of stress using GSR are in part determined by the GSR apparatus and by procedures and instructions used; results of measures such as the Subjective Stress Scale (Kerle & Bialek, 1958) are in part determined by the specific procedures (self-report on adjective check lists, during or after exposure) used in obtaining them. Findings generated solely on the basis of one method of measurement—however many times those findings have been replicated by that method—are still limited in their generalizability to *that* method of measurement.

The methods-variance problem has another application, particularly salient in the context of laboratory experimentation on stress. Methods for manipulation of variables (for example, for experimental induction of stress) are vulnerable to methods variance in just the ways that operations for measurement are.[3] Thus, a finding about the stress generated from laboratory studies using a certain class of stimulus materials (using movies to produce vicarious threat, or using a particular intellectual task) may produce effects which are specific to that class of stimuli. Campbell and Fiske (1959) have made this point central to the development of their multitrait-multimethod strategy. It is here simply applied to the stress area, thereby indicating the need for multiple operations for measurement of stress.

The problem is more complicated than it at first appears. Indeed, it is a part of a basic methodological dilemma which is general to the social sciences but which has especially marked effects in the stress area. The dilemma lies in the desirability of maximizing two mutually exclusive characteristics of a study: standardization and generalizability.

The dilemma of standardization versus generality can be stated as follows. If each of a series of studies uses different samples, different

---

[3] Lazarus' discussion of the methods-variance problem during the conference was particularly helpful in preparing this section. His major contributions in regard to the other issues discussed in this section are also gratefully acknowledged.

measures, different methods of manipulation, their results cannot be compared meaningfully (unless, of course, there exists a strong "theory" within whose nomological network all of these measures and manipulations can be placed). Findings derived from them cannot support each other, since they are in no way replications of each other, regardless of what verbal labels may have been given to the variables manipulated or measured. Without replication we cannot accumulate useful empirical generalizations.

On the other hand, if a series of studies uses the very same measure of stress, and the very same procedures for inducing different degrees of stress, we are faced with the obverse problem. Findings derived from these studies are comparable and can support each other because the studies are to a degree replications. But these findings are generalizable *only* to stress of the particular sort induced by and measured by the particular techniques used. They are not comparable to studies of any other kind of stress.

For accumulation of an integrated body of knowledge about any problem area, we must have *both* stability of findings over studies (by standardization or replication of manipulation and measurement procedures), and generality of findings beyond specific methods (by use of multiple operations for induction and measurements of stress).[4] As Webb et al. (1966) argued convincingly, we gain approximations to knowledge only when and to the degree that there are convergences in results obtained from different operations (for manipulations and measurements). Moreover, we gain such approximations to knowledge only with reference to those populations, situations, and measures which are represented by the concrete cases included in those studies.

There are essentially two strategies for handling this dilemma. One is the development of elaborate programs of study which carry the logic of the Campbell and Fiske (1959) multitrait-multimethod rationale *across* successive related studies and apply it to the manipulation, as well as to the measurement, side of method. This is certainly to be recommended; it is thorough, comprehensive, and methodologically conservative, but it is enormously cumbersome and costly, and perhaps thereby unfeasible.

The other strategy for dealing with the standardization-versus-generality dilemma has already been suggested: development of a broad and comprehensive theory. One function of such a theory is to guide development of operations for manipulation and measurement of the concepts of the theory. Given a theory sufficiently broad so as to encompass all aspects of the problem, and sufficiently operational so as to guide

---

[4] This problem has its counterpart *within* a single study, in relation to the effects of randomization of assignment of cases to conditions on within-condition variance.

the development of manipulation and measurement operations and predict their relationships, results of any one study can then be compared to results of other studies because each can be placed within a structured network of concepts and relations.

But this alternative is easy to wish for, hard to come by. We do not now have such a theory in the stress area; nor does one seem to be incipient. We do have some broad but related concepts and propositions, as indicated in Chapters 2 and 5, which may provide a nucleus for development of a theory adequate to guide our studies. It is a difficult task, but perhaps a feasible goal, for future stress research.

The methods-variance issue has two additional facets in its application to stress research. One of these arises in the context of individual differences (for instance, personality correlates) in stress research and gives rise to some problems for which Opton and Lazarus (1967) propose an "ipsative strategy." The other facet of the methods-variance issue arises in connection with the interpretation of patterns of response. These are the topics of the next two parts of this section.

Individual Differences and the Ipsative Strategy

The individual differences issue in stress research has already been mentioned in preceding chapters. One aspect of this issue—differential sensitivity to the same stress-inducing conditions—is paraphrased in Chapter 5 as: "One man's stress is another man's challenge." (Appley & Trumbull, 1967, paraphrased this issue as "a man is not a man . . . [p. 401].") Another aspect of the issue—differential response, given the perception of threat—can perhaps be paraphrased as: "One man gets angry, another gets ulcers."

The fact of individual differences in sensitivity to stress and/or in response to stress is not at issue; the evidence is ubiquitous. What is problematic is how such differences should be conceptualized.

For research in which stress is defined solely in terms of situation, individual differences in either sensitivity (that is, when is a situation stressful) or in response (that is, how does the individual react to stress) represent error variance—to be prevented by sampling and design, eliminated by statistical control, or neutralized by large samples. For research in which stress is defined solely in response terms, the problem is largely bypassed. By definition, individuals who react in certain ways (those measured) *were* stressed, and individuals who did not react in those ways *were not* stressed, even though both sets were exposed to the same stressing conditions and even though the latter group may have exhibited stress reactions in other ways not tapped by the study's measures.

It is for those studies in which stress is conceived as an organism-environment transaction that the individual differences issue is most crucial, and at the same time is a source of substantively meaningful information rather than just unwanted error variance. If stress is to be construed as the result of an interaction of organism with situation, then it is quite crucial to investigate both: (1) whether different individuals react differently to a given situation; and (2) whether a given individual reacts differently to several different situations.

One particular form of this problem arises in the study of personality correlates of stress. Lazarus and co-workers (Opton & Lazarus, 1967) have urged use of an ipsative strategy to investigate stress as a function of personality characteristics of the individual.

The need for an ipsative strategy arises because of one aspect of the methods-variance problem discussed previously. If a set of individuals vary on a given response measure in reaction to a given (stressor) situation, a lot of that variance may have nothing to do with individual differences in personality. Rather, it may have to do with sources of variance irrelevant to the substantive question being pursued: namely, variance accounted for by particulars of the situation or of the stress measures.

Although the problem is general, it can be illustrated most clearly for physiological measures such as GSR or heart rate. One individual may have a relatively "labile" autonomic system, another a relatively stable one. If you place each of them in a stress situation, the first will show a big reaction and the second will show little or no reaction. What one might wish to infer from these reactions is that the former was more stressed (that is, psychologically threatened) than the latter; but that would not be a valid inference in this instance. If a set of persons showing such response differences was also measured on one or more personality characteristics and correlations were computed between personality measures and stress responses, those correlations would include the unwanted (and unmeasured) difference among individuals that are related to the *methods* component of the particular stress response measure.

The Campbell and Fiske (1959) multitrait-multimethod rationale is applicable here, of course. Its usefulness in eliminating this source of error would depend on the degree to which multiple methods were independent of one another. In terms of the previous illustration, for example, multiple methods consisting of GSR, heart rate and blood pressure might all have the same irrelevant factor (labile versus stable autonomic system) in common. Convergence of a set of methods such as GSR and self-report, though, might offer better evidence for presence (or degree) of psychological stress.

Opton and Lazarus (1967) propose the ipsative strategy as a useful approach to this problem. They maintain that the crucial question for determining personality correlates is not, "Does this fellow react a lot or a little in general?" but rather "Does he react more to situation A than to situation B?" They argue further that people are differentially sensitive to different types of stressor situations (for example, electric shock versus fear of failure), rather than just to stress versus not stress. Moreover, it is likely that different personality characteristics make for sensitivity to different types of stress. (See also Appley & Trumbull, 1967, pp. 10–12 and pp. 401–410.)

Thus, Opton and Lazarus (1967) do not accept the traditional comparison of stress versus control conditions as adequate for exploring personality correlates of stress (although, of course, they do not reject it as a useful device). In terms of the previous example, individual differences in amount of shift in response between a control condition and any *one* stress condition would still reflect the general lability of the autonomic systems of subjects, and this variance would obscure or confound variance related to psychological threat. Moreover, a control versus stress design precludes finding out how *different* personality patterns are associated with sensitivity to *different types* of stress.

An ipsative strategy would expose the same set of individuals to two (or more) different types of stress situations, examine reactions (for example, GSR) to determine which type of stress situation each individual responds to most, and then search for patterns of personality characteristics common to sets of individuals who are (most) sensitive to a particular type of stress.

The ipsative strategy has some limitations, of course. Some of these limitations become apparent when we interpret it in terms of the multitrait-multimethod (MT-MM) rationale. The multiple stress situations seem to be multiple *traits*; and divergence between traits (situations) for any one method (stress measure) becomes the basic score of the individual. In this way, convergence between traits on a given method (which would be method variance, in MT-MM terms) is prevented from occurring. Each individual is typed as more responsive to situation A than to B, or more responsive to B than to A. The fact that an individual is relatively responsive to both, or neither, is obscured. Thus, the ipsative strategy would overlook the possibility that some individuals may be sensitive (in psychological as well as physiological terms) to *all* types of stress used, and that other individuals may be relatively unresponsive to any of them. It might be the case that such groups also show differential personality patterns.

But the ipsative approach contains within it the information needed to test these latter possibilities. For example, by *adding* rather than subtracting individual responses to the different stress situations, one could test the "main effect" of individuals, so to speak, and correlate those total-reaction scores with personality measures. This is analogous to what has been done in most studies of personality and stress, and results have been far from promising. The advantage of the ipsative strategy is that it also permits one to look directly at the relationship between personality, on the one hand, and the *interaction* of person and situation on the other—and to do so while taking into account consistent differences between individuals regardless of situations and consistent differences between situations regardless of individuals.[5]

Comparison to the MT-MM approach raises the question of multiple measures of response to any *one* stress situation. The MT-MM rationale requires convergence of multiple methods (measures) as well as divergence among traits for validity of concepts. But the question of convergence among multiple measures of stress has some complications. These are the topics of the next part of this section.

Problems of Interpretation of Multiple Measures

The MT-MM rationale could insist that it is only when multiple and independent measures (for example, autonomic, self-report and behavior data) agree that one can say that the individual is undergoing stress. High agreement or convergence of multiple measures of stress is a rather rare empirical occurrence, however, even for sets of measures all of which are at the physiological level (see, for example, Lacey's chapter in Appley & Trumbull, 1967). In reaction to a stressing situation: "One man gets angry, another gets ulcers."

Lazarus argues that nonconvergence of measures is "bad" only if stress is viewed as a unidimensional concept. On the contrary, he argues, it is precisely the cases where different stress measures *diverge* that are most interesting, that is, that offer the most opportunity for theoretical insights into how people cope with stress. Each measure of the individual's response contains a kind of method variance—variance related to the specific parameter (for example, heart rate)—as well as a general-stress variance. But in this case, the specific method variance contains important substantive information rather than just error in the methodological sense. The individual's patterns of responses—which parameters he does, and which he does not, show reactivity on—reflect his particular coping techniques.

There are some hazards involved in choosing to interpret nonconvergence of stress measures as a substantive strength rather than a methodological weakness. In the first place, measures may fail to show convergence because one or more of them is really a poor measure, in terms of reliability and validity. Secondly, it is an unfortunate fact of the present state of stress research that many stress studies do not *use* multiple

---

[5] Haythorn pointed out the analogy between the ipsative approach and the interaction term of analysis of variance during the conference.

measures. The point made earlier about the incomparability of studies using different measures still stands; and if they cannot be compared, we can neither establish the convergent validity of those measures, nor investigate the coping meaning of nonconvergent response patterns.

Perhaps the issue can be put in proper perspective by noting that *with* multiple measures of stress within a study, it is possible both to search for trait convergence and to investigate the determinants of non-convergent patterns; *without* multiple measures, it is not possible to do either.

Comparison of Stressors and the Issue of Commensurate Measures

We mentioned in Chapter 2 that the engineering use of the stress-strain concepts contained the decided advantage of having a strong scale of measurement onto which stressor forces of different kinds could be mapped. Not only do studies of social-psychological stress lack such clean metric units (as pounds per square inch per second), but they also suffer from three additional weaknesses of measurement. First, there are no accepted units of measure which can serve as a common metric for stresses of different origins. (How many "ounces" of task failure does it take to equal 100 volts of electric shock?) Second, there are no conceptual tools for mapping units of input (demands) to units of effects (response). (How many "ounces" of task failure yields one increment of subjective threat, or one beat per minute elevation in heart rate?) Lewin cited the advantage of having such commensurate measures, and Kahn (see Chapter 6) argues for them too, on the grounds that they provide considerable conceptual leverage in our attempts to observe and understand the phenomena of our field. Classical psychophysics was, in a sense, an attempt to build such commensurate measures for certain visual and auditory phenomena. Perhaps an analogous effort—a psychophysics of reaction to stress—would be very fruitful as an approach for future research on stress. It would, however, have to take into account learning, adaptation, and individual-differences effects, and also allow for the possibility of nonmonotonic (for instance, U-shaped) demand-response mappings.

There is still a further limitation in the measurement technology of stress. Not only can we not yet map degrees of demand to degrees of stress response, nor map degrees of one type of demand to degrees of another, but we, as yet, do not even have measurement scales stronger than ordinal measurement of many kinds of stress demand (for example, task failure, "disturbing" movies, isolation). It is true that for some demand dimensions, notably those involving physical energy (for example, cold, electric shock, time pressure), interval and even ratio scales can reasonably be assumed. But even for these, there is no reason to presuppose that the *stressing* property of the demand is linearly, or even monotonically, related to the physical energy continuum.

Added to these problems is, of course, the complex of problems which arise from individual differences. Not only are individuals likely to differ in what stresses they are responsive to, how responsive they are, and in what ways (that is, along what response dimensions, by what coping techniques), but it is also quite reasonable to assume that individuals may differ in their *mapping* ratios from one stressor to another. To top it all off, we should expect that whatever individual differences there might be at any of those levels, it is likely that they would change over time—as a function of learning, adaptation, maturation, and, indeed, changes in the person and the situation.

Selection of Criteria and the Issue of Implicit Values

There are several crucial issues related to selection and use of criteria in stress research. One of these, referred to by Weitz (Chapter 8), and also in the discussion of tasks in this volume (Chapter 3), and discussed again in Chapter 5, has to do with the relation between type of criterion and time of measurement within the stress sequence. Some stress reactions are instantaneous and have rapid time decay functions (for instance, GSR); others have relatively slow decay (for example, some forms of task-performance degradation); still others have a considerable time lag between onset of stress and the evidence of its impact (for example, deposits of ketosteroids). Therefore, it is very crucial when and how often the stress impact measure is taken in the stress-stress impact-reaction sequence.

Another issue has to do with selection of appropriate criteria. First, there is the choice of system level; what is good for the organism is often not what is good for the embedding system, and vice-versa. Then, too, there is the question of selection of organismic level—physiological, psychological, social, or task behavior—at which criterion measures will be taken. As already indicated, the use of multiple measures covering more than one level is methodologically crucial whether the interest is in searching for convergence or in interpretation of nonconvergent response patterns. It is also important to measure criteria at various organismic and system levels if we are to carry through the programmatic aim of seeking links in the sequence of stress events, as stated in Chapter 2 and in Kahn (Chapter 6).

There is one further aspect of criterion selection that is less obvious and seldom made explicit. Each time a criterion dimension is selected, stress researchers tend to decide which end of it is good. Sometimes this is done explicitly as when increased task productivity is described as "better" performance. More often, the value aspect of criterion use remains implicit. (Consider for example, the difference between studying conformity versus deviation from group consensus and studying conformity versus independence of judgment!)

In Lazarus' work (for instance, 1966) and in Steiner's (Chapter 10), both of which use GSR as an index of psychological threat, it is easy to fall into the trap of assuming that a low GSR reaction is good. Thus, people who consistently conform, or reject, and so forth, in Steiner's interpersonal disagreement situation, who also have lower GSR responsivity, are somehow handling stress better than others. Likewise, people who successfully intellectualize and thereby reduce the disturbance caused by Lazarus' motion picture material (as indicated by GSR) are somehow adapting better than those who are intensely disturbed by such material. In Kahn's work (Chapter 14) persons with certain personality patterns (for example, high rigidity) perceive less role conflict and ambiguity. Are they better adjusted or healthier or more effective?

It is not hard to conceive of a position which makes the implicit value premise that to be involved with and reactive to environmental conditions—including stressful ones—is a healthy and adaptive posture, and that to be detached from the impact of such conditions is decidedly unhealthy. (Indeed, there seems to be in some of the "repressor-sensitizer" research the implicit value that the sensitizers are the good guys and the repressors the bad guys!)

It is also easy to conceive of situations where a certain type of behavior would seem to offer short-run gains but long-run problems for the individual, or where a certain behavior seems advantageous for the individual but disruptive for the microsettings in which he is behaving (or vice-versa). Even the apparent presumption that effective task performance is an unmixed blessing, for both individual and embedding systems, rests on the value premise that accomplishment of the task itself is good. Although in most cases we might have little reason to question that underlying value premise, many would not accept it for the task of the cadre at Auschwitz, or even for the task of the subject of Milgram's (1965) obedience paradigm.

The central point here is that selection and use of criteria of stress always involve value judgments as to: (1) which behavior dimensions are important; (2) which levels or alternative responses on those behavior dimensions are better, which poorer; and (3) from which point of view are the judgments being made—that of the focal organism, the embedding system, or some other reference point. The point is not that value choices should not be made; without them research could not proceed. Rather, the point is that researchers should be aware of the value choices they have made and of the problems and limitations to which they give rise;

further, they should be prepared to examine their data from points of view corresponding to value premises other than the ones they have chosen.

This value question is related, of course, to the discussion of flexibility of coping in Chapter 3. It is also related to the whole concept of coping. The implication of a term like coping—not only its dictionary meaning but also its conceptual meaning in a great deal of research—is that stress is bad and is therefore to be prevented or reduced. As I have tried to point out in this discussion, and as the U-shaped relation of demand and threat (see Chapters 2 and 5) implies, there are conditions (for example, restricted environments) under which it is reasonable to postulate that certain outcomes of stress-inducing conditions (for example, increased reactivity to increases in a demand condition) are to be actively desired rather than eliminated by coping behavior. It should be noted that the term *defense*, to which coping is sometimes related, has quite the reverse connotation as used in the psychological literature: that the precipitating circumstances are alright, or "real," or to be faced, and that the defensive behavior is an unfortunate "warding off" of those conditions. Neither of these, of course, should be considered an appropriate frame of reference applicable to all environment-organism transactions. The choice of either of them (or of related terms like adaptation) as a focal concept for stress research should be done with full awareness of the value premises upon which the concept rests.

References

Appley, M. H., & Trumbull, R. *Psychological Stress*. New York: Appleton, 1967.

Bronfenbrenner, U. Socialization and social class through time and space. In E. E. Maccoby, T. M. Newcomb, & E. L. Hartley, (Eds.), *Readings in social psychology*. New York: Holt, Rinehart and Winston, 1958.

Campbell, D. T., & Fiske, D. W. Convergent and discriminant validation by the multitrait-multimethod matrix. *Psychological Bulletin*, 1959, **56**, 81–105.

Campbell, D. T., & Stanley, J. C. Experimental and quasi-experimental designs for research on teaching. In N. L. Gage (Ed.), *Handbook of research on teaching*. Skokie, Ill.: Rand McNally, 1963, pp. 171–246.

Collins, B. E., & Guetzkow, H. *A social psychology of group processes for decision making*. New York: Wiley, 1964.

Festinger, L., & Katz, D. *Research methods in the behavioral sciences*. New York: Dryden Press, 1953.

Guetzkow, H. (Ed.) *Simulation in social science: Readings*. Englewood Cliffs, N. J.: Prentice-Hall, 1962.

Hovland, C. I. Reconciling conflicting results derived from experimental survey studies of attitude change. In I. D. Steiner & M. Fishbein (Eds.), *Current studies in social psychology*. New York: Holt, Rinehart and Winston, 1965.

Kerle, R. H., & Bialek, H. M. The construction, validation and application of a subjective stress scale. Staff Memo, Fighter IV, Study 23, February 1958. Presidio of Monterey, Calif.: Human Resources Research Office.

Lazarus, R. *Psychological stress and the coping process.* New York: McGraw-Hill, 1966.

Lindzey, G. (Ed.) *Handbook of social psychology.* Cambridge, Mass.: Addison-Wesley, 1954.

McGrath, J. E. Toward a "theory of method" for research on organization. In W. W. Cooper, H. J. Leavitt, & M. W. Shelly II (Eds.), *New perspectives in organization research.* New York: Wiley, 1964.

McGrath, J. E., & Altman, I. *Small group research: A synthesis and critique of the field.* New York: Holt, Rinehart and Winston, 1966.

Milgram, S. Liberating effects of group pressure. *Journal of Personality and Social Psychology,* 1965, 1, 127–134.

Opton, E. M., & Lazarus, R. S. Personality determinants of psychophysiological response to stress: A theoretical analysis and an experiment. *Journal of Personality and Social Psychology,* 1967, 6, 291–303.

Webb, E. J., Campbell, D. T., Schwartz, R. D., & Sechrest, L. *Unobtrusive measures: Nonreactive research in the social sciences.* Skokie, Ill.: Rand McNally, 1966.

Weick, K. E. Laboratory experimentation with organizations. In J. G. March (Ed.), *Handbook of organizations.* Skokie, Ill.: Rand McNally, 1965.

5

settings, measures, and themes: an integrative review of some research on social-psychological factors in stress

Joseph E. McGrath

A major part of the research effort associated with the conference on social-psychological stress was devoted to a review and integration of current theory and research findings. The aim of that review was to try to identify: (1) the central theoretical propositions which could be said to have received substantial empirical support, and which could therefore be put forth as useful empirical generalizations; and (2) the factors or relationships which seem crucial to the empirical and theoretical status of the stress area, but for which empirical evidence is as yet limited or unclear. We tried to accomplish these aims in part through review and integration of a sample of about 200 research studies.

This chapter is an attempt to describe, in brief, the results of our literature review. It deals, in successive sections, with: (1) the kinds of substantive areas studied under stress research and the kinds of stressing conditions involved in those studies; (2) the kinds of measures used as indices of stress or stress responses; and (3) some general principles which seem to have received substantial empirical support. Some central methodological issues are also noted.

A bibliography of approximately 200 studies, which forms the basis of the material in this review, accompanies this chapter. Before beginning these considerations, a word is in order about the search, sampling, and review procedures used in the literature survey on which this chapter is based.

Early in the project, a broad set of studies of stress was located, read, and abstracted; a prototype of the functional framework described in Chapter 2 was used as the guiding structure for the abstracting process. The search included systematic coverage of a number of standard psychological and sociological journals (for the last ten to fifteen years in most cases); psychological and sociological abstracts; Defense Documentation Service bulletins; and bibliography searches by Interagency Life Sciences Supporting Space Research and Technology Exchange and Scientific Information Exchange. This search was aided greatly by several excellent secondary sources, including Sells (1961), Applezweig (1957), Trumbull (1965). Pertinent references were added from each source read.

The problem of inclusion was a difficult one from the outset, and was resolved only by arbitrary procedures. On the basis of the program's focal interests low priority was given in review to several categories of studies. For example, low emphasis was given to studies of a clinical nature in which stress is treated as a persistent trait of the individual rather than as a state resulting from a transaction between the individual and a concrete situation. Similarly, studies relating physical stressors to physiological outputs were not emphasized. Such studies were of relatively high density in the literature and are indeed valuable, but they are not central to the present focus on social and psychological factors. An arbitrary decision was made to undersample studies in content areas central to the research interests of the conference participants, on the premise that their conference papers would cover that ground adequately. These areas included: studies of interpersonal disagreement and conformity (see Steiner, Chapter 10); studies of community disaster (see Haas & Drabek, Chapter 15); the work of Lazarus and his colleagues on psychological threat (Lazarus, 1966); studies of organizational stress (see Kahn, Chapter 14); and studies of groups in isolation (see Haythorn, Chapter 11; and Altman, Chapter 12).

Detail annotations of over 200 studies were completed. From these an attempt was made to gain both a broad and a detailed picture of social-psychological stress research as represented by that sample of studies. Some of the integrative leverage and insights that were gained from that enterprise are presented in the remainder of this chapter.

SOME VARIETIES OF SETTINGS FOR STRESS RESEARCH

With even a limited exposure to the literature, one is struck by the diversity of research done under the label stress. There are many ways to organize a body of research literature, each of which has its advantages and weaknesses. Several were tried in this research; each produced some worthwhile insights. For the present purpose, however, to give an indication of the range of the field, a straightforward, topically based classification of studies will be presented. The classification is based on the type of setting in which the research took place.

Real Versus Contrived Stress Situations

One of the most obvious ways in which the stress literature can be subdivided is on the basis of research done in real-life settings versus research done in experimentally contrived settings. The crucial distinction here is *not* the data collection methodology used, (that is, laboratory experiment versus field study), but the *phenomenological status* of the study situation within the ongoing life of the subject(S). Essentially, it is based on the answer to the question: Is S in the situation mainly in order to be *in an experiment*; or is the situation an integral part of S's ongoing life? Very few studies in our sample were difficult to classify on this basis.

The distinction between studies in real-life and in contrived settings corresponds closely, though not perfectly, to field study versus laboratory methodology. The advantages of field and laboratory research strategies, and the correlated weaknesses of each, are matters which receive considerable attention in Chapter 4; hence, they will not be discussed here. Suffice it to say that each strategy has its proper place in any programatic approach to stress research, but that neither should be allowed to so dominate the field that the entire research area gets marked indelibly with the particular weaknesses of that strategy.

Studies in Real-Life Settings

Studies of stress done in both real-life and laboratory settings fall rather readily into a number of substantive classes, based on the nature of the situation or conditions presumably giving rise to the stress. For studies in real-life settings within the sample there seem to be nine such classes based on rather global situations. (Symbols in parenthesis refer to study numbers in the bibliography at the end of this chapter.[1])

---

[1] The entries in the bibliography at the end of this chapter are listed according to a letter-numeral code. The letter is the initial of the (senior) author's surname;

1. Studies of stress in *combat* situations. (D3, G9, H4, R1)

2. Studies of stress in (hazardous) *military training* situations, including studies of survival and parachute training, and studies of a variety of simulated hazards in normal training situations. (B1, B7, C2, F5, M7, M22, T6, T5, T3)

3. Studies of stress in *isolated sites*, including studies in the arctic, studies of isolated military bases, submarines, and so forth. While many of these also contain potential environmental hazards, the isolation and confinement aspects seem to be the focal point of stress in these studies. (C8, D4, D5, E3, G10, L4, M6, M9, M11, P8, R2, R3, W5)

4. Studies of *community disasters*. (B10, B20, C3, F4, F10, F11, H7, J2, M13, P2, P3, Q1, S8, W8)

5. Studies of stress in internment and custody (for example, prisons, concentration camps, refugee camps. (B14, C5, H6, S22)

6. Studies of stress resulting from *personal disasters*—so-called life stresses—such as crippling accidents or illnesses, surgery, loss of loved ones. (S2, S7, Z3)

7. Studies of stress in evaluation settings, primarily academic ones. (A3, B2, B3, M8, S1, S3, S23, W2)

8. Studies of stress in *occupational* or *work-role* settings. (B13, E1, G11, G12, K9, M15, N2, R8)

9. Studies of stress arising from the individual's general *sociocultural context* (for example, poverty, slum background, cultural deprivation). (D9, I1, M16)

Studies in Experimentally Contrived Settings

Among stress studies done within experimentally contrived settings, three major classes, each with several subclasses, are apparent within the sample. These classes and subclasses are based on the content of the variables presumably giving rise to the stress.

1. Studies based on manipulations of *physical stimuli.*

   a. Studies of reactions to *shock*, including actual and threatened shock. (B11, B16, D1, E4, F1, F6, J3, K4, K6, K10, L1, L10, M10, M12, M17, R5, S6, S11, W1, W4)

   b. Studies of stress resulting from *puncture* or threat of painful injection. (B4, B18, W11)

   c. Studies of *vicarious* threat from emotionally disturbing stimuli whose content implies threat of physical pain, (for example, a number of studies by Lazarus and his colleagues, presenting the movie *Subincision*). (G7, L5, L7, M14, P10, S18)

---

the numerals are consecutive for each letter of the alphabet. Citations in this chapter to that bibliography use the letter-digit codes rather than the usual reference form. The few references in this chapter that are *not* from this sample use the regular form and are listed in the regular reference section which precedes the bibliography.

d. Studies of the effects of *drugs*. (G6, S5)

e. Studies of the effects of *sleep deprivation*. (G5, L12, M18, M19, M20, O1)

f. Studies of the effects of *distraction* stimuli, both auditory and visual. (This category of studies is often considered as task studies; but they do not involve manipulations of task-inherent variables.) (P14, S21)

g. Studies of effects of *restricted environments*, including studies of sensorially deprived, perceptually impoverished and/or physically constraining environments. (D2, D8, J1, L8, S10, W6, Z7, Z5, Z6)

2. Studies based on manipulation of *social-psychological* conditions.

a. Studies of stress based on *evaluation* threat. These are obviously related to the evaluation category of studies in real-life settings, and also to the task failure category below. (A1, C7, F12, K3, L2, L3, M2, P4, S17, U1)

b. Studies of stress based on *task failure*, including harassment and criticism that is task rather than interpersonal. (This category differs from 2a, above, in that the task failure—actual or manipulated—actually occurs before the stress-reaction measures are taken.) (B5, B12, D6, E5, F2, F3, H3, H8, H9, K1, K7, O2, P7, P11, P12, S4, S15, S16, T1, V1, V2, W3)

c. Studies of stress based on anomalies in *social reinforcement* conditions, including limitation of social interactions, presence versus absence of pleasant or permissive atmospheres, and so forth. This category is related to the isolated site and prison studies in real-life settings, and to the restricted environment category under physical stimuli. (B6, D10, F4, L9, L11)

d. Studies of stress based on *interpersonal disagreement*, including studies of conformity processes and other forms of social influence. (B15, G1, G3, G4, M21, N1, R4, S14, S20)

e. Studies of stress arising from *role* and *status* factors, including studies of role conflict, ambiguity, and status congruence. This category is related to real-life studies of work-role stress. (E2, E7, S11, S24)

f. Studies of *vicarious* stress based on anxiety arousing stimuli whose content implies socioemotional, rather than physical threat. (for example, discussion of Blacky pictures) (G8)

3. Studies based on manipulation of *task-inherent* conditions.

a. Studies of decision making and *risk-taking* tasks, where the presumed stress lies in the decision or risk itself. (A4, A5, B19, H2, K2, Z4)

b. Studies of tasks involving complexity, ambiguity, or conflicting and nondiscriminable cues, or other task parameters, where the stress presumably inheres in the *difficulty* of the task. This category is akin to the task failure category; but here the task "failure" is implied by the difficulty of the task, rather than directly manipulated. (B8, H1, W10, Z1, Z2)

c. Studies of effects of *time pressure*, or *speed pacing*. (C4, P1, P5, U2)

d. Studies of effects of *dull* and repetitive tasks. (G2)

There were also a number of books and articles included in the sample which cannot be classified as in one or another of these categories. Some are very general in scope (for example, Holtzman & Bittermen's factor analysis of a large number of variables, H10; some are theoretical or methodological; some are reviews. These, accordingly, are classified in a general category: A2, B9, B17, C6, D7, D11, F7, F8, H5, H10, K5, K8, L6, M1, M3, M4, M5, P6, P9, P13, R6, R7, S9, S12, S19, T2, T5, T7, W7, W9.

Some Underlying Forms of Stress

The categories used to classify studies, in both real-life and experimentally contrived settings, form a loose taxonomy of nominal classes. Closer consideration of the categories, however, suggests that there are some relationships among them. Several general forms of stress, or rather, stress-inducing conditions, seem to be involved.

First, a number of the categories seem to involve stress based on *actual or anticipated physical injury, pain, or death*—a physical threat or threat to the intact organism. Second, many of the categories seem to involve stress based on *actual or anticipated injury or pain to the psychological self*—for example, negative self-evaluation because of task failure. We might call this ego threat, as distinct from physical threat. It is probably the case that instances of physical threat, at least those of relatively high intensity, also represent threats to the self. Reports of effects of combat, for example, would indicate that threat of loss of self-esteem is a major source of stress. The obverse is not the case, however. Many instances of intense ego threat—such as task failure, evaluation situations—carry no implication of physical harm.

A third form of stress seems to involve the *actual or anticipated disruption of social relationships*—interpersonal threat. In part, such interpersonal threat may be thought of as an indirect form (or special case) of ego threat; for example, interpersonal disagreement may lead to negative self-evaluation by the self and by others. Followers of Mead and Cooley, on the other hand, might argue in quite the reverse way that ego threat is a *derivative* of social relationships. In any case, it seems reasonable to consider that the disruption of social relationships may represent a form of stress distinct from either physical threat or ego threat—one based on the functions of other persons as sources of stimulation, demands, rewards, and definitions of reality.

Finally, in studies of some categories, a major source of stress appears to be a *constraining* and/or *impoverished environment*, which leads to *deprivation*. This is clearly a compound form of stress. The restricted environment may involve deprivation of physical needs (sleep, food, movement), psychological needs (for example, varied stimulation), and/or interpersonal needs (interaction, affection, social comparisons). Furthermore, the restricted environment may combine elements of over- and understimulation—for example, lack of varied physical stimulation and a highly restricted set of others as sources of interpersonal stimulation, accompanied by an enforced intimacy with, or overstimulation from, those others.

Studies in real-life settings tend to involve relatively high levels of several, or even all four, of these forms of stress. Studies in experimentally contrived settings, on the other hand, tend to involve high (or often moderate) levels of only one form of stress. These differences are not surprising. Studies in field settings tend to select relatively extreme situations; these often involve multiple forms, as well as high levels, of stress. On the contrary, laboratory situations are restricted in the degree of intensity of stress which can be generated, for both practical and ethical reasons, and they tend to utilize single forms of stress in the interest of precision and of interpretability of results.

These distinctions between different forms of stress served as focal concepts in the examination of the literature and the attempt to extract general principles from it. There may or may not be similar effects from stress as represented by an electric shock or threat of an injection, and from stress as represented by distraction, failure on a task, or threat of an examination. To the extent that research findings do not show convergences over different forms of stress conditions, it may be that these four forms (or some other set) represent different classes of phenomena, and need to be viewed as more or less separate areas for research. To the extent that research findings do show such convergences of effects, over different forms of stress, then we are more justified in considering these as related phenomena and in seeking general theoretical formulations for social-psychological stress as a unified area of study.

But this classification of study settings and forms of stress deal primarily with the input or antecedent conditions involved in stress situations. Equally important is the matter of different measures of stress, or stress effects, and of convergences of findings across types of measures. The varieties of stress indices which are used in the sample of studies here reviewed are examined in the next part of this chapter.

A CATALOGUE OF SOME INDICES OF STRESS

Along with the categorization of stress studies on the basis of stressor conditions or settings, it is also possible to catalogue operational measures which have been used as indices of stress, or of the direct effects of stress. The categorization of stress indices presented here is organized in terms of two facets, as indicated in Table 5-1. First, it divides indices in terms of the functional level which the measure is presumed to reflect. Second, it classifies measures at each level in terms of the operational procedures used to obtain the data.

Levels

There are three readily discernible levels of measurement in the studies here reviewed. One is the *physiological* level, having to do with body functions and conditions. The second is the *psychological* level, having to do with cognitive, emotional, and motivational functions and conditions. The third can be termed *behavioral*; it has to do with (overt) responses of the organism vis à vis environmental settings, including both interpersonal and task behaviors.

One major clarification of the third functional level is needed. Many stress studies insert the requirement to perform certain tasks (for example, digit-symbol substitution or perceptual recognition) as a device for obtaining a measure of the degree of deterioration (or enhancement) of some psychological process. Although these involve overt behavior, in performance of the task, they are nevertheless interpreted here as indices at the psychological level. Such tasks are used instrumentally for measurement of a psychological process. When there is a task performance which is relevant to the stressor condition (for example, learning a discrimination to turn off a shock), or indigenous to a setting (for example, repair of a damaged radio in a military training situation), then indices derived from it are classified as at the behavioral level.

It may also be worth pointing out that, while our conceptual formulation (in Chapter 2) includes an organization level, this catalogue does not. The reason is simply that no such measures were contained in the sample of literature here reviewed. Haas and Drabek (Chapter 15) have argued for use of organization level measures of stress effects and have suggested some potential measures of this class.

Operations

The second facet in terms of which the catalogue of indices has been organized has to do with the operations or methods used in obtaining the measure. In this regard, we follow the categories and terminology of Webb et al. (1966), using as major classes: subjective report (questionnaires, ratings, and so forth); observation (with or without instruments); analysis of traces accretion and erosion); and analysis of archival records (documents, production records, and so forth). These methods have been used with differential frequency for measures at the different functional levels, but in principle all are applicable at all levels.

Table 5–1, presents a partial catalogue of indices of stress and its effects which were used in the sample of studies reviewed. (The symbols

listed after each subclass of indices are references to the bibliography
of that sample of stress studies, which appears at the end of this chapter.)

TABLE 5–1 A Classification of Indices of Stress

A. *Indices Referring to Physiological Properties*

1. *Subjective Report* a. Items of personality tests referring to somatic symptoms.
(See psychological properties, subjective report.)
b. Checklists or questionnaires about somatic symptoms.
(I1, Z5, Z6, Z7)

2. *Observation* a. Unaided observation of signs of physical tension (for example, perspiration, blushing)
(S14)
b. Observation, via biomedical instrumentation, of ongoing physiological processes. (GSR, EEG, heart and pulse rates; blood pressure and volume; body temperature)
(B2, E4, F5, G4, G5, H8, H9, J3, K4, K9, L1, M12, M14, S5, S6, S10, S18, V1, V2, W1, Z6)

3. *Trace Measures* Biochemical analysis of physiological products, mainly in blood and urine. (For example, adrenaline; corticosteroids, eosinophils; sugar; CO_2)
(B2, B7, B11, B18, D3, G5, J3, K7, L12, M7, S18, U1)

4. *Archival Records* Medical records of physical diseases and symptoms (for example, ulcers, cervical cancer; arthritis)
(R1, S7)

B. *Indices Referring to Psychological Properties*

1. *Subjective Report* a. Personality tests or questionnaires measuring *traits* such as anxiety, stress, fear, (for example, MMPI; Edwards, Bell, Maudsley; Taylor MAS; Endler et al. S-R Inventory; Alexander & Husek Anxiety Differential)
(A3, C1, D4, D5, E5, G8, S13, S23, W2, Z7)
b. Checklists or questionnaires which are direct expression of degree of disturbance in relation to a given situation. (For example, SSS checklist)
(A3, B1, B7, B11, B18, C1, C2, C7, C8, D1,

D2, D8, D9, E3, E4, E5, F5, G7, K6, L1, L3,
L8, M6, M14, M18, O2, S2, S6, S7, S10, S15,
S18, T5, W4, W11, Z5, Z6, Z7)

2. *Observation*   a. Unaided observation of signs of psychological
disturbances (for example, stammering; dis-
orientation; hostility)
F12, G5, L1, L3, L12, M2, O2, P12)

b. Observation, via performance task instruments,
of functioning of ongoing psychological proc-
esses (for example, learning; perception; mem-
ory; problem solving; psychomotor coordina-
tion)
(A1, A4, A5, B2, B4, B5, B6, B7, B8, B11, B12,
C1, C2, C4, C7, D1, D2, D3, E5, E7, F1, F2,
F3, F4, F5, G6, G8, H2, H3, H9, K1, K2, K3,
K10, L1, L8, L11, L12, M5, M17, M22, O1, O2,
P1, P4, P11, P12, P14, R5, R6, S1, S4, S6, S10,
S11, S12, S13, S15, S16, S17, S21, T1, U2, V1,
V2, W1, W2, W3, W10, Z7)

3. *Trace Measures*   Content analysis of products such as interview pro-
tocols, Rorschach, TAT or other "projective tests."
(B7, B12, C1, E5, F5, F6, G6, J3, K3, M2, M18,
P10, P12, S2, V1, Z6, Z7)

4. *Archival Records*   Medical-psychiatric records of psychological disorder and symptoms (for example, neurotic and
psychotic diagnoses; paranoid symptoms)
(M22, R1, S3)

C. *Indices Referring to Properties of Behavior in Settings* (overt; task *and*
social)

1. *Subjective Report*   a. Questionnaires and interviews measuring task-
performance evaluation; level of aspiration; job
satisfaction.
(B3, B5, B15, B19, C8, D5, E7, F2, F3, F4,
G3, G4, G10, K6, P11, W4, Z4)

b. Questionnaires and interviews measuring role
perceptions (conflict, ambiguity, etc.) or other
aspects of interpersonal relations (for example,
attraction to group; sociometric choices)
(B13, C8, D1, G12, I1, M16, S13, S24)

2. *Observation*   a. Observation of quality, speed or success of performance on setting-relevant tasks (for example,
radio repair, escape)

(A4, A5, B7, B16, C2, D2, G1, G7, H2, K6, K9, P5, P14, Z4)
b.   Visual/auditory observation of type and amount of activity; communication; positive and negative effect; influence. (For example, by use of Bales categories)
(A3, B8, B15, D1, D10, E7, G3, G5, H1, L1, L2, L3, L0, M10, M18, M19, M20, N1, P7, P14, S10, S14, S20, W4, Z2, Z5)

3. *Trace Measures*   Analysis of group decisions, task productivity, changes in group structure and membership, and so forth.
(B10, G11, M2, P7, S22, W4)

4. *Archival Records*   Production records; supervisors evaluations; absentee and turnover records; academic achievement records.
(E1, E3, R1, S4, T4, W2)

Indices of Physiological Properties

With the single exception of somatic symptom checklists, often used in studies of sensory restriction and social isolation, subjective report measures are seldom used for physiological indices of stress. The other three methods—observation, trace measures, and archival records—are all used with considerable frequency.

Observation measures.   Although there are occasional uses of direct visual observation of external signs of stress, most observational measures of physiological stress utilize more or less sophisticated biomedical instruments. The most popular of these are measures of the electrical conductivity of the skin (GSR). The GSR actually represents a whole subset of measures, which vary in: (1) where on the body the electrodes are placed (fingers, ankles, and so on); (2) what electrical indices are used (conductivity, resistance, change in resistance); (3) specific (that is, reactions to a particular time-localized stimulus) or nonspecific (that is, changes in level of conductivity); and (4) timing of the measure with respect to experimental conditions. Related to the GSR measures are those which measure amount of perspiration, usually in the fingers or palm of the hand (palmar sweat), but these are actually trace measures.

The second most frequently used set of observation measures of physiological stress are those related to the cardiovascular system: pulse rate, heart rate, systolic and diastolic blood pressure, and blood volume. Far less frequent are measures of respiration: rate and volume. Electrical activity of the brain, especially alpha and theta rhythms as measured by EEG, have been given some attention. At least one study has plotted body temperature shifts.

One major problem for virtually all of these indices is the wide range of individual differences in them, unrelated to specific stressor conditions. Furthermore, such physiological processes show considerable intra-individual variation, related to diurnal cycles or other temporal or environmental conditions, again unrelated to specific stressors. Such inter-individual and intraindividual variation add up to enormous problems of reliability of measurement, requiring elaborate controls and counter-balancing in designs, as well as careful calibration and use of the instruments themselves. Moreover, some of these measures (for example, GSR, palmar sweat, perhaps even heart rate) are probably vulnerable to testing or reactivity effects (compare Webb et al., 1966) by which the measurement procedures themselves alter the properties to be measured. Finally, considering that all these have been used as indices of stress, there is a disappointing lack of convergence or correlation among them. (See H10, also Mandler et al., 1961). This is really not surprising, considering that each of these indices reflect complex and specific physiological processes, which in turn are sensitive to many ongoing body functions and environmental conditions. Nevertheless, the lack of convergence of such measures poses some substantial conceptual problems for stress research.

Trace measures: Biochemical analyses of body products. Most prominent in the class of trace measures are analysis of blood cells and plasma and of urine. The indices of stress have included: (1) eosinophils; (2) corticosteroids; (3) 17-ketosteroids; (4) adrenaline products; (5) ATP; (6) sugar; (7) cholesterol; (8) CO_2; (9) free fatty acids. These are "trace measures," in the terms of Webb et al. (1966). By their nature they are less likely to be vulnerable to reactivity effects. But they are accretions over time. Many of these indices are time-based ratios. All of them require sizable portions of time for substantial accretions to occur. They reflect a summation of deposit over some time period. Hence, they are not very useful for studies of microtemporal factors in stress (for example, cue-to-onset intervals in contrast to the class of observational measures of ongoing physiological process (GSR, pulse, and so forth).

These trace measures also do not correlate as highly with one another as one would expect if they reflected *generalized* stress. They do not show very high correlations with observational measures of ongoing function, but that is not surprising in view of the temporal differences noted.

Archival records: Medical reports of symptoms and diseases. This class of measures differs from the previous ones in that it reflects long-run consequences rather than immediate effects of stress. The class has included measures of occurrence and severity of: (1) ulcers and other alimentary disorders, (2) arthritis, (3) VD, (4) cervical cancer.

Indices of stress based on medical records can enter stress research in either of two ways: as prestudy measures of independent variables, for manipulation or control purposes; and as dependent variable measures of long-run consequences of major stress situations. The latter use (for example, in Kahn et al., 1964; and in Kahn, Chapter 14) usually involves comparisons of rates of occurrence of specific medical diagnoses for populations undergoing different circumstances (for example, those in high versus low conflict roles). These are archival records (compare Webb et al., 1966) hence fairly invulnerable to reactivity effects, although they are quite vulnerable to content, population, and observer biases. Even more than the trace measures, these medical records are limited to studies involving macrotemporal contexts. They are also subject to some of the problems listed for observational measures of ongoing processes. There are presumably many causal influences involved in ulcers or arthritis, for example, and some of them are quite unrelated to environmentally based stressor conditions. But measures based on archival records do have one major advantage shared by many such ultimate criteria: they are mostly indices of permanent, irreversible tissue damage, and their presence and undesirability are not to be contested.

These measures are also not highly interrelated with one another, but one would not expect them to be. Ulcers and allergies are, perhaps, *alternative* indicators of long-run stress. This same notion that multiple measures might represent alternative and substitutable reactions to stress, may be helpful in understanding why there is low convergence in response patterns for other classes of measures—physiological, psychological, behavioral (see Chapter 4).

Indices of Psychological Properties

In contrast to physiological indices, psychological measures of stress make much more use of subjective reports and much less use of trace measures. Like physiological measures, psychological measures rely most heavily on observational indices. As indicated before, the instruments for these observational measures often involve the performance of an imposed task from which measures of specific psychological processes are derived.

Subjective report measures.   Here, we need to distinguish between two subclasses. The first includes trait measures of anxiety, stress-proneness, or the like, usually measured by scales from standardized personality tests. Of these, the Taylor Manifest Anxiety Scale is by far the most frequently used. Others are selected scales of the Minnesota Multiphasic Personality Inventory (MMPI), the Edwards, Bell, and Maudsley inventories, and the Endler et al. S-R Inventory of Anxiousness.

The second group of subjective-report measures of psychological stress involve measures of situation anxiety, including: (1) reports of symptoms of psychological disturbances (hallucinations, delusions, foggy vision, and so forth); (2) direct ratings of anxiety or related properties (fear, uneasiness, guilt, role conflict), with the most frequent method being the Subjective Stress Scale or related adjective checklists; and (3) shifts in attitudes and perceptions (for example, self-other, self-confidence, blaming) which are presumed to be stress effects.

The trait measures are presumably indices of relatively unchanging aspects of the individual. As such, they represent individual properties, rather than properties of the interaction of individual with situation. Their use in stress research is primarily as independent or control variables.

Both types of subjective-report measures are especially vulnerable to reactivity effects. The respondent knows he is being "tested." His behavior is likely to be altered by the social-psychological demands of the testing situation—to please the investigator or to confound him, to uphold social norms about fear or bravery, to exhibit himself in a favorable light. Yet if we are to have a conception of psychological stress which hinges on the subjective experience of threat, then it would seem worthwhile to include in stress studies some direct measures of the individual's threat experience in the situations of concern—preferably *along with* measures of other classes (for example, physiological indices).

Perhaps the most carefully developed and widely used self-report index of situation-based stress is the Subjective Stress Scale (SSS) developed by Kerle and Bialek (1958). It consists of a series of adjectives, ordered unidimensionally from "wonderful" to "scared stiff," from which the respondent is to indicate the adjective which most nearly describes his feelings (at that moment or at some other specified time). Its simplicity and straightforward form are definite advantages. But it is obviously susceptible to response biases and other reactive effects, and probably is limited in its generality to populations for which its scale terms have comparable connotations. There are a number of similar checklists and ratings in this category, some of which are well-developed and some ad hoc. They may have the same strengths, and certainly suffer the same weaknesses, as the SSS.

Observation measures.   Two subclasses of observation measures of psychological indices of stress are worth distinguishing. The first and less numerous subclass includes unaided observations of symptoms of psychological disturbances, such as tension, blushing, fear, and so on. The second and more numerous subclass includes indices of psychological process inferred from performance of tasks. Such tasks are inserted into the situation solely in order to measure those functions; the tasks are not relevant to the stressor or to coping with it, and are not indigenous to the behavior setting.

A very wide range of such imposed tasks, and of measures of psychological function based on them, have been used in stress research. They include tasks designed to measure shifts in visual, auditory, and tactual thresholds, changes in reaction time or latencies, and changes in recall, with respect to stress-relevant stimulus material. This class also includes measures of decrement in cognitive processes, in learning, in short- and long-term memory, in problem solving, in reasoning, and in psychomotor performance.

Measures based on direct observation of symptoms of stress are subject to observer biases, especially since they frequently involve considerable inference by the observer. Observation of task performance minimizes this problem and avoids some of the reactivity effects of self-report measures, but still is vulnerable to reactive effects because this procedure imposes a kind of artificiality on the setting. Imagine a pilot just back from a stressful mission being asked to perform a rotary pursuit task or an anagrams problem. We can scarcely assume that he would take the matter very seriously.

Measures derived from performance of an imposed task also pose a serious conceptual problem. Virtually all uses of such imposed tasks are done with the expectation that task performance will degrade under stress. Just what are the psychological functions which when degraded are evidence of stress? If there are many such functions, then a future question arises as to whether we should expect them *all* to show decrement for *any* stressor condition, whether these decrements are situation specific, or whether they are more or less mutually exclusive *alternative* reactions to stress. Furthermore, if degradation of such functions as reaction time, perceptual thresholds, and so forth, are to be taken as evidences of stress, then it is necessary to determine (or at least control for) sources of interindividual and intraindividual variability in these functions that are unrelated to the stressor conditions we wish to study. (This is parallel to the problem of stability-lability in physiological functions.) It is also possible, unless ruled out by definition, that stressor conditions improve some psychological functions, or do so for some individuals. Indeed, there is some evidence (see the U-shaped hypothesis in the last section of this chapter) that we ought to expect moderate increases in stress to have positive effects, with further increments having negative effects. Given these contingencies, then, it is quite important that at least more than two levels of stress be used in investigating the effects of stress on psychological functions. It is even better, of course, if multiple levels of multiple types of stress are used, and if effects are assessed by means of multiple measures of different types.

Trace measures: Projective tests. One can find a partial analogue to the physiological trace measures in the use of projective tests or similar instruments. Here, the subject is asked to carry out some task, such as writing a story to a Thematic Apperception Test (TAT) picture, and the investigator later scores that product in terms of aggression, dis-comfort-relief, anxiety, or the like. This is not completely a trace measure, as Webb et al. (1966) have used that term, because the subject is aware that he is in a research or contrived setting. But it does share some of the features of trace measures since the attributes of his response which are to be scored are usually unknown to the subject, and indeed these aspects are somewhat a by-product of the performance he is deliberately producing. (For example, the subject may be trying to write a creative story to a TAT card, although the investigator will subsequently score that story with respect to aggression.)

In any case, there has been only limited use of projectives or other quasitrace measures as indices of psychological stress. Such measures suffer from special vulnerabilities regarding scoring reliability, and also share the reactive effects of imposed tasks discussed above. It is perhaps worthwhile to urge effort toward development and use of true trace measures of psychological stress, comparable to biochemical analyses of the blood. But it is quite difficult to anticipate what such measures might be.

Archival records: Reports of psychological symptoms. There are rela-tively few instances, in our sample, of use of medical or other archival records of symptoms of psychological disturbance, or of evidence of psychological function (such as ability tests). When they are used, they usually serve the role of independent variables (neurotics versus normals) in relation to some other class of stress measure. Their potential use as dependent variables measuring stress effects would, of course, require long-term studies, and would have strengths and weaknesses similar to those involved in archival measures of physiological stress.

Indices of Behavior in Settings

This category is to be distinguished from the other categories—especially indices at the psychological level—because it emphasizes task behavior on tasks intrinsic to the settings in which they are measured, rather than tasks imposed solely to measure some performance, and interpersonal behavior rather than the properties of the individual.

Subjective report.   There are two groups of measures in this class. One includes self-report indices (from questionnaires, ratings, interviews) of the subject's confidence or aspirations on his tasks, or his evaluations of his ability to perform them. The second group has to do with the subject's perceptions of his interpersonal milieu: subjective or perceived role conflict, ambiguity, and overload; perceptions of power and attraction in the group, and so forth.

Given the need for inclusion of subjective components (that is, cognitive appraisal, expectations, subjective demands) in the conceptualization of stress, as discussed in Chapter 2, this class of measures is crucial. It represents the more or less direct assessment of perceptions of demands, and of perceptions of demand-capability imbalances (for example, expectation of task success, perceptions of incompatible role demands). Nevertheless, these measures are vulnerable to reactive effects. There is no way of telling, for example, whether the researcher's questions about role demands sensitize the respondent to conflicts he would not otherwise attend to, or lead him to deny conflicts of which he is aware. Again, the remedy is both careful design and use of multiple measures of different classes.

Observation measures.   As with the subjective report category, observation measures can be divided into two groups, roughly task and interpersonal. In the former group are indices of speed, quality, accuracy (or error) or success in performance of setting-relevant tasks (such as radio repair, or escape, in appropriate military training situations). The latter group includes indices of type and amount of activity, territoriality preferences, communication, expression of positive or negative interpersonal affect influence behavior. These are usually obtained by direct visual and auditory observation, sometimes aided by camera, tape recorder or specialized sensing instruments. Examples are given in the chapters by Haythorn (Chapter 11), Altman (Chapter 12), and Haas and Drabek (Chapter 15).

These measures offer the crucial advantage of being relatively nonreactive, provided the measurement operations are carried out so that they are unobtrusive in the setting. They are, however, vulnerable to content biases. In the absence of guiding substantive theory, they also give rise to some crucial conceptual questions: Just what are the parameters of interpersonal interaction which are affected by stressor conditions? How do these vary, over conditions and over individuals? How are these effects mediated by the perceptions, expectations, and capabilities of the organism undergoing the stress condition?

Trace measures.   As with psychological indices, behavioral indices seldom use trace measures. Such measures are most often used in the form of later analyses of task products or of evidences of group structure. These are, like the quasitrace measures discussed for psychological indices, really only partially analogous to the physiological trace measures, and they have the same strengths and weaknesses.

Archival records: Measures of production and academic achievement. This class of measures includes production records, supervisor ratings gathered for company purposes rather than research purposes, and academic achievement records. These measures pose problems of content and population restriction, and of contamination. Many things unrelated to any specific stressor condition affect production or academic achievement. These measures, like other archival records also require long-duration studies. Like physiological disease and psychological disorders, however, they represent a kind of ultimate criterion of effectiveness of social and task behavior in life settings; and, as such, they have a kind of intrinsic validity. But, for the same reasons, they leave a large gap between impact of stressor and its ultimate consequences. They tell us nothing about the psychological experience of stress, or about the processes involved in coping with stress, unless they are used within programatic efforts which try to trace the linkages within the stress sequence (see Chapter 2).

Some Methodological Issues

This partial cataloguing of measures that have been used in the study of stress, and brief comments on their strengths and weaknesses, should make apparent certain crucial methodological issues in the area. One of these is the problem of convergence of multiple measures of stress, both within and between levels. Another is the problem of reactivity— use of measurement operations which alter the property to be measured —which is especially critical in stress research. Still another is the problem of individual differences, in sensitivity to different types of stressors, and in the lability of processes underlying particular indices of stress. These and several related methodological issues in stress research have been discussed in Chapter 4.

The temporal aspects of stress research raise several crucial methodological problems. One has to do with the timing of measures in relation to stressing events. Stress effects presumably may have anticipatory and delayed components as well as immediate aspects. Furthermore, certain types of measures require particular time lags for their use (for example, physiological accretion measures) or have particular time-decay functions (for example, specific GSR effects). Then too, some classes of measures are useful only for studies involving macrotemporal effects (for instance, archival records), while others (such as GSR) can be used for studying processes within microtemporal contexts, but are relatively useless for long-term studies of life stresses. These and some additional temporal aspects of the stress problem were considered in Chapter 3.

These and other weaknesses of method—both in the measurement of stress effects and in the manipulation, control, and measurement of setting and situational conditions—also tend to becloud the import of substantive findings and constrain any generalizations based on them. Thus, the general principles to be discussed in the next part of this chapter must be qualified both in terms of the sampling limitations of the body of literature reviewed and in terms of the methodological limitations of the studies in that sample.

SOME GENERAL THEMES AND VARIATIONS

There are at least five underlying themes, which seem to emerge as reasonable empirical generalizations from detailed scrutiny of the findings in the sample of 200 stress studies reviewed here. These five themes seem to cut across substantive problem areas, although they have not been specifically tested in all areas. The themes are interrelated with one another, as will be apparent in the discussion to follow; and they are related to the propositions of the conceptual paradigm presented in Chapter 2. They are also highly convergent with the central themes and issues drawn by Appley and Trumbull (1967, pp. 400–412), and by Lazarus (1966, pp. 24–29).

The cognitive appraisal theme.   Stress is in the eye of the beholder, and one of the most pervasive themes, both theoretically and empirically, can be stated as follows: *Emotional experiences, and to some extent physiological and performance measures, are in part a function of the perceptions, expectations, or cognitive appraisal which the individual makes of the (stressing) situation* (F10, H4, L6, L7, R1).

For example, this proposition is suggested in the drug studies; physiological effects seem predictable from the biochemical nature of the drug, but feeling states and behavior seem more predictable from knowledge of the subjects' expectations (G6, S5). This same theme occurs in studies of reactions to threat of painful injections or puncture (B4, B18, W11). Furthermore, Lazarus and his colleagues, using vicarious physical threat, have succeeded in manipulating their subjects' cognitive processes or expectations, with associated changes in physiological (for instance, GSR) and psychological indices of arousal (L6, S18). As a related comment, one of the major criticisms of sensory deprivation studies has been that whether or not Ss produce the deprivation syndrome—hallucinations and the like—seems to depend partly upon their knowledge of what one is supposed to experience under the circumstances (J1). While this has been treated as an artifact, limiting external validity (Orne, for example, considers it an instance of experimental demand), it can equally well be construed as a finding of substantive significance which fits nicely with the empirical and theoretical proposition stated above.

This general theme has several aspects.

1. Individual differences. One man's stress is another man's challenge. (E1, G7).
2. Adaptation. Yesterday's novelty is today's routine. (L6, M11).
3. Learning. Expectation is father to perception. (S2, S18, U1).

The cognitive appraisal theme, and its variations, add up to a very general, and conceptually crucial, proposition about the nature of human stress. It presents that old bogeyman of the stress area—individual differences—in a new perspective, one which makes it much more a potentially researchable problem, rather than an inevitable and undesirable source of error variance. Furthermore, some of the other major themes to be discussed here can be construed as special cases of the cognitive appraisal theme.

The experience theme.   "Practice makes better—usually." Another pervasive theme, related to the first, can be stated as follows: *Prior experience, with the task, the stressor and/or the situation, attenuates the effects of stress.* This theme occurs in several variations. For example, prior exposure to shock makes the threat of shock less threatening (E4). Furthermore, disruptive effects of shock and of auditory and visual distractions on task performance tend to "wear off" during extended series of trials, even when the stressor keeps occurring on the later trials (R5). (A caution, however: there is some evidence for a generalization of stress from shock and distractors to later trials even when the stressor is not present on those later trials (K4, M12, S21). Moreover, virtually every study of task performance under stress shows practice or exposure or experience to be effective in reducing performance deterioration (B7, C2, F1, H7, M11, P14, S21, U1). Generally, performance improves with practice on the task, either with a stressor present or for control conditions (although, of course, the former may be accompanied by unmeasured compensatory costs). Finally, a somewhat related point is that subjects will seek information about the occurrence of a potential stressor even when they cannot avoid it, presumably because advance knowledge somehow affects their expectations, and/or their coping responses (L12). (Forewarned is, in some sense, forearmed.) Training, in the sense of deliberate practice in performance of the correct responses, appears to be an unmixed blessing with respect to alleviation of stress effects, and has been highly recommended as a remedy for potential stresses in space missions, civil defense, community disaster, and other real-life situations (F11, M2, R2). Also, prior information (warning) reduces stress and its adverse consequences, provided it is not too little or too late (E4, F11).

However, the one instance in our sample of studies which attempted a deliberate indoctrination of attitudes and expectations (about life on an Arctic base) was unsuccessful (E3). Furthermore, extended practice on a task (overlearning) is *detrimental* to later performance in a stressful situation, if conditions have changed so that the learned response is no longer the "correct" response (C4, P1).

This experience theme is closely related to the cognitive appraisal theme. Exposure or practice can be viewed as another form of change in S's expectations: prior exposure to a stressor lets S know better what is coming. The matter of experience is also part of a complex set of temporal factors, including practice and adaptation effects. Such temporal factors are discussed in Chapter 3.

The negative experience theme.   "Failure breeds failure." A third major theme, which represents a variation of the first and a qualification of the second, can be stated as: *The experience of failure on a task is stressful in itself and has a number of effects which subsequently lead to decreased performance effectiveness.* Induced or actual failure, or evaluation situations involving potential failure, leads to a lowering of level of aspiration, and (therefore?) to a decrement in performance on psychomotor, problem solving, reasoning, learning, and other tasks (A1, F2, H3, H8, K1, O2, P4, S16) but enhances performance on sensori-motor and conditioning tasks (B2, V2). It also leads to rigidity, to quick or impulsive closure, to decisions based on partial information, to increased conformity (A1, C7, D1, D6, P4, R4, S15). There is evidence that task failure is accompanied by increases in the 17-ketosteroids (B5).

Effects of failure can be modified by experience on the task, especially *successful* experience (F2, H7). Thus, this principle can be seen as an extension to the second one: *Prior experience influences stress and its effects.* If that experience is unsuccessful (that is, negatively reinforcing, or of negative affect), prior experience will increase stress and degrade performance. If the prior experience is successful (positively reinforcing, of positive affect, or otherwise leading to learning, mastery or adaptation), stress will be decreased and its negative effects on task performance will be attenuated.

Effects of failure can also be modified by manipulation of the S's expectations of success—for example, by telling him that subsequent tasks will be easy, or easy for him (F3, P11). It is interesting that one study (E5) found Ss able to predict their own subsequent performance levels, although the investigator's measures of personality could not. This suggests that what is being altered here is the S's level of aspiration, and that perhaps failure itself operates similarly, by altering level of aspiration downward. The latter, in turn, makes it clear that the failure theme is a special form of the cognitive-appraisal principle discussed above.

The inverted-U theme.   "Stress comes from too much of a good thing— or not enough of it." Perhaps one of the most widespread ideas in the stress area is the notion (deriving from Selye's pioneer work) that stress represents a kind of abnormal stimulus load, and that stress responses reflect an increase in arousal. There is a related notion, deriving from the work on sensory and perceptual deprivation, that a condition of subnormal stimulus load is also stressful (see Chapter 2). It is not so clear how the deprivation stress relates to either physiological or psychological arousal.

From these two notions, it is a fairly short step to the proposition that stress can be viewed as arising from increments or decrements of some stimulus parameters (intensity, complexity, information, uncertainty, and so forth) away from some optimal zone. A plot of degree of "felt stress" resulting from various magnitudes of a potentially stressing stimulus condition is, therefore, a U-shaped function; while a plot of performance effectiveness over that range of stimulus levels is an inverted U-shaped function.

This hypothesis is very complex, to say the least. First of all, there are problems arising from lack of calibration of degrees of stressor conditions, and lack of comparability of different stressors; these matters are discussed in Chapter 4. The inverted-U hypothesis becomes very complex when we add the individual-differences axiom (optimal level changes for a given individual, as a function of time, development, the state of the organism, and/or learning).

Nevertheless, there appears to be a good bit of evidence supporting (or at least not refuting) the proposition that *the intensity of environmental stimulation (broadly conceived) is curvilinearly related to degree of felt stress and to degree of effectiveness of subsequent performance* (D3, S7, T3; see also Haythorn, Chapter 11, and Steiner, Chapter 10.) For example, degree of time pressure or pacing of a task, plotted against productivity or errors, shows the curvilinear (U-shaped) form (P5). Also, studies using various measures of situational, test, or trait anxiety [for example, Taylor's Manifest Anxiety Scale (MAS)], along with external stressors (such as shock), tend to support the curvilinear-function hypothesis.[2] In a number of such studies, high-anxiety subjects performed *better* than low-anxiety Ss under low or no (external) stress conditions, but performed *poorer* than low-anxiety Ss under high (external) stress. This finding seems to hold for shock, distractors, task-difficulty, pacing, evaluation threat, and task failure as (external) stress conditions, and for performance problem solving, learning and other types of tasks (F3, M5, W3).

The evidence is not all clear-cut, though. For example, there is evidence that *reaction time increases* with degree of task-based conflict on a variety of learning tasks (A4, A5, B8, K2). On the other hand, there is also evidence that *response time decreases* as a function of evaluation threat and task failure, as well as so-called impulsive closure or decisions on the basis of limited information (F5, K3). Steiner (Chapter 10) presents evidence to suggest that Ss who are most stressed (as indicated by GSR) by an interpersonal disagreement situation show *shorter* decision time than Ss relatively unstressed by the same situation; whereas control Ss, performing the same task but without presence of the stressor, showed *even shorter* decision times.

Studies using shock as a stressor have shown conflicting results regarding task performance. Shock impairs time and error scores, distraction does not, and *both* shock and distraction improve those scores (M17). Shock improves performance on reasoning tasks (B11) but impairs performance on a group escape task (K6). Finally, shock does not affect reaction times (F1).

To some extent, dissenting evidence can be rejected by the argument that the conditions of a given study did not encompass a sufficient span of the stimulus continuum to yield the expected U-shaped curve. If degree of stimulus intensity correlates positively and linearly with performance, the high level was not high enough; if degree of stimulus intensity correlates negatively and linearly with performance, the low condition was *in*, rather than below the optimal zone of stimulation or arousal. Until we can calibrate either degrees of stress or degrees of stimulus intensity in some systematic way, such explanations will have an aura of circularity about them. The problem of calibration of stressor is dealt with in Chapter 4.

The social-interaction theme.   "We can't live with people, and we can't live without them." Social interaction is a two-edged sword in the context of stress research. There is at least scattered evidence that presence of, and communication with, other human beings acts to

---

[2] The meaning we have given this result, of course, depends on several qualifying assumptions. First, it is based on the assumption that "anxiety in the person" —trait anxiety—is the same kind of thing as stress arising from an external source. Second, it assumes that such stresses are additive, and this is a tenuous assumption (see discussion of calibration of stressors in Chapter 4.)

attenuate effects of some physical threats, as well as effects of restricted environments (M20, S6, W4). The notion that presence of others increases the stress threshold has been suggested (M9). There is some evidence that the opportunity for social interaction—with its presumed positive reinforcement value—reduces the psychological and psychosomatic symptomatology of Ss under conditions of sensory-perceptual restriction (G12). Furthermore, the attenuation of stress effects is greater if the others are persons with whom S has a prior positive affect relationship (presumably, therefore, a source of more positive reward to him) than if the others are strangers (D2, K7). This differential is further enhanced as a function of the strength of S's affiliation motivation (D8, D9, K7).

But presence of others is not an unmixed blessing, it would seem, especially in the context of long-term isolation in a constraining environment (see Haythorn, Chapter 11). Social interaction and enforced intimacy may be a source of irritation to S. And the crowding of a behavior setting of fixed physical (and interpersonal) dimensions may lead to an increase of the stressing effects of a physical threat, as well as to stress effects deriving directly from restriction of environment. Indeed, presence of, and interdependence with, other people may in itself generate new stresses—ego threats and interpersonal threats—which could not be present if S were in the situation alone.

The degree to which such positive or negative effects will operate appears to depend on: the personality and motivational patterns of the Ss, singly and in relation to each other (for example, D2, D9, G5, S11); the size and the formal and informal structure of the group (for example, M9, S14, S24); features of the ecological setting (G12, M9); and, of course, the nature of the tasks and stressors involved in the situation (F4, H1, O1). (See also, the work of Haythorn and Altman on small groups in isolated and confined settings, Chapters 11 and 12 of this volume.)

It would appear then that social interaction is a kind of stimulation which, like other kinds, has an optimal level. Too little or too much is stressful. Ss will work for social reinforcement (for example, emit operant responses) when deprived of it (D8, D9), just as they will seek sensory-perceptual stimulation, or information, when in a stimulus-deprived environment (Z6); and they will develop means for reducing social interaction if they are satiated (G11). The optimal zone, of course, depends on the behavior setting. It is also likely that the optimal zone varies over individuals and changes or adapts over time for the same individual.

SUMMARY

These five themes add up to something less than a systematic theory of stress, but they do represent a beginning in that direction. It must be kept in mind, of course, that these themes are induced as empirical generalizations from a limited sample of stress research by loose inference processes which overlook many specific points of evidence in order to remain general. They should be viewed as suggestive, not definitive.

Nevertheless, they do represent some general conceptual propositions which, together with the methodological problems noted previously, can be used as a basis for a summary formulation. That formulation, given below can serve three functions: (1) as an overview of some empirical convergences, (2) as a warning of some of the methodological problems which need research, and (3) as a set of substantive issues for future research.

Social-psychological stress can arise from situational conditions which lead to a subjective or cognitive appraisal of threat. The threat can involve actual or anticipated harms to the physical self, the psychological self, and/or interpersonal relations. The threat may also derive from conditions of the physical and/or social environment which deprive the individual of opportunities to satisfy physical, psychological, and/or interpersonal needs.

The occurrence of stress and its effects can be measured at physiological, psychological, behavioral (task and interpersonal performances), and at the organizational level. Within each of these levels, various operational types of measures can be applied: subjective reports, aided or unaided observation, trace measures, archival records. Alternative measures within level and type do not always agree; nor is there always convergence of measures across types and/or levels. Such lack of convergence of measures can be viewed as methodological weakness (alternate measures of the same property—stress—yield different results), or as substantive information (alternative measures represent alternate and more or less substitutable responses to stress).

The effects of stress conditions are mediated through subjective psychological processes (for example, cognitive appraisals of threat, secondary appraisals of coping resources) which are affected by many perspectives of the individual. Because of this, there are substantial interindividual differences in what stimulus situations lend to the perception of threat. Moreover, adaptation effects and learning effects make for intraindividual differences in perception of threat over time, under the "same" stimulus conditions. Finally, many individual physiological, psychological, and behavioral processes vary through time as a function of factors (such as motivation, diurnal cycles) which are more or less orthogonal to environmental stressing events; this introduces further inter- and intraindividual variability in the perception of threat and in responses to it. These considerations, also, are both methodological problems and crucial substantive issues for future stress research.

Stress, and responses to stress, also vary as a function of experience—both experience with the situation or conditions giving rise to stress and practice in behaviors to cope with or avoid the consequences of stressor conditions. Past experience leading to successful mastery or to positive reinforcements tends to reduce the perception of threat (to raise the threat threshold); past experience leading to failure or to negative reinforcements (for example, negative evaluations by others) tend to lower the threat threshold; furthermore, failure and expectations of failure are in themselves threatening.

Situational or stimulus conditions seem to be related to perceived threat and to performance in a curvilinear manner. Extremely low levels or lack of variability of physical and/or social stimulation tend to induce threat and to impair functioning. Extremely high levels or high complexity or ambiguity of physical and/or social stimulation also tend to induce threat and to impair functioning. Moderate intensities tend to be nonthreatening and motivating, and to be conducive to optimum functioning. However, the implied optimal zone probably varies as a function of properties of the physical and social setting, personal attributes, adaptation, and learning. These considerations, too, pose critical methodological problems and offer crucial substantive issues for future investigation.

References

Appley, M. H., & Trumbull, R. Psychological stress. New York: Appleton, 1967.

Applezweig, M. H. Psychological stress and related concepts: A bibliography. Technical Report No. 7, Department of Psychology, Connecticut College, New London, Conn., December 1957.

Kahn, R. L., Wolfe, D. M., Quinn, R. P., Snoek, J. D., & Rosenthal, R. A. Organizational stress: Studies in role conflict and ambiguity. New York: Wiley, 1964.

Kerle, R. H., & Bialek, H. M. The construction, validation, and application of a subjective stress scale. Staff Memo, Fighter IV, Study 23, February 1958. Presidio of Monterey, Calif.: Human Resources Research Office.

Lazarus, R. S. Psychological stress and the coping process. New York: McGraw-Hill, 1966.

Mandler, G., Mandler, J., Kremen, I., & Sholiton, R. D. The response to threat: Relations among verbal and physiological indices. Psychological Monographs General and Applied, 1961, 75, Whole No. 513.

Sells, S. B. Military small group performance under isolation and stress—An annotated bibliography. Arctic Aeromedical Laboratory, Fort Wainwright, Alaska AA1-TR-61-21, Project 8243-11, October 1961.

Trumbull, R. Environment modification for human performance. ONR Report ACR-105, Office of Naval Research, Department of the Navy, July 1965.

Webb, E. J., Campbell, D. T., Schwartz, R. D., & Sechrest, L. Unobtrusive measures: Nonreactive research in the social sciences. Skokie, Ill.: Rand McNally, 1966.

Bibliography of Stress Research
in the Literature Review

A1. Ainsworth, H. Rigidity, insecurity, and stress. *Journal of Abnormal and Social Psychology*, 1958, **56**, 67–74.
A2. Applezweig, M. H., & Moeller, G. *The role of motivation in psychological stress*. New London, Conn.: Department of Psychology, Connecticut College, January 1957, Contract Nonr 996(02), Project NR 171-228.
A3. Armilla, J. Anxiety in taking the role of the leader. *Journal of Abnormal and Social Psychology*, 1964, **68**(5), 550–552.
A4. Atthowe, J. M., Jr. Types of conflict and their resolution: A reinterpretation. *Journal of Experimental Psychology*, 1960, **59**, 1–9.
A5. Atthowe, J. M., Jr. Interpersonal decision making: The resolution of a dyadic conflict. *Journal of Abnormal and Social Psychology*, 1961, **62**, 114–119.

B1. Basowitz, H., Korchin, S. J., & Grinker, R. R. Anxiety in a life stress. *Journal of Psychology*, 1954, **38**, 503–510.
B2. Beam, J. C. Serial learning and conditioning under real-life stress. *Journal of Abnormal and Social Psychology*, 1955, **51**, 543–552.
B3. Beckwith, J., Iverson, A., & Render, M. E. Test anxiety, task relevance of group experience, and change in level of aspiration. *Journal of Personality and Social Psychology*, 1965, **1**(6), 579–588.
B4. Bem, J., Wallach, M. A., & Kogan, N. Group decision making under risk of aversive consequences. *Journal of Personality and Social Psychology*, 1965, **1**(5), 453–460.
B5. Berkeley, A. W. Level of aspiration in relation to adrenal cortical activity and the concept of stress. *Journal of Comparative and Physiological Psychology*, 1952, **45**, 443–449.
B6. Berkowitz, H., Butterfield, E. C., & Zigler, E. The effects of social reinforcers on persistence and learning tasks following positive and negative social interactions. *Journal of Personality and Social Psychology*, 1965, **2**(5), 706–715.
B7. Berkun, M. M., Bialek, H. M., Kern, R. P., & Yagi, K. Experimental studies of psychological stress in man. *Psychological Monographs*, 1962, **76**(15, Whole No. 534), 39 pp.
B8. Berlyne, D. E. Conflict and choice time. *British Journal of Psychology*, 1957, **48**, 106–118.
B9. Berlyne, D. E. Uncertainty and conflict: A point of contact between information-theory and behavior-theory concepts. *Psychological Review*, 1957, **64**, 329–339.
B10. Bernert, E. H., & Ikle, F. O. Evacuation and the cohesion of urban groups. *American Journal of Sociology*, **58**(2), 133–138.
B11. Block, C. H. Interrelations of stress and anxiety in determining problem-solving performance. *Dissertation Abstracts*, 1964, **25**(2), 1316.
B12. Bluhm, P. M., & Kennedy, W. A. Discrimination reaction time as a

function of incentive-related DRQ anxiety and task difficulty. *Perceptual and Motor Skills*, 1965, **20**, 131–134.

B13. Boguslaw, R. Role tensions and role perception: An approach to the analysis of labor-management relations. *Dissertation Abstracts*, 1957, **17**, 2329–2330.

B14. Bondy, C. Problems of internment camps. *Journal of Abnormal and Social Psychology*, 1943, **38**, 453–475.

B15. Boomer, D. S. Subjective certainty and resistance to change. *Journal of Abnormal and Social Psychology*, 1959, **58**, 323–328.

B16. Borah, L. A. The effects of threat in bargaining: Critical and experimental analysis. *Journal of Abnormal and Social Psychology*, 1963, **66**, 37–44.

B17. Bovard, E. W. The effect of social stimuli on the response to stress. *Psychological Review*, 1959, **66**, 267–277.

B18. Brehm, M. L., Back, K. W., & Bogdonoff, M. D. A physiological effect of cognitive dissonance under stress and deprivation. *Journal of Abnormal and Social Psychology*, 1964, **69**(3), 303–310.

B19. Brody, N. On achievement, test anxiety, and subjective probability of success in risk taking behavior. *Journal of Abnormal and Social Psychology*, 1963, **66**(5), 413–417.

B20. Bruning, J. L. Leadership in disaster. *Psychology*, 1964, No. 4, **I**.

C1. Callagan, J. E., Walters, R. H., & Newman, A. F. Effect of Solitary Confinement on Prisoners. *American Journal of Psychiatry*, 1963, **119**, 771–773.

C2. Capretta, P. J., & Berkun, M. M. Validity and reliability of certain measures of psychological stress. *Psychological Reports*, 1962, **10**, 875–876.

C3. Carr, L. J. Disaster and the sequence-pattern concept of social change. *American Journal of Sociology*, 1932, **38**, 207–218.

C4. Castaneda, A., & Palermo, D. S. Psychomotor performance as a function of amount of training and stress. *Journal of Experimental Psychology*, 1955, **50**, 175–179.

C5. Cohen, E. A. *Human behavior in the concentration camp.* New York: Norton, 1953.

C6. Cohn, J. B., & Rubinstein, J. An experimental approach to psychological stress. *Journal of American Psychiatry*, 1954, **III**, 276–282.

C7. Cowen, E. L. The influence of varying degrees of psychological stress on problem-solving rigidity. *Journal of Abnormal and Social Psychology*, 1952, **47**, 512–519.

C8. Crawford, F., & Esch, F. *Situational factors and attitudes expressed toward duty with ARDC.* Technical Research Report No. 3, September 1953, Maxwell AFB, Alabama, Air Research & Development Command, Human Resources Institute.

D1. Darley, M. M. Fear and social comparison as determinants of conformity behavior. *Journal of Personality and Social Psychology*, 1966, **4**(1), 73–78.

D2. Davis, J. M., McCourt, W. F., Courtney, J., & Solomon, P. Sensory deprivation: The role of social isolation. *Archives of General Psychiatry*, 1961, **5**, 85–90.

D3.   Davis, S. W. Stress in combat. *Scientific American*, 1956, **194**(3), 31–35.
D4.   Debons, A. *Survey of human adjustment problems in the northern latitudes—a study of adjustive, non-adjustive behavior as reflected by variations of shifts in disposition by infantrymen assigned to Alaska.* Ladd AFB, Alaska: Arctic Aeromedical Lab., April 1950.
D5.   Debons, A. *Survey of human adjustment problems in the northern latitudes. Study of adjustive, non-adjustive behavior as reflected by variations of shifts in disposition by Air Force personnel assigned to Montana, pre-winter.* Ladd AFB, Alaska: Arctic Aeromedical Lab., February 1951.
D6.   Dittes, J. E. Impulsive closure as a reaction to failure induced threat. *Journal of Abnormal and Social Psychology*, 1961, **63**, 562–569.
D7.   Dohrenwend, B. P. The social psychological nature of stress: A framework for causal inquiry. *Journal of Abnormal and Social Psychology*, 1961, **62**(2), 294–302.
D8.   Dohrenwend, B. S., & Dohrenwend, B. P. Stress situations, birth order and psychological symptoms. *Journal of Abnormal Psychology*, 1966, **71** (3, Pt. I), 215–223.
D9.   Dohrenwend, B. S., & Dohrenwend, B. P. Stress situations, birth order and psychological symptoms. *Journal of Abnormal Psychology*, 1966, **71** (3, Pt. II), 215–223.
D10.   Dorwart, W., Ezerman, R., Lewis, M., & Rosenhaw, D. The effect of brief social deprivation on social and nonsocial reinforcement. *Journal of Personality and Social Psychology*, 1965, **2**(1), 111–115.
D11.   Drabek, T. E., & Haas, J. E. Organizational simulation: A study in method. Paper presented at the Annual Meeting of the Midwest Sociological Society, Madison, Wis., April 21–23, 1966.

E1.   Eckerman, W. C. The relationship of need achievement to production, job satisfaction and psychological stress. *Dissertation Abstracts*, 1964, **24**(8), 3446.
E2.   Ehrlich, H. J., Rinehart, J. W., & Howell, J. C. The study of role conflict: Exploration in methodology. *Sociometry*, 1962, **25**(1), 85–97.
E3.   Eilbert, L. *Indoctrination procedures for personnel assigned to arctic sites.* Final Report, January 1960, Pittsburgh, Penn., American Institute for Research, Contract AF 41(657)-241, Ladd AFB, Alaska: Arctic Aeromedical Lab.
E4.   Elliott, R. Effects of uncertainty about the nature and advent of a noxious stimulus (shock) upon heart rate. *Journal of Personality and Social Psychology*, 1966, **3**(3), 353–357.
E5.   Ericksen, C. W., Lazarus, R. S., & Strange, J. R. Psychological stress and its personality correlates. *Journal of Personality*, 1952, **20**, 277–286.
E6.   Ericksen, C. W., & Wechsler, H. Some effects of experimentally induced anxiety upon discrimination behavior. *Journal of Abnormal and Social Psychology*, 1955, **51**, 458–463.
E7.   Exline, R., & Ziller, R. C. Status congruency and interpersonal conflict in decision-making groups. *Human Relations*, 1959, **12**, 147–162.

F1.   Farber, I. E., & Spence, K. W. Effects of anxiety, stress, and task variables on reaction time. *Journal of Personality*, 1956, **25**, 1–18.

F2.   Feather, N. T. The relationship of expectation of success to need achievement and test anxiety. *Journal of Personality and Social Psychology*, 1965, **1**(2), 118–126.

F3.   Feather, N. T. Effects of prior success and failure on expectations of success and subsequent performance. *Journal of Personality and Social Psychology*, 1966, **3**(3), 237–299.

F4.   Feldman, S. E., & Rice, J. K. Tolerance for unambiguous feedback. *Journal of Personality and Social Psychology*, 1965, **2**(3), 341–347.

F5.   Fenz, W. D. Conflict and stress as related to physiological activation and sensory perceptual and cognitive functioning. *Psychological Monographs: General and Applied*, 1964, **78**(8, Whole No. 585), 33 pp.

F6.   Feshback, S., & Singer, R. D. The effects of fear arousal and suppression of fear upon social perception. *Journal of Abnormal and Social Psychology*, 1957, **55**(3), 283–288.

F7.   Fox, H. M., Gifford, S., Murawski, B. J., Rizzo, N. D., & Kudarauskas, E. N. Some methods of observing humans under stress. *Psychiatry Research Report*, 1957, No. 7, 14–26.

F8.   Freeman, G. L. Suggestions for a standardized "stress" test. *Journal of General Psychology*, 1945, **32**, 3–11.

F9.   Friedsam, H. J. Older persons in disaster. In G. W. Baker, D. W. Chapman (Eds.), *Man and society in disaster*. New York: Basic Books, 1962.

F10. Fritz, C. E. Disasters compared in six American communities. *Human Organization*, 1957, **16**, 6–9.

F11. Fritz, C. E., & Marks, E. S. The NORC studies of human behavior in disaster. *Journal of Social Issues*, 1954, **10**, 26–41.

F12. Funkinstein, D. H. The interrelationship of acute emergency reactions during stress and affective disorder. *American Journal of Psychiatry*, 1956, **112**, 930–932.

G1.   Gallo, P. S. Effects of increased incentives upon the use of threat in bargaining. *Journal of Personality and Social Psychology*, 1966, **4**(1), 14–20.

G2.   Geitwitz, P. J. Structure of boredom. *Journal of Personality and Social Psychology*, 1966, **3**(5), 592–600.

G3.   Gerard, H. B. The anchorage of opinions in face-to-face groups. *Human Relations*, 1954, **7**(3), 313–325.

G4.   Gerard, H. B. Disagreement with others, their credibility and experienced stress. *Journal of Abnormal and Social Psychology*, 1961, **62**, 559–564.

G5.   Gifford, S., & Murewski, B. Minimal sleep deprivation alone and in small groups: Effects on ego-functioning and 24 hour body temperature and adreno-cortical patterns. *Symposium on Medical Aspects of Stress in the Military Climate*, Washington, D. C.: Walter Reed Army Institute of Research, Walter Reed Army Medical Center, 1964.

88   Social and Psychological Factors in Stress

G6.   Goldberger, L. Cognitive test performance under LSD-25, placebo and isolation. *Journal of Nervous Mental Disorders,* 1966, **142**(2), 4–9.

G7.   Goldstein, M. J. Relationship between coping and avoiding behavior and response to fear-arousing propaganda. *Journal of Abnormal and Social Psychology,* 1959, **58,** 247–252.

G8.   Goldstein, R. H. Behavioral effects of psychological stress. *Dissertation Abstracts,* June 1959, **19**(12), 3364.

G9.   Grinker, R. R., & Spiegel, J. P. *Men under stress.* Philadelphia, Penn.: Blakiston, 1945.

G10.   Gross, E., & Miller, C. *The impact of isolation on worker adjustment in military installations of the United States & Japan.* Unpublished research, in part supported by USAF Contract AF-33-(038)-26823. Monitored by HRRI, ARDC, Maxwell AFB.

G11.   Guetzkow, H., & Gyr, J. An analysis of conflict in decision-making groups. *Human Relations,* 1954, **7,** 367–382.

G12.   Gullahorn, J. T. Measuring role conflict. *American Journal of Sociology,* 1956, **61,** 299–303.

H1.   Hamblin, R. L. Group integration during a crisis. *Human Relations,* 1958, **11,** 67–77.

H2.   Hancock, J. G., & Teevan, R. C. Fear of failure and risk-taking behavior. *Journal of Personality,* 1964, **32**(2), 200–209.

H3.   Harleston, B. W. Test anxiety and performance in problem-solving situations. *Journal of Personality,* 1962, **30**(4), 557–573.

H4.   Harris, F. G., Mayer, J., & Becker, H. A. *Experiences in the study of combat in the Korean theater. I. Report on psychiatric and psychological data.* WRAIR-43-55, November 1955, Washington, D. C.: Walter Reed Army Institute of Research, Walter Reed Army Medical Center.

H5.   Harris, W., Mackie, R., & Wilson, C. *Research on the development of performance criteria.* Technical Report No. VI. *Performance under stress: a review and critique of recent studies.* July 1956. ONR Contract Nonr 1241. Los Angeles, Calif.: Human Factors Research, Inc.

H6.   Hayner, N., & Ash, E. The prisoner community as a social group. *American Sociological Review,* 1939, **4,** 362–369.

H7.   Hill, R., & Hansen, D. Families in disaster. In G. W. Baker & D. W. Chapman, (Eds.), *Man and society in disaster.* New York: Basic Books, 1962.

H8.   Hokanson, J. E., & Burgess, M. The effects of status, type of frustration and aggression on vascular processes. *Journal of Abnormal and Social Psychology,* 1962, **65**(4), 232–237.

H9.   Hokanson, J. E., & Burgess, M. Effects of physiological arousal level, frustration and task complexity on performance. *Journal of Abnormal and Social Psychology,* 1964, **68,** 698–702.

H10.   Holtzman, W. H., & Bitterman, M. E. Factorial study of adjustment to stress. *Journal of Abnormal and Social Psychology,* 1956, **52,** 179–185.

I1.   Indik, B., Seashore, S. E., & Slesinger, J. Demographic correlates of psychological strain. *Journal of Abnormal and Social Psychology,* 1964, **69,** 26–38.

J1.   Jackson, C. W., & Pollard, J. C. Sensory deprivation and suggestion: a theoretical approach. *Behavioral Science*, 1962, 7, 332.

J2.   Janis, I. Psychological effects of warnings. In G. W. Baker & D. W. Chapman (Eds.), *Man and society in disaster*. New York: Basic Books, 1962.

J3.   Johnson, H. J. Decision making, conflict and physiological arousal. *Journal of Abnormal and Social Psychology*, 1963, 67, 114–124.

K1.   Kalish, H., Garmezy, N., Rodnick, E., & Bleke, R. The effects of anxiety and experimentally induced stress on verbal learning. *Journal of General Psychology*, 1958, 59, 87–95.

K2.   Kamano, D. K. Relationship of ego disjunction and manifest anxiety to conflict resolution. *Journal of Abnormal and Social Psychology*, 1963, 66(3), 281–284.

K3.   Katchmar, L. T., Ross, S., & Andrews, T. G. Effects of stress and anxiety on performance of a complex verbal coding task. *Journal of Experimental Psychology*, 1958, 55, 559–564.

K4.   Katkin, E. S. Relationship between manifest anxiety and two indices of autonomic response to stress. *Journal of Personality and Social Psychology*, 1965, 2(3), 324–333.

K5.   Kaufman, H. Definitions and methodology in the study of aggression. *Psychological Bulletin*, 1965, 64(5), 351–364.

K6.   Kelley, H. H., Condry, J. C., Jr., Dahlke, A. E., & Hill, A. H. Collective behavior in a simulated panic situation. *Journal of Experimental Social Psychology*, 1965, 1(1), 20–54.

K7.   Kissel, S. Stress-reducing properties of social stimuli. *Journal of Personality and Social Psychology*, 1965, 2(3), 378–384.

K8.   Kollar, E. J. Psychological stress: a re-evaluation. *Journal of Nervous Mental Disorders*, 1961, 132, 382–396.

K9.   Kugelmass, S., & Lieblich, I. Effects of realistic stress and procedural interference in experimental lie detection. *Journal of Applied Psychology*, 1966, 50(3), 211–216.

K10. Kurz, R. B. Effects of three kinds of stressors on human learning and performance. *Psychological Review*, 1964, 14(1), 161–162.

L1.   Lanzetta, J. T., & Driscoll, J. M. Preference for information about an uncertain but unavoidable outcome. *Journal of Personality and Social Psychology*, 1966, 3(1), 96–103.

L2.   Lanzetta, J. T., Haefner, D., Langham, P., & Axelrod, H. Some effects of situational threat on group behavior. *Journal of Abnormal and Social Psychology*, 1954, 49, 445–453.

L3.   Lanzetta, J. T., Wendt, G. R., Langham, P., & Haefner, D. The effects of an "anxiety-reducing" medication on group behavior under threat. *Journal of Abnormal and Social Psychology*, 1956, 52(1), 103–108.

L4.   Law, P. Personality problems in Antarctica. *Medical Journal of Australia*, February 20, 1960, 273–282. (The Sir Richard Stawell Oration, delivered to the Victorian Branch of the British Medical Association.)

L5.   Lazarus, R. S. Laboratory approach to the dynamics of psychological stress. *American Psychologist*, 1964, 19, 400–411.

L6.   Lazarus, R. S., Baker, R. W., Broverman, D. M., & Mayer, J. Personality and psychological stress. *Journal of Personality*, 1957, **25**, 559–577.

L7.   Lazarus, R. S., Deese, J., & Osler, S. *Review of research on effects of psychological stress upon performance.* Research Bulletin 51-28, December 1951. San Antonio: Human Resources Research Center, ATC, Lackland AFB, Texas.

L8.   Leon, H. V., & Frank, G. H. Personality correlates of cognitive disturbances in short term sensory isolation. *Journal of General Psychology*, 1966, **74**, 273–278.

L9.   Lewis, M. Social isolation: A parametric study of its effects on social reinforcement. *Journal of Experimental Child Psychology*, 1965, **2**, 205–218.

L10.   Lockhard, J. A. Choice of warning signal or no warning signal in an unavoidable shock situation. *Journal of Comparative and Physiological Psychology*, 1963, **56**, 526–530.

L11.   Longnecker, E. D. Perceptual recognition as a function of anxiety, motivation, and the testing situation. *Journal of Abnormal and Social Psychology*, 1962, **64**(3), 215–221.

L12.   Luby, E. D., et al. Biochemical, psychological and behavioral responses to sleep deprivation. *Annals of the New York Academy of Science*, 1962, **96**, 71–79.

M1.   Maier, N. R. The role of frustration in social movements. *Psychological Review*, 1942, **49**, 586–599.

M2.   Malmo, R. B., Smith, A. A., & Kohlmeyer, W. A. Motor manifestation of conflict in interview: A case study. *Journal of Abnormal and Social Psychology*, 1956, **52**, 268–271.

M3.   Martin, B. Assessment of anxiety by physiological behavioral measures. *Psychological Bulletin*, 1961, **58**, 234–255.

M4.   Maslow, A. H. Deprivation, threat, and frustration. *Psychological Review*, 1941, **48**, 364–366.

M5.   Matarazzo, R. G., & Matarazzo, J. D. Anxiety level and pursuit-motor performance. *Journal of Consulting Psychology*, 1956, **20**, 70.

M6.   McCollum, E. Survey of adjustment problems in the northern latitudes—Morale survey of Alaskan air command. Project No. 21-01-022, Program C, Pt. 1-C, August 1950. Ladd AFB, Alaska: Arctic Aeromedical Lab.

M7.   McDonald, R. D., & Yagi, K. A note on eosinopenia as an index of psychological stress. *Psychosomatic Medicine*, 1960, **22**, 149–150.

M8.   Mechanic, D. *Students under stress.* New York: Free Press, 1960.

M9.   Milburn, T. W. Space crews, psychology and American society. *Journal of Social Issues*, 1961, **17**(2), 24–28.

M10.   Milgram, S. Liberating effects of group pressure. *Journal of Personality and Social Psychology*, 1965, **1**(2), 127–134.

M11.   Miller, D. A brief review of salient specific findings on morale and human behavior of young men living under the isolation and relative deprivation of radar base habitability. Working paper. Washington, D. C.: *Disaster Research Group, Division of Anthropology and Psychology*, National Academy of Sciences—National Research Council, 1959.

M12.   Miller, L. H., & Shmavonian, B. M. Replicability of two GSR indices as function of stress and cognitive activity. *Journal of Personality and Social Psychology*, 1965, **2**(5), 753–756.

M13.   Moore, H. E. Toward a theory of disaster. *American Sociological Review*, 1956, **21**, 733–737.

M14.   Mordkoff, A. M. The relation between physiological and phenomenological indices of arousal. *Dissertation Abstracts*, 1964, **24**(9), 3852.

M15.   Morris, R. E. Witness performance under stress: A sociological approach. *Journal of Social Issues*, 1957, **12**(2), 17–22.

M16.   Mulder, M., & Stemerding, A. Threat, attraction to group, and need for strong leadership: A laboratory experiment in a natural setting. *Human Relations*, 1963, **16**, 317–334.

M17.   Murphy, R. E. Effects of threat of shock, distraction and task design on performance. *Journal of Experimental Psychology*, 1959 (August), **58**, 1134–1141.

M18.   Murray, E. J. Conflict and repression during sleep deprivation. *Journal of Abnormal and Social Psychology*, 1959, **59**(1), 95–101.

M19.   Murray, E. J., Sabein, E. H., Erikson, K. T., Hill, W. F., & Cohen, M. The effects of sleep deprivation on social behavior. (Experiment No. 1) *Journal of Social Psychology*, in press.

M20.   Murray, E. J., Schein, E. H., Erikson, K. T., Hill, W. F., & Cohen, M. The effects of sleep deprivation on social behavior. (Experiment No. 2) *Journal of Social Psychology*, in press.

M21.   Murray, H. A. Studies of stressful interpersonal disputations. *American Psychologist*, 1963, **18**(1), 28–36.

M22.   Meeland, T., Egbert, R. L., & Miller, I. Field stress: A preliminary study of its structure, measurement, and relationship to combat. Fighter II, Staff memorandum. Fort Ord, Calif., May 27, 1957, U.S. Army Leadership, Human Research Unit.

N1.   Neuringer, C. Reactions to interpersonal crises in suicidal individuals. *Journal of General Psychology*, 1964, **71**, 47–55.

N2.   Nix, H. L., & Bates, F. L. Occupational role stresses: A structural approach. *Rural Social*, 1962, **27**(1), 7–17.

O1.   Orr, D. B. Research behavior impairment due to stress: An experiment in long-term performance. *Journal of Experimental Psychology*, 1964, **68**(1), 94–102.

O2.   Osler, S. F. Intellectual performance as a function of two types of psychological stress. *Journal of Experimental Psychology*, 1954, **47**(2), 115–121.

P1.   Palermo, D. S. Proactive interference and facilitation as a function of amount of training and stress. *Journal of Experimental Psychology*, 1957, **53**(5), 293–296.

P2.   Palmer, G. T., Jr., & Sells, S. B. Behavioral factors in disaster situations. *Journal of Social Psychology*, 1965, **66**(1), 65–71.

P3.   Parad, H. J., & Caplan, G. A framework for studying families in crisis. *Journal of Social Work*, 1960, **5**(3), 3–15.

P4.   Parkes, E. H. The effect of situational stress, set-strength, and trait anxiety on problem-solving rigidity. *Dissertation Abstracts*, 1963, **24**(1), 385.

P5.   Pepinsky, P., Pepinsky, H., & Pavlik, W. The effects of task complexity and time pressure upon team productivity. *Journal of Applied Psychology*, 1960, **44**, 34–38.

P6.   Pepitone, A. Role danger in affiliation and attraction. *Acta Psychologica*, 1961, **18**, 1–10.

P7.   Pepitone, A., & Kleiner, R. The effects of threat and frustration on group cohesiveness. *Journal of Abnormal and Social Psychology*, 1957, **54**(2), 192–199.

P8.   Pepler, R. D. Environmental conditions and behavior: effects of climate conditions limiting performance changes in heat. *Bulletin of British Psychology and Sociology*, 1955, **26** (Inset), 5.

P9.   Phillips, B. N., & DeVault, M. V. Evaluation of research on cooperation and competition. *Psychological Reports*, 1957, **3**, 289–292.

P10. Pomeranz, D. M. The repression sensitization dimension and reactions to stress. *Dissertation Abstracts*, 1963, **24**(6), 2605–2606.

P11. Postman, L., & Brown, D. Perceptual consequences of success and failure. *Journal of Abnormal and Social Psychology*, 1952, **47**, 213–221.

P12. Postman, L., & Bruner, J. S. Perception under stress. *Psychological Review*, 1948, **55**(6), 314–323.

P13. Prokasy, W. F. Berlyne's conflict theory and the acquisition of observing responses. *Psychological Reports*, 1962, **11**(2), 341–342.

P14. Pronko, N. E., & Leith, W. R. Behavior under stress: A study of its disintegration. *Psychological Reports*, 1956, **2**, 205–222. (Monograph Supplement 5)

Q1.   Quarantelli, E. L. The nature and conditions of panic. *American Journal of Sociology*, 1954, **60**, 267–275.

R1.   Reid, D. Sickness and stress in operational flying. *British Journal of Social Medicine*, 1948, **2**, 123–131.

R2.   Rohrer, J. H. Studies of human adjustment to polar isolation and implications of those studies for living in fallout shelters. Working paper. Washington, D. C.: Disaster Research Group, Division of Anthropology and Psychology, National Academy of Sciences—National Research Council, 1959.

R3.   Rohrer, J. H. Studies of human adjustment to submarine isolation and implications of those studies for living in fallout shelters. Working paper. Washington, D. C.: Disaster Research Group, Division of Anthropology and Psychology, National Academy of Sciences—National Research Council, 1959.

R4.   Rosenberg, L. Group size, prior experience and conformity. *Journal of Abnormal and Social Psychology*, 1961, **63**(2), 436–437.

R5. Ross, B. M., Rupel, J. W., & Grant, D. A. Effects of personal, impersonal and physical stress upon cognitive behavior in a card sorting problem. *Journal of Abnormal and Social Psychology*, 1952, 47(2), 546–551.

R6. Ruebush, B. K. Interfering and facilitating effects of test anxiety. *Journal of Abnormal and Social Psychology*, 1960, 60(2), 205–212.

R7. Ruff, G. E. Psychological and psychophysiological indices of stress. In N. Burns, R. Chambers, & E. Hendler (Eds.), *Unusual environments and human behavior*. New York: Free Press, 1963.

R8. Russek, H. I., & Zohman, B. L. Relative significance of heredity, diet and occupational stress in coronary heart disease of young adults. *American Journal of Medical Science*, 1958, 235, 266–277.

S1. Saltz, E. The effect of induced stress on free associations. *Journal of Abnormal and Social Psychology*, 1961, 62(1), 161–164.

S2. Sanua, V. Sociocultural factors in responses to stressful life situations: The behavior of aged amputees as an example. *Journal of Health and Human Behavior*, 1960, 1, 17–24.

S3. Saranson, I. G. The relationship of anxiety and "lack of defensiveness" to intellectual performance. *Journal of Consulting Psychology*, 1956, 20, 220–222.

S4. Saranson, I. G. The effects of anxiety and threat on the solution of a difficult task. *Journal of Abnormal and Social Psychology*, 1961, 62, 165–168.

S5. Schachter, S., & Singer, J. E. Cognitive, social, and physiological determinants of emotional state. *Psychological Review*, 1962, 69, 379–399.

S6. Schachter, S., Williams, T. A., Rowe, R., Schachter, J. S., & Jameson, J. Personality correlates of physiological reactivity to stress: a study of forty-six college males. *American Journal of Psychiatry*, 1965, 121(11), pp. 12–22.

S7. Schmale, A. Object loss; 'giving up' and disease onset: An overview of research in progress, in Symposium on Medical Aspects of Stress in the Military Climate, Washington, D. C., Walter Reed Army Institute of Research, Walter Reed Army Medical Center, 1964.

S8. Schultz, D. P. Theories of panic behavior: A review. *Journal of Social Psychology*, 1965, 66(1), 31–40.

S9. Selye, H. *The stress of life*. New York: McGraw-Hill, 1956.

S10. Silverman, A. J., et al. Psychophysiological investigations in sensory deprivation. *Psychosomatic Medicine*, 1961, 23, 48.

S11. Silverman, R. E., & Blitz, B. Learning and two kinds of anxiety. *Journal of Abnormal and Social Psychology*, 1956, 52, 301–303.

S12. Sinha, D., & Singh, T. R. Manifest anxiety and performance on problem solving tasks. *Journal of Consulting Psychology*, 1959 (Oct.) 23, 469.

S13. Smith, E. E. The effects of clear and unclear role expectations on group productivity and defensiveness. *Journal of Abnormal and Social Psychology*, 1957, 55, 213–217.

S14. Smith, E. E. Individual versus group goal conflict. *Journal of Abnormal and Social Psychology*, 1959, 58, 134–137.

S15. Smock, C. D. The influence of psychological stress on the "intolerance of ambiguity." *Journal of Abnormal and Social Psychology*, 1955, 50(2), 177–182.

S16. Smock, C. D. The influence of stress on the perception of incongruity. *Journal of Abnormal and Social Psychology*, 1955, 50, 354–356.

S17. Smock, C. D. Recall of interrupted and noninterrupted tasks as a function of experimentally induced anxiety and motivational relevance of the task stimuli. *Journal of Personality*, 1957, 25, 589–599.

S18. Speisman, J. C., Lazarus, R. S., Mordkoff, A., & Davison, L. Experimental reduction of stress based on ego defense theory. *Journal of Abnormal and Social Psychology*, 1964, 68, 367–380.

S19. Spiegel, J. P., M.D. The resolution of role conflict within the family. *Psychiatry*, 1957, 20(1), 1–16.

S20. Steiner, I. D., & Johnson, H. H. Category width and responses to interpersonal disagreements. *Journal of Personality and Social Psychology*, 1965, 2(2), 290–292.

S21. Stopol, M. S. The consistency of stress tolerance. *Journal of Personality*, 1954, 23, 13–29.

S22. Strassman, H. D., Thaler, M. B., & Schein, E. H. A prisoner of war syndrome: Apathy as a reaction to severe stress. *American Journal of Psychiatry*, 1956, 112, 998–1003.

S23. Suinn, R. M., & Geiger, J. Stress and the stability of self- and other attitudes. *Journal of General Psychology*, 1965, 73(1), 177–180.

S24. Sutcliffe, J. P., & Hoberman, M. Factors influencing choice in role conflict situations. *American Sociological Review*, 1956, 21, 695–703.

T1. Taylor, J. A. The effects of anxiety level and psychological stress on verbal learning. *Journal of Abnormal and Social Psychology*, 1958, 57(1), 55–60.

T2. Tong, J. E., & Murphy, E. C. A review of stress reactivity research in relation to psychopathology and psychopathic behavior disorders. *Journal of Mental Science*, 1960, 106, 1273–1295.

T3. Torrance, E. P. The behavior of small groups under the stress conditions of "survival." *American Sociological Review*, 1954, 19, 751–755.

T4. Torrance, E. P. Volunteers for experiments involving discomfort. Unpublished Lab. Note CRL-LN-56-203, January 1956. Reno, Nev.: Survival Research Field Unit, USAF Survival Training School, Stead AFB.

T5. Torrance, E. P. A theory of leadership and interpersonal behavior under stress. In L. Petrullo, & B. Bass (Eds.), *Leadership and interpersonal behavior*. New York: Holt, Rinehart and Winston, 1961.

T6. Torrance, E. P., LaForge, G., & Mason, R. Group adaptation in emergencies and extreme conditions. Technical Memorandum OSSP-TM-56-4, December 1956. San Antonio, Tex.: Air Force Personnel and Training Research Center, Air Research and Development Command, Randolph AFB.

T7. Trumbull, R. Environment modification for human performance, ONR Report ACR-105, July 1965, Office of Naval Research.

U1.   Ulrich, C. Measurement of stress evidenced by college women in situations involving competition. *Research Quarterly, American Association of Health and Physical Education*, 1957, **25**, 160–192.

U2.   Usdansky, G., & Chapman, L. J. Schizophrenic-like responses in normal subjects under time pressure. *Journal of Abnormal and Social Psychology*, 1960, **60**(1), 143–146.

V1.   Vogel, W. R., Baker, R. W., & Lazarus, R. S. The role of motivation in psychological stress. *Journal of Abnormal and Social Psychology*, 1958, **56**(1), 105–112.

V2.   Vogel, W. R., Raymond, S., & Lazarus, R. S. Intrinsic motivation and psychological stress. *Journal of Abnormal and Social Psychology*, 1959, **58**, 225–233.

W1.   Wadsworth, H. M. Maertens. The relationship between experimentally induced stress and the characteristic mode of expression and level of anxiety. *Dissertation Abstracts*, 1955, **15**(5), 883–884.

W2.   Wall, H. W., & Guthrie, G. M. Academic stress and perceptual thresholds. *Journal of General Psychology*, 1959, **61**, 269–273.

W3.   Weiner, B. Role of success and failure in the learning of easy and complex task. *Journal of Personality and Social Psychology*, 1966, **3**(3), 339–344.

W4.   Weller, L. The effects of anxiety on cohesiveness and rejection. *Human Relations*, 1963, **16**(2), 189–197.

W5.   Weybrew, B. Psychological problems of prolonged marine submergence. In N. Burns, R. Chambers, & E. Hendler (Eds.), *Unusual environments and human behavior*. New York: Free Press, 1963.

W6.   Wheaton, J. Fact and fancy in sensory deprivation studies. Aeromedical Reviews, Review 5-59, 1959. Brooks AFB, Tex.: Air University, School of Aviation Medicine, USAF.

W7.   Williams, R. N., Jr. Religion, value-orientation and intergroup conflict. *Journal of Social Issues*, 1956, **12**(3), 12–20.

W8.   Wilson, R. Disaster and mental health. In G. W. Baker & D. W. Chapman (Eds.), *Man and society in disaster*. New York: Basic Books, 1962.

W9.   Withey, S. Reaction to uncertain threat. In G. W. Baker & D. W. Chapman (Eds.), *Man and society in disaster*. New York: Basic Books, 1962.

W10.   Worrell, L. Response to conflict as determined by prior exposure to conflict. *Journal of Abnormal and Social Psychology*, 1962, **64**, 438–445.

W11.   Wrightsman, L. S., Jr. Effects of waiting with others on changes in level of felt anxiety. *Journal of Abnormal and Social Psychology*, 1960, **61**(2), 216–222.

Z1.   Zajonc, R. B., & Burnstein, E. Cognitive behavior under uncertainty. *American Psychologist*, 1957, **12**, 388. (Abstract)

Z2.   Zajonc, R. B., & Burnstein, E. The resolution of cognitive conflict under uncertainty. *Human Relations*, 1961, **14**, 113–119.

Z3.   Zborowski, M. Cultural components in responses to pain. *Journal of Social Issues*, 1952, 8(4), 16–30.

Z4.   Ziller, R. C. Four techniques of group decision making under uncertainty. *Journal of Applied Psychology*, 1957, **41**, 384–388.

Z5.   Zuckerman, M., Albright, R. J., Marks, G. S., & Miller, G. L. Stress and hallucinatory effects of perceptual isolation and confinement. *Psychological Monographs: General and Applied*, 1962, **76**(30, Whole No. 549), 15.

Z6.   Zuckerman, M., & Haber, M. M. Need for stimulation as a source of stress response to perceptual isolation. *Journal of Abnormal and Social Psychology*, 1965, **70**(5), 371–377.

Z7.   Zuckerman, M., Levine, S., & Biase, D. V. Stress response in total and partial perception isolation. *Psychosomatic Medicine*, 1964, **26**(3), 250–260.

6

some propositions toward a researchable conceptual- ization of stress

Robert L. Kahn

I would like to propose a series of propositions, for argument or consensus, about stress research.

First of all, it is useful to think of stress, and hypotheses about stress, in terms which are broad enough to include both individuals and organizations, and to include them both as the objects of stress and as active "responders" to stress. Much of the conversation at this conference has been individually oriented, with respect to the endurance of and response to stress. I take it this is happenstance rather than theoretical conviction on our part. I would at least like to make a case that there are parallels between the individual and the organization, as subjects of stress and in terms of the repertoire of possible responses to stress. Further, the similarities are strong enough that we can make some mileage out of them, and the differences are instructive enough that in combination they are likely to improve our theorizing.

The second proposition I would like to advocate is related to definition. The sequence of events which is of interest to the stress researcher *begins* in the environment, with a demand of some sort which the environment is placing upon some system which it contains (usually either an individual or an organization). We stand to learn most about stress by trying to follow that sequence of events through, in reasonably complete form, from environment to stress system. If we do that, I do not really care where the definitional lines fall (that is, which parts of the sequence are called stress, and which are called something else).

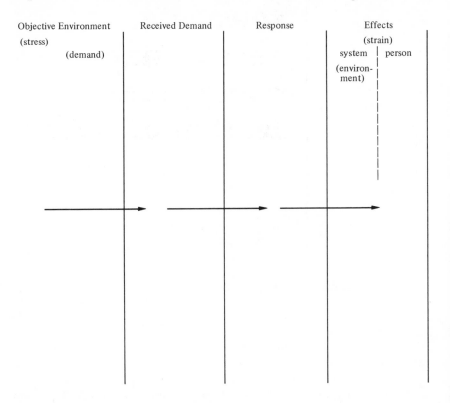

FIGURE 6–1.

The accompanying chart shows essentially the kind of scheme we have tried to use, with some success and some lack of it, in our studies of role and organizational stress. When we begin to talk about stress (regardless of what aspect of the sequence we call stress), we start with some set of facts in the objective environment which demand something, ask something, of an individual system or organizational system located in that environment.

The next stage of interest is in whether that demand is received by, or recognized by, the unit on which it is being made. This is one of the places where the engineering analogy (see Chapter 2) breaks down. The bridge does not "recognize" the load placed upon it. But I think it is essential for the social psychologist to consider the extent to which a demand in the objective environment is recognized or received by the unit which is going to be stressed, or which is having something demanded of it.

Then, there is a further question of how the unit responds immediately. To describe such responses adequately may take us through many categories of variables—physiological, behavioral, affective or emotional, and so on. Distinguishable from such immediate responses are what might be called the enduring consequences, or longer-range effects, of stress and the response to it. Two sets of such effects are of particular interest to me. One is the set of effects on the responding system itself; that is whether the individual's capacities to behave in the future are enhanced, left intact, or reduced, as a result of his trying to work through a particular stress sequence. But it is also of interest to learn what the effects of the stress response are on the environment, particularly on those agencies within the environment which made the initial stressing demand.

Now the thing I am emphasizing is the importance of trying to follow this sequence through, from environment to organism and perhaps back to environment again. My preference is to call the demand in the external environment "stress," and the received demand "strain" or "not strain." But I put those terms in quotes so as to avoid arguing the terminology. I am perfectly willing, however, to argue the importance of following the sequential approach—not necessarily in every piece of research, but as a programatic goal.

If we try to study sequences like this, we become interested in the capabilities of the organization or the individual in several different senses of that word. For example, we are interested in the capacity of the individual or the organization to code accurately what is going on in the environment. We have measured that by looking for congruence between what the individual thinks is happening and what we think independently is happening to him (see Chapter 14, this volume).

The problem of measuring received demand is a difficulty which goes with the postulation of any intrapsychic process. We can only infer the existence of a certain pattern of received demands, and the only thing from which we can make this inference is the behavior, verbal and nonverbal, which a person performs in role. What we have usually done is to rely on the individual actor's verbal responses about what he thought people were demanding of him. The problem may be somewhat easier to study at the level of the organization than at the level of the individual organism, because we can monitor directly many of the communications that take place within an organization, and these often provide clues to the organization's "perception" of environmental situations.

We are also interested in the appropriateness and adequacy of the response to stress. We want to know what performance repertoire the individual has, what calculus he is using to choose some behavior from that repertoire, and how appropriate the chosen response is. Finally, we want to know whether the mustering of the individual's resources to meet a certain demand has enduring effects for good or ill.

To understand this sequence as it moves through time requires some feedback loops. For example, organizations make very different decisions about how to respond to evidence of strain on the capacities of their units. Some may try to build up the capacity of the unit; some may try to avoid the crisis implied. In some situations an appropriate response reduces strain; in others the demand is so great that the strain persists or increases no matter what the response.

In terms of effects—both immediate and longer run—I think we must look at the whole range of consequences both for the system we are studying and for the larger systems in which that individual or organization is embedded. I think performance degradation is a poor place to start because it has the almost unavoidable consequence of directing one's attention toward some particular limited categories of performance, usually defined by the goals of some external system—industrial, military, educational or voluntary. Any event which reorients the individual's performance, so that he ceases doing something that he previously was doing, is defined as degradation if the particular reorientation takes him "off" the particular performance dimensions that happen to have been chosen as criteria. I feel much more comfortable with the proposal that we look at the totality of the effects of stress on the organism, or at least at a wide range of response behaviors.

The conformity situation (as described in Steiner's paper, Chapter 10, of this volume), may be one of those interesting cases where individual comfort and system effectiveness in the performance sense are antithetical. It may be very comfortable for the individual to be a standard "rejector," if the other does not agree with him. But it may make for group or system performance which is relatively unsuccessful, unsophisticated, or inflexible.

Everything cannot be studied simultaneously, of course. We always have to make choices as to what criteria we will emphasize. In part these are value choices, and in part choices that stem from the nature of the hypotheses we are investigating. But my point here is that we need to avoid getting such choices defined into our concepts. If we define stress as anything that reduces an individual's contribution to a particular organization, we are narrower than we want to be; and we can look forward to a whole array of conflicting empirical findings as we look at the individuals in different roles and different organizational memberships and situations. I am pushing for a broader conceptualization of stress than that.

Now let us turn to the third point. A number of the papers and conversations of the conference have discussed stress as change, implying a previous state of equilibrium. There is an implication that stress researchers are particularly interested in situations where there is a change or a sudden surge in environmental demand. I think this view has a certain heuristic value, and in doing more stress research (which I hope to) I will be looking for such situations. But I do not think that change should preoccupy us totally. I do not think we want only to study change as if stable demands, at whatever level, were of no interest to us. I would argue that we do not want either to hypothesize or to define ourselves into a situation where we only study changes, although such situations may be particularly handy and visible indicators of stress.

The fourth point is that any demand, however we conceptualize it, needs to be assessed in relation to the capacities of the system on which the demand is being placed. This puts stress researchers in the fix of having a great need for what Lewinians have called *commensurate measures*. We need very much to conceptualize the capacities of the individual in the same terms, and on the same dimensions, and in the same units, that we use to talk about the demands that exist in the environment. This is the great advantage which engineers have, working with pounds or tons in assessing both the strength of the bridge and the weight upon it. If we psychologists persist in talking about individual capacities in terms of resolved or unresolved Oedipal complexes, for example, and if we talk about demands in terms of interpersonal aggressive acts, we are going to have a difficult time subtracting environmental demand from individual capacity and deciding that a particular situation looks like "more" or "less" than the responding organism can stand.

Commensurate measures do not necessarily have to be in demand or stimulus terms. We may need considerable revision of our data language for describing environments. It may be that part of our problem here is that we have been using a too-colloquial terminology, or a too-physical-istic "pounds-per-feet" kind of terminology, for describing environmental demands. Perhaps, instead, we want to be developing a language more appropriate to the responding organism.

We do this for tests of intelligence, of spatial perception and a number of other attributes. If you want to hire a stenographer you may say, "I have a job that requires 60 wpm of typing and 100 wpm of shorthand. Find a person who takes shorthand at this speed and types at this speed." In this case, you would have defined the task, or at least part of it, in terms of its demand measured in words per minute typed or taken in dictation. The same units—namely, words per minute—make conceptual sense whether you are describing the requirements of the environment or the capacities of the person.

Even though we cannot yet handle this kind of conceptual problem for stress in ways which are equally neat, I would argue that it is worth putting some effort into attempts to do so. We could, of course, try to invent stress-tolerance units or stress-demand units, but I suspect the useful concepts are going to be much narrower than that. Stress-tolerance units would be comparable to manual dexterity units instead of typing words-per-minute units. I think progress probably will come easier at the more specific level.

Finally, I would like to make a point about where I think the engineering metaphor breaks down in stress research. One of the appealing simplicities about analogies with inanimate objects like bridges and buildings is that we can measure the stressor (weight) put on them and see at what point they distort or collapse. But this implies that a situation of no load corresponds to zero stress and represents the condition under which the structure would have its maximum life. Living organisms and living organizations are not like that.

Somehow we have got to develop a set of concepts, which I think we do not yet have in very satisfactory form, that will handle overload and underload (or underutilization) in the same scheme. We somehow have to take account of the fact that, with individuals and organizations, underutilized abilities tend to atrophy. If you do not play the piano, soon you are not a piano player anymore except perhaps in your own self-identity. Similarly with organizations: a fire department that never puts out a fire or never realistically rehearses putting one out, loses its capacity by reason of underutilization. Somehow we have got to take overload or too much demand, and underutilization of too little demand, and get them into the same scheme. We must study the extent to which their effects—the atrophy caused by the underutilization and the breakage caused by overload—are really the same kind of thing, stresses damaging to the system.

We will also have to evolve some distinctions among kinds of overload, at least the gross distinction between qualitative and quantitative overload. The assembly line worker is characteristically overloaded in a quantitative sense; he has more nuts and bolts to turn than he can do conveniently. But he is underutilized or underloaded in a qualitative sense, in that he has capacities that are not being utilized at all.

I do not know how to handle the "normal load" problem. One way to do so is to presume that any ongoing system for example, a department store, in respect to any particular kind of demand—say, selling vacuum cleaners—has some range of inputs which it can handle without either enhancing or incapacitating its existing resources. Whether or not we say that within that range it is not under stress does not really matter. What

I would like to do is to have some way of measuring, quantitatively, how many vacuum cleaner orders this department store can process—say, for example, 1000 a day—and also, a measure of how few can it handle without reorganization or firing people—say 800 a day. Then, for between 800 and 1000 orders a day the system is in equilibrium. Above that something has to happen, and below that it tends to lose some of the capacity it already has. In this frame, our statement that the system is stressed or strained or underutilized acquires more precise meaning.

These few points will not, of course, solve the complex problems of stress research. They represent, however, factors that we have typically failed to take into account in such researches. To that extent they can improve our work.

7 some problems in developing a social psychology of adaptation to stress

David Mechanic

All social-psychological theories in one way or another have implications for understanding adaptation to stress, and several treat adaptive response as central concerns. Thus it is not obvious that a special frame of reference for studying adaptation to stress is either necessary or desirable. The fact that most social psychological theories do not use the concepts of "stress" or "adaptation" is no great disadvantage in understanding personal and social crises since both of these concepts, for the most part, are used as general rubrics, and neither is definite or unambiguous. In one sense the utility of stress concepts is promoted by their lack of specificity, since the use of an ambiguous rubric promotes interdisciplinary links between biology, psychophysiology, psychology, and sociology. These ties, however, are largely superficial; the same concepts have different referents for investigators in these various fields, and the measures which are used to define stress operationally are themselves poorly associated.

Personally I do not believe that it is either possible or fruitful to come to agreement on the referents of the rubrics of stress and adaptation. These concepts take on different meanings depending on the problem being investigated, the methods being used, the theoretical orientations of the investigator, and personal tastes. Although stress researchers have interests in common—and probably benefit from some appreciation of what workers in other disciplines concerned with stress are trying to do— little is gained by trying to force such work into a common mold. Implicit in such attempts at common definition is the idea that it is possible to construct a viable integrated theory of behavior. My impression is that we know far too little to be able to pursue this goal fruit— fully.

I have already noted that adaptation is a common theme in social psychology. I wish to illustrate this by commenting briefly on two prominent developments in recent years in social psychology—those concerning balance theories, and those which perhaps can be characterized as utility-reinforcement theories. Balance theories are heuristic motivational concepts for the most part. As in the case of Festinger's theory of dissonance (1957, 1958), change in attitudes following decision choices, forced compliance, exposure to threatening information, and so on are seen within the context of coping with the discomfort (or stress) resulting from conflicting or incompatible cognitions. In short, this is a theory of stress reduction; and, increasingly, attention is given to specifying the conditions under which one form of defensive procedure would be used in comparison to another (that is, the conditions under which one cognition versus another will be changed, when information will be avoided, when social support will be solicited, and so on). I am not suggesting that Festinger necessarily views the main issue in this way, but it is clear that it is not difficult to view Festinger's concept and other balance theories as well in this light.

To take a somewhat different and less limited example, Thibaut and Kelley in their book, *The Social Psychology of Groups* (1959), present a theory of interpersonal relations and group functioning. Basically, this statement is an attempt to suggest hypotheses concerning the development of dyadic interdependencies, and the theory is concerned with specifying "what the members of the collectivity *should do* if their relationship is to be viable, stable, and optimally satisfactory [p. 4]." In emphasizing how people deal with the problems of interdependency and achieve mutually satisfactory outcomes, Thibaut and Kelley are presenting a functional adaptation approach. As this and other such social-psychological statements show, there are many areas of social psychology where it has been possible to develop a more precise and useful set of concepts than those that characterize stress discussions.

In defending the use of a stress-adaptation perspective, it appears necessary to explain why it is useful in contrast to other more rigorously constructed social-psychological views. Despite its obvious difficulties, this perspective appears to be worthwhile in attacking particular kinds of macroscopic problems of human functioning and in pursuing certain applied interests. Thus, such a framework appears more appropriate in understanding complex as compared with simple task behavior, long-run dynamic responses in contrast to short-run reactions, and circumstances requiring mixed task and interpersonal skills rather than more limited ones. In contrast, most social-psychological theories, experimental work, and field studies emphasize simple tasks, short-run reactions, and the enactment of single skills. In integrating such limited materials, existing social-psychological concepts are more efficient and parsimonious than the more global stress conceptions.

In recent years, social psychology has been increasingly characterized by relatively modest theoretical ideas that are useful in helping to pin down the influence of particular sets of variables, uncontaminated by changing cultural and social influences. Although a stress framework may be useful for summarizing such social-psychological work coming from the fields of interpersonal perception, conflict and dissonance, aggression, emotion, and so on, the more limited but tighter conceptual ideas associated with these subfields are more useful to the investigator than are stress concepts. Stress theory does not really help the experimenter design a better experiment from either a theoretical or methodological standpoint. But in studying more complex situations than the typical experiment or field study usually encompasses, it does help the investigator to ask more meaningful questions and to consider variables he might not have looked at had he used a more limited and conventional perspective.

Current social-psychological theory has an important disadvantage in dealing with particular issues of central concern to stress theorists. Most of such theories are characterized by an extremely passive view of man, and few social-psychological investigations are structured so as to allow study of man's activity in dealing with environmental stimuli. Some experiments allow subjects alternative responses; however, they do not provide them opportunities—ever present in real-life situations—to select alternatives, to seek out optimal opportunities, and in general to structure the situation to their advantage. Since reaction patterns are usually held to a very limited sphere, the researcher ordinarily has little opportunity to observe the considerable flexibility and adaptability which characterize how some people come to terms with their environment and utilize complex skill repertoires.

SOCIAL-PSYCHOLOGICAL THEORY AND THE STUDY OF STRESS

When social-psychological and psychological theories have been used in the study of stress, the views of man implicit in such frames of reference have significantly affected definitions of the general problem. The implications of such underlying views can be seen by briefly comparing the psychodynamic and symbolic interaction perspectives in social psychology.

The study of social stress has been developed largely within the psychodynamic context and has been profoundly influenced by psychodynamic assumptions. This has brought to the study of stress a strong psychobiological, developmental bias which emphasizes dynamic psychological responses and largely ignores the skill components of adaptation. Even within psychology there has been a clear separation between investigators concerned with complex skills and problem solving and those interested in intrapsychic response, although both are central to the study of stress. Those who came to the stress area from the perspective of ego-psychology—although they may have discarded most of the structural assumptions of Freudian psychology—continue to retain Freud's implicit bias concerning man's limited capacities for adaptation. Although they have moved Freud's description of intrapsychic defense from the realm of the pathological to characterize normal psychological processes as well, human adaptation has been seen largely within the context of intrapsychic modes of controlling environmental threat. Implicit in this approach is a certain degree of pessimism about man's efficacy in manipulating his environment. Adaptation is seen mainly as a manipulation of cognitions about the environment rather than the manipulation of the environment itself. Thus, little attention is given to man's intentions and choices, the means he uses to control the alternatives to which he will be exposed, and how he copes in an instrumental sense with situations and other people.

The study of man's manipulation of his environment and symbolic constructions which define threat and help him to deal with it received little attention from other social psychologists as well. From the view of developing a statistical and experimental science of human behavior, it is not surprising that social psychologists found it convenient to ignore man's instrumental capabilities and the importance of his symbolic constructions. The assumption of passivity that developed in much social-psychological thinking—particularly among the behaviorists—had definite methodological advantages. Within the experimental context it has been convenient for the experimenter to control the stimuli affecting behavior, making appropriate measurements of change in response. Indeed, this is the beauty of the experiment; the researcher controls the input, attempting to vary one or possibly two factors at a time. Since he assigns his subjects into experimental and control groups in some unbiased fashion, he can then infer that any changes in response in the experimental group as compared with the control group are attributable to variations in the controlled stimulus. Such an approach leaves little room for assuming that man's symbolic or manipulative abilities must be studied in understanding behavioral response.

Thibaut and Kelley (1959), in attempting to construct their theory of interpersonal interdependency, noted the difficulty in experimental design as a significant problem in developing such constructions.

> In the typical experiment in psychology the subject is in some manner under the management of the experimenter, who controls the presentation of stimuli, the opportunities of behavior available to the subject, and, most importantly, the provision of diverse incentives and rewards for behavior. . . . In these experiments it is usually assumed that the subject has no counter-control over the experiment. What the subject does makes no difference to the investigator . . . and even if it does make a difference it cannot be permitted to cause him to deviate from his prearranged schedule of activities. The situation is sharply different when social interaction is considered. The simplest situation is that in which two subjects interact in a response to a task set by the experimenter. The possibility is now introduced that each subject will exercise control over the other. . . . We now merely note that methodologically the complexity that is added by reciprocal control may be denoted by the loss of a clear separation between independent and dependent variables. Each subject's behavior is at the same time a response to a past behavior of the other and a stimulus of a future behavior of the other; each behavior is in part dependent variable and in part independent variable; in no clear sense is it properly either of them [p. 2].

Thibaut and Kelley note that for the most part psychological investigation has bypassed this issue, and the experimenter continues to maintain control over the independent variable. Thus, the experimental evidence they use in support of their theory comes largely from such traditional experiments. There is, however, a long tradition in social psychology which views social behavior from a perspective of transactive interdependence. Why has this view played such a little part in the development of stress theory?

Symbolic-interaction views such as those of Cooley (1956), Mead (1934), and W. I. Thomas (see Volkart, 1951) developed concurrently with psychodynamic approaches and behavioral experimentation. Within this view, man's nature and social needs are molded and nurtured through psychosocial development and contacts with other people. It is only through other people that children develop investments in living and a view of themselves. It was Mead, especially, who emphasized that the "self" was derived through the interaction of symbolic communications, and thus man's potential capacities were as rich as the symbolic environments that man could create. Although the symbolic-interaction view took account of the fact that man's opportunities could vary as a result of group and class membership, it left considerable room to regard man as an active participant in social processes and to consider the social dialogue among men. Emphasis within this view was thus given to interpersonal influence and its resultants.

W. I. Thomas went one step further than the other theorists in considering the influence of culture and social structure in developing man's capacities to deal with crisis. Unlike the psychodynamists, he argued that control of and adjustment to the environment resulted from the active manipulation of knowledge. Men, of course, must be socialized; they must acquire skills and techniques to mold the environment. It is the culture of the group, he wrote, that limits the power of the mind to adjust to adversity and changing circumstances. If knowledge is insufficient and material resources are scanty, an individual will find no way out of an emergency which under different circumstances would be only the occasion for future progress.

SOCIAL-PSYCHOLOGICAL THEORIES AND TECHNOLOGIES

For the most part, social psychology follows technological innovations rather than theoretical erudition, and not infrequently the theoretical thrust dies out while its methodological counterpart lives on. I believe that one can make a good case for the position that psychodynamic thinking has been so popular among psychologists in contrast to symbolic-interaction views, in part, because it offered an allied technology that was simple and convenient. It is difficult to explain the varying attractiveness of these two conceptual schemes solely on the contents or sophistication of the theories themselves. Unlike the symbolic-interaction theorists, Freud left his followers a simple methodology—a set of modest techniques which facilitated observation and which allowed for easy accumulation of abundant data. Using his technique required no great expertise (in the usual sense of the word), and the interpretations derived from the data were for the most part not easily discredited without attacking the entire system of thought. In contrast, the symbolic interactionists provided a perspective but no methodology, and to this day their central premises and ideas are undeveloped. Each investigator has had to develop his own mode of approach, and this has done little to facilitate the accumulation of a significant body of data.

Similarly, the "traditional" experiment, despite its inappropriateness to many important social-psychological issues, has developed as the main technology in social-psychological investigation because it is a viable method that allows an uncontaminated assessment of the influence of particular variables of interest and importance. Experiments which allow some form of countercontrol are much more difficult to construct and thus pose greater technological problems for the investigator.

Many of the more global theories in social psychology that attempt to deal with complex problem solving in a dynamic sense tend to lack associated methodologies. For example, many of us are impressed by Erving Goffman's (1959, 1961) stimulating insights concerning the techniques individuals use in impression management and in the manipulation of the definition of social situations, but such analytic approaches conspicuously lack a coherent methodology which can be communicated to other research workers and students. Such approaches thus serve as broad frames of reference rather than as useful schemes which promote the growth of research efforts and the accumulation of a growing body of knowledge.

In noting the importance of technologies, a few words are appropriate on their misuse. All too frequently technologies are developed in conjunction with theories that are later discredited or forgotten. If the technology is simple and easily administered it becomes widely used as a standard measure of the variable among persons who no longer have a great interest in the underlying theoretical concerns. Thus, we have a rather large literature on such measures as Srole's anomie scale, the F-scale, the manifest anxiety scale, the Cornell Medical Index, and so on, although the validity of these measures is dubious. If technologies become an end in themselves, investigation becomes trivial. Too many of the measures we use in stress studies have extremely poor validity.

I believe that we are now at a point where it has become obvious that man's manipulative and symbolic processes must be given greater significance within the context of social-psychological theory and research. The issue we face, however, is a technological one: how do we add depth and significance to our inquiries without negating the methodological gains that we have acquired so painfully in the past few decades? It appears that the significant innovations in stress research in recent years—such research efforts as those on sensory deprivation and on cognitive influences on the experience of stress stimuli (Meron, 1957; Lazarus & Opton, 1966; Schachter & Singer, 1962)—were largely based on the development of useful methodologies that could be applied to "natural-like" situations. I believe that further development along these lines can be achieved by more systematic field studies of a prospective nature and by the development of more complicated experimental designs which treat symbolic and behavioral manipulation as central variables. Before elaborating on this point, however, I wish to make clear my assumptions about stress processes.

STRESS VIEWED FROM A SKILLS-ABILITIES PERSPECTIVE

The general question of interest to me—and one toward which stress concepts can be fruitfully directed, in my opinion—is: how do men faced with challenging and threatening circumstances attempt to reverse them or accommodate to them? Since few situations are equally threatening to all men, we first strive to understand why situations are experienced as challenging and threatening by some men and not by others. Moreover, we seek to locate the correlates of varying responses in dealing with the same threatening situations given similar perceptions of challenge. Such questions are more complex and difficult to manage than they appear, but attacking any particular problem within the stress area requires some appreciation of the boundaries of perception and response to life stressors.

Within this context it seems reasonable and convenient to define stress as a discrepancy between a problem or challenge and the individual's capacity to deal with or to accommodate to it. I have come to believe that it is valuable and necessary to separate such discrepancies from *perceived* discrepancies. Many workers in the stress field have been impressed by the substantial degree to which stress reactions are the product of the manner in which persons come to perceive and define stressors, and they have drawn the conclusion which appears to follow from this that emphasis should be given to the individual's definition or perception of the situation (Wolff, 1953; Lazarus, 1966). The importance of perceptions of threat is attested to by a growing literature showing that the anticipation of a stressor is accompanied by substantial indication of physiological and psychological arousal (Lazarus, 1966). I, too, came to a similar conclusion in my study of *Students under Stress* (Mechanic, 1962), but I have become increasingly dubious about the utility of this approach in social research. Although this view is theoretically viable, it appears that if stress study must depend on measuring the individual's appraisal processes, then we find ourselves in a bind similar to the one that has handicapped subjective approaches for so long. The idea of differential cognitive approaches in reactions to stress is useful if we successfully develop techniques for manipulating appraisal processes experimentally, as Lazarus and his co-workers (Lazarus et al., 1962), and Graham and his group (Graham et al., 1962) have done, but my impression is that such manipulations are relatively limited in their scope and applicability. If prediction is an important motivation for building models of stress, it appears necessary to make perceptual variations subsidiary to the central core of stress models. The advantage of objective discrepancies over perceived ones resides in the fact that they can be more easily and rigorously measured. At the ability level, we can achieve a rather high level of prediction relevant to successful coping.

For example, one can objectively measure whether a person has acquired such particular skills as swimming, driving a car, flying an airplane, and so on, and these skills do predict how people perform in such situations. Obviously, deficiencies in self-confidence and perception of inadequacy may detract from performance in particular situations, but the influence of such factors can properly be taken into account in considering the various contingencies affecting performance.

I am sure that the reader is not impressed with the observation that abilities, skill, and experience predict performance. This conclusion, however, takes on a different meaning if we look at the psychological literature dealing with stress. Implicit in typical stress approaches is the idea that the links between abilities and performance are obvious or irrelevant, and that only the psychodynamics of intrapsychic response remain problematic. This assumption, in my opinion, is an erroneous one, and much that is regarded as intrapsychic dynamics can be seen from a skills-abilities perspective. There is an increasing interest in sociology in considering the role of skill acquisition in processes that traditionally have not been regarded as having skill components. Although there is a substantial literature on skill components in criminal behavior and on the acquisition of illegal means (Sutherland & Cressey, 1960; Lemert, 1951; Cloward & Ohlin, 1960), it is only more recently that the skill component has been viewed as a consideration in drug use (marijuana and LSD—Becker, 1963, 1967), suicide (Wilkins, 1967), being mentally ill (Scheff, 1966), and the like. Consistent with this have been such studies as the one by Schachter and Singer (1962) which implies the importance of learning how to define internal arousal; and Schachter (1964, 1967) has attempted to explain compulsive eating as a product of inadequate ability to differentiate hunger from other forms of physiological arousal. In passing, it is worth noting that the process of acquiring most of our skills for dealing with threats (most of which are symbolic and interpersonally organized) is usually indirect and unorganized, and the skills themselves may have no descriptive vocabularies to depict them. Thus these skills may be very unevenly acquired, and deficiencies may not be easily identified until extreme situations develop.

The definition of stress as a discrepancy between challenge and potential response—although somewhat ambiguous—applies usefully to a wide variety of situations and contexts where appraisal is either impossible to measure or it is unimportant. I do not believe that it is fruitful to address ourselves only to stimuli that are perceived as threatening or harmful; more basic to our concern are the varying contingencies under which the same stimulus may arouse fear and threaten harm or appear benevolent. Moreover, although we are defining the concept of stress for social-psychological analysis, it is useful to keep the concept relevant to work continuing in biological and physiological fields as well. For example, situations of sensory deprivation appear to be stressful in that they place a person in a situation of deprived stimulation for which they are experientially, psychologically, and perhaps neurologically unprepared. Such a situation is characterized by a discrepancy between the order or intensity of stimulation and the capacity of the person to adapt to the stimuli. It appears that people have varying capacities to tolerate without ill effects periods of sensory deprivation and that these capacities can be developed with practice. Also, I think it important to note that some stress theorists believe—and there is some evidence to substantiate such a belief—that stress responses follow circumstances that are appraised positively as well as negatively. For example, one theory of stress in the study of schizophrenia holds that a high level of stimulation, regardless of the nature of the appraisal, overstimulates in some unspecific way the individual's neurological apparatus and contributes to florid symptomatology (Brown et al., 1962; Brown, personal communication). This position is consistent with Selye's (1956) concept of stress as the nonspecific changes induced by a variety of agents. We must be careful not to exclude such stress possibilities by fiat. Finally, the difficulty of using the psychological appraisal of harm as a criterion for stress results from the low degree of correspondence between such psychological reports and other measures of behavioral or physiological stress whatever the source of such inconsistencies.

A SOCIETAL VIEW OF PREDISPOSITIONS TO STRESS

I suspect that one achieves a more useful perspective on stress or crisis if he considers stress situations from both a personal and societal perspective at the same time. From the point of view of the person, there are at least three central considerations that must be taken into account in an analysis of how he will deal with a stress situation: (1) the instrumental one—his skills and capacities; (2) his motivation; and (3) his socioemotional state. The enactment of instrumental skills I shall call *coping*; and his socioemotional state (including his feelings of self-confidence and self-esteem) I shall call *defense*. In considering any task or challenge, there are at least three questions that demand some answer: Does he want to deal with the situation? Can he deal with it if he wants to? What kinds of feelings are aroused in him when he faces the situation? Each of these dimensions (and associated questions) has a societal complement which I shall call: (1) preparatory institutions; (2) incentive systems; and (3) evaluative systems. By preparatory institutions, I refer to societal attempts to develop skills and competence among persons to prepare them to deal with societal needs, demands, and challenges. Here I include not only schools and formal learning experiences, but also the many varieties of informal learning that are acquired through parents and peers. By incentive systems, I refer to societal values and the systems of rewards and punishments which organizations and communities develop that push activities in particular directions. These are in a sense the societal "carrots and sticks" that channel motivation into particular spheres of action. By evaluative institutions, I refer to the approval and support, or disapproval and disparagement, resulting from following particular courses of activity.

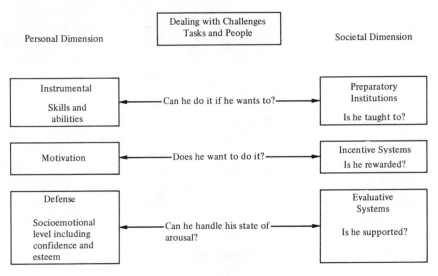

FIGURE 7–1.

There is a direct relationship between each of the analogous variables on what I have described as the personal and societal levels. The levels of skills and competence in any population, for example, are very much dependent on the nature and organization of preparatory systems; motivation is correlated in various ways with incentive systems; and social support and favorable evaluation ordinarily facilitate defensive processes, while opposition and disapproval frequently increase the magnitude of personal distress. Thus far I have not really moved beyond the obvious. Somewhat less visible, however, are the likely relationships among the various subdimensions. For example, the stronger a person's coping skills, the less there is a need for defensive manipulations. Persons who have well-developed skills to meet challenges and environmental demands are less likely to suffer from discomfort and feelings of loss of confidence. In short, the adequacy of preparation is one of the major determinants of what situations are experienced as stressful. Moreover, what people in different groups experience as challenges varies largely because such groups have differing preparatory systems.

The realities of life are of course more complicated than the above statement implies. We know that people with similar instrumental skills and preparation actually perform very differently. It is well known that assessments made during training do not necessarily predict actual successful performance in the real situation. It appears that in situations where motivation is high, the task difficult, and ultimate performance clouded by uncertainties, a high level of discomfort may be aroused despite the person's competence. Thus, the person's socioemotional defenses become important in dealing with the situation. A high level of discomfort interferes with the application of instrumental skills requiring effort and ability. To the extent that a person can control his emotional state, the coping process is facilitated. Thus, how well he performs will depend on the techniques and intrapsychic mechanisms by which he contains his emotional state. Whether his defense restricts, distorts, or falsifies reality has no important meaning in and of itself. The relative usefulness and adequacy of defense processes depend on the way defense affects coping. The primary function of psychological defense is to facilitate the coping process. There are boundaries within which psychological defense must function if it is to be effective. Defense processes cannot be so out of line with social definitions of appropriateness that they lead to negative social evaluation and withdrawal of social support. From the perspective of long-range adaptation, defense processes cannot be so restrictive that they lead the person to avoid taking advantage of preparatory opportunities. I believe that it is important to emphasize that defense is not an end in itself; defense processes divorced from coping or those that hinder the coping process are usually viewed as evidence of emotional disturbance.

Although the perception of a situation is an essential consideration in understanding certain kinds of stressful events, it does not assume central importance in understanding routine everyday situations in which stress may become manifest. On the behavioral level, when individuals have the coping capacities to deal with a situation, it is experienced as routine and ordinary, and behavior frequently takes place in a habituated and unreflective fashion. If one attempts to study persons who cope successfully with stressors (frequently so successfully that they are unaware of variations from ordinary situations), it is extremely difficult to get respondents to recognize and report their own coping skills. There is difficulty in doing this because successful coping requires regularized adaptive responses that have become part of a person's coping repertoire, and these skills can be enacted without any elaborate awareness of the situation. Even those, such as Arnold (1960), who have emphasized subjective appraisal, characterize this appraisal as a "sense judgment" rather than as a more considered thought process. Although intuitively it is necessary to posit some form of appraisal to account for the fact that some stimuli are arousing while others are not, there appears to be little operational benefit from such an assumption.

When in confrontation with a task the person's resources are unequal to the demands of the situation, this usually calls forth a clear appraisal process. In contrast to the posited intuitive or sense judgment, such appraisals have more form, and subjects can report in considerable detail those aspects of the situation that threatened them. But usually this kind of appraisal follows the person's inability to cope successfully; or it occurs during an anticipatory stage when individuals are aware that they will be facing some threatening situation, but they must reserve any attempt to control the situation until the appropriate time comes. In my view, the time dimension is an extremely important factor in stress studies, and it has not received sufficient attention, nor do present concepts of coping effectively conceptualize this variable. I suspect that conscious appraisal is most likely in stress circumstances which have a large anticipatory component, which cover a relatively long time period, and which are characterized by a high level of motivation and vulnerability. To the extent that we feel invulnerable because we have adequate skills or because the probability of danger is very low, an elaborate appraisal is unlikely. The time dimension is important in two ways: (1) when the confrontation is in the future, the "warning period" provides an opportunity to consider and prepare coping strategies; but (2) when an activity is separated in time from the consequences of that activity, it is more difficult to encourage the development of preventive patterns.

Behavioral response in ordinary situations flows smoothly precisely because the person can respond without considerable reflection. Consider the case of a man who falls out of a boat in the middle of a lake. The cognitive theorists would have us imputing various kinds of appraisals to him of danger and how to cope with it. Operationally, I believe it is more valuable to assume that if the person has a well-ingrained skill it will be activated in the appropriate situation and that the degree of stress experienced will in large part be a product of the inadequacy of resources available to the person. This view would also imply that the nonswimmer faced with the situation would quickly become aware of his inability to cope, and that this appraisal would be triggered by the discrepancy between the demands of the situation and the person's inability to activate appropriate skills.

The adequacy of human response is very closely related to the organization of preparatory and incentive systems within a particular social context. The obviousness of this statement should not detract from its importance; and one of the greatest difficulties in the study of stress is that this simple fact is too frequently ignored. More frequently than not, people do well what they learn to do, and areas of social incompetence can frequently be traced back to the inadequacy of preparatory institutions. If one is to send an astronaut into space, every attempt is made to anticipate the problems that will develop and to prepare solutions for these problems (Ruff & Korchin, 1966). To the extent that such solutions can be built into the hardware itself, this is attempted. Other contingencies are dealt with by preparing those who must face particular situations with anticipatory skills and prepared responses. Since such considerations are essential in the development of mechanical systems, it is indeed curious that they play such a small part in social-psychological theories of stress.

Preparatory systems may vary greatly in their effectiveness. For example, in building airplanes one can plan effectively for rare contingencies by insuring that the plane itself has the capacity to survive particular failures, such as a motor stall during take-off. The value and efficacy of other kinds of preparatory systems, such as nuclear fall-out shelters, are, of course, more debatable. It should be clear that preparatory systems involve costs in addition to the economic ones; because human efforts and resources are limited, investment in some kinds of preparatory systems is likely to limit resources for investment in other kinds of preparatory efforts. Thus, each community must make decisions as to the kinds of preparatory efforts that seem most reasonable. Considerations of the importance of the preparation, the likelihood that it can be acquired without training, the magnitude of the threat should the training not be provided, the actual capacity to teach the skills required, the probability of the threat or challenge for which preparation is offered, and many other factors all influence community preparatory efforts. In any particular community, preparatory systems may be more or less congruent with characteristic difficulties that people are likely to face, and they may impart more or less competence to deal with common threats. Communities may fail to provide adequate preparatory resources for many reasons. Frequently the cost seems too high. Also, because typical challenges and difficulties change over time, the preparatory systems have to be relatively flexible and adaptive. But frequently preparatory systems become heavily bureaucratized, and as a consequence they may develop strong resistances to change, in that particular bureaucratic and professional goals and interests are valued more highly than societal instrumental goals.

Societal incentive and evaluative systems also affect preparatory institutions in that they help define the areas of proper concern for training programs. The technology for controlling family size is clearly available; whether a community trains persons to use the technology effectively and provides access to the technology (as in the case of contraceptive devices) depends on social values and the distribution of particular organized groups in the community. It is an unfortunate fact of life that frequently the technology necessary to solve social problems violates the interests or values of particular social groups in the community. When poverty programs stimulate persons in deprived areas to assert their rights and to protest, invariably this has consequences for social groups who have something to gain from the status quo. In short, evaluative institutions influence in important ways what kinds of preparatory attempts are politically feasible. Similarly, societal incentive and evaluative systems structure personal motivation and defense processes. They affect not only what the person wants to do, but perhaps more importantly the means he can apply in dealing with particular challenges.

Effective coping depends on several types of preparation, and much that we have to know to get along in life is not taught in any direct or formal way. A person has to acquire not only task skills, but must as well learn general approaches to problems that occur with some frequency (Torrance, 1965). These inevitably involve such skills as anticipation, information seeking, anticipatory problem solving, rehearsal, task organization, and so on. They include ability to pace activities, preparation of alternative strategies, sensitivity to task and interpersonal cues, and ability to anticipate reactions in the environment.

It is important to consider the difference between skills learned through formal teaching of a direct kind and those which are derived in an incidental fashion through experience. Even within the most concentrated and explicit educational programs, significant failures in imparting skills occur. In contrast, in those situations where learning is covert and perhaps unintentional, it is likely that the failure and error are very large and skills are imparted very unevenly. For example, interpersonal skills are for the most part indirectly learned. More frequently than not, the skill is subtle and not recognized at the verbal level as a skill. Yet, such interpersonal skills in a complex bureaucratic society are central to personal effectiveness on both an occupational and a personal level. Interestingly enough, social psychologists have as yet not developed a very adequate vocabulary to describe these skills, although such descriptions can be gleaned from various social psychological studies (Goffman, 1959). The language available to social psychologists is for the most part a language of emotions and personality traits, and it is extremely difficult to find designations that are descriptive of the way people "handle," "manipulate," or "deal with" other people. In short, we appear to have far too many words to describe internal psychological states and far too few to describe interaction techniques.

THE PROBLEM OF MOTIVATION

It is not realistic to attempt to specify why some people are motivated to deal with challenges while others are not. Except for involuntary situations where persons are given little alternative, the mobilization of effort depends on the personal history of the actor, his aspirations, and the way he comes to view a challenge. Motivation, of course, is also influenced by the societal incentive and evaluative systems. But even within the context of high motivation some persons find themselves able to apply effort to a task, while others of similar aspirations seem unable to persevere in a difficult task. I believe that it begs the question to argue that differences in behavior in such situations are a consequence of differences in motivation. Even where life and death are concerned, there are vast differences in people's staying power and persistence in meeting adversities. There are two basic alternatives in studying such differences. First, we can make some attempt to understand the personalities of the actors involved, and through analyses of their developmental histories attempt to account for their successes and failures. This mode of investigation, thus far, has been less than fully heartening. To explain failures in coping by attributing traits to the personality—inadequacy, rigidity, authoritarianism, lack of an achievement, and so on—tells us little about why such people fail to function successfully. The other alternative, which has not really been exploited, is to study the way people organize and prepare to deal with difficult tasks and how they go about doing this. We really know very little about the ways successful people construct problem solutions and approach difficult situations. There is a great variability among people in the extent to which they experience life as a combination of inevitable and accidental events, and the extent to which they actively seek out alternatives, make choices, and facilitate their own welfare by anticipatory planning. We know that many people regard themselves as relatively powerless to influence and control events, while others have a strong sense of their own potency in affecting their fate and are active in controlling their alternatives and outcomes. We need a much better understanding of these life stances in relation to particular challenges.

At one time or another we have all probably met individuals who appear to be highly motivated, but who are unable to expend effort on any long-range task because when they get down to the task the achievement appears insignificant and the effort too great for the anticipated results. These people tend to be characterized by high motivation which becomes dissipated upon confrontation of tasks. Although such persons probably have different "personality structures" than those who apply themselves more easily, it might be fruitful to approach such performance differences not in terms of the personal histories of such individuals, but rather in terms of how they differentially approach trying tasks. For if we study the way different people approach trying tasks, it becomes possible to locate the coping devices that facilitate persistence and tenaciousness as well as to examine the personality and social characteristics that may influence these.

In some of our own exploratory research on populations that could be characterized as "poor copers," we have been impressed by how frequently these respondents accept their inability to have any control over their situations. They appear to recognize few alternatives and to have no plans or strategies for taking on some of the problems which characterize their lives. This acceptance of "fate" may be regarded as one form of adaptive behavior, since it appeared that such respondents who gave us the impression of "having given up" were less tense and anxious than those who were struggling actively against extremely difficult problems. In any case, it would be important to know to what extent giving up is a product of seeing no alternatives for approaching life problems and to what extent such stances are attributable to other factors.

SOME NOTES ON RESEARCH ALTERNATIVES

If one accepts the assumptions I have presented, then a redirection in the character of social-psychological stress study appears to be indicated. First, I argued that the stress framework is most valuable in understanding complex, long-run responses requiring mixed task and interpersonal skills. Second, I emphasized the need to consider man's activities and plans in coming to terms with his environment. Third, I argued that experimental work must provide greater opportunity for allowing subjects to exercise a more flexible range of manipulative behavior in dealing with fixed stimuli. And finally, I noted that more energy and emphasis must be given to the time dimension in stress response and the components of problem-solving approaches most relevant to performance.

The attack on social-psychological problems involving stress has been less than fully successful, in part because the most impressive methodologies available to social psychologists were not fully applicable to the study of complex skills as they are developed and exercised over time. Although both typical experimental methodologies and correlational studies help illuminate particular stress problems, they do not really capture the development of active mastery. As a consequence, most stress work is approached with a stimulus-response or psychodynamic model, and theoretical concepts of stress which concern themselves with complex responses emphasize cognitive changes in contrast to behavior.

I have already noted that many variables now described within the context of personality, perhaps can be better characterized as skill components. For the most part these skills are subtle and difficult to describe reliably, but if we give more emphasis to measuring such skill components, we will be in a stronger position to evaluate how behavioral efficacy is developed. Cross-sectional approaches that attempt to link particular task and interpersonal skill repertoires to performance hold more promise, I believe, than the more typical personality-type approaches.

The study of long-range stress response will inevitably depend on more adequate observational investigations. Too many of the available observational studies are retrospective, and frequently they lack adequate comparison groups. If main interest is focused on the dynamics of stress response, retrospective data are particularly deceptive and unreliable. As I illustrated in a study of Ph.D. students (Mechanic, 1962), views of the challenging situation changed substantially from one period to another as the stress situation developed and after it was over. Thus, the view of the situation that one might obtain from questioning respondents at any point in time is likely to be unrepresentative of "typical" views over time. This point is also made most convincingly by Davis (1963), who followed polio victims and their families over a period of several years. In questioning families about their experiences in retrospect as to the changes that had occurred in response to the crisis studied, he found that families reported very little change, although his prospective observations reflected very large alterations in family life. The following extract is illustrative:

> Throughout this work we have been concerned with the way in which the child and his family came to conceive of themselves as a result of the child's illness, his separation from the home, and his reincorporation into it as a handicapped person. The data appear to suggest a striking anomaly: although it is clear that much was changed in the family, both objectively and subjectively, by these experiences, it is equally clear that the appreciation by family members of what had transpired in no way matched the magnitude of the changes themselves. Regardless of whether, for example, the families normalized or disassociated the social meaning of the child's handicap, the ebb and flow of daily life appeared to remain sufficiently static to leave them with the conviction that nothing had changed, that the child was essentially the same person he had been prior to his illness, and that everyone in the family felt and acted towards the others as he always had.
>
> It is less important to question the accuracy of such perceptions—that they contradicted certain of the existential realities has been amply documented—than it is to weigh their significance for the organizational stability and psychological continuity of family life . . . the disparity between the changes actually wrought and their reflexive effects on family identity is at the very heart of the question of how a corporate entity such as the family can, in the face of the unexpected, the disruptive, and the transforming, continue to function without breaking drastically from its particular historic identity [pp. 175–176].

Davis' observations, I believe, point to some of the most significant problems in the methodology of field studies. They make clear the need for continuing follow-up, but perhaps even more important for a greater concern with the methodology of field approaches in general. We have yet to demonstrate that we know how to properly tap or make salient to respondents the kinds of material we mean to provide (Mechanic & Newton, 1965). Much of symbolic communication involves implicit as well as explicit meanings (Garfinkel, 1964), and the intention with which a question is posed may vary widely from the frame of reference the respondent puts on it (Brown & Rutter, 1966). One of the major advantages of a continuing investigation through time is that various problem areas can be tapped when they are still salient to the respondent and when they are still imbued with an emotional content.

Finally, let me note that although I have been referring to the study of stress, what we really must study is "situations." In doing this, it is as important to study those who do not feel challenged and who experience no discomfort as it is to study those who are "stressed." In noting variation in response to the same situations we have an opportunity to locate those aspects of approaches and behavioral repertoires that lead to crises and those that make the situation only an occasion for further progress and mastery.

References

Arnold, M. *Emotion and Personality*. Vols. 1, 2. New York: Columbia University Press, 1960.

Becker, H. S. *Outsiders: Studies in the Sociology of Deviance*. New York: Free Press, 1963.

Becker, H. S. History, culture and subjective experience: An exploration of the social basis of drug-induced experiences. *Journal of Health and Social Behavior*, 1967, **8**, 163–167.

Brown, G. W., et al. Influence of family life on the course of schizophrenic illness. *British Journal of Preventive Social Medicine*, 1962, **16**, 55–68.

Brown, G. W., & Rutter, M. The measurement of family activities and relationships: A methodological study. *Human Relations*, 1966, **19**, 241–263.

Cloward, R. A., & Ohlin, L. E. *Delinquency and Opportunity*. New York: Free Press, 1960.

Cooley, C. H. *Social organization and human nature and the social order*. New York: Free Press, 1956.

Davis, F. *Passage Through Crisis*. Indianapolis: Bobbs-Merrill, 1963.

Festinger, L. *A theory of cognitive dissonance*. New York: Harper & Row, 1957.

Festinger, L. The motivating effect of cognitive dissonance. In G. Lindzey (Ed.), *Assessment of Human Motives*. New York: Grove, 1958.

Garfinkel, H. The routine grounds of everyday activities. *Social Problems*, 1964, **11**, 225–250.

Goffman, E. *Presentation of self in everyday life*. New York: Doubleday (Anchor), 1959.

Goffman, E. *Asylums*. New York: Doubleday (Anchor), 1961.

Graham, D., et al. Psychological response to the suggestion of attitudes specific for hives and hypertension. *Psychosomatic Medicine*, 1962, **24**, 159–169.

Lazarus, R. S. *Psychological stress and the coping process.* New York: McGraw-Hill, 1966.

Lazarus, R. S., et al. A laboratory study of psychological stress produced by a motion picture film. *Psychological Monographs*, 1962, **76**, No. 553.

Lazarus, R. S., & Opton, E. M., Jr. The study of psychological stress. In C. D. Spielberger (Ed.), *Anxiety and Behavior.* New York: Academic Press, 1966.

Lemert, E. *Social pathology.* New York: McGraw-Hill, 1951.

Mead, G. H. *Mind, self, and society.* Chicago: University of Chicago Press, 1934.

Mechanic, D. *Students under stress: A study in the social psychology of adaptation.* New York: Free Press, 1962.

Mechanic, D., & Newton, M. Some problems in the analysis of morbidity data. *Journal of Chronic Diseases*, 1965, **18**, 569–580.

Meron, W. The pathology of boredom, Scientific American, 1957, **7**.

Ruff, G. E., & Korchin, S. J. Adaptive stress behavior. In M. H. Appley & R. Trumbull (Eds.), *Psychological stress: Issues in research.* New York: Appleton, 1966.

Schachter, S. The interaction of cognitive and physiological determinants of emotional state. In L. Berkowitz (Ed.), *Advances in Experimental Social Psychology.* Vol. 1. New York: Academic Press, 1964.

Schachter, S. Cognitive effects on bodily functioning: Studies of obesity and overeating. In D. Glass and C. Phaffman (Eds.), *Biology and Behavior: Neurophysiology and emotion.* New York: Rockefeller University Press and Russell Sage Foundation, 1967, pp. 117–144.

Schachter, S., & Singer, J. Cognitive, social and physiological determinants of emotional state. *Psychological Review*, 1962, **69**, 379–399.

Scheff, T. *Being mentally ill: A sociological theory.* Chicago: Aldine, 1966.

Selye, H. *The stress of life.* New York: McGraw-Hill, 1956.

Sutherland, E. H., & Cressey, D. R. *Principles of criminology.* (6th ed.) Philadelphia: Lippincott, 1960.

Thibaut, J. W., & Kelley, H. H. *The social psychology of groups.* New York: Wiley, 1959.

Torrance, E. P. *Constructive behavior.* Belmont, Calif.: Wadsworth Publishing Co., 1965.

Volkart, E. H. (Ed.) *Social behavior and personality.* New York: Social Science Research Council, 1951.

Wilkins, J. The locus of anomie in suicide. Paper presented at the 62nd annual meeting of the American Sociological Association, San Francisco, California, August 1967.

Wolff, H. G. *Stress and disease.* Springfield, Ill.: Charles C Thomas, 1953.

8

psychological research needs on the problems of human stress

Joseph Weitz

Stress is not an area in which I had been actively conducting research, but I became involved with this mercurial concept when the Institute for Defense Analysis (IDA) asked me if I would investigate the stress literature and see if it were possible to indicate gaps in the research in this field. Much of what will be said in this paper is in the report I prepared for IDA (Weitz, 1966).

When starting out on this venture, I naively thought that it would be a good idea to find out what stress is. That is, how do researchers working in this area define stress? You can imagine my dismay when I found a variety of definitions. Some stress researchers define stress in response terms—"a discomforting response of persons in particular situations" (Mechanic, 1962). Others define stress in stimulus terms. Some individuals define it as both a stimulus and a response, and a few discuss stress in terms of an organismic state or an intervening variable.

Parsons (undated) in an earlier paper, was almost ready to give up the ghost as far as a definition of stress is concerned, but more recently (Parsons, 1966) he has regained hope for the usefulness of the word stress and makes a case for defining it as external situations associated with internal states which lead to avoidance and escape behavior. Stress then, for Parsons, is what we escape or avoid. My worry about such a definition is that it seems so broad and all encompassing that it loses meaning.

If we consider learning as improved performance, or even a change in behavior over time (given practice and eliminating maturational effects), then water learns to freeze. Physicists tell us that if you freeze a given quantity of water, melt it, and refreeze it repeatedly it will freeze at higher and higher temperatures. Is the water learning to freeze? It certainly shows a very nice "learning" curve when you plot trials against temperature of freezing.

I might similarly ask Parsons if the act of not ordering (avoiding) parsnips in a restaurant is an indication of stress. If his answer is "yes" (and it is conceivable that it might be), then is this avoidance response in the same class as escaping from a burning building? If both of these avoidance reactions are indicative of stress then doesn't the concept become too general to be useful? After all, most discriminations imply some avoidance reaction. Perhaps I am beating a dead horse, but it would seem that discussion of stress might be more fruitful if all stress researchers were sure they were all discussing the same beast, dead *or* alive.

In view of the fact that I was asked to involve myself with research needs in the area of human stress, I too will assume that certain situational variables lead to a state in the individual called stress (although a definition seems high on the priority list of research needs). This state, in turn, leads to a particular kind of performance which is considered the result of the stress state.

Let us first look at situations which have been thought of as stressful, and consider certain categories of these which have been used in research on stress. These categories should not be thought of as mutually exclusive.

Speeded information processing.   In general, a situation presumably becomes stressful if the inputs are numerous enough to prohibit adequate information processing and the organism becomes overload. The sheer speed of the input cannot be the determiner of stress, since there are apparently wide individual differences in when (or if) performance becomes degraded. Degradation of performance is the measure most frequently used to indicate the presence of overloading. The degradation may be so extreme as to lead to immobilization.

Related to the process of overloading is the condition of temporal uncertainty. One possible way of explaining why overloading and temporal uncertainty of stimulus occurrence may have similar effects is to consider the individual as "overloading" himself in the condition of temporal uncertainty. That is, where there are a variety of delays between events to which the individual must respond, he may be introducing (internally) additional inputs which are inappropriate and hence lead to something like the overloading condition.

Environmental stimuli. The stimulus situation here consists of noxious environmental stimuli. Such conditions as extremes of temperature, noise, vibration, and so forth, would fit in this category. While many of the situations evoking stress would logically fall under this heading, we will consider here only those which are generally agreed upon as noxious.

Perceived threat. Here the emphasis is on *perceived*. It is apparently not necessary for a situation to be such that the individual is actually experiencing pain or some other debilitating stimulation. It is enough that he perceives the situation as potentially dangerous. Parachuting, combat, examinations, conferences, and so on, may all produce what is thought of as stress, with concomitant stressful responses.

Physiological variables. We are concerned here with stimulus conditions provided by disease, drugs, sleep loss, weightlessness, and so forth. It is obvious that this set of variables might well overlap with those in other categories or at least be related to them. For example, there is undoubtedly a relationship between certain physiological stimuli and perceived threat, and there will indeed be overlap between some of the so-called physiological stimuli and those classified in this paper as environmental.

Isolation. Isolation might be thought of as a special case of environmental and perhaps of the perceived-threat categories. Under conditions of isolation, stress is especially likely to be experienced when there is a perceived threat and there is no possibility of social contact. For isolation to produce stress, it is apparently not necessary for the situational conditions to be those of sensory deprivation. Social deprivation alone would seem to be sufficient to produce the stress response in some individuals (Lazarus, 1966).

Confinement. This is to be differentiated from isolation inasmuch as there is no necessary implication of physical restraint in isolation, whereas restraint is implied in confinement. Similarly, it is not necessary that confinement be associated with isolation. The two, however, are frequently associated when manipulated as independent variables in studies of stress.

Blocking and frustration.   This might well have been subsumed under the environmental category, but is differentiated here since it is thought of as not necessarily noxious. This rubric is used to denote a barrier, either physical or psychological, which inhibits task completion. Defining the situation in this manner, we might consider it to overlap with overloading, since overloading is one way of inhibiting or blocking task completion.

Group pressure.   Here the stimulus condition for stress derives from established social norms of a group or role expectations imposed upon the individual. Fear of failure is the frequent result of such impositions, and it is this which apparently leads to the stress state.

The above categories of stimulus conditions cover, in a broad way, most of the situations, or independent variables, manipulated in research on stress. These categories share one characteristic: all of them lead to degraded performance for some individuals if the stimulus conditions are of sufficient strength and are continued for a long enough period of time. Any of them, however, might lead initially to improved performance in certain cases.

When we consider the performance or the response of the individual during or following the stress state, we are really discussing the criteria for the identification of stress; from this point of view, such responses are the dependent variables. If, on the other hand, we accept the definition that stress is a response, then we may theoretically be measuring the stress itself. Somehow this latter concept is difficult for me to accept.

In any event, the resultant response of one "under stress" is either enhancement or decrement of performance. Most investigators studying stress have been more interested in the degradation of performance. This is especially true of investigators concerned with military matters.

When we consider taking criterion measures we are faced with the problem of *when* to take them. In another context I have shown that the effect of an independent variable is apparent or not, depending upon the time the criterion measure is taken (Weitz, 1962). Incidentally, it has been found that if the task is easy, the criterion measure must be taken relatively early in the performance in order to show an effect of the independent variable; if the task is more difficult the effect of the independent variable will show up somewhat later.

If we are investigating performance degradation under stress, the time at which performance measures are taken must be considered. The same, of course, would be true for performance enhancement. Depending upon when the criterion measure is taken, evidence of the effect of stress may or may not be found.

In general, most of the research on stress uses speed, accuracy, errors (or some such measure) as indications of the behavioral concomitants of the stress situation. Related to these performance measures are what might be thought of as their extremes—immobilization or inappropriate responses.

Much research on stress, as you know, has involved physiological measures as dependent variables. Unfortunately, there seems to be less than a perfect relationship between the physiological and the so-called psychological responses. Part of this lack of consistency between the two classes of measures may result from the fact that, in much of the research on stress, task-relevant performances are not used as the basis for psychological measures. In addition, performance measures are frequently taken outside of the immediate stress situation. If the physiological effects are lasting, and a change in motivation occurs during performance which is not task relevant, than we would expect little relation between physiological and performance measures.

A typical form of the research alluded to above would take baseline performance measures prior to introducing a stress situation, and later obtain performance measures after removal of the stress stimuli. This type of research is exemplified by the paradigm in which a pilot is given a psychomotor task prior to flying a mission and is retested on it upon his return. Here the performance required is not task relevant and the subject is removed from the stress stimuli before the post-testing.

It may well be that removal from the stressful situation leads to a different motivational state on the part of the subject, and this, in turn, is expressed in *less* degraded performance than would be anticipated. However, the physiological states engendered by the stress may remain. If this is so, we would obtain the rather low relationships frequently reported between physiological and psychological measures. More will be said about this later. I would like now to suggest some alternative directions for research in this area.

First of all, there seem to be some basic questions yet unanswered beside that of "What is stress?" As a start, one wonders not only about the generalizability of the definition, but also, regardless of the definition one adopts, about whether or not there is generalization of stress. Are individuals more or less stress resistant regardless of the situation, or is so-called stress, and the stress response, situation specific for an individual?

For example, one might interpret the report of Ruff and Korchin (in Appley & Trumbull, 1967) as indicating that astronauts have low stress reactions regardless of the situation. It has been reported that some of the astronauts did not perceive the manned space flights as particularly stressful. Is the presence or absence of stress in the eye of the experimenter? Almost certainly this is true, but if this is not recognized it confounds our understanding of the generalization of stress.

Assuming that the stimulus situations listed earlier in this paper evoke stress, then we are really asking a question concerning the likelihood of an individual responding in a similarly stressed manner to a number of these situations. We might find that individuals are more likely to exhibit stressed behavior to a variety of stimuli within a particular situational category. That is, an individual might exhibit stress to all noxious stimuli (environmental) but not to conditions of isolation. Another possibility is that both of these types of generalization, or neither of them, exist. The individual may exhibit the stress response to what appears to be a random set of stimulus situations and hence stress might be thought of as situation specific.

These possibilities have some practical as well as theoretical implications. One practical implication is that if the stress response for most people is situation specific, and we are interested in assigning people to jobs, we have a classification rather than a selection problem. On the other hand, if stress is exhibited across a variety of stimulus situations then we are dealing with the more typical selection problem, and might well introduce stress measures into our selection battery.

In order to determine something of the nature of the generalization of stress one could devise a relevant task[1] to be performed under a variety of presumed stress situations. If there is similar degradation of performance (or perhaps enhancement?) across all stress situations, then there is evidence of generalization. If, on the other hand, there is performance degradation in some situations but not in others, we might be inclined to think of stress as more nearly situation specific.

It would also be interesting to investigate the possibility that the effect of stress is task specific rather than situation specific. It is possible that stress interferes more with the performance of certain kinds of tasks than with others (for example, psychomotor versus intellectual). An investigation which would be of interest in this general area is a study of the interaction of type of stressor and type of task. Systematic research in this problem of generality versus specificity of stress would seem fruitful.

In addition to studying the problem of generalization of stress there seem to be some other worthwhile paths to travel. If uncertainty can lead to stress and stress responses, does knowledge concerning the source of the uncertainty affect the potential for the existence of stress? That is, there are certain occasions where the uncertainty is in the situation whereas at other times the uncertainty stems from the performance of the individual. The need here is a determination of the effect of two conditions on the establishment of stress: (1) where the individual has

---

[1] The performance demanded might be one which leads to escape from the stress situation.

control of the situation and (2) where he has no control over events in the situation. Variations on these two themes would include the subject's knowledge, or lack of it, as to whether or not he had control.

An obvious example of one individual having more control over the situation than another is a pilot of an aircraft versus a passenger. For the pilot, if there is any uncertainty it is more likely to be in himself; while for the passenger, the uncertainty is more likely to be in the situation. It has been reported that pilots in training are less likely to get air sick than other members of the crew on the same flight. Could this be related to different sources of uncertainty leading to differential stress (assuming that air sickness is in part related to stress)?

There are a variety of ways in which the uncertainty problem might be investigated. Again, the findings would have practical implications, especially in the area of training and task structuring. From a theoretical point of view a study attacking this problem may cast some light on the stimulus conditions necessary for the establishment of stress.

Earlier, I mentioned that in a number of studies of stress, the dependent variable was performance which was not task relevant. That is, performance decrement was measured on some activity unrelated to the stress situation, or in some instances even after the subject has been removed from the situation evoking the presumed stress. If a new nontask-relevant activity is introduced into the stress situation, it may actually be a relief to the individual, and hence he will not exhibit degraded performance. This might be true especially in the research paradigm where the subject is tested after removal from the stress situation. Here, if there is in fact elation, certain kinds of performance may be improved, but other types might show degradation. One possible type of task which could be used to show a decrement in performance is one demanding fine discriminations. Presumably people in elated states find this type of task extremely difficult. If it were shown that elation or relief *did* lead to poorer performance on a certain class of tasks, perhaps we could use these tasks, after removal of the subject from the stress situation, and infer stress *was* present since elation or relief is *now* present and performance on these tasks are degraded. This procedure may seem indirect but I doubt that these kinds of inferences are any less warranted than those we usually make concerning an undefined concept.

As mentioned previously, if these assumptions concerning relief or elation and task relevance are warranted, then it is not surprising that we find little relation between physiological and performance measures.

It is obvious from this paper that one of my major interests has to do with criterion measurement. Considering three dimensions of criteria: (1) type, (2) time of measurement, and (3) level of difficulty, I have shown that conclusions concerning the effect of an independent variable are modified when these parameters are manipulated (Weitz, 1963).

This, in itself, may not be of great significance, but investigating the effect of changing these criterion dimensions helps one understand the operation of the independent variable.

In research on stress, time of measurement and type of criteria may be of especial interest. For example, how does the time of measuring performance relate to the apparent presence or absence of stress? Is there an adaptation phenomenon in stress, and, if so, what is the course of the adaptation? It would not be too difficult to design studies where dependent performance measures were taken at different times after the induction of stress. In certain experimental designs, different groups might have to be used to avoid practice effects. However, other designs could be devised where this would not be necessary.

In the case of different types of criteria, reference was made earlier to the problem of whether or not the effects of stress were observable in certain kinds of performance and not in others. Klein (1957) sheds some light on this problem in his study showing that the relationship between stress and performance is more dependent upon the performance measure than on the method of inducing stress.

It would seem worthwhile to conduct a study of stress using different performance criteria for the evaluation of the effect of stress. For example, do we come to similar conclusions concerning the nature of stress when we use speed in contrast to accuracy as the criterion? If we found differential effects in these two measures we might gain some insight concerning the operation of stress. Certainly, the concept of types of criteria must be basic to the use of various physiological measures as dependent variables.

Why not investigate, systematically, the effect of using different task-relevant performance criteria at different points in time—prior to, during, and after the induction of stress? The results may tell us a little more than we now know about this mysterious animal.

Another area which seems to need more research is that of finding methods for reducing the debilitating effects of stress. There is an implicit assumption that something like overtraining is valuable for diminishing the damaging effects of stress on that performance which is overtrained. We have crews rehearse ditching procedures, children go through fire drills, and so forth. Is there a more expedient method of training individuals to perform appropriately when stress is introduced into the system? Is overtraining equally effective in reducing performance decrement in different types of activities? If research were undertaken in these areas we might learn more about stress, how to combat its ill effects, and we might *even* learn more about human performance.

Harris et al. (1956) indicated that there were very few studies which investigated the effect of superimposing short-term stress on longterm existing stress. That report was published in 1956. If it is still true today, it seems unfortunate, because in real life this is not an unusual occurrence. We frequently encounter the situation where there is an existing state of anxiety (stress?) and a new short-term stressor is introduced. It would seem worthwhile to investigate the interaction of various degrees of the two stress components.

Lastly I would like to suggest that further work be undertaken in studying the effect of group size and cohesiveness on performance of individuals when stress is introduced. Can the effect of stress be changed by manipulating group cohesiveness and size?

I have tried to describe some of the areas where further research might be desirable. Obviously this is not intended as a comprehensive list of gaps in our knowledge concerning stress, and furthermore, some of the suggested areas may be in the process of being studied, so that the number of gaps may not be so great.

Probably one of the biggest deficiencies in our knowledge about stress stems from the paucity of studies of stress under natural, or what may be called field, conditions. This of course is related to the problem of using task relevant measures in the study of stress. When S. R. Wallace was chairman of the Joint Discussion Forum on Behavioral Sciences, he said:

> Stress simulation in the laboratory achieves precision and control at the possible expense of introducing extraneous factors, such as subjects' resistance to ostensible invasions of privacy, overcompliance in attempting to fit the stereotype of the "good" subject, etc. Further the laboratory approach always assures him of protection and control over the duration or intensity of the stressor. [Weitz, 1966, p. 36.]

If Wallace is correct, and it seems probable that he is, we might be gaining an inaccurate picture of the effect of stress on performance. If we take our research out of the laboratory into "field" situations we are more likely to get task-relevant performance to measure, but will have to be ingenious in the ways we measure it. It would be unfortunate if the uncertainty principle plagued us after all of our efforts.

References

Appley, M. H., & Trumbull, R. *Psychological stress.* New York: Appleton, 1967.

Harris, W., Mackie, R. R., & Wilson, C. L. Performance under stress: A review and critique of recent studies. ONR Technical Report VI, July 1956, Contract Nonr 1241(00), Office of Naval Research.

Klein, S. J. The measurement of stress and its relationship to performance. February 1957, 366, Naval Air Material Command (ACEL), Phila., Pa.

Lazarus, R. S. *Psychological stress and the coping process.* New York: McGraw-Hill, 1966.

Mechanic, D. *Students under stress.* New York: Free Press, 1962.

Parsons, H. D. What the Navy's anti-air warfare training program can learn from air defense system training experience. Contract Nonr 1345(02), Office of Naval Research (undated).

Parsons, H. D. Stave: Stress avoidance/escape. System Development Corporation, August 1966.

Weitz, J. Criteria for Criteria. *American Psychologist*, 1963, **16**, 228–231.

Weitz, J. Stress. IDA/HQ 66-4672, April 1966, Institute for Defense Analysis.

CHAPTER

9 | on the nature of stress

S. B. Sells

The organization of this conference so closely following the publication of the York University symposium on stress (Appley & Trumbull, 1967) attests to the complexity and elusiveness of the problem of stress. As a participant in that symposium, I was impressed by the difficulty of embracing the diverse material presented in a unified summary statement. This was neatly expressed by one of the participants (Cohen, 1967), who noted that "stress is one of those peculiar terms which is understood by everyone when used in a very general context but understood by very few when an operational definition is desired which is sufficiently specific to enable the precise testing of certain relationships [p. 78]. Psychologists have experienced similar difficulties with fatigue, motivation, and other concepts.

In the general context there appears to be a common principle, involving biochemical, physiological, psychophysiological, and individual and group behavioral processes in relation to injury; illness; environmental extremes; task demands; threat to person, prestige, or survival; interpersonal relations, and group activities. That common principle involves insult to the organism and degradation of function, produced in the face of noxious stimulus events, and the evocation of coping mechanisms to counter the effects. The sequence of these events was generalized by Selye (1956) in the General Adaptation Syndrome, with its stages of alarm, resistance, and exhaustion. Various writers have identified these in most of the contexts and processes in which *stress* has been studied. However, as a unifying principle, it is questionable whether these stages are more informative than those of noxious stimulation, coping, and disorganization when coping is unsuccessful. Effective research or application of stress principles must refer back to the specific processes and proceed in the context of the disciplines involved.

At this level generality vanishes. Most so-called stress mechanisms are highly specific, although their action is dependent on the simultaneous occurrence of other responses with which their effects may combine (for example, cold and fear) or which may partially cancel each other (for example, noise, an overarousing stimulus versus sleep loss, an underarousing stimulus). Motivation, group support or pressure, level of physiological adaptation to the situation, conditioning and prior experience in the situation, expectations and confidence in one's reactions, competency, equipment, associates and superiors, represent additional variables that may affect the responses that occur. The fact that for almost every stimulus variable there is a continuum from activation to response facilitation, to impairment, to disorganization, and that these levels may follow a time course, increases the complexity of these multivariate problems.

At the level of specific mechanisms, one may quite properly ask whether a separate concept such as stress is needed, and why the existing concepts and principles of the several scientific disciplines should not be adequate to account for the so-called stress reactions. The most common approach to the definition of stress appears to accept specificity, but to find value in identifying a class of specific reaction mechanisms involving noxious stimulation, impairment of function, and associated states. No assumptions concerning a common principle are needed in this approach. A volume on stress would consist of a compendium of data on a wide range of specific response mechanisms, by a wide sampling of individuals, to a wide range of stimulus situations involving discomfort, physiological impairment, and performance impairment of varying degrees of intensity. In my opinion, however, the justification for doing this would have to be administrative and not scientific. This would be similar to collections related to sanitation, disease prevention, and the like. Such an enterprise would be, at best, a technological exercise, and hardly the justification for a scientific symposium.

Selye himself recognized the distinction between the *specific* aspects of reaction to disease, which he accepted as such, and the *nonspecific* aspects, which he defined as stress. His GAS is concerned with systemic stress, which is superimposed on the specific processes and effects and is claimed to account for genuine phenomena not embraced by the specific processes. This belief in a nonspecific common state in stressed organisms arises from an assumption of a unity in the total psychophysiological system which critics believe may turn out to be an oversimplification when sufficient data are available to evaluate it accurately.

At the biological level, stress has generally been conceptualized as an insulting agent, generally external to the organism, to which the organism responds. The *stressor* is thus something that happens to the organism.

This view has generally prevailed in medicine and in psychiatry, as illustrated by the following quotation from Sir Charles P. Symonds (1947), who set forth the view of the Royal Air Force Medical Service on flying stress:

> Flying stress might usefully be employed . . . to designate the special strains or stresses to which flying personnel are exposed. It might well in this sense be used in a quantitative way to denote the amount of strain to which a man has been put. Thus a man who had had a crash without injury to himself or others might be said to have been exposed to slight flying stress; a man who had had a similar crash with painful injury to himself or fatal injury to others, to moderate flying stress, and so on. Such estimates, especially as recorded by commanding officers would be of considerable value to the medical branch if the man subsequently became ill with psychological disorder. There will still be problems of flying stress for discussion by executives and medical officers: for example, how much flying stress can the average man stand without breaking down; what are the most important elements in flying stress for fighter, bomber, and reconnaissance personnel; what psychological types stand up to flying stress best or worst? But it should be understood once and for all that flying stress is that which happens to the man, not that which happens in him: it is a set of causes, not a set of symptoms [p. 21].

The paradigm implied by this quotation, which was widely used by Allied flight surgeons in World War II, was that symptoms were the resultant of varying profiles of *stress intensity* and *individual predisposition*. Stress was presumed to be a function of the dangers and threatening circumstances of combat flying, and predisposition, of the personality and background of the individual. Psychiatrists often took into account, on the predisposition side, not only information from personal history and personality assessment, but also such factors as separation anxiety, guilt-proneness, and the like. They also made allowances for weight loss, fatigue, and other developments in the field. Stress was evaluated on the basis of experiences in combat missions, losses in battle, calculated chances of survival of particular missions, and other factors of this kind. While far from precise, it must nevertheless be conceded that this paradigm resulted in a calculus of human endurance that greatly increased the effectiveness of the Western Allies. However, it is really a rough rule of thumb and breaks down rapidly when one attempts to represent the variables precisely for the interaction equation.

Psychologists vary on the issue of whether stress is an external entity or state of the organism. Dr. Weitz (1966) feels that stress is a stimulus variable, while Appley and Trumbull (1967) have taken the position that "stress is probably best conceived *as a state of the total organism under extenuating circumstances* rather than as an event in the environment" [p. 11].

The latter view is one that I endorse without qualification, but with some elaboration. As I view it, stress does occur under extenuating circumstances, but I believe that these circumstances can be specified. As an interactionist (Sells, 1963, 1966), I believe that a "state of the organism" is more appropriate than either external or internal loci, since the interaction of the two, producing a state, is more consistent with the data of behavior. My concern, at this time, is to present a theory and definition of stress which adds explanatory information beyond that involved in various specific mechanisms and applies meaningfully to response variation among individuals and within individuals over time.

Appley and Trumbull (1967, p. 401) in summarizing their symposium, concluded: (1) that individual differences in reactions to situations are great; (2) that stress measures reflecting different organismic subsystems and different criteria are largely unrelated; (3) that responses vary from situation to situation and that variation is greatest between laboratory and life situation; (4) that the social context is of major importance in understanding stress reactions and that social and other environmental supports have often been overlooked in evaluating particular behaviors; (5) that stress, as other behavior, is best understood as *interaction* of individual and situation; and (6) that in evaluating such interactions, "private" or inner events should be taken into consideration. While agreeing with these six statements, I find them more general than the stress context would suggest.

The theory of stress that I wish to present is consistent with these generalizations. It is interactional; it provides for individual differences, variability of measures, variability of situations, social context, and implicit, inner reactions. In keeping with the contemporary emphasis on cognitive control, it assumes that response control is in the cognitive system and that stress reactions are a function of cognitive control rather than the emotions. I believe that this theory integrates most of the psychological (and physiological) stress phenomena that I have encountered during the past twenty years, but I will leave it to this critical audience to test its utility.

Briefly stated, I believe that a state of stress arises under the following conditions:

1. The individual is called upon in a situation to respond to circumstances for which he has no adequate response available. The unavailability of an adequate response may be due to physical inadequacy; absence of the response in the individual's response repertoire; lack of training, equipment, or opportunity to prepare.

2. The consequences of failure to respond effectively are important to the individual. Personal involvement in situations can be defined in terms of importance of consequences to the individual.

Stress intensity depends on the importance of individual involvement and the individual's assessment of the consequences of his inability to respond effectively to the situation.

In his review of the stress literature, Weitz (1966 and Chapter 8 of this volume) mentioned eight common types of stress situations that have been investigated: speeded information processing, environmental extremes, perceived threat, disturbed physiologic balance, isolation, confinement, blocking and frustration, and group pressure. It appears to me that each of these is stressful when the individual is unable to respond effectively and to the degree that the consequences are significant to him. Some individuals, because of training, conditioning, habituation, prior experience, equipment, expectation, support, or other mitigating factors may be able to perform effectively under stimulus conditions that far exceed the capabilities of others. The onset of stress is to be determined and understood in these various situations, not in terms of the stimulus parameters above, or of the personality profiles of the participants, although these are relevant, but in every case in terms of the individual's ability to make an effective response and his assessment of the consequences of failure.

This approach owes debts to Irving Janis (1958), who has emphasized the importance of preparatory communication and the "work of worry" in meeting life stress, and to Saul Rosenzweig (1944) who has indicated how stress is related to frustration. Miller's (see, for example, Miller, 1962) information processing model is related, but as a special case.

Among the advantages of this definitional paradigm are:

1. That it provides a general concept of stress, independent of specific mechanisms, which appears to embrace a wide range of situations, personalities, and events.

2. That it indicates an unrestricted range of measures to mitigate

stress, by conditioning, training, equipment and system design, preparatory communication, warning, and perhaps even manipulation of costs and rewards.

3. That it requires no special concepts of stress behavior; on the contrary, it utilizes established principles of behavior for understanding. Yet it provides a new principle to distinguish stress from other phenomena of human behavior.

References

Appley, M. H., & Trumbull, R. (Eds.) *Psychological stress.* New York: Appleton, 1967.

Cohen, S. I. Central nervous system functioning in altered sensory environments. In M. H. Appley and R. Trumbull (Eds.), *Psychological stress.* New York: Appleton, 1967, pp. 77–118.

Janis, I. L. *Psychological stress.* New York: Wiley, 1958.

Miller, J. G. Information input overload. In M. C. Yovits, G. T. Jocobi, and G. D. Goldstein (Eds.), *Self organizing systems.* Washington, D. C.: Spartan, 1962.

Rosenzweig, S. An outline of frustration theory. In J. McV. Hunt (Ed.), *Personality and the behavior disorders.* Vol. 1. New York: Ronald Press, 1944.

Sells, S. B. An interactionist looks at the environment. *American Psychology,* 1963, **18,** 696–702.

Sells, S. B. Ecology and the science of psychology. *Multivariate Behavioral Research,* 1966, **1,** 131–144.

Selye, H. *The stress of life.* New York: McGraw-Hill, 1956.

Symonds, Sir Charles P. Use and abuse of the term flying stress. In Air Ministry, *Psychological disorders in flying personnel of the Royal Air Force, investigated during the War, 1939–1945.* London: H. M. Stationery Office, 1947, pp. 18–21.

Weitz, J. Stress. IDA/HQ 66-4672, April 1966, Institute for Defense Analysis.

CHAPTER

10

strategies for controlling stress in interpersonal situations[1]

Ivan D. Steiner

In a series of recent studies (Steiner & Rogers, 1963; Steiner & Johnson, 1964; Johnson, 1966; Steiner, 1966) the writer and his colleagues have examined four responses that a person may produce when he finds his own views are contradicted by those of a respected associate. The individual may adjust his own opinions to agree with the associate's judgments (conform), reject the associate as a person who is less competent than he was originally thought to be, devaluate the importance of the issue about which disagreements have occurred, or under-recall the frequency or extent of the disagreements. Each of these responses has been conceived as a means of reducing the stress which is presumed to exist when an individual unexpectedly finds himself in disagreement with a respected associate.

[1] This research was supported in part by a grant from the United States Public Health Service, National Institutes of Health, No. M-4460.

Evidence from the previous studies in this series suggests that these four responses are functional alternatives, and that any one of them—or a combination of all four—may be used to reduce the stress that is engendered by interpersonal disagreements. However, when free to choose their own responses, some subjects have manifested a significant tendency to rely upon a single response instead of using two or more simultaneously. Different individuals have revealed preferences for different responses, and these preferences have been found to be related to scores on personality variables (Steiner, 1966). The data suggest that some (but not necessarily all) individuals have learned to employ favored techniques for reducing the stress created by interpersonal conflicts.

If each of the four responses listed above provides relief from stress, persons who elect to use any one of them should show less arousal after encountering interpersonal disagreements than should persons who use none of them. Partial support for this conclusion has been provided by Back, Bogdonoff, Shaw, and Klein (1963) who found that conformity in an experimental situation was accompanied by a decrease in free fatty acid in the blood, and by Buckhout (1966) whose conforming subjects showed a significant decrease in heart rate.[2] Although these studies suggest that conformity is a stress-reducing response to interpersonal disagreements, they provide no direct information about the consequences of rejection, devaluation or under-recall. The present study tests the hypothesis that all four reactions have the effect of suppressing arousal levels.

People who have learned to rely heavily upon a specific stress-reducing technique should manifest comparatively low levels of arousal when they confront situations in which disagreements are likely to occur. Goldin (1964) has suggested that defensive strategies that have worked in the past provide the individual with assurances that he can handle future conflicts that may arise, and has argued that successful reliance on a defensive technique may be associated with low anxiety when the individual subsequently faces threatening situations. Similarly, Hoffman (1957) has contended that persistent conformity may be a device for avoiding anxiety rather than a response to anxiety. It may serve as a dependable, ready-made solution to almost any interpersonal problems that arise. Thus the steadfast conformer is forearmed in a fashion that should permit him to maintain a relatively low level of arousal. The present research tests the contention that low levels of arousal *before*

---

[2] Lacey and Lacey (1958) have suggested that increased heart rate and blood pressure are associated with reduction in sensitivity to stimulation and with "rejection of the environment." Decreased heart rate is associated with increased sensitivity to stimulation. Consequently, Buckhout's findings may reflect subjects' styles of responding to stress, rather than the intensity of the stress they are experiencing.

disagreements have occurred will be associated with strong use of one or another of the four balance-restoring responses when disagreements actually occur.

Buckhout's (1966) data may be interpreted as running contrary to this hypothesis. The initial base-line heart rate of subjects who conformed to social pressures was found to be higher than that of "anticonformers" (that is, subjects who produced a boomerang effect). However, it is possible that many of Buckhout's anticonformers were people who relied heavily upon rejection, devaluation, or under-recall, and that his findings do not reveal a difference between conformers and subjects who do not have any ready-made strategy for coping with interpersonal disagreements.

In addition to testing hypotheses concerning the arousal levels of subjects, the present research explores the amount of time elapsing between the receipt of dissonant information and the subject's announcement of his own judgment. Long response latencies have sometimes been interpreted as indicating that a task is difficult or that a subject has little confidence in his decision (Johnson, 1957). But long response latencies have also been cited as evidence of low vigilance and low arousal (Buck, 1966; Dardano, 1962). Benton, Hartman, and Sarason (1955) found that subjects who scored high on the Taylor MAS had short latencies when responding to TAT cards, but Kamin and Clark (1957) obtained an opposite finding for subjects who worked on a simple discrimination task. Thus the available evidence appears to support either of two contradictory predictions: subjects who are highly anxious when they confront interpersonal disagreements will express their own views more rapidly than will subjects who are less anxious, *or* subjects who are highly anxious will express their own views more slowly than will less anxious subjects. Informal observations made during previous studies in this series suggest that the former of these two hypotheses is a more valid statement *when the task involves interpersonal disagreements.* Although we have never before collected data on decision times, we have repeatedly observed that subjects who do not make strong use of any of the four balance-restoring techniques have seemed anxious, and have announced their judgments very soon after hearing the contrary views of their associates. We suggest that very rapid responses are symptomatic of an attempt by the subject to insulate himself from the source of threat (that is, the contrary opinions of the associate). Subjects who have learned to rely upon conformity, rejection, under-recall, or devaluation are presumably less threatened by dissonant messages; they can afford to delay their responses and give the appearance of weighing the merits of their associate's views.

The strategy of the present study is to divide subjects into two types on the basis of their reactions to a series of interpersonal disagreements.

One type consists of subjects who have manifested strong use of con-formity, rejection, devaluation, *or* under-recall. The other type includes all subjects who have not manifested strong use of one of these responses. The two types of subjects are compared with respect to (1) their pre-disagreement arousal levels, (2) their postdisagreement arousal levels; and (3) their decision times. Three hypotheses are tested:

> *Hypothesis I.* Subjects of Type 1 (those who make strong use of *one* of the four balance-restoring responses) will show *less arousal* than sub-jects of Type 2 *before* disagreements occur.
> *Hypothesis II.* Subjects of Type 1 will show *less increase* in arousal after disagreements have occurred than will subjects of Type 2.
> *Hypothesis III.* Subjects of Type 1 will have *longer decision times* than will subjects of Type 2.

PROCEDURES

Subjects

The sixty experimental and fourteen control subjects were male students enrolled in the introductory psychology course at the University of Illinois. They received research credit for their participation in the experiment.

The Experimental Session

Subjects came one at a time to a laboratory room where they were joined by another male student who was serving as the experimenter's accomplice. The same student acted as the accomplice in all sessions. The subject and the accomplice were seated at opposite sides of a table and were separated by a small plywood partition approximately 10 inches high which obscured each person's view of the opposite side of the table but did not otherwise interfere with vision. The experimenter explained that the subjects were participating in a study of impression formation and that he would ask each of them to supply certain information which the other person could use in forming an accurate perception. In answer to the experimenter's questions the participants then revealed their home town, class in the university, major subject, and reported whether their academic average was higher or lower than *B*. In order to guarantee that the accomplice would be viewed favorably he always reported that he was from Chicago, was a junior majoring in physics, and had an average that was higher than *B*. Use of this bogus "information" in earlier studies had almost invariably created a very favorable impression of the accomplice.

At this point the subject and the accomplice were asked to rate one another on fourteen six-step graphic rating scales. Nine scales called for ratings of the partner's personality and five required judgments about the partner's probable knowledge and skill in subject areas over which the subject and accomplice were subsequently to be tested.

After the rating scales had been collected, the experimenter attached zinc electrodes to opposite sides of the index finger of the subject's non-preferred hand. Electrodes were coated with Beck-Lee microhm electro-cardiograph jelly and were held in place by surgical tape. The subject's hand was lightly strapped to a short board which kept it immobilized for the duration of the experimental session. While the accomplice received identical treatment the experimenter assured the participants that no electrical shock would be employed and that they would experience no discomfort whatever.

The subject's electrodes were connected to a Hunter Deceptograph which produced a continuous record of skin resistance on a tape which moved at the rate of six inches per minute. The electrodes applied to the accomplice's finger were not connected to the recording device. Five minutes after the subject's electrodes had been applied, the experimenter balanced the input circuit and made certain that the sensitivity control of the recorder was set at a low level. The latter step was taken because we desired to obtain data on base rates rather than information about momentary changes associated with specific events. The basal or "background" level of skin conductance has been regarded as an indicant of general activation or arousal (Woodworth & Schlosberg, 1954; Montagu & Coles, 1966). Fixed resisters were employed to check the calibration of the recording instrument.

After adjusting the recording apparatus, the experimenter announced that he would administer a test that would be answered orally. Participants were informed that they should pay attention to one another's answers so they could improve upon the accuracy of their initial impression of one another. The experimenter then exposed thirty-two cards, on each of which was a multiple-choice question with three alternative answers. The questions called for judgments about political and social events, the characteristics of animals, the sizes and shapes of geometrical designs, and number series which had been included in IQ tests. Each card was displayed for 30 seconds and the experimenter asked the accomplice to announce his answers first. The accomplice's first ten answers were those most frequently given by subjects in a preliminary study who had responded privately to the thirty-two questions. However, starting with question 11 the accomplice sometimes gave answers which had *least* frequently been given by subjects in the preliminary investigation. The questions to which he gave least popular answers were numbers 11, 13, 14, 17, 22, 24, 26, 27, 28, 30, and 32 in the series.

When the accomplice announced his answer to a question, the experimenter closed an electrical switch which activated an event marker on the recording instrument. The switch was kept in the closed position until the subject announced his answer to the same question. Thus the record included an indication of the amount of time elapsing between the accomplice's and subject's responses.

After all cards had been exposed, the subject and accomplice once more rated one another on the fourteen graphic-rating scales described above. They also responded to a questionnaire concerning the significance of people's answers to the thirty-two questions, and they recorded written estimates of the number of times each had disagreed with his "partner." These data will be discussed later.

The Control Group

Fourteen control subjects received the same treatment as did the sixty experimental subjects except that the accomplice always gave answers which were most popular among the subjects of the preliminary study, who had responded privately without hearing anyone else's replies. (It should be noted, however, that the "most popular" answers had not been universally preferred by subjects in the preliminary study. On the average these subjects had disagreed with the "most popular" answers 9.93 times out of thirty-two.)

Response Scores

Conformity.   The subject's conformity score was obtained by counting the number of times out of thirty-two he had agreed with the answers given by the accomplice. Scores for the sixty experimental subjects ranged from 23 to 10 and the mean was 16.0.

Under-recall.   After all thirty-two cards had been exposed the subject was asked to express a written estimate of the number of times he and his partner had disagreed with one another. The subject's estimated number of disagreements was subtracted from the actual number to obtain his under-recall score. Scores ranged from +12 to −5, with a mean of +5.0.

Rejection.   Subjects rated the accomplice before exposure to the thirty-two cards and again after exposure. Ratings given to the accomplice on each of the fourteen six-step graphic scale were scored by assigning a value of six to responses at the most favorable end of the scales and a value of one to responses at the least favorable ends. The sum of the numerical values for the second set of ratings was subtracted from the sum of the values for the first set of ratings to yield the subject's rejection score. Scores ranged from +11 to −15 with a mean of +1.6.

Devaluation.   The postsession questionnaire included ten six-step graphic scales on which the subject indicated the strength of his belief that a person's answers to the thirty-two questions reveal his intelligence, knowledge, general sophistication, and ability to think rationally. Scales were scored by assigning the value of six to responses indicating disbelief, and the value of one to responses indicating very strong belief. Scores ranged from 46 to 18 with a mean of 29.3. High scores suggest that the subject tended not to believe that his associate's or his own answers to the thirty-two questions were indicative of important personal qualities.

Categorization of Subjects

For purposes of analysis subjects were categorized on the basis of their responses to the experimentally created disagreements. All sixty experimental subjects were ranked with respect to their use of conformity, and then reranked on each of the other three responses. Thus, every subject received a rank score on each of four responses. A subject was categorized as a high scorer on a given response if he ranked in the top quarter of the distribution on that response but was not in the top quarter of any of the other three distributions. Use of these criteria identified eight persons as conformers, eight as devaluators, seven as under-recallers, and two as rejectors. In order to obtain a larger number of cases in the latter category, the selection criteria were relaxed slightly. Four additional subjects who were in the top ten percent of rejection but also ranked in the top quarter on one other response were added to the rejection category. These four subjects ranked at least seven steps higher on rejection than on any other response. Finally a seventh subject was added because he fell at a 73rd percentile on rejection and was in the bottom quarters of the other three distributions.

Analysis involved a comparison of the skin conductances and decision times of the subjects in the categories described above. Each category was compared with every other category, with the control group, and with the thirty experimental subjects who were not categorized as strong users of *any one* of the four responses.

Two additional sets of categories were employed in an effort to determine whether the strong use of a single response has implications for anxiety control which differ from those inherent in the simultaneous use of several responses. In constructing the first of these sets of categories, each subject was given an initial score equaling his inverted rank score on the response he had used most strongly (for example, the person in the sample who had conformed most often received an initial score of 60). The *mean* of the subject's inverted rank scores on the other three responses was subtracted from his initial score, yielding a "rank-difference" score which indicated the extent to which he had employed one response more than the other three. For purpose of analysis the sixty subjects were dichotomized at the median of the distribution of rank-difference scores (at 23.9).

The final categorization of subjects was based on their total use of all four responses. Each subject's four inverted rank scores were summed to yield a "total-rank" score. Subjects were dichotomized at the median of this distribution (122.9).

Conductance Scores

A continuous record of each subject's basal skin resistance was available. In order to reduce these data to manageable proportions the following steps were taken. A reading was made of the subject's skin resistance at the moment when he announced each of his thirty-two answers. These values were averaged for blocks of five answers (trials), and the reciprocal of the obtained average for any block was recorded as the subject's *conductance* score (in micromhos) for that block. Conductance scores were computed for trials 6–10, 11–15, 16–20, 21–25, and 28–32, as was the subject's initial conductance score (the reciprocal of his basal skin resistance before the first of the thirty-two cards was shown).

Decision Time

The amount of time elapsing between the accomplice's announcement of his answer and the subject's reply was determined for each trial. These decision times were then summed across the five trials in each of the blocks described above.

RESULTS

Initial Levels of Skin Conductance

Table 10–1 reports the means of the initial conductance scores of subjects grouped according to criteria described above. It is to be noted that experimental and control subjects did not differ in arousal level before the first test card was exposed. Among experimental subjects, those who obtained high total rank scores manifested the same initial level of arousal as did those who obtained low total rank scores. But, as anticipated, subjects who subsequently showed a strong tendency to conform, under-recall, reject, *or* devaluate (the C-U-R-D category in Table 10–1) manifested lower initial levels of arousal than did other experimental subjects (the non-C-U-R-D category). Although this finding does not quite reach the .05 level of significance by two-tailed *t* test, it suggests that people who have learned to rely heavily upon a single strategy experience little arousal when confronting situations in which interpersonal disagreements are likely to occur. The direction of the difference between high and low rank-difference scorers is also consistent with this conclusion, though the obtained *t* value does not approach significance ($.20 < p < .30$, by two-tailed test).

TABLE 10–1 Initial Conductance Scores (Micromhos) of Subjects Categorized According to Several Criteria

Categories of Subjects	n	M	SD	t
Experimental Ss	60	31.39	7.73	0.61
Control Ss	14	29.98	7.87	
C-U-R-D Ss°	30	29.52	5.33	1.92°°
Non-C-U-R-D Ss°	30	33.25	9.20	
High rank-difference Ss	30	30.33	6.62	1.07
Low rank-difference Ss	30	32.45	8.61	
High total rank Ss	30	31.47	8.56	0.08
Low total rank Ss	30	31.30	6.85	
Conforming Ss	8	28.95	5.77	
Under-recalling Ss	7	31.26	4.99	
Rejecting Ss	7	28.11	5.02	
Devaluating Ss	8	29.80	4.77	

° The C-U-R-D category consists of the experimental subjects who ranked high on the use of *one* of the four responses (conformity, under-recall, rejection, *or* devaluation). The non-C-U-R-D category includes the remainder of the experimental subjects.
°° $.05 < p < .10$.

The last four rows of Table 10–1 report the initial conductance scores of subjects who were categorized as making strong use of specific response strategies. The *n*s for these categories are small and none of the differences between these four types of subjects is significant.

Changes in Skin Conductance

Table 10–2 reports data concerning changes in conductance levels as subjects proceeded through the thirty-two test cards. Changes across two time intervals were regarded as especially critical: the change from the

block of trials just preceding the accomplice's first expression of unpopular beliefs (trials 6–10) to the first block in which such beliefs were
expressed (trials 11–15), and the change from the block just preceding
the accomplice's first expression of unpopular beliefs (trials 6–10) to
the final block (trials 29–32). Indices of these changes were obtained by
subtracting the subject's earlier conductance score from his later conductance score. Differences between the mean changes of various categories of subjects were evaluated by t test. Although the variances
involved in some of the comparisons are significantly different, the
demonstrated robustness of the t statistic (Boneau, 1960) appears to
justify the use of this technique.

TABLE 10–2 Mean Increases in Micromhos of Skin Conductance

Categories of Subjects		Increases in Micromhos of Skin Conductance from Block 1 (Trials 6-10) to:						
		Block 2 (Trials 11-15)			Block 5 (Trials 28-32)			
	n	M	SD	t	M	SD	t	
Experimental Ss	60	2.47	2.73	6.52†	5.30	3.49	6.35†	
Control Ss	14	.14	.35		1.86	1.13		
C-U-R-D Ss*	30	.60	.67	7.23†	3.50	2.18	4.68†	
Non-C-U-R-D Ss*	30	4.34	2.75		7.10	3.61		
High rank-difference Ss	30	1.41	1.97	3.26**	4.07	2.03	2.95**	
Low rank-difference Ss	30	3.53	2.97		6.52	4.14		
High total rank Ss	30	2.40	2.14	.19	5.46	3.14	.71	
Low total rank Ss	30	2.54	3.22		5.13	3.78		
Conforming Ss	8	.60	.69		3.67	1.35		
Under-recalling Ss	7	1.00	.86		4.67	3.48		
Rejecting Ss	7	.27	.20		2.43	1.34		
Devaluating Ss	8	.54	.54		3.22	1.38		

* The C-U-R-D category consists of the experimental subjects who ranked high
in the use of *one* of the four responses (conformity, under-recall, rejection, *or* devaluation). The non-C-U-R-D category includes the remainder of the experimental
subjects.
** $p < .01$.
† $p < .001$.

It is evident that the conductance levels of all categories of subjects
tended to increase over blocks of trials. However, the increases for control
subjects are significantly smaller than those for experimental subjects.
Among the latter, those who showed strong reliance upon a single response strategy (the C-U-R-D category) manifested smaller increases
in arousal than did other experimental subjects (the non-C-U-R-D

category). Similar patterns are revealed by the two categories based on rank-difference scores: subjects who used one response strategy to a high degree showed less increase in conductance than did subjects who did not emphasize a single response. It should be noted that the differences between groups reported in Table 10–2 are about as large for changes from block 1 to block 2 as they are for changes from block 1 to block 5. The first few trials on which the accomplice gave unpopular answers were sufficient to produce marked differences between the arousal levels of subjects who did and subjects who did not emphasize a single response. Subsequent trials did little to increase these differences.

Although strong use of a single response strategy was associated with small increase in skin conductance, high total use of all four strategies was not. The difference between subjects who obtained high versus low total rank scores was negligible.

The last four rows of Table 10–2 report the change scores of subjects who emphasize specific response strategies. The ns for these categories are very small, and none of the differences between the four types is significant.

Decision Times

The subject's decision time for a block of five trials was computed by summing his five decision times for that block. Scores obtained in this manner were then averaged across members of a category. Figures 10–1 and 10–2 report these means.

Although the decision times of various categories of subjects differed somewhat even before the accomplice began to give unpopular answers (trials 6–10), none of these initial differences is large enough to approach statistical significance. However, it should be noted that all categories of experimental subjects increased their decision times when the accomplice began to announce unpopular answers (trials 11–15), whereas the decision times of control subjects decreased slightly. The mean *change* in decision time from trials 6–10 to trials 11–15 was 3.44 seconds for the sixty experimental subjects. For the fourteen subjects, it was —.71 seconds. The difference between these two mean change scores is significant at the .02 level ($t = 2.51$).

Starting with trials 16–20, the decision times of both control and experimental subjects became rather erratic, possibly due to differences in the character of the questions that were included in the several blocks of trials. But it is apparent from Figure 10–1 that subjects who relied heavily upon a single response strategy (the C-U-R-D and the high rank-difference categories) consistently responded more slowly than did other experimental subjects, and that control subjects responded more rapidly than did any category of experimental subjects. Table 10–3 presents a comparison of the total decision times (for twenty-five trials) of subjects grouped according to the criteria described earlier. The pattern of findings closely parallels that shown in Table 10–2: experimental subjects differ from control subjects, C-U-R-D subjects differ from non-C-U-R-D subjects, and high rank-difference subjects differ from low rank-difference subjects. But total rank on all four response strategies is unrelated to

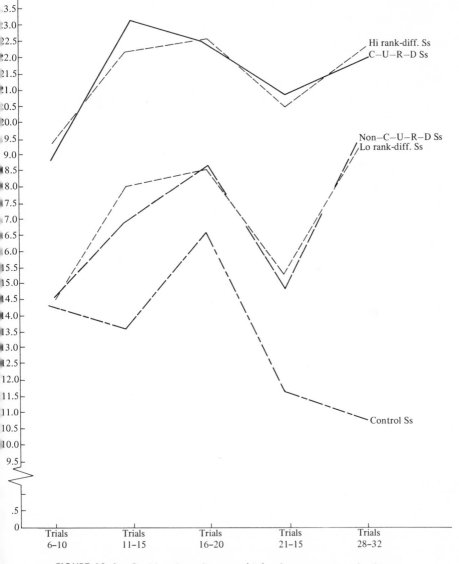

FIGURE 10–1. Decision times (in seconds) for five categories of subjects.

decision time, and people who employed any one specific response strategy to a high degree are not significantly different from those who emphasized any other specific strategy. As hypothesized, subjects who emphasized a single response strategy (the C-U-R-D and the high rank-difference categories) gave their replies more slowly than did other experimental subjects.

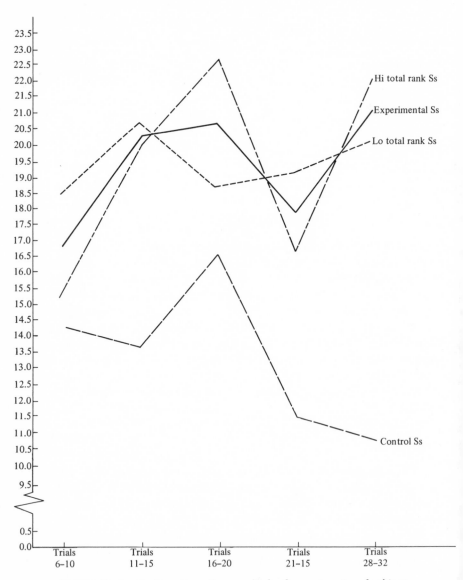

FIGURE 10–2.   Decision times (in seconds) for four categories of subjects.

TABLE 10–3 Total Decision Times for Five Blocks of Trials

Categories of Subjects	n	M	SD	t
Experimental Ss	60	96.75	38.38	2.71**
Control Ss	14	67.21	22.72	
C-U-R-D Ss	30	107.97	42.61	2.37*
Non-C-U-R-D Ss	30	85.53	29.66	
High rank-difference Ss	30	107.10	42.73	2.17*
Low rank-difference Ss	30	86.39	30.11	
High total rank Ss	30	96.34	35.97	.08
Low total rank Ss	30	97.16	40.65	
Conforming Ss	8	106.41	30.86	
Under-recalling Ss	7	93.22	29.49	
Rejecting Ss	7	119.47	50.58	
Devaluating Ss	8	112.38	50.26	

$* \ p < .05$
$** \ p < .02$

Skin Conductance and Decision Time

The findings reported above suggest that skin conductance is negatively correlated with decision time. Obtained correlation coefficients tend to support this expectation, but at rather low levels of significance. For all sixty experimental subjects, the correlation between initial skin conductance and total decision time was $-.28$ $(p < .05)$, and for the control subjects, the correlation was $-.20$ (not significant). Correlations between skin conductance and decision time were predominately negative for each block of trials, but the obtained relationships were rarely strong enough to be statistically significant. No consistently significant differences were found between the correlations for different categories of subjects.

DISCUSSION

We have reported data indicating that disagreements with respected associates are uncomfortable or stressful and that many individuals take steps to control that stress. Some people appear to have ready-made response strategies which permit them to maintain low levels of arousal in the face of impending disagreements and to avoid severe stress when disagreements actually occur. But other people seem not to have learned to rely upon a particular protective device, and these individuals manifest high levels of arousal both before and after disagreements have arisen.

The data of this study suggest that they are also inclined to announce their views very soon after hearing the contrary opinions of an associate.

Perhaps rapid responses after hearing the contrary judgments of an associate are symptomatic of a defensive strategy we have not yet examined in detail. By answering almost immediately the individual is able to maintain the appearance of being isolated from the associate. He can seem to rely entirely upon his own resources and to avoid any evaluation of the merits of the associate's judgments: "My associate may be right or wrong, but I am paying no attention to him. If I happen to agree with him it is not because I am submissive; and if I disagree with him (as is often the case), it is not because I am being defiant. As anyone can see, I am answering immediately, and I am not even bothering to evaluate his opinions. My answers may be wrong, but no one can say I am being nasty or genuinely disagreeable."

This interpretation of the behavior of the non-C-U-R-D subjects is reminiscent of Horney's (1945) description of persons who avoid the stresses of interpersonal entanglements by "moving away from people." Unlike other individuals who are said to "move against people" (the rejectors in this study), or to "move toward people" (conformers), the non-C-U-R-D subjects seem to isolate themselves from the threatening situation. However, we are inclined to believe that their isolation is more a pose than a reality, for their high average arousal levels suggest that they were rather strongly affected by hearing the accomplice's contrary opinions. Perhaps "moving away from people" is a more successful strategy in many "real-life situations" than it was in the present study.

If the short decision times of non-C-U-R-D subjects are indicative of an attempt by these persons to isolate themselves from the source of threat, subjects in this category who made the least use of any other defensive strategy should have manifested the greatest tendency to give rapid responses. Those who found no other acceptable means of coping with the problem should have been most inclined to increase the tempo of their answers (or *least* inclined to *decrease* their tempo). To test this derivation, subjects in the non-C-U-R-D category were dichotomized on the basis of their total rank scores. The decision times of subjects who made the least total use of conformity, under-recall, rejection, and de-valuation (low total rank subsample) were found to be a little longer than those of high total rank subjects *before* the accomplice began to give unpopular answers (3.2 seconds per response versus 2.8 seconds). But by the last block of trials the former subjects were answering more rapidly than were the latter (3.39 seconds per response versus 4.64 seconds). While the differences do not reach acceptable levels of significance, the data are consistent with the conclusion that rapid responses are character-istic of those who have found no other means of coping with interpersonal disagreements. The two subcategories of non-C-U-R-D subjects were very similar to one another with respect to both initial and final conductance levels. For the entire non-C-U-R-D group the correlation between *changes* in decision times and *changes* in conductance levels, while positive, was very low ($r = .11$). Thus it appears once more that the rapid expression of answers was not a highly successful technique for controlling stress.

If the tendency to give rapid responses was a simple reaction to stress, and if it was totally ineffective as a means of controlling stress, the correlation between arousal level and decision time should have been negative. Those persons who were most aroused should have answered most rapidly. Among C-U-R-D subjects the obtained correlation was $-.45$ ($p < .05$), but for the non-C-U-R-D category it was only $-.07$. The failure of the latter correlation to approximate that for the C-U-R-D category suggests that decision times may have reflected different processes in the two groups. If some of the non-C-U-R-D subjects employed rapid responses as a means of controlling stress, and if this strategy was even partially successful for a few of these people, the correlation should have been lower for non-C-U-R-Ds than for C-U-R-Ds. (If the strategy were highly successful for many subjects, the correlation for non-C-U-R-Ds should have been strongly positive.) Although the pertinent findings are not very strong, they suggest that some of our non-C-U-R-D subjects obtained a modicum of relief by giving very rapid answers.

By comparison with the experimental groups, control subjects gave very rapid responses. But it should be remembered that the accomplice always expressed popular answers during control sessions. Thus control subjects generally obtained consensual validation for decisions they had already reached. They had little reason to reflect upon the comparative merits of two different answers, and were seldom caught on the horns of a perplexing dilemma. Their rapid replies were probably a consequence of low stress, whereas the comparatively short decision times of non-C-U-R-D subjects were symptomatic of attempted isolation from a threatening situation.

Our data suggest that the effects of stress on decision time are curvilinear, at least in the types of situations examined by this research. Very low stress (control group) encouraged rapid responses, whereas moderate stress (the C-U-R-D category) seemed to induce individuals to hesitate long enough to evaluate the possible advantages of alternative replies. When stress was high (the non-C-U-R-D category), many subjects apparently tried to avoid the threatening aspects of the situation by isolating themselves from the source of contrary opinions. Their rapid responses are interpreted as symptomatic of this strategy.

Throughout this report, we have treated conformers, under-recallers, rejectors, and devaluators as though they were completely interchangeable members of the C-U-R-D category. Because the *n*s for these four types were very small, only extremely large differences between them would have been statistically significant. And we did not obtain extremely large differences. But there are some moderate-sized differences that deserve comment. In particular, the under-recallers seem not to have followed the pattern set by the other three groups. They started with higher initial skin conductances, manifested larger increases in conductance as they proceeded through the thirty-two trials, and gave their answers more rapidly than did conformers, rejectors, or devaluators. With respect to all three of these indices under-recallers look more like non-C-U-R-Ds than do any of the other three types. It appears reasonable to suggest that under-recall is a technique which does not yield very good *immediate* control of stress, and that its "beneficial" consequences may become apparent only after the individual has had time to convince himself of the validity of his inaccurate memories. If this is the case, under-recallers should show much less arousal when they are reminded of the experiment at some later time than they do immediately after the experiment. We have no data with which to test this prediction.

Implicit in this research has been the assumption that people obtain more control over stress through the use of their favorite strategies than they might gain by employing less-favored techniques. Thus we have contended that strong use of a single response is more effective than is the moderate use of two or three responses, and the data seem to support this argument. But additional research is needed to test the comparative effects of favored and nonfavored strategies. Perhaps subjects who have been identified as favoring a particular response (say, rejection) can be put in a situation where use of their favorite reaction is experimentally blocked. If nonfavorite responses are not highly effective, these persons should make even more use of an experimentally "induced" strategy than should other subjects who naturally favor the induced strategy. Thus rejectors who find themselves in a situation which encourages conformity and makes rejection very difficult should conform even more strongly than subjects for whom conformity is the preferred response (more conformity should be required of the former subjects in order to achieve the same amount of control over stress). We are contemplating a series of studies to explore this notion.

It must be acknowledged that we are not at all sure that people's preferred strategies are stable across different types of situations, though we have found considerable stability across very similar situations (Steiner, 1966). Probably preferences for particular response strategies are learned in much the same fashion as are other kinds of coping responses, a "hierarchy of habit strengths" being developed as the individual is selectively reinforced for behaving in various ways. If this is the case, the individual undoubtedly learns that certain kinds of responses are effective under only certain types of circumstances

(Mowrer, 1960) and allows himself to be guided by different "habit family hierarchies" in different classes of situations. The research reported in this paper has involved a preliminary examination of the response preferences that are expressed in a particular class of situations. Additional research is needed to identify the critical boundaries of this class, and to determine how response preferences change when various parameters of the situation are altered.

It is apparent that the data of this study represent reactions under a very limited range of conditions. The experimental situation involved disagreements with a stranger about issues that were probably not highly important to the subject. The accomplice did not communicate criticisms or express open hostility. Furthermore, the subject probably realized that few if any adverse consequences would follow from the experimental encounter; the accomplice was a person whom the subject might never see again, who had no enduring control over the subject's goal achievements, and whose competence to render judgments was not completely unimpeachable. Consequently, it may be surmised that the conflict created by the experimental manipulations was less intense or threatening than are many of the disagreements that occur outside the laboratory. Whether the findings of this study are representative of outcomes that would be obtained under more stressful circumstances remains to be determined.

References

Back, K. W., Bogdonoff, M. D., Shaw, D. M., & Klein, R. F. An interpretation of experimental conformity through physiological measures. *Behavioral Science*, 1963, 8, 34–40.

Benton, A. L., Hartman, D. H., & Sarason, I. G. Some relations between speech behavior and anxiety level. *Journal of Abnormal and Social Psychology*, 1955, 51, 295–297.

Boneau, C. A. The effects of violations of assumptions underlying the *t* test. *Psychological Bulletin*, 1960, 57, 49–64.

Buck, L. Reaction time as a measure of perceptual vigilance. *Psychological Bulletin*, 1966, 65, 291–304.

Buckhout, R. Changes in heart rate accompanying attitude change. *Journal of Personality and Social Psychology*, 1966, 4, 695–699.

Dardano, J. F. Relationships of intermittent noise, intersignal interval and skin conductance to vigilance behavior. *Journal of Applied Psychology*, 1962, 46, 106–114.

Goldin, P. C. Experimental investigation of selective memory and the concept of repression and defense: A theoretical synthesis. *Journal of Abnormal and Social Psychology*, 1964, 69, 365–380.

Hoffman, M. D. Conformity as a defense mechanism and a form of resistance to genuine group influence. *Journal of Personality*, 1957, 25, 412–424.

Horney, K. *Our inner conflicts.* New York: Norton, 1945.

Johnson, H. H. Some effects of discrepancy level on responses to negative information about one's self. *Sociometry,* 1966, **29,** 52–66.

Johnson, L. C. Generality of speed and confidence of judgment. *Journal of Abnormal and Social Psychology,* 1957, **54,** 264–265.

Kamin, L. J., & Clark, J. W. The Taylor Scale and reaction time. *Journal of Abnormal and Social Psychology,* 1957, **54,** 262–263.

Lacey, J. I., & Lacey, B. C. The relationship of resting autonomic activity to motor impulsivity. In *The brain and human behavior* (Proceedings of the Association for Research in Nervous and Mental Disease). Baltimore: Williams & Wilkins, 1958.

Montagu, J. D., & Coles, E. M. Mechanism and measurement of the galvanic skin response. *Psychological Bulletin,* 1966, **65,** 261–279.

Mowrer, O. H. *Learning theory and the symbolic processes.* New York: Wiley, 1960.

Steiner, I. D. The resolution of interpersonal disagreements. In B. Maher (Ed.), *Progress in experimental personality research.* Vol. III. New York: Academic Press, 1966.

Steiner, I. D., & Johnson, H. H. Relationships among dissonance reducing responses. *Journal of Abnormal and Social Psychology,* 1964, **68,** 38–44.

Steiner, I. D., & Rogers, E. D. Alternative responses to dissonance. *Journal of Abnormal and Social Psychology,* 1963, **66,** 128–136.

Woodworth, R. S., & Schlosberg, H. *Experimental Psychology.* (3rd ed.) London: Methuen, 1954.

11 interpersonal stress in isolated groups

William W. Haythorn

A paper addressed to the topic of interpersonal stress should begin with a definition of terms, particularly since the term *stress* is used to reference a wide variety of physiological, behavioral, and cognitive phenomena. Unfortunately, the term does not lend itself to easy definition, as several symposia and literature reviews indicate (for example, Appley & Trumbull, 1967; Lazarus, 1966).

According to Appley and Trumbull (1967), the term stress was introduced into the life sciences by Selye in 1936. Selye's (1956) concept of stress is physiological in nature, with particular emphasis on endocrine functions. Deevey (1962) describes Selye's model in the following terms:

. . . a remarkably bureaucratic hook-up between the adrenal cortex, acting as the cashier's office, and the pituitary, as the board of directors. Injury and infection are common forms of stress, and in directing controlled inflammation to combat them the cortex draws cashier's checks on the liver. If the stress persists, a hormone called cortisone sends a worried message to the pituitary. Preoccupied with the big picture, the pituitary delegates a vice-presidential type, ACTH or adrenocorticotrophic hormone, whose role is literally to buck up the adrenal cortex. As students of Parkinson would predict, the cortex takes on more personnel and expands its activities including that of summoning more ACTH. The viciousness of the impending spiral ought to be obvious and ordinarily it is; but while withdrawals continue the amount of sugar in circulation is deceptively constant (the result of another servomechanism), and there is no device, short of autopsy, for taking inventory at the bank. If the pituitary is conned by persisting stress into throwing more support to ACTH, the big deals begin to suffer retrenchment. A cutback of ovarian hormone, for instance, may allow the cortex to treat the well started fetus as inflammation to be healed over . . . leaving hypertension aside . . . the fatal symptom may be hypoglycemia. A tiny extra stress, such as a loud noise (or, as Christian would have it, the sight of a lady rabbit), corresponds to an unannounced visit by a Bank Examiner; the adrenal medulla is startled into sending a jolt of adrenalin to the muscles, the blood is drained of sugar, and the brain is suddenly starved [pp. 583–584].

In this view, the term stress would be limited to the physiological state in which the organism is aroused through the activity of the endocrine system, and particularly that of the adrenal gland. The most common physiological measures of stress are biochemical indicators of the degree to which such endocrine induced arousal has occurred. This operational definition of stress, however, has not been universal for physiologists, and is considerably different from that usually used to define psychological stress. The latter has been defined variously as the reaction to noxious stimuli, a state of subjective emotional discomfort, stimulus overload, physical threat, and so on. Perhaps the most generally acceptable operational definition of psychological stress would be one propounded by Parsons (1966), which describes stress as a very broad term covering a considerable variety of conditions underlying avoidance and escape responding. This view has the advantage of requiring that a condition labeled stressful be capable of demonstrably instigating avoidance and/or escape responses. This definition, though a disturbingly broad one, has much to recommend it to the behavioral scientist.

It must simply be admitted that no very specific definition of stress has been offered that is generally satisfactory to investigators in the field. In this paper, stress will be regarded rather broadly as an intraorganismic state, largely instigated by environmental stimuli, and capable of generating fight or flight response tendencies on the part of the organism. Some degree of organismic arousal is implied, but it is not necessary to assume a unidimensional arousal system. It is not at variance with Lacey (1967), who casts considerable doubt on the unidimensionality of organismic arousal under conditions commonly called stressful.

Stress, then, will be regarded in this paper as an intervening variable between environmental stimuli and behavioral responses. It is only one of many such intraorganismic intervening variables and can therefore not be expected to account for a majority of variance in social behavior except in the most extreme situations. It is regarded as a variable capable of assuming many values from very low to very high, and is presumed to have an arousal value to the organism, generating an instigation to fight or flight behavior.

The intricacies of the various physiological subsystems involved in this arousal are beyond the scope of this paper. Lacey (1967) has offered evidence of at least a degree of dissociation between somatic and behavioral arousal. Lacey, Bateman, and Van Lehn (1953) argue that the autonomic nervous system responds to experimentally induced stress "as a whole" in the sense of all autonomically innervated structures seemingly being activated concomitantly in the direction of sympathetic predominance. It does not respond as a whole, however, in the sense of all autonomically innervated structures showing equal increments or decrements of function. However that may be, there seems to be general agreement that the organism is alerted for fight or flight behavior under conditions of stress.

This arousal, activation, or alerting aspect of stress is presumably functional under conditions in which fight or flight behavior is appropriate. Under situational conditions calling for task performance, however, the functional value of such a mechanism has not been so clear. Much of the relevant literature assumes a performance decrement under experimental conditions thought to be stressful. Indeed, as Appley and Trumbull (1967) point out, some concepts of stress require performance decrement in a situation in order to qualify it as stressful. In the work of Kerle and Bialek (1958), Berkun, Bialek, Kern, and Yagi (1962), Lanzetta (1955), and others, however, stress is regarded as a continuous variable ranging from a mild degree of discomfort and anxiety to extreme degrees of fear. Both Lanzetta (1955) and Berkun et al. (1962) report a curvilinear relationship between stress and performance effectiveness, with increase in stress leading to improvement in performance up to moderate levels beyond which increasing stress leads to progressively more impaired performance. This would seem to be consistent, or at least not inconsistent, with Selye's (1956) concept of autonomic arousal, with the performance decrement perhaps coinciding with the level at which the liver is unable to provide the sugar demanded by the adrenal medulla. This possible linkage between physiological and psychological concepts of stress is certainly not yet empirically established. At any rate, the curvilinear inverted-U relationship between stress and performance is consistent with data reported by Haythorn and Altman (1967a), which showed an increase in performance effectiveness with increased stress induced by isolation and personal incompatibility—up to moderate levels of subjectively reported stress beyond which there was either no further performance enhancement or a performance decrement.

It would be a mistake to leave the problem of the definition of stress without mentioning the role of perception. Appley (1962) and Cofer and Appley (1964) both emphasize the importance of the organism's perception of threat to his well being or integrity. Lazarus (1966) also considers perceptual and evaluative processes to be critical in determining stress response. For example, Lazarus (1966) comments that "for threat to occur, an evaluation must be made of the situation, to the effect that a harm is signified. The individual's knowledge and beliefs contribute to this. The appraisal of threat is not a simple perception of the elements of the situation, but a judgment, an inference in which the data are assembled to a constellation of ideas and expectations [p. 44]." Lazarus (1966) goes on to indicate that changing the background of cognition may change the evaluation of threat, thereby considerably modifying the stress response. Schachter and Singer (1962) contribute further to an understanding of the role of perception through their work on the labeling of emotional states. It seems to be established that, to a remarkable degree, subjective emotional experiences can be modified through cognitive and social factors.

INTERPERSONAL STRESS

The primary concern of this paper is with interpersonal stress in isolated groups. One can speak of interpersonal stress to the degree that individuals perceive or behave as though they perceive other individuals as stressors. Some social psychological research has indicated that when small groups have a common external reference as the source of stress, they turn to each other for mutual support. Under these circumstances, there is apparently an increased group cohesiveness and a higher level of cooperation (Lanzetta, 1955). However, from the work of Ulrich and associates (for example, Ulrich & Azrin, 1962; Ulrich, Wolff, & Azrin, 1964) and others, it appears likely that individuals tend to turn aggressively on each other when under stress from unknown or unclear sources. In other cases, it appears that the needs and behavioral patterns of some individuals are incompatible with the needs and behavioral patterns of others. Under both of these conditions, we would expect a degree of interpersonal stress to develop.

Several sources of interpersonal stress in isolated groups can be identified. Interpersonal incompatibility can be said to exist when: (1) the individual needs of group members are competitive such that satisfying the needs of one individual automatically frustrates the needs of another; (2) incongruencies between the need patterns of group members exist such that an interpersonal relationship satisfactory to one member would be unsatisfactory to the other; and (3) there is a low level of complementarity of need patterns such that the kinds of responses one member seeks from others are not likely to be generated by the behavioral predispositions of those others. All three kinds of incompatibility would be likely to generate interpersonal stress, but they would differ in the degree to which fight as compared to flight response tendencies would be instigated. Competitive incompatibility, one might assume, would make fight responses salient, while incongruent or noncomplementary incompatibilities would be more likely to instigate flight or withdrawal patterns.

Social isolation per se is thought to generate interpersonal stress, aside from incompatibility considerations, because it denies satisfaction of certain kinds of social needs and distorts certain normal social processes. For example, an isolated small group has fewer opportunities for social comparison than are normally available. This fact would seem to impair the isolated group member's ability to evaluate the adequacy of his performance, the validity of his opinions, and the appropriateness of his emotional responses, leading perhaps to a decreased accuracy and stability of such self-evaluations (Festinger, 1954; Radloff, 1966).

Lack of privacy has also been mentioned as a source of dissatisfaction in isolated, confined groups (Wilkins, 1967). Even though isolated from other social contacts, such that loneliness is frequently reported (Gunderson, 1963), there is also a relatively high frequency of individual responses indicating a desire to be alone. The close confinement enforces socialization to a greater degree than many crew members would prefer. This enforced interaction tends to accelerate the normal acquaintance process (Altman & Haythorn, 1965), perhaps overexposing group members to each other such that the acquisition of interpersonal information proceeds at a rate in excess of the normal ability of group members to develop shared values and expectations. The normal acquaintance process permits the interpersonal information exchange process to proceed at a rate that can be paced to the preferences of the individuals involved so that if incompatibility is detected relatively early in the game and at relatively superficial levels of exchange, the relationship can be either terminated or maintained at a superficial level. In isolated groups, it is apparently more likely that the exchange will proceed simply because there are few alternative stimuli and little variety in the other sources of social interaction. This lack of variety is reported by Shultz (1965) as a more important source of stress in Antarctic situations than the physical dangers and hardships.

There seems to be considerable agreement that isolated, confined groups develop a significant degree of interpersonal irritability, for a wide variety of reasons. In Antarctic weather stations, however, such interpersonal irritability does not often lead to interpersonal aggression.

Mullin (1960) reports the suppression of interpersonal hostility, and Ruff, Levy, and Thaler (1959) report suppression, denial, and undoing as the most common mechanisms for dealing with hostility. There appears to be recognition that alienating other group members under conditions of isolation and close confinement is dangerous, and is therefore avoided. The normal opportunities individuals have for displacing aggression generated in the work situation to people and objects outside the work situation is not available to members of isolated groups. It seems entirely reasonable to suppose, as Mullin (1960) suggests, that the suppression of aggressive tendencies contributes to the widespread prevalence of headaches and insomnia reported in many isolated group situations.

One further source of interpersonal stress in social isolation is the obvious lack of visibility of the larger society. Leadership and other behavioral patterns are clearly determined to some degree by role expectations and behavioral prescriptions of larger segments of organizations and societies than are fully represented in the small group. When groups are isolated from contact with the larger society, these prescriptions and expectations cannot be as frequently and strongly reinforced as they normally are. There appears, under these conditions, to be a strong tendency for group behavior to become more directly a function of the needs, abilities, and expectations of the immediate group members and less related to those of the larger society than is normally the case. Leadership under such circumstances is unable to rely as strongly on formal role relationships and must depend more on the individual capabilities of the men to whom leadership is assigned. This problem has often been noted as a significant source of difficulty for men in isolated groups.

A number of interpersonal adjustment processes can be identified as relevant to the reduction of interpersonal stress. If another individual is seen as a threat to their own well being, aggressive behavior is very salient for many individuals. Withdrawal is another highly salient response pattern, particularly likely to be chosen under conditions where aggressiveness is censured or perceived as likely to be unsuccessful. Social imbalance (Heider, 1958; Newcomb, 1961), which has been viewed as one source of interpersonal stress involving evaluative discrepancies between the life spaces of interacting individuals, can be reduced by developing common attitudes and beliefs. The pressure toward uniformity in small groups is a well-known adaptive mechanism for reducing such imbalance (compare Hare, 1962). More recently, attention has been given to territoriality behavior as a means of relieving interpersonal stress (Altman & Haythorn, 1967a).

In Thomas Mann's *Joseph in Egypt*, Joseph views each man as living in the center of his own little universe and is much impressed with the divine wisdom that causes these separate universes to overlap in ways that contribute to the progress of each individual through life. Lewin (1951) expressed a rather similar view in his concept of overlapping life spaces in interpersonal interaction. Isolated small groups present a situation in which overlapping of life spaces is forced to an unusual degree. Confined together, deprived of access to other individuals, isolated group members tend to use each other as significant sources of stimuli and are driven to share life experiences and exchange interpersonal information to a significantly greater degree than are individuals who are freer to avoid each other and to seek alternative companions.

A VIEW OF PERSONALITIES IN GROUPS

Personality incompatibility is obviously a very complex topic, complete coverage of which is far beyond the scope of this paper. In order to achieve a manageable degree of simplicity, it seems necessary to adopt a relatively limited theory of personality. The view adopted here owes much to Lewin (1951); Maslow (1943); Kelly (1955); Harvey, Hunt, and Schroeder (1961); and others. Personality is seen as a concept used to reference the organizing function in individual development. According to Harvey, Hunt, and Schroeder (1961), personality development is seen as being directed toward a greater degree of differentiation and integration. At the lowest level of development, organic tissue needs are seen as paramount. This also is the position of Maslow (1943). A somewhat higher level of organizational functioning is represented by safety and security needs, emphasizing the secure viability of the organic whole. At this level of functioning, the individual is likely to be stimulus-bound, concretistic in his thinking, and relatively intolerant of ambiguity. A major concern at this level of functioning is with unambiguously defining the nature of the environment in which the organism exists. This level of organization corresponds roughly with the safety and security needs of Maslow (1943) and the System 1 organization of Harvey, Hunt, and Schroeder (1961).

With increasing freedom from physical threat, it is assumed that the individual becomes increasingly concerned with self-identity. This level of organization is characterized by behavior seemingly directed to individuation, and includes behavior variously defined as dominance-oriented, control-oriented, status-oriented, and so forth. The essence of this level of organization is its emphasis on the individual's control of his environment, particularly with reference to the behavior of other people. (Harvey, Hunt, & Schroeder, 1961, call this System II functioning, and Maslow, 1943, identifies it as reflecting ego needs.)

A still higher level of differentiation and integration, according to

Harvey, Hunt, and Schroeder (1961), is shown by the individual who is primarily concerned with interpersonal relationships as these are expressed in affiliative, affectionate, group-oriented behavior. In the view adopted in this paper, group orientation represents concern for a greater whole than that of the individual and in that sense can be seen as directed towards a higher level of integration than that represented by self-oriented behavior. The "urge to merge" in group behavior is seen in the present framework as directed to a larger and more stable level of organization.

It is assumed here that task or achievement-oriented behavior grows out of an identification with the needs of society, and in this sense represents a still higher level of organization than that of the individual concerned primarily with the affiliative relationships among people. The achievement motive as commonly measured, of course, contains elements of fear of failure and needs for recognition which would be more representative of self-oriented levels of functioning. We would like to include at this higher level only those aspects of achievement orientation that grow out of a recognition or identification with the view that contributions to effective task accomplishments are favorably evaluated by a larger society.

Maslow (1943) argues for a still higher level of functioning directed to cognitive and esthetic needs. Although these will not be dealt with subsequently in this paper, the importance of philosophies, religions, and scientific theories to mankind support the view that such needs are indeed influential in human affairs. They are especially relevant to Kelly's theory of personality, with its emphasis on the importance of the anticipation of events (Kelly, 1955).

The relevance of the foregoing concept of personality to the present paper lies in the bearing it has on social isolation and interpersonal compatibility. It has been argued elsewhere (Haythorn, 1957) that the relationships between the need patterns of different individuals could be classified for purposes of compatibility analysis as: (1) congruent versus incongruent, (2) complementary versus noncomplementary, and (3) competitive versus noncompetitive. Congruent relationships are those in which similar needs are conducive to mutual need satisfactions, as for example, when two individuals are both affiliation oriented, leading them to interact in mutually satisfying ways. A complementary relationship is one in which individuals with different needs and abilities find their need-oriented behavior mutually satisfying, as when one individual with high dependency needs interacts with another with high nurturant needs. A competitive relationship is one in which an interactive relationship satisfying the needs of one individual frustrates the needs of the other, as when both have high dominance needs or one has a high need for affiliation and the other a high need for autonomy. We would argue here that incongruent, noncomplementary, or competitive dyadic relationships tend to be stress inducing in the sense that, by definition, they frustrate interpersonal needs and are likely to be perceived as threatening to the personality organizations of the individuals concerned. Social isolation and confinement of hypothetically incompatible dyads is thought likely to magnify such interpersonal stress because the individuals concerned are neither able to escape each other nor to seek social satisfactions in interaction with alternative others.

A STUDY OF ISOLATED DYADS

A study directed to the investigation of this general hypothesis, reported elsewhere (Altman & Haythorn, 1965; Altman & Haythorn, 1967a; Altman & Haythorn, 1967b; Haythorn & Altman, 1967a; Haythorn & Altman, 1967b; Haythorn, Altman, & Myers, 1966), composed pairs of men to fit a Greco-Latin square such that one third of the pairs were homogeneously high, one third homogeneously low, and one third heterogeneous with regard to each of four personality dimensions: dogmatism, need achievement, need dominance, and need affiliation. These four personality variables were selected as representative of variables found by other investigators to be significant determinants of group behavior (for further discussion of the rationale for choosing these four variables, see Haythorn, Altman, & Myers, 1966). They are thought to coincide roughly with the four levels of personality organization described by Harvey, Hunt, and Schroeder (1961) and the security, ego, affection, and self-actualizing needs of Maslow (1943). Similarly composed dyads were assigned to both social isolation and control conditions. The former condition involved confinement of the pair of men to a small room for ten days during which they were deprived of contact with anyone other than the other member of the pair. Control dyads worked in the same rooms on the same tasks for an equivalent ten days, but they ate in the regular Navy mess, returned to the barracks at night, were free to leave the room between tasks for short periods of time, and otherwise worked in the rooms much as anyone else on the base might.

Stress in this study was measured by subject responses to an adjective list developed by Kerle and Bialek (1958), consisting of 15 adjectives scaled by a Thurstone procedure to represent varying degrees of subjective stress. This Subjective Stress Scale has also been used by Berkun et al. (1962), who offered validation data in addition to that generated by the authors of the scale. It has also been found useful by Myers, Murphy, Smith, and Windle (1962) in distinguishing sensory deprived subjects from controls. Myers et al. (1962) also developed an Isolation

Symptomatology Questionnaire which was administered to the subjects in the present experiment. Both of these instruments showed statistically significant effects of the experimental manipulations.

It had been hypothesized in designing the study that both social isolation and group composition would be significant sources of stress to our subjects. Experimental results confirmed both of these general hypotheses. That the stress was not trivial was indicated by the fact that two of the nine isolated dyads were unable to complete ten days of social isolation, while two more developed a level of interpersonal conflict that could easily be defined as severe. There were no such difficulties in the control dyads. In addition, analysis of the responses to the Subjective Stress Scale and the Isolation Symptomatology Questionnaire yielded a high number of statistically significant results, summarized in Table 11–1.

TABLE 11–1 Summary of Results of Stress and Symptomatology Analyses[a]

A. DOGMATISM

Condition	Hypothesis	Measures
Social isolation	$LL_I > LL_c$ [*]	SSS_{now}
Interpersonal stress	$HL > LL$	3. Reminiscence and memory 7. Navy assignment $(-)$
Both	$HL_I > HL_c$	SSS_{now} 1. RVS† 8. Self-appraisal 14. Hunger 16. Temporal disorientation
	$HL_I > LL_I^U HH_I$ [**]	1. RVS (HH) 1. RVS (LL) 8. Self-appraisal (LL) 14. Hunger (HH) 16. Temporal disorientation (HH) 16. Temporal disorientation (LL)
Personality	$HH > LL$	7. Navy assignment 18. Restless acts

[a] Results based on analyses of variance. Differences were in expected direction to statistically significant degree ($p < .05$) except when indicated by $(-)$. The latter indicates difference in opposite direction.

[*] Indicates hypothesized direction of difference. HH = homogeneously high; HL = heterogeneous; LL = homogeneously low; I = isolation; c = control.

[**] LL_I U HH_I = isolated homogeneously low *or* isolated homogeneously high dyads.

† RVS = Reported Visual Sensation.

TABLE 11–1 Summary of Results of Stress and Symptomatology Analyses *(Continued)*

B. DOMINANCE

Condition	Hypothesis	Measures
Social isolation	$HL_I > HL_c$	SSS_{now} 14. Hunger
Interpersonal stress	$HH > HL$	2. Dreams 15. Tedium of time
	$LL > HL$	SSS 2. Dreams 15. Tedium of time 19. Anger 20. Regret participation 22. Low feeling of well-being
Both	$HH_I > HH_c$	SSS_{now} 12. Religion
	$HH_I > HL_I$	SSS_{now} 12. Religion 14. Hunger
Personality	$HH > LL$	SSS_{now} 3. Reminiscence and memory $(-)$

C. AFFILIATION

Condition	Hypothesis	Measures
Social isolation	$HH_I > HH_c$	SSS_{now} $SSS_{then-normal}$ 2. Dream $(-)$ 3. Sex
	$LL_I > LL_c$	SSS_{now} $SSS_{then-normal}$ 5. Novelty and surprise 9. Self-appraisal 9. Inefficiency of thought 17. Restlessness 22. Feeling of well-being
Interpersonal stress	$HL > HH$	
	$HL > LL$	
	$HL_I > HL_c$	9. Inefficiency of thought $(-)$ 20. Regret participation $(-)$ 21. Worry and fright $(-)$
Both	$HL_I > LL_I{}^U HH_I$	2. Dreams (HH) 21. Worry and fright (LL, $-$)
Personality	$HH > LL$	

TABLE 11-1 Summary of Results of Stress and Symptomatology Analyses *(Continued)*

D. ACHIEVEMENT

Condition	Hypothesis	Measures
Social isolation	$HH_I > HH_c$	SSS_{now} 9. Inefficiency of thought ($-$) 13. Religion ($-$) 15. Tedium of time ($-$)
	$LL_I > LL_c$	SSS_{now} 12. Religion 19. Hunger ($-$) 20. Regret participation ($-$) 22. Low feeling of well-being ($-$)
Interpersonal stress	$HL > HH$	2. Dreams
	$HL > LL$	SSS_{now} 2. Dreams
Both	$HL_I > HL_c$	3. Reminiscence and memory 5. Novelty and surprise 9. Inefficiency of thought 12. Religion 19. Hunger 20. Regret participation
	$HL_I > HH_I^U LL_I$	3. Reminiscence and memory (LL) 5. Novelty and surprise (HH) 9. Inefficiency in thought (LL) 12. Religion (HH) 15. Tedium of time (LL) 15. Tedium of time (HH) 19. Hunger (LL) 19. Hunger (HH) 20. Regret participation (LL) 20. Regret participation (HH)
Personality	$HH > LL$	SSS_{now}

The table attempts to present statistically significant results in a matrix that separately identifies the effects of social isolation and interpersonal stress with regard to each of the four personality dimensions. The rows of the matrix separate social isolation, interpersonal stress, joint effects of isolation and interpersonal incompatibility, and simple personality differences. The four parts of the table deal with the four personality dimensions by which groups were composed. The hypothesized relationship in each cell of the matrix is shown, and each measure either consistent or inconsistent with the hypothesized relationship to a statistically significant degree is listed. A minus sign following the identification of the measure indicates that the direction of the obtained difference was opposite from that hypothesized.

The basis on which hypothesized differences were determined in Table 11–1 were as follows: (1) *Social isolation* per se was expected to be stressful. A pure test of this, however, obtains only for hypothetically compatible dyads. Therefore, the hypothesized difference stated in Table 11–1 under social isolation is that the hypothetically compatible crew compositions in isolation would report more subjective stress and emotional symptomatology than would their control counterparts. (2) *Interpersonal incompatibility* was also expected to generate elevated levels of subjective stress and symptomatology. This expectation is confirmed when the mean differences between hypothetically incompatible and compatible compositions are in predicted directions and variance associated with those differences is significantly greater than interaction variance. (3) *Both* sources of stress apply in hypothetically incompatible isolated dyads. The hypothesized differences are therefore that incompatible isolated dyads will show more stress than their control counterparts and/or will show more stress than compatibly composed isolated pairs. (4) Some differences were apparently simply a function of *personality* per se. These were assessed by comparing the responses of subjects in homogeneously high dyadic compositions with those in homogeneously low groupings with regard to that personality variable. The hypothesized direction of the difference in Table 11–1 is stated as homogeneously high showing more stress than homogeneously low, although no particularly strong arguments for the difference being one way as opposed to another can be offered.

As the table shows, by far the majority of statistically significant differences were in the hypothesized directions, indicating that both social isolation and hypothetically incompatible dyadic compositions produced higher levels of subjective stress and isolation symptomatology, and that the effects of incompatibility were especially pronounced under conditions of isolation. This latter statement holds for all personality variables except affiliation, where hypothetically incompatible combinations (heterogeneous) tended to report less isolation symptomatology than their control counterparts or compatible (homogeneous) compositions in isolation.

This study, then, supports the general hypothesis that social isolation and interpersonal incompatibilities elevate subjective experiences of stress. In a recent study by Altman, Wheeler, and Taylor—as yet unreported—pairs of men were socially isolated and subjected to a greater degree of stimulus reduction than was the case in the study just described. Very

little data from the more recent study has been analyzed, but at least one
piece of data is readily available: the frequency of aborted missions,
that is, isolated pairs who terminated their experimental run before the
scheduled termination, was approximately 50 percent. This observation
lends additional support to the view that social isolation of very small
groups can be highly stressful to a rather large percentage of personnel
in the population from which our samples have been drawn. It would
seem that interpersonal stress, whether deriving from incompatibility
among members of the isolated group or the lack of sufficient variety and
numbers of alternate others, is a significant source of variance in isolated
group adaptation and performance.

In addition to our concern with subjective stress, we have also
examined the effects of our experimental variables on task performance
(Altman & Haythorn, 1967b); interpersonal information exchange (Altman & Haythorn, 1965); and territoriality and social behavior (Altman &
Haythorn, 1967a). Our underlying conceptual model envisioned environmental and group compositional variables interacting to determine intra-
group processes which, in turn, determined performance effectiveness.
Using the data from this study, we now believe that additional specifications can be given to the conceptual model, as represented in Figure 11–1.

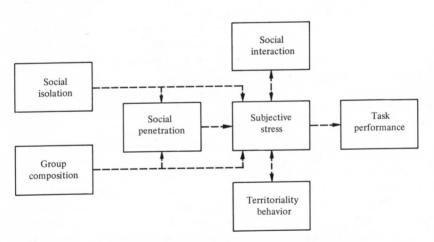

FIGURE 11–1. Conceptual model of relationships among independent, intervening,
and dependent variables in socially isolated groups.

Our results indicate statistically significant relationships between social
isolation and group composition as independent variables and interpersonal exchange (social penetration), social interaction, territoriality behavior and task performance as dependent variables. Our current view
of these relationships is (1) that subjective stress is an intervening vari-

able that is elevated by social isolation and incompatible group compositions (Haythorn, Altman, & Myers, 1966); (2) that a degree of social penetration (that is, interpersonal information exchange) is necessary for perceptions of interpersonal threat to occur; (3) that such social penetration is accelerated by social isolation (Altman & Haythorn, 1965); (4) that social interaction and territoriality behavior are affected by the level of subjective stress and, in turn, may elevate or reduce it (Altman & Haythorn, 1967a); and (5) that there is an inverted-U relationship between stress and performance, such that mild to moderate levels of stress enhance the attention subjects give to the task and therefore improve performance, but that higher levels of stress result in performance decrement, probably because fight or flight responses become so salient as to interfere with those response patterns more appropriate to the task (Haythorn & Altman, 1967a; Altman & Haythorn, 1967b).

FURTHER RESEARCH NEEDS

In summary, stress is viewed here as one of many intraorganismic variables moderating the relationship between environmental stimuli and behavioral responses. Interpersonal stress is not different from other stresses in this regard, the difference being only in the nature of the stress-inducing stimuli. From this point of view, the task for social psychologists interested in stress is to identify environmental and group compositional situations which generate interpersonal stress, and to trace out the individual and group processes by which subjects adjust to that stress. A small start in this direction has been offered but clearly the gaps in our knowledge far exceed the amount of reliable information. Further research is obviously needed, as is also more sophisticated model building.

It seems unlikely that many would take issue with the statement that not much is known about group behavior under stress. For that matter, not much is known about individual behavior under stress. In viewing the social psychological research requirements in this area, several shortcomings seem particularly noteworthy:

1. There have not been many longitudinal studies. The adaptive processes of groups under stress are poorly understood. It seems likely that the relationships among environmental stimuli, perceived threat, physiological states, and interpersonal behavior change over time. Improvements in methodology are required before we can track these changes in relationships adequately, but efforts in that direction seem promising.

2. The chain of events between environmental modifications and behavioral responses contains many intervening links, undoubtedly com-

plicated by numerous multiple interacting relationships with subtle feedback loops. Assuming this to be the case, it seems necessary to pursue research that is both intensive and extensive in dependent variable measurement. That is, attempts to measure as many of the intervening states and events as possible seems desirable. There is undoubtedly a great need for simpler, more traditional research designs, but a strong case seems to exist for the argument that multivariate designs with a large number and variety of dependent measures—approaching real-world complexity in stimulus and response richness—is indispensable to a thorough understanding of group behavior under stress.

3. The foregoing emphasis on realistic degrees of complexity, of course, places a great strain on our ability to construct symbolic analogues of the processes under investigation. A growing capability to build computer models of complex organizational processes represents a very promising methodological solution to this problem. Computer simulation of complex processes is already well established in economics, operations research, and industrial engineering. Some progress along this line is also evident in social psychology (see, for example, Tomkins & Messick, 1963). It seems probable that increasing attention will be given to this method of representing process data.

4. In addition to the foregoing, much more research on interpersonal compatibility within a more sophisticated framework of group compositional variables seems indicated. Any two individuals are likely to be competitive in some ways, complementary in some ways, and have some degree of incongruent needs. Each of these probably has its own implications for interpersonal stress and behavior. Too much of our current research in this area is limited to the similarity-attraction hypothesis or the complementary-needs hypothesis, both of which seem to be empirically established within certain contexts, and neither of which by itself accounts for very much of the variance in interpersonal compatibility and associated interpersonal behavior.

References

Altman, I., & Haythorn, W. W. Interpersonal exchange in isolation. *Sociometry*, 1965, 28, 411–426.

Altman, I., & Haythorn, W. W. The ecology of isolated groups. *Behavioral Science*, 1967, 12, 169–182. (a)

Altman, I., & Haythorn, W. W. The effects of social isolation and group composition on performance. *Human Relations*, 1967, 20, 313–340. (b)

Appley, M. H. Motivation, threat perception and the induction of psychological stress. *Proceedings of Sixteenth International Congress of Psychology*, Bonn. Amsterdam: North Holland, 1962, pp. 880–881.

Appley, M. H., & Trumbull, R. On the concept of psychological stress. In

M. H. Appley & R. Trumbull (Eds.), *Psychological stress*. New York: Appleton, 1967.

Berkun, M. M., Bialek, H. N., Kern, R. P., & Yagi, K. Experimental studies of psychological stress in man. *Psychological Monographs*, 1962, **76** (15, Whole No. 534).

Cofer, C. N., & Appley, M. H. *Motivation: Theory and research*. New York: Wiley, 1964.

Deevey, E. S. The hare and the haruspex: A cautionary tale. In E. Josephson & M. Josephson (Eds.), *Man alone: Alienation in modern society*. New York: Dell, 1962, 583–584. (Reprinted from the *Yale Review*, Winter 1960.)

Festinger, L. A theory of social comparison processes. *Human Relations*, 1954, **7**, 117–140.

Gunderson, E. K. Emotional symptoms in extremely isolated groups. *Archives of General Psychiatry*, 1963, **9**, 362–368.

Hare, A. P. *Handbook for small group research*. New York: Free Press, 1962.

Harvey, O. J., Hunt, D. E., & Schroeder, H. M. *Conceptual systems and personality organization*. New York: Wiley, 1961.

Haythorn, W. W. A review of research on group assembly. Research Report AFPTRC-TN-57-62, May 1957, Lackland, AFB, Tex., Air Force Personnel and Training Research Center.

Haythorn, W. W., & Altman, I. Personality factors in isolated environments. In M. H. Appley & R. Trumbull (Eds.), *Psychological stress*. New York: Appleton, 1967. (a)

Haythorn, W. W., & Altman, I. Together in isolation. *Transaction*, 1967, **4**, 18–22. (b)

Haythorn, W. W., Altman, I., & Myers, T. I. Emotional symptomatology and subjective stress in isolated pairs of men. *Journal of Experimental Research in Personality*, 1966, **1**, 290–305.

Heider, F. *The psychology of interpersonal relations*. New York: Wiley, 1958.

Kelly, G. A. *The psychology of personal constructs*. New York: Norton, 1955.

Kerle, R. H., & Bialek, H. M. *The construction, validation, and application of a subjective stress scale*. Staff Memorandum, Fighter IV, Study 23, February 1958, Presidio of Monterey, Calif., Human Resources Research Office.

Lacey, J. I. Somatic response patterning and stress: Some revisions of activation theory. In M. H. Appley & R. Trumbull (Eds.), *Psychological stress*, New York: Appleton, 1967.

Lacey, J. I., Bateman, D. E., & Van Lehn R. Autonomic response specificity: An experimental study. *Psychosomatic Medicine*, 1953, **15**, 8–21.

Lanzetta, J. T. Group behavior under stress. *Human Relations*, 1955, **8**, 20–53.

Lazarus, R. S. *Psychological stress and the coping process*. New York: McGraw-Hill, 1966.

Lewin, K. Intention, will, and need. In D. Rappaport, *Organization and pathology of thought*. New York: Columbia University Press, 1951, pp. 95–151.

Maslow, A. H. Higher and lower needs. *Journal of Psychology*, 1943, **25**, 433–436.

Mullin, C. S. Some psychological aspects of isolated antarctic living. *American Journal of Psychiatry*, 1960, 117, 323–325.

Myers, T. I., Murphy, D. B., Smith, S., & Windle, C. Experimental assessment of a limited social and sensory environment. Summary results of the Human Resources Research Office (HUMRRO), U.S. Army Leadership Human Research Unit, February 1962.

Newcomb, T. M. *The acquaintance process.* New York: Holt, Rinehart and Winston, 1961.

Parsons, H. D. STAVE: Stress avoidance/escape. Santa Monica, Calif.: System Development Corporation, August 1966.

Radloff, R. Social comparison and ability evaluation. *Journal of Experimental Social Psychology*, 1966, Supplement 1, 6–26.

Ruff, G. E., Levy, E. Z., & Thaler, V. H. Studies of isolation and confinement. *Aerospace Medicine*, 1959, 30, 599–604.

Schachter, S., & Singer, J. Cognitive, social and physiological determinants of emotional state. *Psychological Review*, 1962, 69, 379–399.

Schultz, D. P. *Sensory restriction: Effects on behavior.* New York: Academic Press, 1965.

Selye, H. *The stress of life.* New York: McGraw-Hill, 1956.

Tomkins, S. S., and Messick, S. *Computer simulation of personality,* New York: Wiley, 1963.

Ulrich, R., & Azrin, N. H. Reflexive fighting in response to aversive stimulation. *Journal of Experimental Analysis of Behavior*, 1962, 5, 511–521.

Ulrich, R., Wolff, P., & Azrin, N. H. Shock as an elicitor of intra- and inter- species fighting behavior. *Animal Behavior*, 1964, 12, 14–15.

Wilkins, W. Group behavior in long-term isolation. In M. H. Appley & R. Trumbull (Eds.), *Psychological stress,* New York: Appleton, 1967.

12

the ecology of interpersonal relationships: a classification system and conceptual model[1]

Irwin Altman and Evelyn E. Lett

On the behavioral or response side, research on stress has emphasized physiological, verbal, and cognitive motivational processes. In the present paper we consider another level of analysis—an ecological one—which involves the mutual interaction of man and his environment (see Weick, Chapter 16, for a methodological analysis of this issue). The basic thesis of this paper is that man actively uses his physical environment to cope with stressful situations, as well as being affected or stressed by the environment. From our point of view an ecological analysis of stress phenomena includes the ways in which spatial and object properties of the environment (*environmental props*), and

[1] The research reported here was conducted under Bureau of Medicine and Surgery, Navy Department, Research Task MF 022.01.03.1002, Subtask 1. The opinions and statements contained herein are the private ones of the authors and are not to be construed as official or reflecting the views of the Navy Department or the Naval Service at large.

various forms of nonverbal behaviors such as eye contact, gestures, body positions, and so forth (*self-markers*) are used to cope with or manage stressful situations. As pointed out earlier (see Chapter 3), such coping responses may be anticipatory, with environmental-prop and self-marker behaviors exhibited to prevent the occurrence of a stressful state, or reactive and in response to such a situation.

The ecology of human behavior—the nature of the mutual interaction between man and his environment—is certainly not a new topic. Kurt Lewin and others signaled the need for such research many times. Over the course of the last three decades, however, only a few men such as Roger Barker and his associates have studied the person-environment unit as an integral entity (Barker & Wright, 1955; Barker, 1963; Barker & Gump, 1964). But the last five to ten years have seen an upsurge of such research. Psychologists, psychiatrists, architects, geographers, and others have come to view their separate disciplines as too provincial to handle the complex relationships which man, alone and in groups, has with his environment. Recognition of the importance of these relationships has led to the formulation of problems in terms of "interpersonal-ecological," "sociophysical," and "environment-behavioral" considerations—all of which attempt to link man and his environment.

The present paper offers a classification model to integrate existing knowledge and to provide a conceptual framework which can guide and stimulate future research and theory in one aspect of this field—interpersonal relationships. The framework is based on the general assumption that ecological processes are part and parcel of ongoing social interaction events. As such, their study may provide important advances in our understanding of interpersonal acquaintance processes and interpersonal conflict and stress. The first section of the paper reviews some major institutional and research trends in the field. The proposed classification system is then discussed, followed by an application of it to the area of interpersonal conflict and stress.

PERSPECTIVES ON THE FIELD AND NEED FOR A CLASSIFICATION SYSTEM

A number of considerations make this a propitious time to develop a conceptual framework bearing on the ecology of interpersonal relationships. These involve the diversity of disciplines engaged in research, the range of subject matters studied and methodologies employed, and a number of institutional events which signal the potentially rapid growth of the field. Before considering these trends, a few statements of definition are necessary.

For us, an ecological orientation to interpersonal behavior includes the study of how man mutually interacts with his physical environment in the course of managing his relationships with others. In a sense, we propose a simple *ABX* model, where *A* and *B* refer to social actors and *X* includes physical aspects of the environment, for example, specific props such as furniture, areas such as offices.

An important definitional issue revolves around the term "environment" as part of a social interaction system. Too often, researchers have overemphasized the impact of the environment on behavior and neglected behavioral *use* of the environment. Man does not just respond or adapt to inputs but literally uses and shapes the environment in his interpersonal exchanges with others. Without understanding how people use objects in their environment, we can, at best, only develop a limited understanding of interpersonal processes of conflict and compatibility. A comprehensive ecological orientation must stress linkages in both directions—man's use of and effect on the environment and the effect and impact of the environment on man's behavior.

Furthermore, interpersonal dynamics are not restricted to verbal interaction, subjective perceptions, or reports of sociometric attraction. Another assumption underlying our approach is that gestures, body postures, and other nonverbal behaviors are important aspects of the ecology of interpersonal behavior and should be incorporated into a general model.

The tenor of recent interest in interpersonal ecology is reflected in a number of ways. Several writers have called for more research on the mutual interaction of man and his environment (Sommer, 1959; Sells, 1966). Sommer states:

> Surprisingly little is known about the way people use space. Social scientists in the field of human ecology have been concerned primarily with the distribution of such things as social classes, economic institutions, and mental illness. An almost unexplored area is micro-ecology or the way that people in pairs or small groups arrange themselves [p. 247].

From another perspective, some recent philosophical and methodological concerns in social psychology have arisen from and led to ecological considerations. Many researchers have expressed increasing concern with the current emphasis on short-term, artificially contrived laboratory studies, and have called for unobtrusive naturalistic investigations, with less sole reliance on fragmented behavioral responses, subjective perceptions, and verbal reports (see especially Webb, Campbell, Schwartz & Sechrest, 1966). This concern probably has and will continue to sensitize us further to man-environment relationships.

Other evidence of an institutional nature comes from: a special issue of the *Journal of Social Issues* wholly devoted to ecological problems (Kates & Wohlwill, 1966); the recent founding of university programs in architectural and environmental psychology; the appearance of behavioral scientists in schools of architecture, and their increasing role in the design of military housing, space and undersea systems; the establishment of an interdisciplinary journal, a series of informal conferences among interested researchers, and some preliminary plans to organize a "society" under the auspices of the American Association for the Advancement of Science. Secular attention to problems of an expanding and mobile population and the popular response to recent books on aggression and man's territorial behavior (Lorenz, 1966; Ardrey, 1966) also suggest an awakening interest in ecological matters.

Research on Ecological Aspects of Behavior

A more important indicator of the growth of the field comes from its research wherein one sees a diversity of content and methodology. It is this diversity, along with the rapidly accumulating volume of research, that highlights the need for an organizing framework and set of concepts to help assess and guide research.

Generally speaking, the field appears to be characterized by many lacunae of internally coherent but isolated programs of research. For example, Kuethe and his associates (Kuethe, 1962a, 1962b, 1964; Fisher, 1967; Kuethe & Weingartner, 1964) focus on physical distance and use of intervening environmental objects in interpersonal situations—by casual acquaintances versus good friends, adults versus children, normals versus emotionally disturbed subjects and homosexuals.

Hall (1955, 1959, 1963, 1966), an anthropologist, emphasizes *proxemics*, or the way in which man consciously and unconsciously structures his microspace. He proposes a system to describe four social distances in interpersonal relationships. At one extreme are intimate distances of less than 18 inches which usually occur in private among intimates; at the other extreme are public distances of 12 feet or more, which generally occur in formal or public situations. Associated with each social distance are cue and information exchange properties such as kinesthetic or possible body contact, thermal, olfactory, visual and oral-aural. He also briefly describes use of spatial objects and props, and distinguishes between fixed feature space (actual and hidden designs that govern behavior in buildings and communities) and semifixed feature space (more mobile aspects of design).

A different approach is taken by Scheflen (1964, 1965a, 1965b), a psychiatrist, who calls for a nonreductionistic, Gestalt, systems orientation to the study of ecological dynamics in psychotherapeutic situations. His strategy is to identify natural units of behavior which consist of content, tone, and style of verbal communication, physical movements and body positions, facial expressions, olfactory cues, changes in skin color, pupil dilation, and the like. Scheflen also posits the existence of a finite and identifiable set of behavioral complexes that reflect interpersonal events.

Several other approaches stem from clinical psychology and psychiatry. Esser (1964), Esser, Amparo, Chamberlain, Chapple, and Kline (1965), Almond and Esser (1965) studied territorial behavior in psychiatric wards; Horowitz (1963) and Horowitz, Duff, and Stratton (1964) analyzed territorial behavior in interaction painting between a therapist and patient; Winick and Holt (1961) reported on the significance of chairs and seating positions in group therapy situations.

Others have emphasized the importance of nonverbal acts, including facial expressions, body movements, and gestures, in both therapeutic and normal interaction settings. Hutt and Ounsted (1966) and Hutt and Vaizey (1966) examined social-distance and eye-contact behavior of autistic and normal children. Ekman and his associates have developed theory and methods for analysis of facial and body movements in therapy, along with other nonverbal behaviors (Ekman, 1965; Ekman & Friesen, 1967a, 1967b, 1967c); and Loeb (1966) studied grasping behavior. Along the same lines, Rosenfeld (1965, 1966a, 1966b) investigated the role of smiling and approval gestures in interpersonal dynamics; Exline (1963, 1965), Argyle and Dean (1965) and others have studied eye contact in interpersonal relationships. A recent overview of current work on nonverbal aspects of behavior appears in Davitz (1964).

Sommer, a social psychologist, has done extensive work in this area. He has studied schizophrenics (Sommer, 1959); seating with respect to a leader (Sommer, 1961); the limits of comfortable conversation distance (Sommer, 1961); how people position themselves in libraries so as to avoid others (Sommer, 1966); and seating preferences in different types of classrooms as a function of distance and accessibility to an instructor (Sommer, 1967a). In a review paper, Sommer (1966) organized studies of human microecology in terms of territorial behavior, density and crowding, personal space, seating-position and social-distance dynamics, and research on nonverbal communication. He has also reviewed the research on small group ecology (Sommer, 1967b).

It is interesting to note that much ecological work is linked to early studies of animal behavior, for example, territoriality in birds (Howard, 1948), territorial and ecological behavior of captive animals (Hediger, 1955), effects of overcrowding (Calhoun, 1956, 1962; Christian, 1960, 1961).

There has also been a broad range of methodology used in the study of ecological processes. At one end of a continuum are relatively carefully controlled studies conducted in laboratory settings using simulated persons. Little (1965) and Kuethe (1962a, 1962b, 1964) had subjects work with doll-like figures. Others undertook experiments in naturalistic situations such as cafeterias, or employed observational studies without experimental intrusion (Sommer, 1959, 1961, 1967b; Barker & Wright, 1955; Barker, 1963). A fair amount of energy is also being devoted to the development of methodology, both at tactical and strategic-philosophical levels. Scheflen (1965b) proposes a general philosophy of methodology while Ekman and Friesen (1965, 1967a, 1967b, 1967c), Loeb (1966), Exline (1963, 1965), and others offer techniques for molecular analysis of specific behaviors.

At a more general level, there has not yet appeared a general framework of important variables nor a programatic strategy for research; and only a few guiding theoretical concepts have been postulated. Furthermore, one gets the impression that much of the work is fairly basic and seeks to establish certain fundamental facts about the ecology of social behavior, for example: good friends stand closer to one another than do casual acquaintances, people who want privacy in public seat themselves as far from others as possible, those who sit close to professors talk more, and so forth. Of course, there are some important theoretical notions available, which we shall examine later in this paper. Basically, they revolve around homeostatic equilibrium concepts and seem quite similar in spite of the fact that they originate from such widely divergent areas as studies of social force fields in animal behavior (McBride, 1964; McBride, James, & Shoffner, 1963); approach-avoidance behavior in animals and children (King, 1966a; King, 1966b; McBride, King, & James, 1965); eye contact and distance in normal human beings (Argyle & Dean, 1965) and in autistic children (Hutt & Ounsted, 1966; Hutt & Vaizey, 1966).

The Utility of a Classification System

The newness and diversity, the relative paucity of theory, and the expected blossoming of the field of ecological research compels us to try to develop a classification system to integrate existing and future knowledge. Such a system can also aid in bridging the gap between ecologically oriented studies and other social-psychological phenomena such as compatibility and conflict.

There are several advantages to be gained from such an effort. A good classification system can provide a standard metalanguage to describe all concepts and variables in a field. After translation into the language of taxonomy, it is then possible to compare any finding with any other one. One also can determine well-established findings, areas of confused or uncertain results, and relatively neglected areas of study. Moreover, if the taxonomy has an underlying ordering principle, it can be used to predict new relationships, and if such predictions are upheld the classification system and its underlying structure are confirmed. Thus, it can also contribute to theory development.

Work on taxonomies to synthesize research information has a long history in the natural sciences but only a short one in the behavioral sciences. (See Altman, 1968, for an overview of recent efforts.) Berelson and Steiner (1964), March and Simon (1958), Collins and Guetzkow (1964), and Price (1968) built propositional inventories or sets of general statements derived from empirically supported relationships. A few researchers have offered formal classification systems with one or more classification dimensions and categories, unit property descriptions, a rationale for dimensions and principles for ordering them. Our work on small groups (McGrath & Altman, 1966) was one such attempt, using operational rather than conceptual definitions of variables.

In proposing a classification system for ecological aspects of interpersonal behavior we face some unique circumstances. Taxonomies typically have been developed in heavily researched fields (for example, organizational behavior, small groups, and now "stress") where impetus has come from the overwhelming cascade of unorganized facts. The area of man-environment relationships is different, for there has been only a relatively small amount of research, although it appears that the next few years will show a mushrooming of studies. This newness of interest should make it easier to be comprehensive, to track development of the field, and to contribute to its growth as it happens—rather than just to "dig out" from under a one- or two-decade period of accumulated, unorganized facts.

But there are some disadvantages to taxonomic work in a new area. Absence of a large body of knowledge makes it difficult to determine the "correct" classification dimensions; there is no institutional wisdom to rely on in assessing the probable usefulness of the system; one is unable to anticipate wholly the eventual scope of the field and the likely need for major revision of the system. Furthermore, we shall face the unique difficulty of trying to integrate knowledge from diverse disciplines, each with its own jargon and modes of stating and solving problems.

The type of classification we hope to develop for the ecology of interpersonal relationships is more than a set of pigeonholes to catalogue and store facts. It is meant to be a dynamic model and framework which will lay the basis for more sophisticated theory development. It is a framework because classes of relevant antecedent, intervening, and consequent variables are identified. It has some properties of a model in that certain links and directions of causation are hypothesized between variable classes in different parts of the framework. It is a dynamic model because relationships among parts of the model are seen as changing through time and as a function of shifting states of the ecological system. We do not yet presume to offer a theory, since the nature and intensity of relationships between variables are not hypothesized, nor are more than a few predictive statements offered at this time.

THE CLASSIFICATION MODEL

From a representative bibliography of empirical and nonempirical studies we identified a series of ecological indicator variables (such as distance, seating position, gestures, eye contact) and determined their linkage to dependent psychological processes and antecedent predictor factors. This simple tabulation yielded a general map of major variables, concepts, and measures which one might expect to find from a more thorough literature review. Some of the main dimensions of the taxonomic model were then induced from the tabulation, although we would be hard put to specify exactly the nature of that induction process!

Overview of the Classification Model

The classification system to be offered is conceptualized as dynamic, with internal feedback mechanisms continuously adjusting the state of the ecological system (See figure 12–1). The model first hypothesizes a series of antecedent factors which serve as initial determinants of subjective expectations of situational definitions. The latter are personal estimates by social actors about what a particular social interaction calls for by way of appropriate behaviors, role relations, and general situational demands. These in turn mediate ecologically oriented overt behaviors—use of environmental props and self-markers. As the figure suggests, the use of specific environmental props (objects, areas, and space) is integrated with use of the "self" (gestures, positions, and other nonverbal cues) into an over-all complex behavior pattern or behavior syndrome which is conveyed during a temporal period of social interaction. The model then hypothesizes that an internal, subjective evaluation and assessment process occurs, during which social actors determine whether the interaction was desirable and in accord with their earlier definition of the social situation. To the extent that it is not, they are hypothesized to undertake a series of readjustment processes to preserve their original expectations, or to develop a new situation definition. In either case, a series of feedback loops may alter the state of the antecedent factors, the situation definition, and the use of environmental props and the self. This results in a system continually changing through time as a function of external and internal events. Because it is conceived of as a dynamic model, any class of factors theoretically can be, at one time or another, independent or dependent variables.

The model also takes into account the fact that these processes are applicable at both individual and group levels, as illustrated by the terms "person," "dyad," in several parts of the diagram. With this sketch in mind, let us now trace the logic of each step of the classification model.

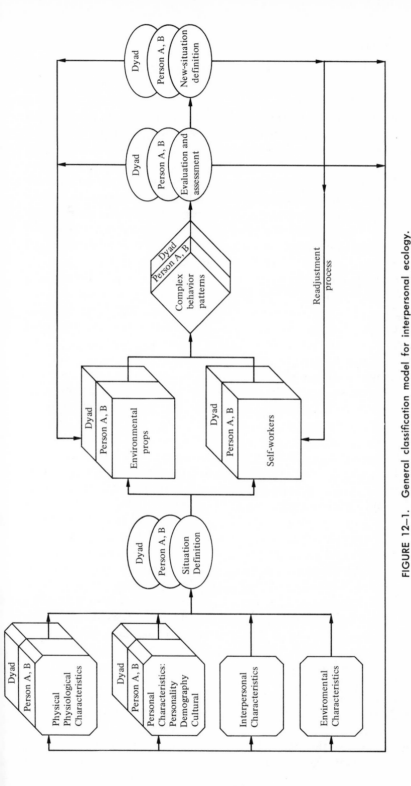

FIGURE 12–1. General classification model for interpersonal ecology. The terms enclosed in circles reflect internal subjective processes. Those in rectangles indicate overt behavioral events. The diamond-shaped enclosure indicates an integrated complex of specific behavioral events.

185

Then we shall attempt to apply it to a few cases of interpersonal conflict and stress.

Antecedent factors. Several classes of antecedent variables are hypothesized as initial determinants of ecological processes, although they themselves are subject to change through feedback mechanisms to be discussed later. *Physical and physiological factors* encompass both momentary and relatively enduring states of the parties to the interaction. Examples include height, weight, and socially important physical characteristics such as blemishes, scars, disfiguring properties or stigma (see Goffman, 1963, for a thorough treatment of the role of physical stigma in interpersonal dynamics). Also included are dynamic physiological processes, such as those investigated by Christian (1960; Christian, Flyger, & Davis, 1961) and others on changes in adrenal functioning as a result of overcrowding, changes in GSR under different social distance and angle of approach conditions (McBride et al., 1965).

Next is the effect of a series of *personal characteristics* on ecological processes. These are grouped into three subclasses: demography, personality, and cultural characteristics. Demography refers to the usual set of biographical background characteristics, including age, sex, and education. Relevant studies in this category are those concerned with relationships between educational and socioeconomic factors and propinquity (Maisonneuve, Palmade, & Fourment 1952), sex and seating position (Sommer, 1959), sex and eye contact (Exline et al., 1965). Personality properties include a vast array of labels, categories, and dimensions used to describe transitory and relatively permanent properties of individuals. These include social-legal classifications, social and personal needs (need affiliation, need achievement). For example, Fisher (1967) studied social distance patterns of normal and disturbed children; Esser (1965; Esser et al., 1966) analyzed territorial behavior of schizophrenics; Hutt and Ounsted (1966) and Hutt and Vaizey (1966) compared normal, autistic, and brain-damaged children regarding distance and eye-contact behavior. At this point in the history of the proposed model no particularly compelling basis for describing personality is evident. Cultural properties cover a similarly broad range, including primary and secondary group features, characteristics of larger reference groups, and cultures as a whole. The work of Hall (1966) and Watson and Graves (1966) on crosscultural social-distance patterns is relevant here.

Each of the preceding classes can be used to describe individual actors in a relationship but, equally important, should be used to specify the "mix" or composition of individual characteristics. For example, in the personality area it is critical to portray each person's need achievement level and also the "mix" of need achievement characteristics within a group (for example, homogeneous high, homogeneous low, heterogeneous). For this reason personal, physiological, and cultural classes allow for individual and group composition description.

The third class of antecedent factors, *interpersonal properties*, includes properties of the group as a whole, such as past history as a group and level of compatibility among members. As examples of this class, Little, Ulehla and Henderson (1968) studied the relationship between value congruence of group members and social distance; Rosenfeld (1965, 1966a, 1966b) examined effects of interpersonal approval on social distance, smiling, and gestures; Stass and Willis (1967) found relationships between perceived compatibility and eye contact and pupil dilation; Lott and Sommer (1967) investigated seating positions as a function of role and status relationships.

Environmental factors encompass the set of events which impinge on the group from the outside. Representative studies in this area would include those examining relationships between seating arrangements and communication (Steinzor, 1950; Sommer, 1959); room design and participation (Sommer, 1967a); propinquity and sociometric patterns (Byrne & Buehler, 1955); living arrangements and interaction patterns (Blake, Rhead, Wedge, & Mouton, 1956); crowdedness and territorial behavior (McBride et al., 1963).

Situation definition. The model proposes that these antecedent factors contribute to a global personal definition or expectancy about the situation. This step, signified by a circle in Figure 12–1, is seen as an internal, subjective process which mediates between the complex of antecedent factors and resultant ecological behaviors. Goffman (1959) and others have emphasized the importance to subsequent behavior of an individual's personal definition of what a social situation calls for and what he wants the situation to be like.

One way to describe subjective expectancies may be to first distinguish between two classes of events: boundary phenomena and internal management phenomena. Several writers describe a person as having "boundaries" surrounding him, referred to as a personal bubble (Stern, 1938), or proximate and distal zones (Hall, 1966). This view is similar to so-called "onion-skin" theories of personality in which different layers of the psychological self are differentially accessible to others and in which different levels of intimacy of interaction occur. Thus, boundary phenomena refer to shifts in behavioral acts or role relationships as individuals move to new interpersonal interaction zones. Internal management refers to interaction patterns *within* a boundary zone such as interaction between friends or co-workers, which occurs in a delimited universe of discourse. A second set of distinctions specifies subjective expectations about motivational states and desires regarding boundary and internal management phenomena. Person A can want person B to enter into a particular kind of relationship or to maintain a desired level of relationship. Similarly, B can have various motivating states regarding A. These can lead to many possible dyadic combinations of subjective situation definitions. A may want B to change the relationship in one direction, but B may not want to do so; A may desire to have B leave a particular kind of association and B may not want to leave. An inconsistency between A's and B's personal definition of the situation is a potential determinant of interpersonal conflict and stress. That is, discrepancies in expectations about what a situation or relationship calls for may lead to perceptions that the other person's use of environmental props, self-markers, and Gestalt profiles are inappropriate and that the over-all relationship is not a satisfactory one.

Environmental props.   Assuming that the social actors have personal expectations about the situation, the model hypothesizes that they then use various environmental props and self-markers (see Figure 12–1) consistent with and designed to confirm their subjective perceptions.

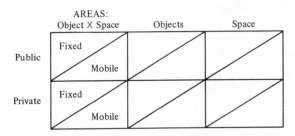

FIGURE 12–2.   Environmental prop dimensions.

Figure 12–2 summarizes three dimensions to describe environmental props. The first distinguishes between objects in the environment, space per se, and the combined use of objects and space—the latter constituting an area. The range of potential objects in the environment is, of course, very broad and can include almost any thing or person. The use of space generally maps to physical distance and/or angle of location and is a very popular dependent measure used in actual situations and in simulations.

The second dimension refers to fixity-mobility of objects, and is partly related to Hall's (1966) distinction between fixed feature, semifixed feature, and informal space. Fixed objects are not normally movable during an interpersonal encounter. A conference table is a fixed environmental object because it is ordinarily in a permanent location, while chairs around a table have some limited degree of mobility. The distinction between fixed and mobile is usually a cultural or mutually agreed upon one.

The third dimension involves a public-private distinction. Things unique to a person, possessed or used consistently by him, and which cultural practice specifies as such, are personal. A public prop is commonly used by several people, does not have any unique defining characteristics which attach it to a specific person, and is generally available for use by people at large. Clothing, a watch, and a briefcase are generally classified as personal or private objects. A family bedroom or bathroom would be classified as a personal area. A conference room, auditorium, or cafeteria would be relatively public areas. Of course, the relative privacy of a prop can shift over time and as a function of the situation or the relationship between group members.

We have found these distinctions to be useful in accounting for territorial behavior in isolated groups (Altman & Haythorn, 1967a). Over a 10-day period territoriality developed first for fixed private objects (beds), then for fixed public areas (location around a table), and lastly for mobile public objects (chairs). Other studies also can be classified differentially according to this system. Some emphasized understanding use of space (distance) but did not distinguish between public and private spaces (Kuethe, 1962a, 1962b, 1964; Fisher, 1967). Little (1965) did much the same, although he also examined distances between people in a public area (Object × Space). Hall (1966) attempted to understand use of space in both public and private areas. One can further distinguish between research investigations in terms of the antecedent variables which were related to use of environmental props. For example, Little (1965) studied interpersonal characteristics (friends and casual acquaintance), whereas Fisher (1967) focused on differences in personality (homosexuals versus normals) as determinants of use of space.

Another way to describe environmental props of the above types is in terms of their function, or what is being done with them, for example, giving, taking, holding, using as a barrier, sharing, and so forth. This is a more subjective level of analysis but reflects dynamic, functional characteristics which may be useful in future extensions of the model.

Use of self-markers.   Not only do people use environmental props consonant with their personal definition of a situation but they also employ themselves—their bodies and bodily characteristics—which we term self-markers. Self-marker dimensions can be roughly categorized into use of the body, including positions and movements, and sensory-perceptual processes such as olfaction, kinesthesis, visual contact, and vocal contact.

A differentiation also should be made between relatively static or dynamic conditions, for example, a relatively enduring head position versus changing head movements, a continuous gaze versus intermittent eye contact. The nature and use of nonverbal self-marker cues is a rapidly developing area of interest and is well summarized in writings by

Davitz (1964), Weick (1968), and others. It is interesting to note that analysis of nonverbal self-marker behaviors has developed as a relatively independent field of study heavily researched by clinical psychologists.

Complex Behavior Patterns

The next stage of the model, complex behavior patterns, is at a more molar, system-oriented level. An overview of this type of approach is offered by Scheflen (1964, 1965a, 1965b). Although Hall (1966) does not explicitly call for a holistic approach to proxemics, his summary profile of various social distances implies global behavioral syndromes. The concept of complex behavior patterns suggests that overt use of the environment and of the self leads to a behavioral syndrome, unique profile, or general image. Scheflen (1965a) illustrates this in describing a quasicourtship syndrome in psychotherapy. This is an organized behavioral complex including a high state of muscle tonus, a specific configuration of musculature around the eyes, erect torso, brightening of the eye, preening (hair combing, adjusting of clothing), movement of the body and head so as to face the other person, invitational statements and soft or drawling language, gaze holding, demure gestures, head cocking, and rolling of the pelvis. At a more analytic and perhaps empirically testable level, it is possible to identify several classes of complex behavior patterns:

Environmental-prop behavior complexes.   Combined use of different classes of environmental props, such as distance and seating positions or distance and object placement. Typically, behavioral elements in this and the following classes are either not studied in combination or tend to be confounded. Confounding is especially evident in studies of seating locations around a table, where distance and angle of location are generally not separable.

Self-marker behavioral complexes.   Combined use of different classes of self-markers, such as eye contact and smiling, smiling and gestures, and so on. While there are a number of researchers whose work falls in this category, as noted earlier, much of it does not view such behaviors in an integrated sense but rather views each self-marker as a parallel event. We need to understand smiling eye-contact *syndromes*, not just smiling behavior considered as a parallel process.

Self-marker environmental-prop behavior complexes.   Combined use of self- and environmental-prop behaviors such as distance and gestures, distance and eye contact, and so forth. Again, relatively few studies investigate these behavior classes as a syndrome although there are some beginnings in this direction, such as the work of Argyle and Dean (1965), who showed eye contact falling off with decreased distance and that of Lewit and Joy (1967), who found differences in distance between figures as a function of their "action or kinetic" status.

In addition to these complex behavior patterns involving individual use of props and self-markers, the behavior exhibited in interactive settings also can be considered from the point of view of *functional fit* of the behavior of two or more interacting individuals. Considering the case of a dyad, one can distinguish between whether the behavioral acts of

	Similar Acts	Different Acts
Facilitative Acts	Congruent	Complementary
Nonfacilitative Acts	Competitive	Antagonistic

FIGURE 12–3.   Group composition dimensions.

the two participants are (1) similar or different, and whether they are (2) facilitative or nonfacilitative. Facilitative acts are those generally considered by a culture to be positive, helpful and nonhostile while nonfacilitative acts are the obverse. The combination of similarity and facilitation dimensions generates, for a dyad, the four types of behavioral acts shown in Figure 12–3—congruent, complementary, competitive, and antagonistic. Some of these categories have been found to be particularly important in consideration of group composition factors. An example of the congruent case is two high need-affiliation individuals who have similar and facilitative need characteristics. For ecological behavior, two people shaking hands represents a congruent act—facilitative in that it is a normally approved way of greeting someone, and similar in terms of the actual movement. A more facetious example would be two people holding each other up to prevent one another from falling. A complementary act would occur if one person were falling and if another person were holding him up. These are different but facilitative acts (at least on the part of one member). A competitive relationship would be exemplified by two individuals who were both highly dominant or who were attempting to push one another down, exhibiting similar but nonfacilitative acts. Finally, antagonistic behavior would occur if one person were trying to keep from falling and the other were pushing him to accelerate his fall. Such behavior is generally considered nonfacilitative in our culture, and obviously dissimilar. Although existing ecological work has not made such distinctions, they fit in with research in the group-composition area and have particular relevance to issues of interpersonal conflict and compatibility.

Evaluation and Assessment Processes

Use of environmental props and self-markers, and the presence of an over-all complex behavior pattern, takes place over time, during a period of social interaction. During and following such interaction, the model hypothesizes the occurrence of an evaluation and assessment process. This internal, subjective process involves individuals posing a self-directed question: "Did what happened agree with my previous definition of the situation?" Each person determines whether his previous expectations about what the situation called for were confirmed or disconfirmed, and whether a desirable or undesirable state of affairs now exists. Two options exist if there is a discrepancy between desired expectations and outcomes. One alternative is to generate a new definition of the situation, which might involve use of new environmental props and self-markers. Another option is to maintain the original situation definition, involving some readjustment in use of environmental props and self-markers, but still in support of the prior definition of the situation. Such readjustments might involve adding new types of behaviors, or changing the intensity and temporal continuity of ones already exhibited.

Now consider an example of the total process. Dancing with someone else's husband or wife first involves a subjective definition of what behavior is appropriate. Specific self-marker and available environmental-prop behavior would then occur in accordance with that definition. Body distance, head position, body movements, types of body contact, hand and arm contact, and verbal behaviors would lead to an over-all profile of behavior manifested through time. Theoretically, periodic evaluations and assessments by both parties as to whether his and her own behavior and the behavior of the other was appropriate to their original definition of the situation would then occur. Let us assume, however, that one party defines the situation as an opportunity to promote a more personal relationship. He or she then might exhibit behavior in accordance with such a desire through use of voice, kinesthetic, visual behavior, and so on. This would probably result in an evaluation and assessment by the "victimized" person that the partner's behavior was not appropriate to the situation. One alternative might be to try to define the original situation more clearly to the rule-breaker. This could be done by maintaining further distance, increasing body rigidity and use of arm musculature, assuming a less friendly tone of voice, and by avoiding or using disapproving eye-contact mechanisms. Thus, mobilization of additional ecological resources is postulated, in terms of number, type, intensity, and temporal continuity, to preserve the original definition of the situation. Another option, as previously indicated, might involve a *new* definition of the situation. While the partner's behavior might have been discrepant with original expectations, it may be evaluated as unexpectedly pleasant and desirable, resulting in a redefinition of the situation and subsequent behavioral changes. From this example it can be seen that the classification model is intended to reflect the operation of a dynamic system, with adjustive feedback mechanisms responsive to ongoing events, and reverberating effects taking place throughout the system as the situation changes.

APPLICATION OF THE CLASSIFICATION MODEL

The present statement of the classification system is an initial one, obviously requiring further development in several areas. We are not certain that all important dimensions have been identified. Additional work is necessary on categories of dimensions already identified. The differential importance of various parts of the model, and dimensions and categories in those parts, are not now indicated. In spite of its early stage of development, however, the proposed model can be applied to the analysis of aspects of interpersonal compatibility, conflict, and stress. (Incidentally, there is relatively little ecologically oriented research on these issues.)

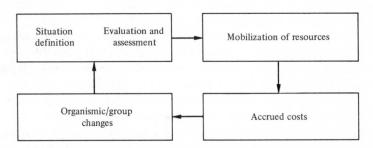

FIGURE 12–4.   Ecology system feedback mechanisms.

Referring to Figure 12–4, let us assume that one source of inter-personal conflict or stress derives from a discrepancy in the "fit" of one's prior expectation or situation definition with the evaluation and assess-ment of a subsequent social interaction. As illustrated by the example of dance partners, an attempt to retain an original definition of the situa-tion requires an adjustment process involving mobilization of resources. This might include changes in intensity, frequency, type and temporal continuity of use of self-markers and environmental props. The person brings to bear more and more resources as he strives to maintain an acceptable situation definition. There are, however, a variety of costs incurred in the process of mobilizing ecological resources. These feed back to personal, physiological, and interpersonal antecedent factors, referred to in Figure 12–4 as organismic changes. Such alterations in the individual or group, in turn, affect the situation definition which then feeds through the rest of the system. If a state of imbalance (expectation-assessment discrepancy) persists, the organism is hypothesized to go through a cyclical process involving increased mobilization of resources, increased costs, and further organismic changes. Such changes can lead to extensive psychological, physiological and interpersonal costs and eventually cause individual or interpersonal deterioration. Although we cannot now specify completely all parameters of such a derivation, there are a few studies consistent with these ideas which may provide the springboard for further linking of interpersonal conflict and ecological processes.

Christian et al. (1960) concluded that a mass, unexplained die-off of a herd of Sika deer was caused by physiological imbalances of adrenal and other internal organs resulting from social pressures associated with overcrowding. During the period of the die-off the food supply was adequate, there were no radical changes in the over-all environment, and analysis of later-generation deer indicated no adrenal abnormalities. Thus, it was concluded that overcrowding somehow led to altered physiological functioning which eventually resulted in physiological deterioration. These findings are consistent with our model. As the population increased, there probably was more and more intrusion into one another's territory and family-unit areas, more competition for females, increased needs to protect young, and generally more physical contact. It probably became necessary for animals to mobilize more and more resources (fighting, appropriate signals, heightened alertness) to establish desirable physical and social-psychological boundaries. But the problem was not really resolvable since geographical size of the area was fixed. Thus, it might be hypothesized that a vicious cycle of repeated attempts at readjustment, incurred costs, and resultant organismic changes took place. Eventually this probably led to serious physiological malfunctioning and death.

A similar sequence of events can be inferred from the overcrowding and "behavioral-sink" studies of Christian (1961) and Calhoun (1956, 1962). In a classic study, Calhoun (1962) demonstrated that overcrowding in rats led to abnormal social behaviors, as well as possible physiological upsets, and a resultant higher mortality rate. A rat pen was designed with food and water in a central location and in side areas. Dominant male rats eventually controlled the side areas and established harems and family units. Most other males were excluded from these areas and a crowded behavioral sink developed, composed of a large number of males and females. Comparison of behavior indicated extreme deviations by the overcrowded animals. Many females died in pregnancy, lost their litters, were less adept at building nests, and were less effective in caring for their young. Among males there also was evidence of behavior pathology; for example, they engaged in cannibalism, sexual deviations, social withdrawal, eating and drinking and moving about only when others were asleep. In a related study and review of other research, Christian (1961) found that crowded mice showed similar behavior deviations as well as increased adrenocortical activity, lowered resistance to disease, and smaller litters of newborn whose growth was stunted at the time of weaning. In terms of our model, it seems reasonable to infer a cyclical series of attempts by these crowded animals to establish proper and acceptable boundaries between themselves and others, followed by frustration and failure. Presumably, they continued to mobilize resources to achieve a satisfactory situation but eventually incurred severe social and physiological costs.

At the human level, an investigation of isolated groups also fits this conceptualization (Altman & Haythorn, 1967a; and Altman & Haythorn, 1967b). Pairs of men confined to a small room for ten days showed systematic patterns of territorial behavior, social activity, and stress reactions as a function of interpersonal compatibility and environmental factors. Over days, isolated groups exhibited increased territoriality for chairs and areas of the room and increased social withdrawal from one another. Furthermore, groups incompatible on certain social needs demonstrated relatively high levels of territorial behavior but differential social activity and stress reactions. For example, incompatible dominance groups (both members high dominant) showed a great deal of social activity (talking and doing things together) and high stress reactions, whereas those pairs who were incompatible on need affiliation (one high and one low) withdrew from one another but showed little stress. Thus, certain patterns of interpersonal incompatibility led to socially active territorial acts, whereas others resulted in more passive, low-stress withdrawal behaviors. Of relevance to the classification model is the idea that the incompatible dominance groups may not have resolved their group organization and living habits. They were continuing to mobilize resources to achieve a satisfactory level of functioning but were paying a price in terms of reported stress. The incompatible affiliates, on the other hand, apparently had resolved their relationship, showed no unusual stress patterns, exhibited a low level of social intercourse, and remained in their own part of the environment. Thus, these results reasonably fit aspects of the ideas presented in Figure 12–4 and also illustrate the intrinsic communality of social-psychological and ecological processes.

The conceptual model proposed here is obviously homeostatic and presumes that we are dealing with a "system"—an integrated organization having interdependent parts, compensatory feedback mechanisms, and continuously operating in a dynamic fashion. This type of thinking is quite evident in most existing theoretical frameworks bearing on ecological aspects of behavior. For example, McBride and his associates (McBride, 1964; McBride et al., 1963) postulated a social-force theory to account for social distance behavior in animals. Animal social organizations were hypothesized to develop to a point where attraction-repulsion forces are in a state of balance and responsive to dominance characteristics of group members and environmental characteristics such as food supply, geography, density and overcrowding. Force fields around animals shifted as a function of changes in such factors and as a function of momentary social situations. For example, although chickens normally regulate social distance by head turning and facing, these force fields were "tuned out" in certain social situations, for example, feeding and sleeping. To be somewhat anthropomorphic, it appears that differential mobilization of resources occurs for different "personal definitions" of the situation.

At the human level, Argyle and Dean (1965) proposed a homeostatic model of ecological behavior linking social distance and eye contact. Eye contact was seen as determined by a series of approach forces (affiliation, need for feedback) and by a counterbalancing set of avoidance forces (fear of disclosing, fear of being rejected), which contribute to a dynamic equilibrium process. The level of equilibrium is partly a function of the "intimacy" of the social relationship and is achieved through an interplay of such factors as eye contact, physical proximity, and smiling. If the equilibrium is disturbed, a compensatory shift in these ecological behaviors is predicted to occur. We would hypothesize such shifts to be mediated by personal definitions and subsequent assessments and evaluations of behavior.

Another aspect of current theorizing and of our model is the explicit interdependency of what have been termed environmental props and self-markers. The importance of the interaction and compensatory relationship between such behaviors is most evident in the Argyle and Dean, and the McBride studies, where systematic shifts in eye contact occurred with changing distance between social actors. Thus, environmental-prop and self-marker behavior should not be considered separate areas of study but should be studied in a way that conceives of them as combining to form a complex behavior pattern or syndrome.

Future Directions

Our attempt to develop a general classification of the ecology of interpersonal relationships has made salient some areas of needed research. At the most general level, we see the need for further development of theoretical models to help guide the future direction of the field. What is required is not a separate theory of ecological processes but the marriage of ecological concepts with general theorizing in a field. For interpersonal behavior, this means seeing how concepts of group composition, interpersonal compatibility and interpersonal conflict affect, and are affected by concomitant ecological processes. This will have a two-way impact. It will tie in use of the environment and of the self with general social psychology. Perhaps more important, the view from the perspective of ecological processes may stimulate the development of new concepts and methods for studying interpersonal relationships. The model proposed in this paper is designed to be one step in this direction.

More specifically, there just has not been, at the human level, very much ecologically oriented research bearing on problems of interpersonal conflict and stress. Clearly, more is needed, and it should have several characteristics previously implied in this paper. First, a good criterion language of ecological behavior is necessary. It is important that this language be more than just methodologically pure. It must include underlying concepts that can lead to general theory. Next, an empirical fund of knowledge needs to be accrued. It must not be collected in a "shot gun" fashion but should follow a programatic strategy. This means that research should tap several aspects of a model such as the one proposed in this paper. But this is not simple in the present case. The classification model contains a mixture of overt behavioral processes such as environmental props and self-markers, complicated integrations of these in the form of complex behavior patterns, and internal subjective processes involving situation definition, evaluation, and assessment. These subjective, intraindividual processes precede, accompany and follow overt events and require different methodological skills and have different problems associated with their study. But only through incorporation of both objective and subjective processes will it be possible to establish the types of links which seem necessary.

The most essential aspects of the model for understanding interpersonal compatibility, conflict, and stress are those involved in the hypothesized feedback mechanisms, referred to earlier as readjustment processes. These include mobilization of ecological resources and resultant costs. Although conceptually and methodologically difficult to handle, research is needed in this area. This will require longitudinal studies to track behavior through time, and development of a metric for assessing dynamic changes in such behavior. It is only through research oriented toward understanding such dynamics that we can proceed toward general theory and toward the meshing of ecological aspects of behavior with other levels of human functioning.

References

Altman, I. Choicepoints in the classification of scientific knowledge. In B. Indik and K. Berrien (Eds.), *People, groups and organizations: An effective integration*. New York: Columbia University Press, 1968.

Altman, I., & Haythorn, W. W. Interpersonal exchange in isolation. *Sociometry*, 1965, **28**(4), 411–426.

Altman, I., & Haythorn, W. W. The ecology of isolated groups. *Behavioral Science*, 1967, **12**(3), 169–182. (a)

Altman, I., & Haythorn, W. W. The effects of social isolation and group composition on performance. *Human Relations*, 1967, **20**(4), 313–340. (b)

Almond, R., & Esser, A. H. Tablemate choices of psychiatric patients: A technique for measuring social contact. *The Journal of Nervous and Mental Disease*, 1965, **141**, 68–82.

Ardrey, R. *The territorial imperative*. New York: Atheneum, 1966.

Argyle, M., & Dean, J. Eye-contact, distance and affiliation. *Sociometry*, 1965, **28**, 289–304.

Barker, R. G. (Ed.) *The stream of behavior*. New York: Appleton, 1963.

Barker, R. G., & Gump, P. *Big school, small school*. Stanford, Calif.: Stanford University Press, 1964.

Barker, R. G., & Wright, H. F. *Midwest and its children*. New York: Harper & Row, 1955.

Berelson, B., & Steiner, G. A. *Human behavior: An inventory of scientific findings*. New York: Harcourt, Brace & World, 1964.

Birdwhistell, R. *Introduction to kinesics*. Louisville, Ky.: University of Louisville Press, 1952.

Blake, R. R., Rhead, C. C., Wedge, B., & Mouton, J. S. Housing architecture and social interaction. *Sociometry*, 1956, **19**, 113–139.

Byrne, D., & Buehler, J. A. A note on the influence of propinquity upon acquaintanceships. *Journal of Abnormal and Social Psychology*, 1955, **51**, 147–148.

Calhoun, J. B. A comparative study of the social behavior of two inbred strains of house mice. *Ecological Monographs*, 1956, **26**, 81–103.

Calhoun, J. B. Population density and social pathology. *Scientific American*, 1962, **206**, 139–148.

Christian, J. J. Phenomena associated with population density. *Proceedings of the National Academy of Sciences*, 1961, **47**, 428–449.

Christian, J. J., Flyger, V., & Davis, D. E. Factors in the mass mortality of a herd of sika deer *cervus nippon*. *Chesapeake Science*, 1960, **1**, 79–95.

Collins, B., & Guetzkow, H. *A social psychology of group processes for decision making*. New York: Wiley, 1964.

Davitz, J. R. Communication of emotional meaning. New York: McGraw-Hill, 1964.

Ekman, P. Communication through nonverbal behavior: A source of information about an interpersonal relationship. In S. Tomkins & G. E. Izard (Eds.), *Affect, cognition and personality*. New York: Springer, 1965, pp. 390–441.

Ekman, P., & Friesen, W. V. Head and body cues in the judgment of emotion: A reformulation. *Perceptual and Motor Skills*, 1967, **24**, 711–724. (a)

Ekman, P., & Friesen, W. V. Nonverbal behavior in psychotherapy research. In J. Shlien (Ed.), *Research in Psychotherapy*, Vol. III. Washington, D. C.: American Psychological Association, 1967, pp. 1–76. (b)

Ekman, P., & Friesen, W. V. Origin, usage, and coding: The basis for five categories of nonverbal behavior. Paper presented at symposium on Communication Theory and Linguistic Models in the Social Sciences, Torquato Di Tella Institute, Buenos Aires, Argentina, October 1967. (c)

Esser, A. H. Social contact and the use of space in psychiatric patients. Paper presented at the American Association for the Advancement of Science, Berkeley, Calif., December 1965.

Esser, A. H., Amparo, S., Chamberlain, R. N., Chapple, E. D., & Kline, N. S. Territoriality of patients on a research ward. *Recent Advances in Biological Psychiatry*, 1964, **7**, 37–44.

Exline, R. Explorations in the process of person perceptions: Visual interaction in relation to competition, sex and need for affiliation. *Journal of Personality*, 1963, **31**, 1–20.

Exline, R., Gray, D., & Schuette, D. Visual behavior in a dyad as affected by interview content and sex of respondent. *Journal of Personality and Social Psychology*, 1965, **1**(3), 201–209.

Fisher, R. L. The social schema of normal and disturbed school children. *Journal of Educational Psychology*, 1967, **58**(2), 88–92.

Goffman, E. *The presentation of self in everyday life.* New York: Doubleday, 1959.

Goffman, E. *Stigma: Notes on the management of spoiled identity.* Englewood Cliffs, N. J.: Prentice-Hall, 1963.

Hall, E. T. The anthropology of manners. *Scientific American*, 1955, **192**, 85–89.

Hall, E. T. *The silent language.* New York: Doubleday, 1959.

Hall, E. T. A system for the notation of proxemic behavior. *American Anthropologist*, 1963, **65**, 1003–1025.

Hall, E. T. *The hidden dimension.* New York: Doubleday, 1966.

Haythorn, W. W., & Altman, I. Personality factors in isolated environments. In M. H. Appley & R. Trumbull (Eds.), *Psychological stress: Issues in research.* New York: Appleton, 1967, pp. 363–386.

Haythorn, W. W., Altman, I., & Myers, T. I. Emotional symptomatology and subjective stress in isolated groups. *Journal of Experimental Research in Personality*, 1966, **1**(4), 290–306.

Hediger, H. Studies of the psychology and behavior of captive animals in zoos and circuses. New York: Criterion Books, 1955.

Horowitz, M. J. Graphic communication: A study of interaction painting with schizophrenics. *American Journal of Psychotherapy*, 1963, **17**, 230–239.

Horowitz, M. J., Duff, D. F., & Stratton, L. O. Body-buffer zone. *Archives of General Psychiatry*, 1964, **11**(6), 651–656.

Howard, D. *Territory and bird life.* London: Collins Publication Company, 1948.

Hutt, C., & Ounsted, C. The biological significance of gaze aversion with particular reference to the syndrome of infantile autism. *Behavioral Science*, 1966, **11**, 346–356.

Hutt, C., & Vaizey, M. J. Differential effects of group density on social behavior. *Nature*, March 1966, No. 5030, 1371–1372.

Kates, R. W., & Wohlwill, J. F. Man's response to the physical environment: Introduction. *Journal of Social Issues*, 1966, **22**, 15–21.

King, M. G. Interpersonal relations in pre-school children and average approach distance. *Journal of Genetic Psychology*, 1966, **109**(1), 109–116. (a)

King, M. G. Social reflexes nos. 1 and 2 in relation to approach and avoidance tendencies. *Journal of Genetic Psychology*, 1966, **109**(1), 101–107. (b)

Kuethe, J. L. Social schemas. *Journal of Abnormal and Social Psychology*, 1962, **64**, 31–38. (a)

Kuethe, J. L. Social schemas and the reconstruction of social object displays from memory. *Journal of Abnormal and Social Psychology*, 1962, **65**, 71–74. (b)

Kuethe, J. L. Pervasive influence of social schemata. *Journal of Abnormal and Social Psychology*, 1964, **68**, 248–254.

Kuethe, J. L., & Weingartner, H. Male-female schemata of homosexual and nonhomosexual penitentiary inmates. *Journal of Personality*, 1964, **32**, 23–31.

Lewit, D. W., & Joy, V. D. Kinetic versus social schemas in figure grouping. *Journal of Personality and Social Psychology*, 1967, **7**(1), 63–72.

Little, K. B. Personal space. *Journal of Experimental and Social Psychology*, 1965, **1**, 237–247.

Little, K. B., Ulehla, Z. J., & Henderson, C. Value congruence and interaction distances. *Journal of Social Psychology*, 1968, **79**, 249–253.

Loeb, F. Grasping: The investigation of a recurrent behavior pattern. Paper presented at American Psychological Association, New York, 1966.

Lorenz, K. *On aggression*. New York: Harcourt, Brace & World, 1966.

Lott, D. F., & Sommer, R. Seating arrangements and status. *Journal of Personality and Social Psychology*, 1967, **7**, 90–94.

Maisonneuve, J., Palmade, G., & Fourment C. Selective choices and propinquity. *Sociometry*, 1952, **15**, 135–140.

March, J. G., & Simon, H. A. *Organizations*. New York: Wiley, 1958.

McBride, G. A general theory of social organization of behavior. St. Lucia, Australia: University of Queensland Papers, 1964, **1**, 75–110.

McBride, G., James, J. W., & Shoffner, R. N. Social forces determining spacing and head orientation in a flock of domestic hens. *Nature*, 1963, **197**, 1272–1273.

McBride, G., King, M. G., & James, J. W. Social proximity effects on galvanic skin responses in adult humans. *Journal of Psychology*, 1965, **61**, 153–157.

McGrath, J. E., & Altman, I. *Small group research: Synthesis and critique of the field*. New York: Holt, Rinehart and Winston, 1966.

Price, J. L. Organizational effectiveness: An inventory of propositions. Homewood, Ill.: Richard D. Irwin, 1968.

Rosenfeld, H. M. Effects of an approval-seeking induction on interpersonal proximity. *Psychological Reports*, 1965, **17**, 120–122.

Rosenfeld, H. M. Approval-seeking and approval-inducing functions of verbal and nonverbal responses in the dyad. *Journal of Personality and Social Psychology*, 1966, **4**, 597–605. (a)

Rosenfeld, H. M. Instrumental affiliative functions of facial and gestural expressions. *Journal of Personality and Social Psychology*, 1966, **4**, 65–72. (b)

Scheflen, A. E. The significance of posture in communication systems. *Psychiatry*, 1964, **27**, 316–331.

Scheflen, A. E. Quasi-courtship behavior in psychotherapy. *Psychiatry*, 1965, **28**, 245–257. (a)

Scheflen, A. E. Systems in human communication. Paper presented at American Association for the Advancement of Science, Berkeley, Calif., December 1965. (b)

Sells, S. B. Ecology and the science of psychology. *Multivariate Behavioral Research*, 1966, **1**, 131–144.

Sommer, R. Studies in personal space. *Sociometry*, 1959, **22**(3), 247–260.

Sommer, R. Leadership and group geography. *Sociometry*, 1961, **24**, 99–110.

Sommer, R. The ecology of privacy. *The Library Quarterly*, 1966, **36**, 234–248.

Sommer, R. Classroom ecology. *Journal of Applied Behavioral Science*, 1967, **3**(4), 489–503. (a)

Sommer, R. Small group ecology. *Psychological Bulletin*, 1967, **67**(2), 145–152. (b)

Stass, J. W., & Willis, F. N., Jr. Eye contact, pupil dilation, and personal preference. *Psychonomic Science*, 1967, **7**, 375–376.

Steinzor, B. The spatial factor in face to face discussion groups. *Journal of Abnormal and Social Psychology*, 1950, **45**, 552–555.

Stern, W. *General psychology.* H. D. Spoerl (Transl.) New York: Crowell-Collier and Macmillan, 1938.

Watson, O. M., & Graves, T. D. Quantitative research in proxemic behavior. *American Anthropologist*, 1966, **68**(4), 971–985.

Webb, E. J., Campbell, D. T., Schwartz, R. D., & Sechrest, L. *Unobtrusive measures: Nonreactive research in the social sciences.* Skokie, Ill. Rand McNally, 1966.

Weick, K. Systematic observational methods. In G. Lindzey and E. Aronson (Eds.), *Handbook of social psychology.* New York: Addison-Wesley, 1968.

Winick, C., & Holt, H. Seating position as nonverbal communication in group analysis. *Psychiatry*, 1961, **24**, 171–182.

13 | tasks and task performance in research on stress[1]

J. Richard Hackman

INTRODUCTION: THE USE OF TASKS IN STRESS RESEARCH

Tasks are widely used in research on stress—as well as in most other areas of behavioral research. In some applications, tasks are central to research designs, as when stress conditions are induced by variations of the difficulty or the ambiguity of experimental tasks. In other cases, tasks are peripheral to the major research purposes: for example, when tasks are given to subjects either as "something to do" while other variables

---

[1] An earlier version of this paper was presented at the Conference on Social and Psychological Factors in Stress sponsored by the Air Force Office of Scientific Research (AFOSR) at the University of Illinois in May 1967. Revision of the paper was supported in part by AFOSR grant AFOSR–68–1600 (Effects of Task Characteristics on Performance). Thanks are due Miss Ann Garvin for her assistance, and to the numerous individuals who read and commented on an earlier draft of the manuscript.

are being studied, or when they are used only as a vehicle performance data.

Not very much is known about tasks. There is no gene definition of the concept, few systematic means of describing tiating among them, and little understanding of how tasks affect behavior. This is unfortunate, since rather compelling evidence has now accumulated which indicates that tasks control substantial behavioral variance in many kinds of research settings.[2] Thus, to the extent that we are unaware of the ways tasks influence behavior, we also are often unaware of the ways in which our major independent variable—in this case, stress —is affecting our subjects.

This paper is an attempt to lay the groundwork for more effective use of tasks in research on stress, and for better understanding of how task-induced stress relates to behavior. This introductory section will review how tasks have been used in previous research on stress. In the next section, several issues which must be confronted in dealing systematically with tasks in any substantive area are reviewed, a general definition of the concept is suggested, and a framework for analyzing the behavioral effects of tasks is proposed. Finally, several implications of the definition and a framework for understanding task performance under stress are examined, and some steps toward the development of a taxonomy of task-based stressors are suggested.

Previous Use of Tasks in Stress Research

The abstracts of published stress-relevant research assembled by the staff of the AFOSR conference (see Chapter 5) provided an opportunity to determine the ways tasks have been used in stress research.[3]

Of the approximately 200 abstracts in the stress conference collection, 140 were relevant empirical studies (that is, were not review, theoretical, or purely methodological pieces). [See references and Chapter 2.] Of these, specifiable tasks were used in almost 70 percent of the studies, again testifying to the heavy use of tasks of one sort or another in behavioral research. Most of the studies in which specific tasks were not used were field studies which frequently involved naturally occurring stress— such as disasters, serious illness, combat, or living in a hostile or isolated environment.

---

[2] See, for example, Hackman, 1968; McGrath and Altman, 1966; Morris, 1966; Weick, 1965.

[3] As might be expected, just what is and what is not considered a "task" varies from author to author and from abstractor to abstractor. Since a general definition of the concept will be proposed later in this paper, I will accept the usages of the researchers and abstractors for present purposes, with the knowledge that this undoubtedly will result in some inconsistencies.

The tasks which have been used in stress research are a heterogeneous lot. Listed below are ten general types of tasks which frequently were used in the studies reviewed:

Decision-making tasks
Discussion tasks, frequently with built-in conflict or risky alternatives
Items or subtests from aptitude or achievement tests
Learning tasks
Memory tasks, especially digit span
Miscellaneous parlor and board games
Motor coordination tasks
Perceptual tasks, usually focusing on perceptual speed, accuracy, and discrimination
Problem solving tasks, especially anagrams
Reaction time tasks

The kinds of *uses* to which tasks were put also varied widely from study to study. Most frequently, tasks were associated with the induction of stress, in the measurement of its effects, or both. The reviewers' data indicate that, of those studies in which tasks were used, tasks or task-relevant factors were involved in the stress induction in 72 percent of the cases. Task factors served as the *only* stressor in about half of these studies, and as one of several sources of stress in the other half.

An example in which task factors represented the only stressor is the rather ingenious study of collective behavior in a simulated panic situation by Kelley, Condry, Dahlke, and Hill (1965). In this experiment, the experimenter explained to the subjects that the study was about:

> Behavior under threat, the situation being one where a number of people have to use a single, limited exit to escape from an impending danger within a limited time. The threatened penalty for failure to escape was, in most cases, one or more painful shocks. The fact that only one person at a time could escape was made clear by explanation and demonstration [p. 27].

Although the details differed from one experiment to the next, in all cases the subject could see signal lights showing his own position vis-à-vis the danger situation and similar lights showing the position of each of the other subjects. At the beginning of a trial, each subject's light indicated that he was in "danger." By manipulating a switch, he could attempt to escape—at the same time changing his signal light and making his attempted escape visible to all the others. When only one subject had his escape switch on for three seconds, his signal light turned green, indicating that he had escaped. If two or more subjects simultaneously turned on their escape switches, no one could escape. Thus, in this study, the task—here represented by the shock and signal light apparatus and by the "rules of the game"—served as the only source of experimental stress.

An example of a study in which both task and nontask factors contributed to the stress induction is that of Ainsworth (1958). As part of his induction of stress, Ainsworth varied two factors relevant to a mathematical problem-solving task: time limit and perceived importance. In addition (in the high-stress condition), he introduced the presence of a "mathematics expert," who watched over the subjects' shoulders as they worked. Ainsworth treated the effects of his three stressors (time limit, importance, and observation) as cumulative, and his data suggest that this indeed may have been the case. Nevertheless, an early review by Lazarus, Deese, and Osler (1951) implies that inductions of stress grounded in the task itself may operate in very different ways from certain other kinds of inductions, such as failure. To the extent that the kinds of effects obtained from task and nontask stressors are qualitatively different, the numerous studies in which part of the stress manipulation is task-based and part is external to the task must be interpreted with caution.

Thus far we have discussed only the ways in which tasks have been used to induce conditions of stress. As was mentioned earlier, tasks serve a second important function in stress research: they frequently provide a means of generating output measures, through which the *effects* of stress may be objectively assessed.

In 88 percent of those studies in which specifiable tasks were used, some kind of task-generated output data were collected. For example, in a study by Smock (1955) the task was considered to be independent of the stress induction (threat to the subjects' self concepts and rejection by the experimenter) and was conceived of only as a means of gathering output data relevant to the hypotheses of the study. Smock was interested in the degree to which psychological stress results in increased intolerance of ambiguity. To test this proposition, several series of fifteen stimulus cards which varied in ambiguity were designed. The first card of each series was highly ambiguous; in each succeeding card more stimulus elements were added until a complete design or picture emerged on the final card. It was hypothesized that under stressful conditions, subjects would exhibit intolerance for ambiguity by identifying the stimulus before adequate information was available to them.[4] By simply

---

[4] Smock did not view the "ambiguity" of the initial cards in a series as adding to the stressfulness of the situation, even though ambiguity is frequently used as a task-based stressor. If indeed subjects did perceive the ambiguity of the cards as stressful, the amount of stress on the subjects probably would have decreased throughout the course of each fifteen-card series—perhaps affecting the obtained results.

noting which card in the series evoked the first attempted identification of the final pattern, Smock achieved a quantitative, operational measure of his dependent variable.

Several other task-based output measures which have been used frequently in stress research are listed below:

Rigidity
Performance effectiveness, creativity, accuracy, speed
Riskiness of decision
Amount of cognitive restructuring
Attitude change
Perceptual speed, threshold
Conformity

Finally, we may note that although a wide heterogeneity of tasks has been used in research on stress, and although these tasks have served several different functions in such research, only rarely has *more than one* task been used in a particular study. Of the approximately 100 studies reviewed in which tasks were used, about seventy employed only a single form of a single task, and most of those studies involving more than one task were multistage experiments with different tasks used to test different hypotheses. Virtually no studies made any attempt to sample tasks or to vary them systematically within a design—so as to avoid the task-specificity of results which reliance on a single task necessarily implies.

DEALING WITH TASKS SYSTEMATICALLY: SOME ISSUES AND PROPOSALS[5]

Cronbach (1957) has pointed out the importance of being able to describe differences in situations in systematic terms. As an example, he suggests: "Research on stress presents a typical problem of organization. Multivariate psychophysical data indicate that different taxing situations have different effects. At present, stressors can be described only superficially, by inspection [p. 677]." One pervasive aspect of the situation is the task and (as was noted earlier) tasks frequently serve as a source of stress, both inside and outside the laboratory. Thus, before we make substantial progress in alleviating the difficulties to which Cronbach alludes, it may be necessary to develop means of describing and comparing tasks in systematic terms, and to devise some conceptual tools for

---

[5] This section is, in part, a summary of material presented elsewhere (see Hackman, J. R. *Toward understanding the role of tasks in behavioral research.* Interim Scientific Report, Air Force Office of Scientific Research grant AFOSR–68–1600. New Haven, Conn.: Department of Administrative Sciences, Yale University, August 1968). The assertions and positions presented in this section are discussed and elaborated upon in more detail there.

examining the ways task-based factors influence behavior in stressful situations. This section attempts to make some beginning steps toward developing these capabilities.

Approaches to Describing Tasks[6]

One means of describing tasks is to observe and record what people working on the tasks actually do. In this method, called the *task-as-behavior-description* approach, the emphasis is not on what tasks require performers to do, or on what they should do to be successful, but rather on their *actual* behavior in response to the task. The behavior-description approach has been a dominant one in research on jobs and job characteristics by industrial psychologists. For example, McCormick (1965) has derived dimensions of jobs by factor analysis of specific aspects of job behavior, and Dunnette (1966) has reviewed the numerous attempts to define and describe managers' jobs by variants of the behavior-description approach.

Even though the task-as-behavior-description approach may be useful in grouping and identifying behaviors emitted by people working on tasks or jobs, it probably will not prove useful in understanding how tasks affect behavior. It appears that some researchers concerned with job and task descriptions, in effect, have substituted a dependent variable class for what should be an independent variable class. If what we are interested in are the effects of tasks and task characteristics on behavior, it is essential that we develop a means of describing and classifying the independent variables (tasks) other than in terms of the dependent variables (behaviors) which we ultimately wish to predict.

A second approach to task description focuses on the pattern of abilities or personal characteristics which are required for successful task completion, and is called *task-as-ability-requirement*. Thus, tasks can be described and compared on the basis of, say, the degree to which finger dexterity is important for successful performance, or the degree to which high intelligence is required for problem solution. Ferguson (1956) suggests that ability requirements may be useful in differentiating among learning tasks, and a similar position is taken by Hare (1962, p. 251) for group tasks. This approach also has been popular in describing industrial jobs and tasks. Lytle (1946), tracing the history of job evaluation procedures, found heavy reliance on this approach, and recent studies by Orr (1960) and by McCormick, Finn, and Scheips (1957) utilize it.

Neither the task-as-ability-requirement approach nor the behavior-description approach described above focus on the characteristics of the

---

[6] Three of the approaches to be discussed (task as behavior description, task as behavior requirement, and task qua task) were originally proposed by McGrath and Altman (1966) in their review and critique of the small group field.

task itself in making descriptions or differentiations of tasks. The ability-requirement approach differs from the behavior-description approach mainly in that it elects relatively enduring aspects of the performer as the basis of description, rather than aspects of the performance itself. Thus, it appears that this position, too, is not an appropriate one for the analysis of the impact of tasks and task characteristics on behavior.

As described by McGrath and Altman (1966), the *task-qua-task* approach asks: "What pattern of stimuli is impinging on the subjects? [p. 75]" In this view, task-qua-task properties are "objective" task properties—the physical nature of the task, its subject matter, the characteristics of the stimulus materials involved. Although many task-qua-task dimensions refer primarily to the physical nature of the stimuli which confront a performer (for example, stimulus input rate), the term legitimately applies to any aspect of the actual task materials. Thus, dimensions describing the actual instructions given to performers or the nature of the task content would be task-qua-task characteristics.

Several researchers (for example, Arnoult, 1963; Sells, 1963, pp. 7–8; Barker & Gump, 1964, p. 6) have argued that describing tasks and situations in their own terms is the most appropriate starting point for developing understanding of their effects on behavior. The main argument against treating tasks in task-qua-task terms is that it may not be feasible to do so (see Altman, 1966). This is because: (1) there is an enormous number of possible task-qua-task dimensions which might be employed, and (2) these dimensions are usually quite "distant" from behavior, which may tend to obscure their behavioral links. Nevertheless, there are some important conceptual advantages associated with the use of task-qua-task descriptors in examining task effects on behavior, and it is my view that the potential of the approach should be extensively explored before judgments of feasibility are made.

The *task-as-behavior-requirement* approach asks the general question: "What behaviors *should* be emitted, given the task, to achieve some particular outcome state (frequently, task success)?" The concept of "critical demands" suggested by Roby and Lanzetta (1958) is an example of the task-as-behavior-requirement approach. Other applications of this approach have been made by Steiner (1966, p. 274), Altman (1966), and Gagné (1964).

Behavior requirements can be conceptualized as mediating between behaviors which a performer emits and the output states which result from these behaviors. Consider, for example, an experimental game which requires subjects to allocate materials (for example, money) among several areas (such as, advertising media) so as to maximize their "payoffs" (total sales). The particular outcome which a subject will obtain on any given trial is determined wholly by the mathematical structure of the payoff function. This function, then, translates behaviors into out-

comes, and the experimenter (assuming he knows the operating characteristics of his payoff function) can specify precisely what the behavior
requirements are for any of a wide variety of particular outcomes (for
instance, maximization of sales for a given sum of money spent).

As another example, assume a subject is given a concept-formation
task in which he is to indicate whether or not particular stimuli are instances of some concept. If the concept "rule" is that a stimulus is an
instance only if it contains, say, curved lines, this rule represents a
behavior-outcome link (or behavior requirement) in the same sense as
the payoff function in the previous example. That is, the rule mediates
between the actual behavior of the subject (that is, saying "instance" or
"not an instance") and the outcome for him (that is, being correct or
incorrect).

When the links between what a performer does (that is, his behavioral process in working on the task) and the outcomes he receives
are determined by the task, as in the two examples above, such links
will be referred to as task-based *process-outcome links*. Process-outcome
links subsume behavior requirements as the term has been used in this
paper, and represent an important way in which tasks can influence the
nature of task performance.

Of the approaches to task description reviewed above, the task-qua-
task and the task-as-behavior-requirement strategies seem to hold the
greatest potential for furthering our understanding of how tasks influence
behavior, including the question of how task-based stress affects performance. Thus, these two approaches will be relied upon heavily in
subsequent sections of this paper.

The Problem of Task Redefinition

One conceptual difficulty associated with using the task-qua-task approach for defining and describing tasks is that the task which is actually
worked on by performers is not the one which is available for description
in objective terms. This, of course, is because tasks which are given to
performers are routinely "redefined" by them to be consistent with their
needs, values, and goals before actual work begins. Several researchers
(for example, Pepinsky & Pepinsky, 1961, pp. 219–220; Weick, 1965; Hare,
1962, pp. 248–249) have discussed the importance of the redefinition
process, and some have implied that descriptions of externally imposed
tasks may be of marginal validity and usefulness because of subjects'
often rather idiosyncratic redefinitions of tasks.

Clearly, if we attempt to deal with tasks and task effects without
recognizing the importance of the redefinition process, we will be ex-
cluding by fiat much of the substantive richness associated with task
performance, as well as a sizable portion of legitimate behavioral

variance. Such a course would seem indefensible. On the other hand, if redefinition is included as part of definitions and descriptions of tasks, virtually the whole problem of human motivation would be introduced into the descriptive enterprise, and it would be impossible to discuss task dimensions or effects without including enormously detailed specifications of the characteristics and motives of the particular persons who would be working on the tasks. Such a course would seem to negate the possibility of developing a general theory of tasks toward which so many researchers (as examples, McGrath & Altman, 1966; Weick, 1965; Hoffman, 1965) have claimed we should aspire.

The solution to this dilemma may lie in recognizing that, although the objective and redefined tasks occupy different temporal positions in the performance sequence, they both are still tasks, and therefore can be described and differentiated on the same dimensions. Thus, the redefinition process can be viewed as that sequence of (mostly covert) behavior that occurs between the time a performer receives the task and the time he begins actual work on it; and the problem of redefinition can be discussed in substantive rather than in definitional terms. This is the general strategy which will be followed here.

A Definition of Task and a Framework for Assessing Task Effects[7]

Consistent with a general task-qua-task approach to definition and description, the following definition of the concept *task* is proposed:

A task is assigned to a person (or group) by an external agent or is self-generated, and consists of a stimulus complex and a set of instructions which specify what is to be done vis-à-vis the stimuli. The instructions indicate what operations are to be performed by the performer(s) with respect to the stimuli and/or what goal is to be achieved.

Let us examine this definition part by part. First, a task may be either *assigned* or *self-generated*. If a person decides to draw a picture of a mountain scene, a self-generated task exists; if an art instructor presents a person with a mountain scene and tells him to draw a picture of it, an assigned task exists.

Assigned tasks exist in the real world; (that is, they exist independent of the performer). Thus, they may be described and compared in objec-

---

[7] The definition of the concept "task" to be proposed here draws heavily on the characterization of the "external problem situation" which has been made by Gagné (1966) for application to the study of human problem solving. A major point of difference between the present definition and Gagné's is our inclusion of "self-generated" tasks as instances of the concept.

tive (for example, task-qua-task) terms. Therefore, it is meaningful to speak of different individuals being given the *same* assigned task, and it is possible to vary systematically the objective parameters of assigned tasks in an experimental situation. That a subject may (and will) redefine an assigned task in terms of his own idiosyncratic needs, values, or goals is irrelevant to the problem of defining and describing tasks qua tasks.

There are obvious and substantial difficulties associated with the objective description of self-generated tasks. In one sense, the self-generated task is redefined by the performer as it is generated or selected and does not exist in objective reality at all. Nevertheless, according to the definition of *task* presented above, self-generated tasks, like assigned tasks, consist of a set of stimulus materials and a set of instructions. Whether an individual is told to look at a TAT card and write a story about it, or whether he decides to do so on his own, he is still dealing with the stimulus material on the TAT card, and he is still responding to the instruction: "Write a story." The problem is to find a means of identifying self-generated task materials and measuring their character-istics—a problem of considerable magnitude, considering that the task may not even exist outside the performer's consciousness or the group's interaction process. Nevertheless, recent work on the roles of verbal reports and conscious intentions in performance (for example, Dulany, 1968; and Locke, 1968) suggests that development of an adequate methodology for dealing with the self-generated tasks of individuals is by no means out of the question.

The definition proposed here also asserts that tasks must include some *stimulus material* and some *instructions*. Thus, the instruction, "Think!" would not be a task, but, "Think about this picture and tell me what it means" would be. If there is no stimulus material there is no task. The definition specifies two types of instructions: instructions about *goals* which are to be achieved and instructions about what *operations or actions* are to be performed. Most tasks probably will have instructions about both goals and operations: for example, "Minimize the wavering in the tone you hear [instructions about goals] by adjusting the four knobs on this panel [instructions about operations]." It is possible, how-ever, to have tasks without instructions about goals ("Watch this motion picture"), or without instructions about operations ("Make this broken radio work again"). But some instructions—either about goals or about operations—is essential to the definition. Merely giving a person a broken radio, for example, would not be assigning him a task.

By specifying explicitly the three aspects of tasks (that is, the stimulus materials, the instructions about goals, and the instructions about opera-tions), the definition may facilitate the organization and comparison of the variety of task dimensions which have been central to much research on physchological stress. A tentative taxonomy of task-based stressors which is based on the present definition will be presented later in this paper.

To trace out the means by which differences in these aspects of the task realized their behavioral effects, however, some framework or model of the task performance process is needed. A general framework for sorting out some of the classes of variables which may be important in understanding task effects on behavior is presented in Figure 13–1. The framework is not intended to be a model of the task performance process in any formal sense; no particular predictions derive directly from it. Instead, the usefulness of the framework may be in providing a context in which substantive relationships may be placed and compared, and in which new hypotheses about substantive relationships may be generated. It is in this spirit that the framework will be used in this paper to address issues of particular relevance to stress research.

The core of the framework is the sequence of boxes connected by arrows. A few characteristics of the performer which seem especially likely to be important in understanding task behavior are grouped near the bottom of the figure. The locus of their interactions with the main performance sequence are not indicated in the figure, but will be pointed out as the framework is described in the text. The framework will be described in time sequence; that is, by reading from left to right.

The box farthest to the left represents the objective task as it is presented to the performer(s). Consistent with the definition which has been proposed, the task is seen as having three components: stimulus material, instructions about operations, and/or instructions about goals. As was discussed earlier in this paper, the objective task is not necessarily the one actually dealt with by any given performer(s) because of the process of task-redefinition. Because the information included in the objective statement of the task must be perceived and coded by the subject before it becomes useful to him, all of the factors which affect the dynamics of perception (needs, values, and so forth) potentially will contribute to task redefinition. Four factors that seem likely to be especially important are: (1) the degree to which the performer understands the task (and if he misunderstands, in what ways); (2) the degree to which he accepts the task and is willing to cooperate with its demands; (3) the idiosyncratic needs and values which the performer brings to the task situation; and (4) the impact of his previous experience with similar tasks.

To the extent that subjects do not understand and/or do not accept the objective task, there is likely to be a considerable difference between the objective and the redefined task. In this case, the impact of needs, values, and perhaps even past experience with superficially similar tasks

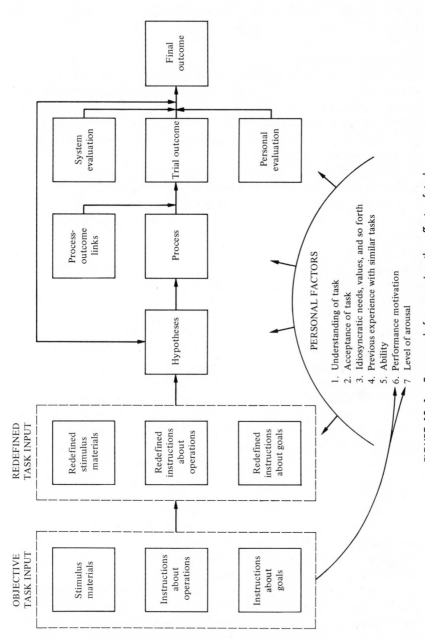

FIGURE 13–1. Framework for assessing the effects of tasks.

213

will play a relatively large role in determining the nature of the redefined task.

The framework proposes that, after a subject has cognitively rede-fined a task and, so to speak, "has it in his head," he formulates some "hypotheses" about how he ought to perform. These hypotheses probably are of two types: hypotheses relevant to the strategy of performance which will be used (that is, "How should I go about dealing with this task?") and hypotheses relevant to the actual behaviors which will be performed ("Given that I am going to approach the problem in this way, just what should I do or say?"). Breer and Locke (1965, p. 12) also point out the role of hypothesis formation in task performance, and the notion has considerable similarity to the concept of "plans" proposed by Miller, Galanter, and Pribram (1960).

The specific hypotheses which are generated will depend, of course, on the characteristics of the performer as well as upon the redefined task. Of particular importance in this regard may be any previous experience which the performer has had with the task or with tasks which seem to him to be similar. If in the past an individual has been given, say, highly difficult mathematical problems to solve and has found that he succeeded on these problems most frequently when he broke them into parts before starting actual work, he is very likely to hypothesize that this strategy also will be applicable in the present situation. Rotter (1955), in discussing the impact of the psychological situation, uses expectancy theory concepts to make much the same point. In essence, Rotter suggests that situation-based cues (in the present case, character-istics of tasks) are related through previous experience to expectancies about what kinds of behaviors will be reinforced.

The next stage in the task-performance sequence is called *process* and refers simply to the "doings" of performance. The process that occurs is seen in the framework as following directly from the hypotheses about what ought to be done. Like the other stages which have been discussed, process is moderated by personal factors. In this case, the performer's task-relevant abilities and his motivation to perform should be especially critical personal factors.

It should be noted that the individual's performance motivation is not merely the motivation that the person brings with him to the per-formance situation. The characteristics of the task itself (especially the stimulus materials) can strongly affect the performer's level of motiva-tion in at least two ways. For example, Scott (1966) has shown how certain task factors can increase the level of arousal of individuals in work situations through activation of the reticular formation, and Hunt (1963) reviews the role of stimulus factors in activation and motivation in more general terms. McClelland and Atkinson (for example, McClelland et al., 1953) take a somewhat different approach to the same issue. These authors suggest that stimulus materials (as well as other conditions) may serve as cues for the arousal of certain motives (for example, achievement or affiliation) which subsequently can affect the level or direction of performance.

The actual behavior or process of performance results in a tentative or trial outcome.[8] Two general kinds of trial outcomes (and ultimately, final outcomes) are noted in the framework: objective outcomes and personal outcomes. The former are simply the products of the performance process (a written passage, a configuration of lights on a panel, an assembled device, physical locomotion); the latter are the performer's own reactions to the task experience (attitude change, frustration, GSR).

The means by which particular responses are translated into particular outcomes are what we have termed process-outcome links. These, it will be recalled, are those aspects of the task or the situation which determine what outcomes result from various behaviors on the part of the performer. The payoff matrix in the experimental game and the rule in the concept-formation task described earlier both are examples of process-outcome links which are based in the task itself.

The framework suggests that after a trial outcome has been obtained (whether explicitly or via a covert trial-and-error sequence), some evaluation of this outcome is made. The source of this evaluation may be either the person, the system in which the performance is taking place, or both. Examples of system evaluation would be the appearance of the correct pattern of lights on a panel in a board-wiring task, or a communication from a supervisor that one's job performance was not adequate. Personal evaluation is merely the degree to which the performer feels that the particular trial outcome is "good enough," regardless of whether or not any evidence of system evaluation is present. If there is no system evaluation, the decision as to when any given trial output will be accepted as final output is strictly a function of the subject's evaluation. When there is system evaluation, it may be all-encompassing (for instance, no outcome is successful until all five lamps are lighted), or it may operate in conjunction with personal evaluation (such as, "You may stop when you feel that you have lighted as many of the five lamps as you possibly can").

If evaluation is negative, the task performance process is seen in the framework as recycling back to the hypothesis box, where the subject

---

[8] It should be noted that a trial outcome need not exist for every task. For example, if a performer were permitted only one attempt at solution and the task conditions were arranged so as to insure that this solution resulted directly from his *first* approach to the task, the notion of a trial outcome would not be necessary. However, it is difficult to imagine a task in which even covert trial and error processes are completely ruled out so as to eliminate the possibility of *any* trial outcomes.

presumably will try something different to see if he can improve his trial outcome. If evaluation is positive, the trial outcome will become the final outcome and the performance sequence will terminate.[9]

This concludes our discussion of problems and issues associated with attempts to develop means of dealing with tasks systematically. Subsequent sections will draw on the proposals made and conclusions reached here in an attempt to further understanding of performance under conditions of stress.

TASK PERFORMANCE UNDER STRESS: SOME IMPLICATIONS OF THE FRAMEWORK

Human reactions to stressful situations are complex. They represent a tangled net of physiological, psychological and social responses which, at times, seem to defy analysis. As Lazarus (1964, p. 410) has pointed out, progress toward understanding the dynamics of behavior under stress is not likely to be achieved by simple and repeated stimulus-response experiments:

> The theoretical and methodological problems inherent in the field of psychological stress will never be solved merely by repeated demonstrations that this or that condition will result in a blood chemistry effect, a change in affect, or an autonomic nervous system reaction—unless at the same time attention is given to the psychological processes involved, and to the empirical conditions which identify these processes.

The framework proposed in the previous section represents one way of conceptualizing some of the psychological processes associated with task performance. To the extent that researchers induce stress conditions by means of changes in tasks or task characteristics, they would seem obliged to look "inside" a framework such as this in order to make progress in sorting out the several kinds of cognitive and behavioral variations which may be associated with the inductions. This position implies that it is not enough to know, say, that increasing task load increases performance variability, or that dealing with threatening stimulus materials decreases the riskiness of decisions. Rather, for more complete understanding of how persons react to stressful situations, data are required on how these input-output changes come about; that is, whether the results are caused by particular kinds of task redefinitions, particular ways of forming behavioral hypotheses, or what. Thus, the framework should be useful both in interpreting and comparing past research on stress, and in programing future research in such a way that the *why*

---

[9] The general process suggested here is similar to the "Test-Operate-Test-Exit" (TOTE) unit proposed by Miller, Galanter, and Pribram (1960).

and *how* of substantive results can better be ascertained. In the following paragraphs, some of these possibilities will be explored.

The Importance of the Redefinition Process

One of the themes which has been prominent in discussions of psychological stress is the importance of the person's perception or appraisal of the objective environment in understanding individual reactions to objective stress. As Lazarus (1964) notes regarding psychological threat:

> The threat is not simply out there as an attribute of the stimulus. Rather, it depends for its threat value on this appraisal process, which in turn depends upon the person's beliefs about what the stimulus means for the thwarting of motives of importance to him [p. 404].

The framework proposed here recognizes the importance of the appraisal process for performance situations involving task-based stress, in that the redefined task is seen as mediating between the objective task and the hypotheses which the performer makes about how he ought to proceed. This redefinition is viewed as an interaction between the objective task and the characteristics of the person; identical objective-task stressors may result in quite different levels of experienced stress for different individuals. The relative impact of the personal component of the interaction may vary according to the nature of the task or situation. For example, if an objective task is high on ambiguity (a common task-based dimension of stress), and if the performers have a divergence of needs, values, and prior task experiences (which will usually be the case), considerably more interindividual performance variability should be expected—because of the redefinition process—on this task than on one which is low on ambiguity.

The redefinition process may be especially potent in another variety of stress research—those studies in which the *stimuli* are threatening or frightening to the subject. In these cases, we would expect that the nature of the objective stimulus situation might arouse subjects' mechanisms of perceptual defense to a greater degree than would more innocuous stimulus material. Here again, the result might be a greater variance among subjects' redefined tasks (and by implication, greater performance variability among subjects) than would have been obtained for tasks involving nonthreatening stimuli. The mechanisms suggested by these two examples may help to explain the common finding that performance variance increases under conditions of stress.

Although stress researchers generally agree on the importance of the redefined or appraised environment in determining a person's reactions to a supposedly stressful task or situation, just how redefinition should be dealt with conceptually and methodologically remains unclear. There are, for example, substantial methodological difficulties associated with attempts to measure and directly manipulate a person's cognitive appraisal of a situation, as Mechanic (Chapter 7) points out:

> It appears that if stress study must depend on measuring the individual's appraisal processes, then we find ourselves in a bind similar to the one that has handicapped subjective approaches for so long. The idea of differential cognitive approaches in reactions to stress is useful if we successfully develop techniques for manipulating appraisal processes experimentally . . . but my impression is that such manipulations are relatively limited in their scope and applicability. If prediction is an important motivation for building models of stress, it appears necessary to make perceptual variations subsidiary to the central core of stress models.

These views lead Mechanic to suggest increased use of objective characteristics of tasks and situations which can be more easily and rigorously measured. This is an emphasis that this writer would find hard to dispute—given the essentially objective nature of the task-qua-task approach to task definition and description proposed in this paper. Nevertheless, the view presented here has been that, although the objective approach does provide highly important real-world referents for concepts and variables, the approach probably cannot be of much help in ascertaining the dynamics or the "how" of reactions to stress.

The major difficulty surrounding the use of cognitive concepts (for example, "appraisal," "redefinition") is, as Mechanic notes, essentially a methodological one. It is the view of this writer that such methodological problems ought not to determine the substantive directions which stress research takes, at least not until they have proved themselves insurmountable. Two researchers (Lazarus et al., 1962; Graham et al., 1962) cited by Mechanic have developed techniques for manipulating the appraisal process experimentally. This fact provides a basis for some optimism about the possibility of overcoming the substantial methodological difficulties associated with the use of cognitive states in stress research.

Part of the difficulty of dealing with concepts such as appraisal and redefinition may derive from the tendency to consider these cognitive states as inputs to models of stress and, to some extent, to research designs. The framework proposed here suggests that it is more appropriate to consider the redefinition of objective tasks as a part of the performance process itself. This process is seen as beginning with a task and a performer, with cognitive redefinition resulting from the interaction between these two inputs.

Viewing redefinition as a stage of performance rather than as an input yields some advantages: performers and objective tasks can be described more efficiently and reliably than can redefined tasks, and relatively stable conceptual "anchors" for the beginning of the performance process are provided. In addition, study of the redefinition phenomenon itself may be facilitated, as will be suggested below.

Consider a hypothetical experiment in which a subject is given an information handling task in which the rate of stimulus presentation is very high. For subjects with low ability to handle cognitive material, a syndrome of behavior is observed which can be described as ego-defensive: making an elaborate show of not caring about the task, and purposely mishandling some of the data to show that poor performance derived from a lack of desire to perform the task, not a lack of ability. Now consider a second experiment. An individual is given a task which requires him to assist in moving human cadavers in a city morgue. In this situation, some subjects who have high measured anxiety about death and little experience with death-situations are seen frequently talking in loud voices about irrelevant matters, making gross jokes about the cadavers, and generally behaving in a manner designed to convince others that this job does not bother them at all.

Although the tasks in the two examples given above are quite different, in both cases some subjects are found to engage in ego-defensive behavior. Because we know *both* the input factors (the nature of the task and certain attributes of the person) and the task behavior (acting ego-defensively), we are in a position to make inferences about the presence and nature of a common redefinition process which may mediate between the input and output states. For the examples given above, it seems likely that the tasks in both situations were appraised as threatening to those subjects who exhibited ego-defensive behavior. In the first case, a low-ability subject would soon realize that the stimulus was being presented at a faster rate than he was able to handle, and that he would fail the task. So threatened, he might attempt to find a way of behaving which, although it would not prevent him from failing, would at least protect his ego in the failure situation. The second task would be threatening to a person with little familiarity with death or cadavers, not because of intellective or motor factors as in the first example, but because of the test it makes of the subject's ability to deal with an emotional strain, and he also might attempt to behave in a manner which would not reveal his difficulty in dealing with the anxiety-arousing task.

Thus, the redefinition process has assumed the status of an intervening variable, which can be studied by systematic variation of input states and assessment of output states. When, as in the example, different experimental manipulations yield similar patterns of behavior, it can be hypothesized that a common redefinition process may be mediating both relationships. Based on the characteristics of the substantive variables involved, speculations about the nature of this presumed common process can be made, and testable predictions about additional input states which should give rise to the mediating process can be generated.

A recent study by Opton and Lazarus (1967) examines the interaction between the task and the performer in a stress situation, and is suggestive of additional analyses along the lines discussed above. A group of undergraduate students were given two tasks (in counterbalanced order): one was to watch a film of three "rather harrowing" accidents in a sawmill, of which the latter two could be anticipated by the subjects before they occurred; the other was to experience an electric shock which was to occur at the conclusion of a series of seven audible clicks presented at five-second intervals. In both tasks, the source of stress was in the stimulus materials which were ultimately presented to the subjects. During the waits for the presentation of these materials, the subjects experienced increasing levels of arousal.

In both situations, stress was assumed to inhere in anticipation threat —waiting for the bloody accident to occur in one case, and waiting for the shock to occur in the other. Nevertheless, using an ipsative strategy, the authors were able to identify two distinct groups of individuals within the subject population; one group responded more strongly to the motion picture experience, the other responded more strongly to the shock experience. Subjects responding relatively more strongly to the film described themselves as "lacking in impulse expression, socially inhibited, introverted, submissive, suggestible, obedient, insecure, passive, anxious, and not caring about friends." Subjects responding relatively more strongly to the threat of shock described themselves in opposite terms. Although this finding further substantiates the importance of the performer-task interaction in determining responses to stress, it also has implications for further research on the redefinition process itself.

Why did one group of subjects respond relatively more strongly to the film and the other more strongly to the threat of shock? It may be that the film was in fact a more threatening stimulus to one group and the shock more threatening to another because of the different configurations of personal attributes which characterized the two groups. Since the Opton and Lazarus study provides information on the modal personal characteristics of the groups, it is possible to speculate as to why they may have differentially redefined the task stimulus materials so as to render them differentially threatening. Let us briefly pursue one possible hypothesis, and suggest some research which might be done to test it.

The group which responded relatively more strongly to the film presentation consisted basically of people who described themselves as oriented inwardly; they were passive, inhibited, introverted, submissive, and so forth. These individuals may have been indicating that they probably would not be comfortable in a socially live, give-and-take, risky, real-world situation. Fantasy may play an important role in their lives, perhaps substituting for actual life experiences when there are high levels of fright, risk, or excitement involved. Thus, these individuals may have developed a style of strong personal response to fantasy situations, based on a life history in which affectively "strong" data were treated on the level of fantasy.

The electric shock, on the other hand, is a highly personal, "here-and-now" experience; the shock, when it comes, is felt, not imagined. The individuals in the second group described themselves as being relatively extroverted, dominant, active, and generally involved in real-world matters. They may have developed a personal style which would lead them to respond more strongly to this real-life situation than to the more imaginary, fantasy-world experience represented by the motion picture.

If these speculations about why the two groups responded differently to the two tasks have any validity, then these two groups ought to differ in other kinds of stress situations which are quite different from the manipulations of the Opton and Lazarus study but which maintain the distinction between the fantasy world and the real world. A bargaining situation in which two individuals must work out a division of labor on a series of tasks, some of which are very attractive and some of which are highly distasteful, might provide an appropriate setting for this kind of experiment. In one condition, the subjects would bargain directly with another person about whom they had considerable personal information; in the other, communication would be through messages transmitted by note and the other party could be completely unknown to the subject. The latter condition should permit considerably more room for fantasy experiences about the other person and about the bargaining process than the former. If so, and if the stakes in the bargaining were sufficiently important to engender a state of arousal in the subjects, we would expect subjects similar to the fantasy group in the Opton and Lazarus study to respond relatively more strongly in the indirect communication condition, and subjects similar to the Opton and Lazarus real-world group to respond relatively more strongly in the direct munication condition.[10] Finally, it would seem appropriate to interview the subjects about their perceptions of the task, the other party, and the bargaining process, since these data could provide direct indications of the kinds of task redefinitions made by the two groups of subjects. Given the limitations of verbal reports of cognitive states, it would be important to attempt to corroborate the self-report data with the obtained behavioral measures. Nevertheless, even apparently inconsistent interview data could

---

[10] It should be noted that the concern here is with the *relative* strength of response of the two groups in each of the conditions, not the absolute level of response. It is not unlikely that all subjects would experience the direct confrontation as more stressful than the indirect one.

be helpful in calling attention to previously overlooked variables which might be important in understanding the redefinition process.

The extended and speculative discussion above represents, of course, only one possible means of going about investigating the redefinition of task stressors. Its intent was not to recommend the particular approach which has been described. Instead, the discussion has been an attempt to suggest by example that just because the redefinition of task stressors is a cognitive phenomenon, its study does not have to be outside the realm of experimental investigation.

The Central Role of Behavioral Hypotheses

The framework presented in Figure 13–1 suggests that after individuals in a task-performance situation have redefined the objective task, they develop some hypotheses about what kinds of behavior are appropriate or desirable for that task. These hypotheses are viewed in the framework as: (1) being strongly influenced by the task input, and (2) having a direct impact on the behavior which subsequently is emitted and the outcome which ultimately is obtained. For example, if subjects in an experimental game are told that their goal is to beat the other players, quite different hypotheses about behavioral strategy probably would be developed—and thus quite different behavior exhibited—than if they are told to "work together so everyone does as well as he can."[11]

Few experimental studies have directly addressed the question of how individuals develop particular behavioral strategies in response to tasks and situations. If there are common "types" of behavioral strategies which are usually employed by subjects for certain kinds of tasks, this lack of information is unfortunate: we may be missing the opportunity to make relatively compact descriptions of how individuals react to different types of task-based stress. It might be, for example, that individuals under one type of stress commonly adopt a strategy of attack, while individuals under stress of another kind tend to adopt a strategy of escape. If we could specify the characteristics of those tasks and situations which give rise to these different kinds of hypotheses about strategy (and if we better understood their behavioral consequences), study of the onset and consequences of stress could be made considerably more efficient and systematic.

The research program of Steiner (see Chapter 10) demonstrates the usefulness and relevance of studying the behavioral strategies of in-

---

[11] This general kind of manipulation is often used to induce "conflict" in experimental subjects, and is frequently interpreted as a form of social-psychological stress.

dividuals under stress. Steiner has focused on stress which is produced when a person discovers that his own views on some matter are contradicted by those of a peer whom he respects. He specifies four predominant strategies for stress reduction in this situation:

> The individual may adjust his own opinions to agree with the associate's judgments (conform), reject the associate as a person who is less competent than he was originally thought to be, devaluate the importance of the issue about which disagreements have occurred, or under-recall the frequency or extent of the disagreements.

Steiner has found that different individuals tend to rely on different behavioral strategies in the stress situations he has studied, and that preferences among the four strategies are related to the personality characteristics of the individuals. This finding fits well with the implication of the present framework that the nature of behavioral hypotheses depends on the interaction between task characteristics and personal characteristics.

Steiner has not investigated strategy selection in situations other than that of interpersonal conflict, and it is apparent that other kinds of strategies would be appropriate in other task situations. For example, the strategy of physical attack is obviously inappropriate for Steiner's interpersonal-disagreement situation, and the strategy of conformity used by some of Steiner's subjects is not meaningful for individuals watching a frightening motion picture.

A brief examination of the stress literature has suggested the existence of at least four general types of behavioral strategy for dealing with stress. For each of the general types, several specific forms of response were identified, which presumably would be differentially useful in different situations. The forms of response within the four groups may or may not cluster empirically, and they undoubtedly are not exhaustive; they are presented here only to illustrate the kinds of hypotheses which subjects seem to generate about appropriate behavior under stress, and to suggest that it may be possible for the same general type of response to appear in various forms to "fit" different task or situational demands.

One category of strategies is characterized by an explicit movement against the stressful situation or its agent, or against some substitute target. Included are aggression, attack, hostility, and Steiner's strategy of rejecting the competence of one's partner. A second category is nearly the opposite of the first, and is characterized by movement *away* from the source of stress. Included are strategies of avoidance, withdrawal, resignation, inaction, and escape, and perhaps Steiner's "devaluate" strategy. The third category subsumes submissive and/or collaborative movement toward the source of difficulty. Included are ingratiation, cooperation, and Steiner's conformity. The final category is a distortion of the situation, and involves processes which are generally ego-defensive. This category includes most of the traditional psychological defense mechanisms. Some of these mechanisms in themselves may not be conscious strategy choices (for example, subjects probably do not consciously choose to under-recall an upsetting experience). Instances of these strategies found in the literature include blame assignment, reaction formation, denial, intellectualization, displacement, and Steiner's under-recall.

Additional work toward systematizing general behavioral strategies such as these, and toward identification of the task and personal characteristics which lead an individual to hypothesize that one or the other of them will be the "best" for him in a particular stress situation would seem to carry much potential for developing additional insights into stress behavior.

How Task-based Stress Affects the Performance Process

One of the most common and important functions which tasks serve in stress research is as a means for inducing stress in experimental subjects. This state of affairs in the laboratory parallels life in the real world: many tasks are performed each day by almost everyone, and associated with many of these tasks is some degree of stress.

In this section we will examine those points of the task performance process (as conceptualized by the framework in Figure 13–1) at which task-based stress influences the direction of behavior. Three different types of influence will be suggested, and some inferences about the kinds of behavioral reactions they may imply will be made.

The explicit and implicit demands of the objective task itself represent one of the ways tasks influence behavior. This kind of effect is called influence through hypothesis control. The name was selected because the first conscious response a performer makes to a new task invariably is an attempt to decide how to go about dealing with it—or in terms of the framework, to formulate some hypotheses about strategy. Thus, to the extent that performers typically generate, say, hypotheses X and Y— but not hypotheses W and Z—about how they should respond to a particular task, that task is affecting their behavior through what we are calling hypothesis control.

Frequently it is the instructional aspects of the task which affect the performer's hypotheses. If instructions are sufficiently detailed and explicit, the appropriate behavioral hypotheses are, in effect, dictated to the performer. For example, there is little doubt about the nature of the appropriate hypotheses for a task which contains these instructions: "First, take the bolt from the red bin with your left hand, and the nut from the blue bin with your right hand. Then, move your right hand horizontally toward the left hand until the nut touches the threaded end of the bolt." On the other hand, a task such as "Fix this radio" leaves virtually all of the responsibility for hypothesis generation to the performer. Tasks with very detailed instructions (as in the former example) should lead to more uniform performance across individuals, since they leave less room for individual differences to affect the kinds of hypotheses which are generated. Tasks similar to the latter example might be expected to generate more involvement and motivation on the part of the performer, since he has considerably more responsibility for formulating the behavioral hypotheses he will use.

Although the discussion above focuses on the relationship between explicit instructions and hypothesis generation, it should be noted that tasks can influence performers' behavioral hypotheses by implicit demands as well. Consider, for example, a task with very straightforward and innocuous instructions (for example, "Draw a sketch of what you are looking at right now"). If the stimulus material for this task is frightening or otherwise threatening to the performer (if what is being "looked at" is a number of uncaged snakes on the floor), the hypotheses which are generated probably will have nothing to do with drawing an adequate sketch, but will focus instead on possibilities for escaping the situation. Although the explicit demands of the task are, in this case, ignored, the task still affects behavior by influencing the performer's behavioral hypotheses.

It appears from the above discussion that task-based stress may operate through hypothesis control in at least two ways. First, a task may give rise to hypotheses about appropriate behavior which are either threatening or otherwise unacceptable to the performer, resulting in experienced stress. This can occur via explicit demands of the task (that is, the task in effect dictates the unacceptable behaviors), or via more subtle or implicit demands (that is, hypotheses are generated by the performer but they imply behaviors which are threatening or unacceptable to him). Secondly, stress may be induced by the very lack of explicit instructions. When the task provides few or no clear cues about what should be done (for instance, a task high on ambiguity), performers may have difficulty developing criteria for choosing among a large number of possible hypotheses—or they may not be able to generate any relevant hypotheses whatever. In either case, experienced stress may be the result.

Finally, let us examine how performers may react to task-based stress which has been introduced through hypothesis control. Whether the source of the stress lies in the demands of the task or in the fact that there are no clear demands, performers may react by generating hypotheses about how to *adapt* to the stressful situation. Thus, hypotheses aimed at coping successfully with the performer's feelings of stress may largely replace hypotheses about how to perform the task. And such redirection of planning away from the task will, of course, usually result in a decrement in performance effectiveness.

Tasks also can influence behavior in ways which bypass the hypotheses a performer develops about behavioral strategy by effecting changes in the performer himself. One important type of such direct impact is through changes in the *arousal level* of the performer. Performance is indirectly affected by the changed level of arousal, since this factor is among those which affect the actual "process" of behavior in the performance sequence.

There is some evidence to suggest that the main behavioral effect of having an optimally high level of activation is to increase the attentiveness and perceptual- and response-readiness of the performer. If this is so, then simply being optimally aroused per se probably would not lead directly to substantial changes in a performer's observable behavior. Instead, it should enhance the ability of the performer to attend to and react to other aspects of the situation or task so as to increase the magnitude of any behavioral effects which may be associated with them. A performer might, for example, be more sensitive to subtle task demands; this could affect the kinds of behavioral hypotheses which he would generate.

When arousal is at a nonoptimal level—that is, either especially high or especially low—performers frequently report experiencing stress. For example, Weick (see Chapter 16) has suggested that stimulus intensity is both a common and an important source of psychological stress. When the magnitude of stimulation is very great, regardless of the source of the stimulation or the nature of the surrounding situation, people seem to feel uncomfortable and stressed. Low levels of stimulation (or the absence of stimulation) also are stressful. Scott (1967) has shown that when tasks are dull, repetitive, and familiar, individuals will experience uncomfortably low levels of arousal. Performers frequently react to this state of affairs by engaging in behaviors designed to increase their stimulus inputs, usually with unfortunate consequences for performance effectiveness.

The third means by which task stressors can affect behavior is through what we will call influence through control of process-outcome links, or, more briefly, *process-outcome control*. It will be recalled that process-outcome links mediate between actual behavior and the outcomes which result from this behavior. The magnitude of behavioral effects associated with these links must be nearly zero as a person begins a task, and probably grows over time to become the most important of the three kinds of task-based influence. At the outset of a performance period, those characteristics of a task which are obviously a part of the objective task itself will have a very strong impact on behavior; no behavior has yet been emitted, and thus the performer can have no firsthand knowledge about the nature of the link between what he does and what outcomes he obtains. Thus, as the performance process begins, a substantial portion of the behavioral variance will be controlled by those aspects of the task which lead subjects to make particular kinds of hypotheses about what they ought to do. As performance continues over time with the task (or with similar tasks), however, the performer learns what outcomes result from particular patterns of behavior, and he finds, perhaps, that he can change his outcomes by changing his behavior. What he is doing over time is learning the nature of the process-outcome links. Since the existence and nature of these links are determined through the performer's own personal experience, they are likely to assume increasing potency as performance continues. Ultimately, the performer may base his behavior entirely on what he has learned about the process-outcome links, virtually ignoring the demands of the objective task.

One type of stress frequently induced in experimental subjects through process-outcome control is failure stress. When a task is "wired" so that no matter what behaviors are emitted by a performer, an unsatisfactory outcome is obtained (as is the case for insolvable problems and for true dilemmas), the performer necessarily will experience failure. For example, Kissel (1965) gave subjects a perceptual-reasoning task consisting of five line drawings which were to be traced without lifting the pencil from the paper or retracing a line. The problems were insolvable and successfully induced a state of failure stress in the subjects. Feather (1966) has used a series of insolvable anagrams for much the same purpose.

Another way in which stress can be induced through process-outcome control is for the nature of the process-outcome links to be *changed* during the performance process. For example, Palermo (1957) used a task in which subjects were required to pair stimulus lights to buttons (which turned off the lights). Midway through the experiment (and unknown to the subjects), the task was changed in such a way that two of the lights needed re-pairing with buttons. Thus, the process-outcome links which the subjects had learned no longer were applicable. Ross, Rupel, and Grant (1952) gave subjects a concept-formation task in which, unknown to the subjects, the stimuli were to be sorted according to color until ten correct responses had been obtained; at this point, the sort was to be based on form, and finally the basis was changed to number of elements. The subjects were not told that the "rules" were changed at any time in the task, and the only outcomes they obtained were the experimenter's comments of "right" and "wrong." Finally, Hamblin (1958) studied crisis in a social situation by changing the rules during a golf-shooting game. Each time a correct rule was discovered by the players (through trial and error) another rule was changed, insuring that the process-outcome links remained obscure throughout the experiment.

Stress induced through manipulation of process-outcome links is considerably different from the two types discussed previously, in that there need be nothing in the task which is initially presented to the performer which appears stressful to him. Thus, we might expect that the impact of stress on the performance process would be initially "softer" when it is induced through control of process-outcome links than when it is based in the actual task materials presented to the performer at the outset of the performance period. For this reason, inductions of stress through process-outcome control could prove to be particularly useful in studies of the onset and development of stress. In such applications, the physiological and cognitive reactions of performers could be continuously monitored as they gradually came to realize that their behavior was ineffectual in obtaining the kind of outcomes to which they aspired, and the impact of this realization on subsequent performance strategy and behavior could be assessed. Further, researchers interested in failure stress could, by using process-outcome control techniques, avoid some of the difficulties in the usual manipulations of failure (for example, by communicating false norms or by simply asserting that the subject had failed). These latter strategies are "all-at-once" information inputs which may not fit with the subjects' perceptions of their performance, and which are mostly irrelevant to the task performance itself. In process-outcome control, the stress grows out of the subjects' task experiences and thus is likely to be both more meaningful and more realistic to them.

TOWARD A TAXONOMY OF TASK-BASED STRESSORS

In this section we will attempt some beginning steps toward a taxonomy of task-based stressors. The taxonomy is relevant mainly to those task characteristics present (and visible to the performer) during the performance sequence. Such task-qua-task characteristics represent the most frequent means by which task stress is induced in experimental subjects in laboratory and field settings. Task stressors which operate mainly through process-outcome control will not be discussed further here.

One facet which will be useful in differentiating among the task-qua-task stressors is the aspect of the task which gives rise to the stress experience. In the task definition presented earlier in this paper, three such aspects were identified: the stimulus materials, the instructions about operations, and the instructions about goals. There is no a priori reason to expect that the kinds of task effects which derive from these different aspects of the task will operate in the same or even in comparable ways. Consider, for example, the task stressor ambiguity. Although some effects of ambiguity might be comparable for the stimulus and the instructional aspects of the tasks, certainly not all of them would be. In one case, the stimulus materials with which a subject was to work might be perfectly clear and straightforward but the instructions about what he was to do highly obscure and ambiguous. The subject probably would react to this situation quite differently than he would to one in which the instructions about what to do were very clear but the stimulus materials were ambiguous. Similar kinds of differences in reactions to changes in a single task dimension with respect to different aspects of the task might be obtained for other task-based inductions of stress as well. To the extent that the two aspects of tasks do imply differential subject reactions, we must be careful to specify which aspect of the task we are dealing with— and, indeed, to make sure we realize just what is being manipulated and what is not.

The second facet which will be utilized in the taxonomy of task stressors is the substantive type of stress involved. A review of the stress literature has yielded three very general substantive types of stress which frequently have been induced through manipulation of task characteristics:

1. *Time sequencing.* Especially high or low rates of information processing or response are required by the task.
2. *Complexity-interpretability.* Especially high or low levels of complexity or ambiguity are present in the task.
3. *Threat or punishment.* The task requires or strongly implies that the performer will or may have to endure some form of physical or psychological punishment.

A tentative taxonomy of task-qua-task stressors, based on these two facets, is presented in Table 13–1. The taxonomy is partitioned first according to the three substantive "types" of task-stress which have been identified, and second (within each type) according to the aspects of the task which may be utilized in the induction of stress. Examples of typical stress inductions are provided within each substantive type-task aspect combination.[12]

Stress occurs for the first two substantive categories (that is, time sequencing and complexity-interpretability) at both especially high and especially low levels of intensity. Thus, for example, while too rapid a rate of stimulus presentation in an information processing task is stressful, so is too slow a rate. The same is true for response rates. Several

---

[12] Not all aspects of tasks are included for each substantive type of stress; when a particular task aspect was found to be not appropriate or not relevant with respect to a substantive type, it was excluded from the taxonomy. Also, it should be noted that characteristics of the instructions themselves are included as aspects of the task, as well as the characteristics of the actual operations and goals which are specified by the instructions. As will be seen below, for some stressors, the stress may reside in the instructions about "what to do" as much as in the actual "doings" of performance.

TABLE 13–1 A Tentative Taxonomy of Task-Qua-Task Stressors

Time sequencing
1. Of stimuli
   a. high rate of presentation
   b. low (or constant) rate of presentation
2. Of operations specified in instructions
   a. high rate of response
   b. low rate of response (or no response)
   c. inappropriate time limit
   d. repetitive response

Complexity-Interpretability
1. Of stimuli
   a. high complexity
   b. high ambiguity/low interpretability
   c. low discriminability
2. Of instructions themselves
   a. high complexity
   b. high ambiguity/low interpretability
3. Of operations specified in instructions
   a. high complexity
   b. extreme simplicity
   c. low variety/high repetitiveness
4. Of goals specified in instructions
   a. ambiguity of nature of goal
   b. ambiguity as to when goal is achieved

Threat or Punishment: Physical and Psychological
1. Of stimuli
   a. threatening
   b. punishing
2. Of operations specified in instructions
   a. threatening
   b. punishing
3. Of goals specified in instructions
   a. threatening
   b. punishing

---

studies (for example, Usdansky & Chapman, 1960; Kurz, 1964; Palermo, 1957) have studied the effects of instructions which emphasize the importance of rapid response rates, and Scott (1966) includes in his review a discussion of the apparently stressful effects of tasks which limit the frequency or rate of task-relevant responses that can be made by the subject.

There are substantial numbers of studies which examine the effects of the complexity-interpretability of task stimulus materials on performance and personal reactions, although in some of these the complexity-interpretability manipulation is not dealt with conceptually as stress. For example, Hokanson and Burgess (1964) varied task complexity by presenting subjects with four, eight, sixteen, or thirty-two digit symbol pairs, modified from the Wechsler Adult Intelligence Scale (WAIS) Digit Symbol Subtest. Studies by Bluhm and Kennedy (1965), Johnson (1963), and Murphy (1959), all utilize geometric discrimination tasks, for which the experience of stress derives from the performer's difficulty in making adequate discriminations.

Pepinsky, Pepinsky, and Pavlik (1960) have provided data on *instructional* complexity-interpretability through the use of assembly tasks which were either simple or operationally complex. The opposite pole of the continuum has been addressed by Geitwitz (1966), who induced a high (and apparently stressful) level of boredom by giving subjects a task which required them to make checks on a piece of paper over a relatively long period of time. This task combined the presumably stress-producing effects of extreme simplicity, low variety, and high repetitiveness.

The last substantive type of stress (physical and psychological: threat or punishment) appears to require relatively more information about the nature of the performer population to determine the stressfulness of a given task, because what is highly threatening or punishing to one performer may not affect another so strongly. Nevertheless, the stress literature indicates that there are many kinds of threats and punishments which seem to be stressful to such substantial numbers of people that they may be considered intrinsically stressful, and on this basis they are included in the taxonomy.

A study by Capretta and Berkun (1962) provides an example of a task in which the stimulus material is physically threatening. In this experiment, subjects were required to run across a three-rope toggle bridge, some 200 feet long and 50 feet above the ground. Clearly, this stimulus situation was more threatening to the subjects than the control situation, which consisted of a "short, mock bridge," 1 foot off the ground. The pervasive dimension of stimulus intensity discussed by Weick (see Chapter 16) may partly fall into the physical-threat category as well: as stimulation becomes extremely intense and overloads a person's receptors, physical pain usually is experienced. To the extent that there is also psychological punishment associated with intense stimulation (as is often the case), stimulus intensity should serve as a "double-barreled" stressor and might give rise to especially pronounced reactions.

Operations and goals specified in task instructions, as well as the stimulus material, can give rise to experiences of physical threat or punishment, although examples in the literature are scarce. A task which involves innocuous stimulus materials but that is physically threatening, for example, might require an individual to drive a car at high speeds down a road with many curves. Neither the car nor the road (the stimulus materials) would be considered stressful by themselves; but physical threat would derive from the instructions to "drive fast" in this situation. Finally, a task which would involve physically threatening goals might be one which requires a subject to determine by trial and error the correct setting of a series of electrical switches—with success being achieved when the subject received a strong electric shock as a result of his switch manipulations.

Several studies involve task stimulus materials which may be said to carry implications of psychological threat or punishment. In a study by Ainsworth (1958), subjects were told (as part of the stress induction) that a test which they were taking was especially important, because it was "related to academic success." Because failure on such a test would be quite disturbing to a group of students, the test presumably became more threatening as a result of this manipulation. Similarly, Beckwith, Iverson, and Reuder (1965) utilized an upcoming examination as a discussion topic among college students on the (apparently justified) assumption that the topic would be intrinsically anxiety arousing for these subjects.

There are relatively few studies in the literature which deal directly with psychological threat or punishment which is inherent in the operations or goals specified in the task instructions. An example of a task in which stress is inherent in operations would be one in which a subject was instructed to scrape his fingernails repeatedly across a blackboard. The stimulus materials are innocuous, and no *physical* threat or punishment is involved in this simple task, but many persons find the experience quite difficult to handle emotionally and become quite upset by it. Weick (see Chapter 16) suggests a task in which the stress inheres in the goal specified by the task. The subject is simply asked to blow up a balloon until it breaks. The goal—having the balloon break while it is still being blown up—is upsetting to most people, but neither the stimulus materials nor the operations are in themselves stressful.

Although the task characteristics and dimensions discussed above are not specified "operationally" (that is, the actual experimental operations involved in specifying the values of the tasks on the dimensions are not indicated), they have been treated in relatively "molecular" terms. Thus, instead of utilizing broad concepts such as "difficulty" (as is done by some of the researchers cited), terms such as "complexity" and "interpretability" and "discriminability" were used and applied to specific aspects of the task, such as the stimuli or the instructions. This was done both because it was felt that the more molecular terms would communicate the general category of operations used to specify the concept with less surplus meaning than would broader terms, and because in many cases the broader terms involve more than one aspect of the task. It is possible to use this latter feature and describe many relatively "molar" task stressors in terms of the more specific terms used in the taxonomy presented above. For example, a difficult task could be one in which a subject was required to make discriminations (instruction about operations) regarding ambiguous stimuli (characteristic of the stimulus materials) in a short time (instruction about operations). A risky task could be one which requires a subject to *make decisions* (instruction about operations) which could result in physically (or psychologically) harmful outcomes (characteristics of goals). Finally, a task with intrinsic conflict could require a subject to make choices (instruction about operations) among equally attractive alternatives (characteristics of stimulus materials).

Further, the patterns of behavior which are obtained in response to task-based stress may depend partly on both (1) the aspect of the task which gives rise to the stress (that is, the stimulus materials or the instructions), and (2) the substantive type of stress involved (time-sequencing, complexity-interpretability, or threat-punishment). If this is so, these characteristics of task stressors should be carefully specified in research, since there are many ways tasks can be difficult or risky or conflict-laden, and there is no *a priori* reason to assume that broad constructs such as these are psychologically unitary. Only when it is determined that the empirical relationships between some molar task state (such as difficulty) and behavior are similar regardless of which molecular task characteristics are used in defining or manipulating that state, should the impact of the molar state be discussed in causal terms. The taxonomy of task stressors presented above encompasses most of the ways relatively molecular task characteristics have been used in the creation of stressful states. Thus, by facilitating identification and comparison of similar patterns of task-behavior relationships, it may provide a basis for the identification of important general constructs for describing stress inductions.

TASKS AND SITUATIONS: A CONCLUDING COMMENT

Tasks are ubiquitous in stress research, and they are important; they make differences in the ways performers respond, differences which we do not understand very well at present. What I have tried to do in this paper is to examine some literature on tasks and stress, to suggest some distinctions, and to make some speculations which may be helpful in paving the way toward bettering our understanding of tasks, task characteristics, and their effects in stressful situations.

Yet what we are really studying is neither tasks nor stress per se, but *situations*. The task is just one aspect of the general situation which confronts a performer, whether he is under stress or not. And, as Mechanic (see Chapter 7) notes, it is important that we study those who do not feel challenged in presumably stressful situations as well as those who do experience stress. The ultimate payoff of any research on tasks, or on stress, or on tasks in stress situations is the gaining of additional insight into how people perceive and react to the life situations which they experience. Continued research toward this end—regardless of the particular substantive field in which it takes place—will, in the opinion of this writer, be well worth the effort it demands.

References

Ainsworth, L. H. Rigidity, insecurity, and stress. *Journal of Abnormal and Social Psychology*, 1958, **56**, 67–74.

Altman, I. Aspects of the criterion problem in small group research: II. The analysis of group tasks. *Acta Psychologica*, 1966, **25**, 199–221.

Arnoult, M. D. The specification of a "social" stimulus. In S. B. Sells (Ed.), *Stimulus determinants of behavior*. New York: Ronald Press, 1963.

Barker, R. G., & Gump, P. *Big school, small school*. Stanford, Calif.: Stanford University Press, 1964.

Beckwith, J., Iverson, M., & Reuder, M. Test anxiety, task relevance of group experience, and change in level of aspiration. *Journal of Personality and Social Psychology*, 1965, **1**, 579–588.

Bluhm, P. M., & Kennedy, W. A. Discrimination reaction time as a function of incentive-related DRQ anxiety and task difficulty. *Perceptual and Motor Skills*, 1965, **20**, 131–134.

Breer, P. E., & Locke, E. A. *Task experience as a source of attitudes*. Homewood, Ill.: Dorsey, 1965.

Capretta, P. J., & Berkun, M. M. Validity and reliability of certain measures of psychological stress. *Psychological Reports*, 1962, **10**, 875–876.

Cronbach, L. J. The two disciplines of scientific psychology. *American Psychologist*, 1957, **12**, 671–684.

Dulany, D. E. Awareness, rules, and propositional control: A confrontation with S-R behavior theory. In D. L. Horton & T. R. Dixon (Eds.), *Verbal behavior and general behavior theory*. Englewood Cliffs, N. J.: Prentice-Hall, 1968.

Dunnette, M. D. Identification and enhancement of managerial effectiveness. Part II: Research problems and research results in the identification of managerial effectiveness. Richardson Foundation Survey Report, 1966, mimeo.

Feather, N. T. Effects of prior success and failure on expectation of stress and subsequent performance. *Journal of Personality and Social Psychology*, 1966, 3, 237–299.

Ferguson, G. A. On transfer and human ability. *Canadian Journal of Psychology,* 1956, **10**, 121–130.

Gagné, R. M. Human tasks and the classification of behavior. Paper delivered at the Tenth Annual Seminar Series, Psychology in Management, Occupational Research Center, Purdue University, April 1964.

Gagné, R. M. Human problem solving: Internal and external events. In B. Kleinmuntz (Ed.), *Problem solving: Research, method and theory.* New York: Wiley, 1966.

Geitwitz, P. J. Structure of boredom. *Journal of Personality and Social Psychology,* 1966, **3**, 592–600.

Graham, D., et al., Psychological response to the suggestion of attitudes specific for hives and hypertension. *Psychomatic Medicine,* 1962, **24**, 159–169.

Hackman, J. R. Effects of task characteristics on group products. *Journal of Experimental Social Psychology,* 1968, **4**, 162–187.

Hamblin, R. L. Group integration during a crisis. *Human Relations,* 1958, **11**, 67–77.

Hare, A. P. *Handbook of small group research.* New York: The Free Press, 1962.

Hoffman, L. R. Group problem solving. In L. Berkowitz (Ed.), *Advances in experimental social psychology,* Vol. II. New York: Academic Press, 1965.

Hokanson, J. E., & Burgess, J. E. Effects of physiological arousal. *Journal of Abnormal and Social Psychology,* 1964, **68**, 698–702.

Hunt, J. McV. Motivation inherent in information processing and action. In O. J. Harvey (Ed.), *Motivation and social interaction.* New York: Ronald Press, 1963.

Johnson, H. J. Decision making conflict and physiological arousal. *Journal of Abnormal and Social Psychology,* 1963, **67**, 114–124.

Kelley, H. H., Condry, J. C., Jr., Dahlke, A. E., & Hill, A. H. Collective behavior in a simulated panic situation. *Journal of Experimental Social Psychology,* 1965, **1**, 20–54.

Kissel, S. Stress-reducing properties of social stimuli. *Journal of Personality and Social Psychology,* 1965, **2**, 378–384.

Kurz, R. B. Effects of three kinds of stressors on human learning and performance. *Psychological Reports,* 1964, **14**, 161–162.

Lazarus, R. A laboratory approach to the dynamics of psychological stress. *American Psychologist,* 1964, **19**, 400–411.

Lazarus, R., Deese, J., & Osler, S. Review of research on effects of psychological stress upon performance. Research Bulletin 51-28, 1951, Lackland AFB, San Antonio, Tex., Human Resources Research Center.

Lazarus, R. S., Speisman, J. C., Mordkoff, A. M., & Davison, L. A. A laboratory study of psychological stress produced by a motion picture film. *Psychological Monographs,* 1962, **76** (Whole No. 553).

Locke, E. A. Toward a theory of task motivation and incentives. *Organizational Behavior and Human Performance,* 1968, **3**, 157–189.

Lytle, C. W. *Job evaluation methods.* New York: Ronald Press, 1946.

McClelland, D. C., Atkinson, J. W., Clark, R. A., & Lowell, E. L. *The achievement motive.* New York: Appleton, 1953.

McCormick, E. J. Job dimensions: Their nature and possible uses. Paper read at American Psychological Association convention, Chicago, September 1965.

McCormick, E. J., Finn, R. H., & Scheips, C. D. Patterns of job requirements. *Journal of Applied Psychology*, 1957, **41**, 358–364.

McGrath, J. E., & Altman, I. *Small group research: A synthesis and critique of the field.* New York: Holt, Rinehart and Winston, 1966.

Miller, G. A., Galanter, E., & Pribram, K. H. *Plans and the structure of behavior.* New York: Holt, Rinehart and Winston, 1960.

Morris, C. G. Task effects on group interaction. *Journal of Personality and Social Psychology*, 1966, **5**, 545–554.

Murphy, R. E. Effects of threat of shock distraction and task design on performance. *Journal of Experimental Psychology*, 1959, **58**, 134–141.

Opton, E. M., Jr., & Lazarus, R. S. Personality determinants of psycho-physiological response to stress: A theoretical analysis and an experiment. *Journal of Personality and Social Psychology*, 1967, **6**, 291–303.

Orr, D. B. A new method for clustering jobs. *Journal of Applied Psychology*, 1960, **44**, 44–49.

Palermo, D. S. Proactive interference and facilitation as a function of amount of training and stress. *Journal of Experimental Psychology*, 1957, **53**, 293–296.

Pepinsky, H. B., & Pepinsky, P. N. Organization, management strategy, and team productivity. In L. Petrullo & B. M. Bass (Eds.), *Leadership and interpersonal behavior.* New York: Holt, Rinehart and Winston, 1961.

Pepinsky, P., Pepinsky, H., & Pavlik, W. The effects of task complexity and time pressure upon team productivity. *Journal of Applied Psychology*, 1960, **44**, 34–38.

Roby, T. B., & Lanzetta, J. T. Considerations in the analysis of group tasks. *Psychological Bulletin*, 1958, **55**, 88–101.

Ross, B. M., Rupel, J. W., & Grant, D. A. Effects of personal, impersonal and physical stress upon cognitive behavior in a card sorting problem. *Journal of Abnormal and Social Psychology*, 1952, **47**, 546–551.

Rotter, J. B. The role of the psychological situation in determining the direction of human behavior. In M. R. Jones (Ed.), *Nebraska symposium on motivation.* Lincoln, Neb.: University of Nebraska Press, 1955.

Scott, W. E., Jr. Activation theory and task design. *Organizational Behavior and Human Performance*, 1966, **1**, 3–30.

Scott, W. E., Jr. The behavioral consequences of repetitive task design: research and theory. Paper presented at American Psychological Association convention, Washington, D. C., 1967.

Sells, S. B. Dimensions of stimulus situations which account for behavior variance. In S. B. Sells (Ed.), *Stimulus determinants of behavior.* New York: Ronald Press, 1963.

Smock, C. D. The influence of psychological stress on the "intolerance of ambiguity." *Journal of Abnormal and Social Psychology*, 1955, **50**, 177–182.

Steiner, I. D. Models for inferring relationships between group size and potential group productivity. *Behavioral Science*, 1966, **11**, 273–283.

Usdansky, G., & Chapman, L. J. Schizophrenic-like responses in normal subjects under time pressure. *Journal of Abnormal and Social Psychology,* 1960, **60,** 143–146.

Weick, K. E. Laboratory experimentation with organizations. In J. G. March (Ed.), *Handbook of organizations.* Skokie, Ill.: Rand-McNally, 1965.

14

status and conflict: two themes in the study of stress[1]

Robert L. Kahn
John R. P. French, Jr.

INTRODUCTION

The program of research which will be discussed in this paper is, in a sense, an offshoot of earlier studies on factors that influence the effectiveness of large-scale organizations, initiated in the Survey Research Center of the University of Michigan in 1947. The earlier program has been concerned primarily with the ways in which individual behaviors contribute to organizational effectiveness: it asks what the individual can

---

[1] This paper summarizes some of the research in a program of studies on mental health in industry. Colleagues in this work include Sidney Cobb, John R. P. French, Jr., Stanislav Kasl, George Brooks, Jerald G. Bachman, and Robert P. Quinn. The text and materials of this paper are drawn from a number of sources from within the program. Extended quotations and adaptations are made from the following: Cobb & Kasl, 1966; French, 1963; French & Kahn, 1962; Kohn et al., 1964.

do directly or indirectly for the organization. The newer pr
research asks instead what the organization does for (or to) the in

Like all choices of research topics, this one involves a val
ment, in this case one that assumes we already know much about performance or productivity and the ways of attaining these things, but less
about the human costs and benefits involved in our ways of organizing
for production, about the meaning of work, and about the mental and
physical outcomes of organizational life. In short, this newer program is
intended as an environmental approach to mental health. As such, it is
complementary to the more usual approaches of individual counseling
and therapy, which seek the causes of pathology in genetic and historical
terms. It focuses on the effects of contemporary environmental factors on
the mental and physical health of adults, with special emphasis on social
psychological factors in large-scale organizations. Still more specifically,
the program concentrates on the *social* aspect of the work situation—its
relationship to other aspects of the person's life and environment, and its
direct effects on his health.

The scope of the program is broad, and committed to the quantitative
study of problems and variables which appear in several related disciplines, the essential merger being between social psychology and
medicine. This is an oversimplification, of course. A still greater oversimplification, but an instructive one, is to say that social psychology
provides most of the independent variables for the research, and medicine
provides the dependent variables. The research method employed primarily is the quantitative, intensive field study, which has had a parallel
development in epidemiology and in the behavioral sciences. This approach is supplemented by the techniques of biochemistry and physiology,
by the experimental designs which originated in research on small groups,
and by the large-sample procedures of survey research.

APPROACH TO PROGRAM PLANNING

The word *program* has enjoyed marked popularity in the research
vocabulary of the past ten or fifteen years, and in becoming popular it
has become much abused. In this paper the word is meant to convey two
essential ideas: (1) the existence of a general theoretical or perhaps
metatheoretical framework within which explanation is sought and in
terms of which explanation is defined; and (2) the conduct of research
within this framework in such a way that the theoretical relationships
among projects are specified and the research results are cumulative.

The general explanatory framework for our program is represented
in Figure 14–1. The figure specifies immediately the six panels of concepts
which are of concern. The categories of relationships and hypotheses

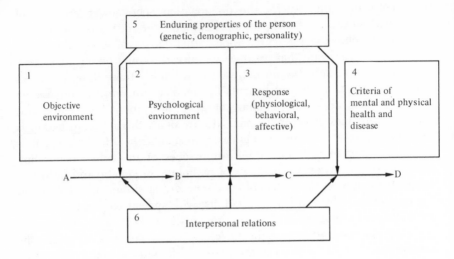

FIGURE 14–1.

are represented by the arrows which also illustrate the directions of causality to be emphasized. Hypotheses of the $A \rightarrow B$ category have to do with the effects of the objective environment on the psychological environment—for example, the extent to which one's status in an organization determines the extent to which he perceives others to esteem him. Hypotheses of the $B \rightarrow C$ category relate facts in the psychological environment (conscious and unconscious representations of the objective world as it exists for the person) to the immediate response which is evoked in the person. For example, the perception that one is held in low esteem by others may evoke feelings of anger, elevation of the blood pressure, or resignation from the job. The $C \rightarrow D$ category of hypotheses deals with the effect of specific responses on criteria of health and illness. The effect of anger on rheumatoid arthritis illustrates the $C \rightarrow D$ category.

Finally, the categories of hypotheses just described must be qualified by an additional class, represented by the vertical arrows in the figure. This class of hypotheses states that relationships between objective and psychological environment, between psychological environment and response, and between responses and criteria of health are all modified by enduring characteristics of the person and by interpersonal relations. For example, the extent to which a person shows strong affective responses (shame, anger, and so forth) to being held in low esteem by others may depend upon the extent to which he esteems himself. Thus the personal attribute of self-esteem conditions the relationship between the psychological environment and the response which it evokes. In similar fashion, other properties of the person and his interpersonal relations act as *conditioning variables* in the hypotheses which we have described above.

The research aims of the program are represented by all four classes of hypotheses, in combination. We are attempting to develop a theory of mental health, taking into account the facts of personality and genetic endowment insofar as they are necessary to make sense of the effects of the contemporary environment on the person. Given this framework, it is clear what constitutes an adequate explanatory sequence—a chain of related hypotheses beginning with some characteristic of the objective environment, ending with some criterion of health, specifying the intervening variables in the psychological environment and response categories, and stating the ways in which this causal linkage is modified by differing characteristics of the individual and differing interpersonal relations. Such a causal chain we call a *theme*, and we have attempted to state the aims of each research project in terms of one or more themes.

RESEARCH RESULTS

The following sections of this paper will illustrate several of the major themes which we have attempted to develop in this program. Each of them is represented by one or more specific projects. These themes include status and status incongruency as a determinant of health, role conflict and ambiguity, shift work as a factor in personal and family adjustment, and others.

Status and Health[2]

The first step was an exploratory study seeking correlations between job status and the frequency of diagnosed illnesses on voluntary dispensary visits in a large public utility (Kasl & French, 1962). This measure of illness reflects both the incidence of disease and the tendency to visit the company dispensary. The main findings were in the expected direction: among blue-collar workers and also among supervisory personnel there was a substantial inverse relationship between status and our index of dispensary visits. Our second project in this research replicated the first study in a quite different industry but with substantially the same results: again, the lower the status of the blue-collar workers, the higher the index of illness; and the same inverse relationship held separately within management personnel. In both companies the magnitude of this relationship was very substantial; the four correlations range from −.57 to −.83.

In all these correlational studies, however, it is impossible to disentangle the effects of status from the effects of *selective factors*; for example, management may select out and promote those employees with

---

[2] This section is quoted, with revisions, from French, 1963.

better health, especially those with better mental health, thus producing the obtained findings that higher status persons are healthier. More generally, we can say that any cross-sectional study which relates position in the social environment with measures of mental health is confounded; it may be that the environmental variable produces the health or it may be that healthy people achieve or are given different positions in the environment. Since our objective is to discover the effects of the industrial environment, this confounding is a serious problem. Therefore, an additional longitudinal study was made to control on the possible effects of selective factors. We wished to control for the effects of enduring personality characteristics which may have been the basis for achievement by the individual of a high status position. These differences in personality and in physical constitution were controlled by comparing the same persons over time. In line with the assumption that one's status position affects one's health, we predicted that those men whose status was increased by promotion should get healthier while those who were demoted should become less healthy as indicated by more visits to the dispensary. The data confirmed these predictions; those who were promoted were healthier after promotion, even though they were older, whereas those who were demoted became less healthy than they had been previously.

The findings of these three preliminary studies indicated that low status produced illness, but were unsatisfying because of the large theoretical gap between status and illness. We had succeeded in establishing a relationship between a characteristic of the objective environment and the health of the person without providing any empirically tested theory of the intervening processes. In accordance with our strategy of "gap filling," our next step was to provide such an interpretation in terms of self-identity theory. Following the general paradigm of Figure 14–1, we developed the theme illustrated in Figure 14–2.

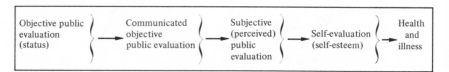

FIGURE 14–2.

Our first step was to conceptualize status in the organization as objective public evaluation or esteem. There are various dimensions of status such as education, occupation, level in the hierarchy, pay level, and so forth, but for each of these dimensions there is social agreement with respect to evaluation. Most people agree it is good to have a high-ranking occupation or a high level of education and it is bad to have a low-skill job or a subordinate position in the organization. In this conceptualization, the public which makes the evaluation is defined as the reference group for the person; it may consist of an organization, a small group, or another person. There may be different publics for different individuals, and a given individual may have several relevant publics.

Usually the objective esteem which some referent public has for a person gets communicated, to some extent, to him; hence the arrow linking objective public esteem to communicated objective public esteem. We assume also that in the psychological environment of an individual there exists some conception of how he is evaluated by the relevant publics. And our first general hypothesis for filling the gap between objective status and health asserts that objective public evaluation influences subjective public evaluation. The next hypothesis assumes that subjective public evaluation affects self-evaluation. The final link in the theme, as shown in Figure 14–2, hypothesizes that self-esteem (evaluation) influences health and illness.

Our fourth study was aimed at testing this theory about the steps intervening between status and health. In addition to objective measures of status and the same index of dispensary visits used previously, we also secured measures by questionnaire of subjective public esteem and self-esteem. In this questionnaire we attempted to measure the valued characteristics of the various jobs and the valued characteristics of the employees along eighteen commensurate dimensions. We asked, for example, how much administrative ability was required in each job, and we asked each employee how much administrative ability he had. Thus the attributes and evaluations of both jobs and persons could be compared on the same scale. Our first assumption, that there is social agreement concerning the evaluation of jobs, was strongly confirmed for the ordering of the fifteen jobs on the general prestige and respect which the job commands. Furthermore, this ordering of jobs according to subjective status agrees well with the ordering of the same jobs according to the objective status of the job as indicated by the level of pay. Our second major finding showed that attributes and evaluations of the job were attributed to the job holders. Subjects were asked to rate the characteristics of two unknown men when the only information given about these men was the jobs held—a third-level management job and a low-skill craft job. The subjects consistently rated the manager higher on such dimensions of the occupational subidentity as ambition, education, administrative skill, and tendency to work hard. That these differences were not a part of a simple halo effect was shown by the fact that there were no differences between the two men on such nonoccupational dimensions of the self as honesty, sense of humor, and helpfulness.

This process of attribution of job characteristics to job holders applies to the self as well as to others, as demonstrated by the finding that the profile of self-description given by men on the same job tends to be similar. Since people attribute to themselves the evaluations which they and others hold of their jobs, we found, as expected, that objective measures of job status such as pay were positively related to self-esteem. Finally, we found the predicted negative correlation ($r = -.47$) between self-esteem and our index of illness.

In any cross-sectional study relating status to self-esteem, the direction of causation is equivocal: either high esteem from others (that is, high status) causes high self-esteem, or high self-esteem and its consequent behavior produces esteem from others. In our theory we assume the former, but the latter interpretation could not be ruled out in the cross-sectional study just reported.

Our fifth study, therefore, was a field experiment designed to test the effects of objective public esteem on self-esteem, while controlling for the possible reverse effects of self-esteem on objective public esteem. This experiment was conducted in the T-groups at a human relations training conference (Sherwood, 1965). These "sensitivity-training" groups were somewhat like therapy groups where communication about the self and others was especially frank and open. We assumed that objective public esteem would produce a corresponding communicated objective public esteem, but no measures of this latter variable were obtained, so it remains as a theoretical gap in this experiment.

At the beginning and at the end of the training, we measured the subject's self-esteem, the esteem he perceived from others, and the esteem objectively accorded to him by each of the other members of the group. As shown in Figure 14–2, we hypothesized that objective public esteem would influence subjective public esteem only to the extent that the public had reference power, that is, the public as a reference group to whom the subject is attracted (French & Raven, 1959). Accordingly, the reference power of other members of the training group was measured by means of a sociometric questionnaire. As predicted, we found that subjective public esteem changed more toward the objective public esteem accorded to the person by referent members of the group than toward esteem from members he did not like. Finally, we found, as predicted, that the person's self-esteem changed during the two weeks to become closer to the subjective public esteem.

In order to fill the gap in our knowledge about communicated objective public esteem, a sixth study was conducted in sensitivity-training groups. This was a preliminary experiment in which the amount of communicated objective public esteem was directly manipulated. Data were collected on how each member evaluated every other member on a series of human relations skills. In different experimental treatments, we varied amount of feedback to the subject of these written evaluations from others and of verbal feedback from two members of the same T-group.

As predicted, the more the T-group communicated the objective public esteem, the more the subject's self-esteem changed in the direction of agreeing with the communicated objective public esteem.

A seventh project in this research continuity examined the effects of communicated objective public esteem in a dyadic rather than in a group context. We chose to study the effects of the appraisal system in a large industrial organization because we suspected that these annual appraisals constituted a stressful situation involving severe threats to self-esteem. Ninety-two members of management were interviewed before and again after their annual appraisal by their supervisors. During the appraisal interview trained observers recorded quantitatively the behavior of both the appraisee and his supervisor. The number of criticisms made by the supervisor and the frequency of praise were recorded as measures of communicated objective public esteem. Ten weeks after this appraisal we obtained from both the supervisor and the appraisee their ratings on the amount of improvement in performance shown by the men. We found that the appraisals were indeed threatening to self-esteem; 82 percent of the men reported afterwards that the evaluation by the supervisor was lower than their own self-evaluation. The number of threats to self-esteem observed in the interview was related to the amount of defensive behavior and to negative attitudes toward the appraisal system. Contrary to the usual assumptions of the appraisal system, we hypothesized that threats to self-esteem would be sufficiently demoralizing to inhibit, rather than promote, subsequent performance improvement, especially for those persons low in self-esteem. The findings confirmed this expectation, and there was a significant interaction between person and environment. For those persons who were already low in occupational self-esteem, the greater the threat to self-esteem, the worse the subsequent performance; but there was no such effect of threat for those who were high in occupational self-esteem. This study shows that self-esteem is not only influenced by the social environment, but it is also a more or less stable characteristic of the person that conditions the effects of the social environment on performance, on negative attitudes toward the appraisal system, and on subjective public esteem.

None of the seven studies reported up to this point have examined physiological variables intervening between social status and health; our efforts to fill this gap are illustrated by two studies of peptic ulcer. In a study of shift workers, we carried one step further our findings on self-esteem. Among 132 male employees we found a significant inverse relation between self-esteem and an index of peptic ulcer; the lower the self-esteem, the higher the index of ulcer. We expected this inverse relation in view of Vertin's finding that skill level is inversely related to ulcer and our own finding that skill is positively related to self-esteem. Another finding revealed that self-esteem was correlated with serum pepsinogen, which, in turn, was significantly related to the index of ulcer. It is a plausible hypothesis that self-esteem influences ulcer via its effect on pepsinogen.

The second study of ulcer compared craftsmen, foremen, and executives (Dunn & Cobb, 1962). On several measures of peptic ulcer the foremen were highest and the executives were lowest. These findings were to be expected on the basis of previous studies despite the myth of "executive ulcer." We were surprised to find, however, that the mean serum pepsinogen values were highest for executives and lowest for foremen. Thus the group with the highest pepsinogen had the lowest ulcer rate, while the group with the lowest pepsinogen had the highest ulcer rate. This finding was unexpected in view of the usual positive relation between pepsinogen and ulcer, so we checked this relation within each of the two larger groups. Within the group of 364 executives and also within the group of 263 craftsmen, we found the usual positive relation. It remains a mystery for future research to discover just how job status interacts with pepsinogen levels to influence peptic ulcer.

A final example of our current work on the relationship between status and health involves the disease of rheumatoid arthritis. There is an accumulation of evidence that social psychological factors are implicated in this disease. For example, Dublin (1933) found that rheumatoid arthritis was more prevalent among people in the lower socioeconomic classes. The Pittsburgh Arthritis Study reported the prevalence of rheumatoid arthritis to be two to three times as great among people in the lowest education group as among those higher in education. King and Cobb (1958, 1959) found that rheumatoid arthritis was associated with a discrepancy between income and education; that is, the onset of the disease was more likely among people whose education would have led to an expected income higher than that actually received. They also reported relatively high prevalence of the disease among women who experienced some discrepancy between the requirements of the familial role and their own sense of identity. In a related paper, Cobb (1959) proposed that the concept of resentment (contained or unexpressed hostility) be considered an intervening variable between the social and familial sources of such resentment and the disease of rheumatoid arthritis.

More recently Cobb and Kasl (1966) have described research testing the hypothesis that certain social incongruities contribute to chronic anger and irritation and by this path to rheumatoid arthritis. Their research involved a group of 155 women, forty-nine of whom had been classified as rheumatoid arthritics.

In looking at the problem of status incongruence, Cobb and Kasl used the occupation of the man of the family as the reference point. This was classified on the Duncan Scale of relative status. Congruence or incongruence of each man's occupation was judged in relation to the educational level of his wife and in relation to his own education. These relationships were in turn examined in relation to the frequency of rheumatoid arthritis and self-reported anger among the daughters in these families. The data are summarized in Table 14-1.

TABLE 14-1 The Relation of Status Incongruence in Parents to Rheumatoid Arthritis and Anger-Irritation in Their Daughters

	n	Daughter's Frequency of Rheumatoid Arthritis		Daughter's Frequency of Anger-Irritation	
		%	p	%	p
Mother's Education > Father's Occupation (Incongruent)	67	43		55	
			< .05		< .005
Mother's Education < Father's Occupation (Congruent)	54	26		31	
Father's Education and Occupation (Incongruent)	46	50		61	
			< .02		< .005
Father's Education and Occupation (Congruent)	69	29		35	
Daughter's Frequency of Anger-Irritation (High)	61	44			
			< .001		
Daughter's Frequency of Anger-Irritation (Low)	94	20			

Rheumatoid arthritis is significantly more frequent among those women who had mothers with education inappropriately high for the social stratum defined by their father's occupation. Moreover, high anger-irritation is very significantly more common among these daughters of "overeducated" mothers, and high anger-irritation is associated with excessive frequency of rheumatoid arthritis. Following the chain starting with the incongruence of father's own education with his occupation, we see the same effect.

The nature of these relationships and their place in the framework of our research program is shown in Figure 14-3. The long line from parents' status incongruence to daughter's rheumatoid arthritis represents the modest association of these two. The line is given a direction because it is quite clear that the daughter's rheumatoid arthritis could not have caused the parents' status incongruence. Therefore, if there is a causal relationship here, it must flow in the direction indicated. The same reasoning applies to the arrow from parents' status incongruence to daughter's anger-irritation, but not to the last line connecting daughter's anger-irritation to daughter's rheumatoid arthritis. It is conceivable that at least part of the daughter's anger and irritation might be a result of the disease rather than a cause of it. The arrow from other factors is to remind us that the etiology of this disease is surely multiple and that social psychological phenomena are not *the* cause or even the major part of the causation. They are implicated, nevertheless, and the manner and degree of the implication is beginning to become clear.

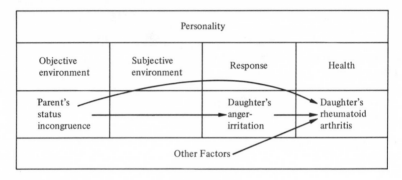

FIGURE 14–3.

Role Conflict[4]

The notion of status incongruency suggests that the potent aspect of status for health may not be position per se, but an incompatibility of two positions simultaneously occupied by the same person or perhaps the incompatibility of two aspects of a single position so occupied. This brings us close to a second major theme in our research: role conflict.

Our studies of role conflict and ambiguity in industry are among a number of researches which share a common and distant goal: to make understandable the effects of the contemporary environment on the person including his physical and mental health. We begin by thinking of the environment of any individual as consisting very largely of formal organizations and groups. From this point of view the life of the person can be seen as an array of roles which he plays in the particular set of organizations and groups to which he belongs. These groups and organizations, or rather the subparts of each which affect the person directly, together make up his objective environment. Characteristics of these organizations and groups (company, union, church, family, and others) affect the physical and emotional state of the person and are major determinants of his behavior.

---

[4] Adapted from Kahn et al., 1964.

The first requirement for linking the individual and the organization is to locate the individual in the total set of ongoing relationships and behaviors comprised by the organization. The key concept for doing this is office, by which we mean a unique point in organizational space, where space is defined in terms of a structure of interrelated offices and the pattern of activities associated with them. Associated with each office is a set of activities or potential behaviors. These activities constitute the *role* to be performed by any person who occupies that office. Each office in an organization is directly related to certain others, less directly to still others, and perhaps only remotely to the remaining offices included in the organization. Consider the office of press foreman in a factory manufacturing external trim parts for automobiles. The offices most directly related to that of press foreman might include general foreman and superintendent, from which press foreman's work assignments emanate and to which he turns for approval of work done. Also directly related to the office of press foreman will be the foreman of the sheet-metal shop, which provides stock for the presses; the inspector who must pass or reject the completed stampings; the shipping foreman who receives and packages the stampings; and of course, the fourteen press operators for whose work press foreman is responsible. We can imagine the organizational chart spread before us like a vast fish net, in which each knot represents an office and each string a functional relationship between offices. If we pick up the net by seizing any office, we see immediately the other offices to which it is directly attached. Thus, when we pick the office of press foreman, we find it attached directly to nineteen others—general foreman, superintendent, sheet-metal foreman, inspector, shipping room foreman, and fourteen press operators. These nineteen offices make up the *role set* for the office of press foreman.

In similar fashion each member of an organization is directly associated with a relatively small number of others, usually the occupants of offices adjacent to his in the work flow structure. They constitute his role set and usually include his immediate supervisor (and perhaps his supervisor's direct superior), his immediate subordinates, and certain members of his own and other departments with whom he must work closely. These offices are defined into his role set by virtue of the work flow, technology, and authority structure of the organization. Also included in a person's role set may be people who are related to him in other ways—close friends, respected "identification models," and others, within or outside the organization, who for one reason or another are concerned with his behavior in his organization role (see Figure 14–4).

All members of a person's role set depend upon his performance in some fashion; they are rewarded by it, or they require it in order to perform their own tasks. Because they have a stake in his performance, they develop beliefs and attitudes about what he should and should not

do in his role. These preferences, which we will refer to as role expectations, are by no means restricted to the job description as it might be
given by the head of the organization or prepared by some specialist in
personnel.

For each person in an organization then, there is a pattern of role
expectations which exists in the minds of members of his role set, and
represents standards in terms of which they evaluate his performance.
The expectations do not remain in the minds of members of the role set,
however. They are communicated in many ways—sometimes directly,
as when a supervisor instructs a subordinate in the requirements of his
job; sometimes indirectly, as when a colleague expresses admiration or
disappointment in some behavior. The crucial point is that the activities
which define a role consist of the expectations of members of the role set,
and that these expectations are communicated or sent to the *focal person*
(the person occupying the role being studied).

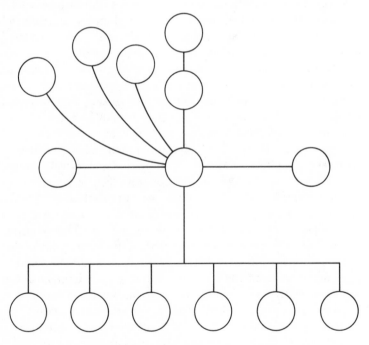

FIGURE 14–4.   Focal person and role set.

It is apparent from the approach to social role described above that
various members of the role set for a given office may hold quite different
role expectations toward the focal person. At any given time, they may
impose pressures on him toward different kinds of behavior. To the

extent that these role pressures are felt by him, he experiences psychological conflict. In the objective sense, then, *role conflict* may be defined as the simultaneous occurrence of two or more sets of pressures such that compliance with one would make more difficult or render impossible compliance with the other. For example, a person's superior may make it clear to him that he is expected to hold his subordinates strictly to company rules and to high production schedules. At the same time, his subordinates may indicate in various ways that they would like loose, relaxed supervision, and that they will make things difficult if they are pushed too hard. The pressures from above and below in this case are incompatible, since the style of supervision which satisfies one set of pressures violates the other set. Cases of this kind are so common that a whole literature has been created on the problem of the firstline supervisor as the man in the middle, or the master and victim of double-talk.

Several types of role conflict can be identified. One might be termed *intrasender conflict*: different prescriptions and proscriptions from a given member of the role set may be incompatible, as for example when a supervisor requests a man to acquire material that is unavailable through normal channels and, at the same time, prohibits violations of normal channels.

A second type might be termed *intersender conflict*: pressures from one role sender oppose pressures from another sender. The pressures for close versus loose supervisory styles cited above constitute an example of this type of conflict.

A third type of conflict we refer to as *inter-role conflict*. In this case the role pressures associated with membership in one organization are in conflict with pressures which stem from membership in other groups. For example, demands on the job for overtime or take-home work may conflict with pressures from one's wife to give undivided attention to family affairs during evening hours. The conflict arises between the role of the person as worker and his role as husband and father.

All three of these types of role conflict begin in the objective environment, although they will regularly result in psychological conflicts for the focal person. Other types of conflict, however, are generated directly by a combination of environmental pressures and internal forces. A major example is the conflict which may exist between the needs and values of a person and the demands of others in his role set. This fourth type of conflict we will call *person-role conflict*. It can occur when role requirements violate moral values—for example, when pressures on an executive to enter price-fixing conspiracies are opposed by his personal code of ethics. In other cases a person's needs and aspirations may lead to behaviors which are unacceptable to members of his role set; for example, an ambitious young man may be called up short by his associates for stepping on their toes while trying to advance in the organization.

All the types of role conflict discussed above have in common one major characteristic—members of a role set exerting pressure to change the behavior of a focal person. When such pressures are generated and sent, they do not enter an otherwise empty field; the focal person is already in role, already behaving, already maintaining some kind of equilibrium among the disparate forces and motives which he experiences. Pressures to change, therefore, represent new and additional forces with which he must cope; by definition they threaten an existing equilibrium. Moreover, the stronger the pressures from role senders toward change in the behavior of the focal person, the greater the conflict created for him.

This approach to the understanding of behavior in organizations in general and the understanding of role conflict in particular is summarized in Figure 14–5, which illustrates a *role episode*: that is, a complete cycle of role sending, response by focal person, and the effects of that response on the role senders.

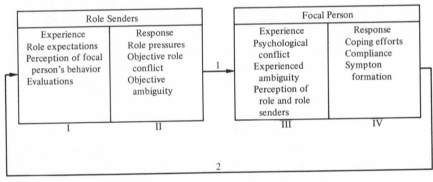

FIGURE 14–5.   A model of the role episode.

The four boxes in Figure 14–5 represent events that constitute a role episode. The arrows connecting them imply a causal sequence. Role pressures are assumed to originate in the expectations held by members of the role set. Role senders have expectations regarding the way in which the focal role should be performed. They also have perceptions regarding the way in which the focal person is actually performing. They correlate the two, and exert pressures to make his performance congruent with their expectations. These pressures induce in the focal person an experience which has both perceptual and cognitive properties, and which leads in turn to certain adjustive (or maladjustive) responses. The responses of the focal person are typically perceived by those exerting the pressures, and their expectations are correspondingly adjusted. Thus, for both the role senders and the focal person the episode involves experience and the response to experience. Let us look in more detail at the contents of the four boxes in Figure 14–5 and at the relations among them.

A role episode starts with the existence of a set of role expectations held by other persons about a focal person and his behavior on the job. Speaking of the members of a person's role set as a group is a matter of convenience. In fact, each member of the role set behaves toward the focal person in ways determined by his own expectations and his own anticipations of the focal person's responses. Under certain circumstances a member of the role set, responding to his own immediate experience, expresses his expectations overtly; he attempts to influence the focal person in the direction of greater conformity with his expectations. Arrow 1 indicates that the total set of such influence attempts affects the immediate experience of the focal person in a given situation (Box III). This experience includes, for example, the focal person's perception of the demands and requirements placed on him by members of his role set, and his awareness or experience of psychological conflict. The specific reactions of each focal person to a situation are immediately determined by the nature of his experience in that situation. Any person who is confronted with a situation of role conflict, however, must respond to it in some fashion. One or more members of his role set are exerting pressure on him to change his behavior, and he must cope somehow with the pressure they are exerting. Whatever pattern of response he adopts may be regarded as an attempt to attain or regain an adequately gratifying experience in the work situation. He may attempt a direct solution of the objective problem by compliance or by persuading others to modify their incompatible demands. He may attempt to avoid the sources of stress, perhaps by using defense mechanisms which distort the reality of a conflicting or ambiguous situation. There is also the possibility that coping with the pressures of the work will involve the formation of affective or physiological symptoms. Regardless of which of these, singly or in combination, the focal person uses, his behavior can be assessed in relation to the expectations of each of his role senders.

The degree to which the focal person's behavior conforms to the expectations held for him will affect the state of those expectations at the next moment. If his response is essentially a hostile counterattack, members of his role set are apt to think of him and behave toward him in ways quite different than if he were submissively compliant. If he complies partially under pressure, they may increase the pressure; if he is obviously overcome with tension and anxiety, they may "lay off." In summary, the role episode is abstracted from a process which is cyclic and ongoing; the response of the focal person to role pressure feeds back on the senders of those pressures in ways that alter or reinforce them. The next role sendings of each member of the set depend on his evaluations of the response to his last sendings, and thus a new episode begins.

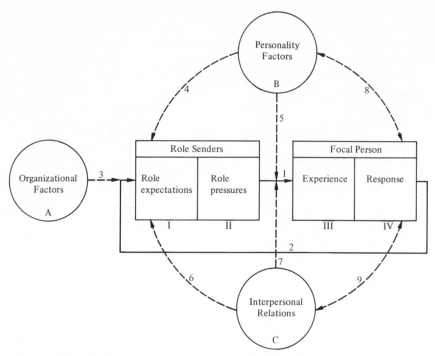

FIGURE 14–6.   A theoretical model of factors involved in adjustment to role conflict and ambiguity.

In order to understand more fully the causal dynamics of such episodes and their consequences for the person's adjustment, the model must be extended to include three additional classes of variables—organizational factors, personality factors, and the character of interpersonal relations between the focal person and other members of his role set. Taken in combination, these factors represent the context within which the episode occurs. In Figure 14–6 the role episode is shown in the context of these three additional classes of variables. Figure 14–5 forms the core of Figure 14–6. However, the circles in Figure 14–6 represent not momentary events but enduring states of the organization, the person, and the interpersonal relations between focal person and other members of his role set. An analysis of these factors makes more understandable the sequence of events in a role episode. Figure 14–6 provides a convenient framework within which to summarize the major research findings obtained from an intensive study of fifty-four role sets in a number of different industries, and from a national survey of approximately 1500 households.

The experience of role conflict is common indeed in the work situation. Almost half of our respondents reported being caught "in the middle" between two conflicting persons or factions. These conflicts are usually hierarchical; 88 percent of the people involved in them report at least one party to the conflict as being above them in the organization. Somewhat less than half report that one of the conflicting parties is outside the organization. One of the dominant forms of role conflict is overload, which can be thought of as a conflict among legitimate tasks, or a problem in the setting of priorities; almost half of all respondents reported this problem.

The intensive study, in which role senders and focal persons were interviewed independently, deals more directly with the causal sequences initiated by conditions of conflict. Measures of objective conflict, as derived from the expectations of individual role senders, are strongly associated with the subjective experience of conflict, as reported by the focal person, who is target of incompatible expectations. These, in turn, are linked to affective and behavioral responses of that person.

For the focal person, the emotional costs of role conflict include low job satisfaction, low confidence in the organization, and high scores on the multi-item index of tension. The most frequent behavioral response to role conflict is withdrawal from or avoidance of those who are seen as creating the conflict. Symptomatic of this is the attempt of the person experiencing the conflict to reduce communication with his co-workers and to assert (sometimes unrealistically) that they lack power over him. Case material indicates that such withdrawal, while a mechanism of defense, is not a mechanism of solution. It appears to reduce the possibility of subsequent collaborative solutions to role conflict.

Organizational Determinants of Conflict

The major organizational determinants of conflict include three kinds of role requirements—the requirement for crossing organizational boundaries, the requirement for producing innovative solutions to nonroutine problems, and the requirement for being responsible for the work of others (Arrow 3).

Let us consider first the requirement for crossing a company boundary. Both the frequency and the importance of making contacts outside one's company are associated with the experience of role conflict. Crossing the company boundary is associated also with experienced tension, but the relationship is curvilinear; greatest tension is experienced by those who have discontinuous contacts outside the organization. We propose the hypothesis that in positions which require extracompany contacts on a continuous basis, there are special facilities or some other organizational acknowledgment of boundary difficulties which renders them less painful.

Hypothetical explanations for the stressfulness of boundary crossing are available primarily from case materials. It appears that the person who must frequently deal with people outside the company usually has limited control over these outsiders. He cannot strongly influence their demands and the resources which they supply to him. Moreover, a person in a boundary position is likely to be blamed by people in his own company for what his outside contacts do or fail to do. They in turn may blame him for shortcomings in his own company. The difficulties of living at the boundary of an organization are intensified when the boundary dweller must coordinate his extraorganizational activities with people in other departments within the company.

In general, living "near" a departmental or other intraorganizational boundary has effects very like those just remarked for boundaries of the organization itself. Nearness to a departmental boundary and frequency of dealing across such boundaries are associated with felt conflict and with experienced tension.

Roles which demand creative problem solving are associated with high role conflict and with tension. The occupants of such roles appear to become engaged in conflict primarily with older, and often more powerful, individuals in the organization who want to maintain the status quo. Among the major role conflicts which persons in innovative jobs complain of is the conflict of priority between the nonroutine activities which are at the core of the creative job and the routine activities of administration or paper work. These latter, according to the people who fill innovative positions, are unduly time consuming, disrupt the continuity of their creative work, and are generally unpalatable.

There is considerable evidence that organizations exercise selective effort in choosing people for innovative positions. People in such positions tend to be characterized by high self-confidence, high mobility aspirations, high job involvement, low apathy, and a tendency to rate the importance of a job extremely high compared to the importance of other areas of their lives.

Supervisory responsibility emerges as a major organizational determinant of role conflict. Either the supervision of rank-and-file employees or the supervision of people who are themselves supervisors appears to have substantial effects on the degree of objective conflict and the amount of experienced conflict. In combination, direct and indirect supervisory responsibility produce very substantial role conflict and tension. There is a systematic relationship also between rank and role conflict, as there is between rank and tension. The often heard assertion that the lowest levels of supervision are subjected to the greatest conflict is not borne out by these data. Rather, there is a curvilinear relationship in which the maximum of conflict and conflict experience occurs at what might be called the "upper middle" levels of management. We interpret this in part as a consequence of the still unfulfilled mobility aspirations of middle management, in contrast to the better actualized aspirations of top management people.

Interpersonal Relations as Determinants of Role Conflict

The sources of pressure and conflict for a person can be expressed rather fully in terms of his interpersonal relations with these pressure sources. The greatest pressure is directed to a person from other people who are in the same department as he is, who are his superiors in the hierarchy, and who are sufficiently dependent on his performance to care about his adequacy without being so completely dependent as to be inhibited in making their demands known (Arrow 6). The people who are least likely to apply such pressures are a person's peers and role senders outside his own department.

The kinds of pressure which people are prepared to apply, as well as the degree of that pressure, vary considerably with their formal interpersonal relationship to the potential target of their pressures. Thus, supervisors seem to refrain from exerting coercive power where it might impede the performance of the focal person and perhaps reflect upon the supervisor himself. On the other hand, the techniques used by subordinates to apply coercive power are precisely those which threaten the efficiency of the organization. They include the withholding of aid and information.

When a person is surrounded by others who are highly dependent on him and who have high power over him and exert high pressure on him, his response is typically one of apathy and withdrawal (Arrow 7). Moreover, under such circumstances, his experience of role conflict is very high and his job satisfaction correspondingly reduced. Emotionally he experiences a sense of futility and attempts a hopeless withdrawal from his co-workers.

There is significant evidence that close and positive interpersonal relations between a focal person and members of his role set can mediate substantially the effects of role conflict (Arrow 7). A given degree of objective role conflict is experienced as less stressful in the context of positive affective relations with others. Nevertheless, experienced conflict and ambiguity appear to cause deterioration in interpersonal relations (Arrow 9). Thus, a consequence of role conflict is decreased trust, respect, and liking for co-workers, and in the presence of experienced ambiguity there is a similar attempt on the part of the focal person to weaken interpersonal relations. As with conflict, this weakening of interpersonal relations is self-defeating, since he finds himself withdrawing in the face of ambiguity from the very persons from whom he requires information.

The Place of Personality Variables in the Study of Conflict

Several personality dimensions mediate significantly (Arrow 5) the degree to which a given intensity of objective conflict is experienced as strain by the focal person. These personality dimensions include emotional sensitivity, sociability, and flexibility-rigidity. With respect to sociability, we find that the effects of objective role conflict on interpersonal bonds and on tension are more pronounced for people who are unsociable (independent). The independent person, in other words, develops social relations which, while often congenial and trusting, are easily undermined by conditions of stress. The preference of such people for autonomy becomes manifest primarily when social contacts are stressful, that is, when others are exerting strong pressures and thereby creating conflict for the persons. In similar fashion, emotional sensitivity conditions vary sharply the relationship between objective conflict and tension, with emotionally sensitive persons showing substantially higher tension scores for any given degree of objective conflict. There is also a tendency for people of different personality characteristics to be exposed by their role senders to differing degrees of objective conflict (Arrow 4). Thus, people who are relatively flexible are subjected to stronger pressures than those who have already demonstrated by their rigidity the futility of applying such pressures.

A more recent study by Allen Kraut (1965) replicated many of the findings which I have just summarized and extended our research on role conflict in two additional respects—by obtaining comparable measures of objective and subjective conflict which had not been available from the previous research, and by bringing into the predictive scheme objective measures of individual and organizational performance.

Kraut's study was conducted in the sales department of a large corporation and utilized a population of 151 sales offices. In each of these offices data were obtained from the manager and a sample of salesmen, 823 of whom were included in the total sample. In general, the findings from this study are congruent with those of the earlier researches. Role conflict is associated with low satisfaction with the job, the organization, and especially with the manager ($r = .39$). Role conflict is related also to an index of tension, to the frequency with which symptoms having to do with mental health are reported, and to an index of job-related stress ($r = .39$). (These findings are not mediated by the factor of personal flexibility, contrary to the previous research.)

A significant pattern of relationships emerged with respect to objective versus subjective (perceived) role conflict; that they are related is not surprising. More important, perhaps, is the tendency of salesmen to perceive the expectations of their supervisors differently from the supervisors' actual statement of their expectations. Moreover, the distortion is persistently in the direction of the salesman's perceiving his supervisor to be nearer his own position than is in fact the case. The effect of this distortion is to understate the conflict; subjective conflict is significantly less than objective conflict. In fact, the level of distortion is about as great as the level of acknowledged conflict. Table 14–2 presents summary scores which incorporate differences in four content areas: *influence* appropriate for the salesman, *support* to which the salesman is entitled, *rules orientation*, and *cooperation*.

TABLE 14–2 Means and Standard Deviations of Salesmen's Scores on
Objective and Subjective Role Conflict

D Score	Mean	Standard Deviation
Objective conflict	2.07	.77
Subjective conflict	1.87	1.00
Distortion	1.99	.78

The presence of such distortion suggests that the process may be serving as a means of coping with conflict, and raises the question as to its effectiveness for this purpose. To the extent that distortion is effective in mediating the effects of role conflict for the individual, we would expect that objective conflict would be correlated less highly with the various criteria of dissatisfaction and discomfort than would subjective conflict. This is indeed the pattern. The presence or absence of objective role conflict adds very little to the predictive ability of the subjective conflict score, whereas the subjective data add greatly to the predictive power of the objective conflict score. Since these findings could also be interpreted as reflecting a familiar artifact of research methods—namely, the tendency to generate higher correlations "within-method" than "across-method"—interpretation had best be conservative.

The second extension of the Kraut study was the relating of conflict to individual and unit (office) performance. In this respect, his research brought under empirical consideration an issue which traditionally has been handled by assumption, both by social theorists and practitioners. For example, Simmel in his classic essay on the subject (see Simmel, 1950) comes very near to making conflict an unvarying organizational benefit—provided that it does not assume the form in which the aim is "mutual annihilation of the combatants." Boulding (1962), on the other hand, while considering the notion of some optimum level of conflict, asserts that "there is a great deal of evidence that conflict in its nonsport aspect is usually felt as too much." Managers show similar differences of opinion. There are those who insist on "keeping the animals stirred up," as their uncomplimentary metaphor puts it, and those for whom any sign of conflict signifies personal failure and organizational threat.

Though not so extreme in formulation, Kraut's hypothesizing was closer to the last of these interpretations. His prediction was that role conflict would be negatively related to individual and office performance. His findings, however, gave little support either to the theorists of intra-organizational peace or war; the correlations between conflict and performance (while significantly negative in a statistical sense) are too small to be significant for the organization.

Shift Work

Our interest in patterns of shift work stems from the likelihood that such requirements will increase not only the difficulty in performing the work role, but will affect also the opportunity and ability of the individual to perform other major life roles—for example, those of husband and father, citizen and friend. In other words, we expected that shift work would create a kind of role conflict we had not studied: conflict *between* two or more of the life roles of the individual, rather than conflict between the expectations of a single role. The research on shift work patterns was conducted by Floyd Mann and his colleagues in five plants which included 950 employees working four different shift patterns—day, afternoon, night, and rotating shifts. In the process of developing the questionnaires and interview schedules, both husbands and wives were interviewed. (The results of this research are described fully in Mott, et al., 1965.)

Shift work does apparently increase the experienced difficulty of the individual with his major life roles. Men working the afternoon shift are more likely to report difficulty with their role as father and in the performance of miscellaneous household functions. Men working the night shift are more likely to report difficulty with their role as husband, including the sexual relationship and the providing of adequate protection to their wives and families. Men working rotating shift patterns described all of the above difficulties and in addition reported that the rotating shift pattern interfered with the formation of friendships and with their opportunities to see friends.

Mott and his colleagues find reduced integration of the shift worker in a number of social relationships. They find less functional integration in marriage, in terms of the adequacy of coordination of activities, problem solving in family affairs, and sharing of responsibilities. The reported amount of strain and tension in marriage was greater among shift workers than day workers. Findings with respect to the integration of the individual in the community showed a similar pattern. The shift worker was less likely to be a member of community organizations, less likely to be an active participant in the organizations to which he did belong, and still less likely to be a leader in such organizations.

Shift workers, especially those who reported difficulty with the shift-work pattern, were commonly bothered by problems of the time-oriented bodily functions—sleep, appetite, and elimination. They were also more likely to report colds, headaches, infectious diseases, ulcer, and rheumatoid arthritis.

The psychological effects of shift work appeared to be strongly mediated by the extent to which the shift worker felt that the shift-work pattern interfered with his other life activities. Where such felt interference was high, the shift worker was likely also to experience low self-esteem and high anxiety.

All the findings on the reported effects of shift work are mediated by additional factors of personality, family relations, and background, although not always in obvious fashion. For example, neuroticism appears to mediate inversely the relationship between shift work and experienced difficulty. People who score high on the neuroticism measure report themselves to be less bothered by shift work than people who score low.

The attitudes and behaviors of the wives of shift workers appear to be particularly important as mediating factors. For example, those shift workers whose wives make substantial adjustments in the schedule of meals, of sleep, of quiet, and of social life are much less affected themselves in the adverse ways described above. It seems that the fact of shift work presents the wife with a great deal of additional power over the husband. She can, if she chooses to do so, exclude him from a great deal of the family and marital relationships, and do so in ways that do not expose her to general social criticism. There is also a suggestion in some of the interview material that wives and husbands can use the fact of shift work in a collusive fashion to "hide" from each other in time in a way that is analogous to people hiding from each other in space.

CONCLUSION

Our current research is concerned with the effects of several kinds of environmental stress, primarily in the work situation and secondarily in the family. For the most part, the stresses with which we are concerned can be understood in terms of status and status incongruence, and in terms of such related concepts as role and role conflict.

The research includes studies of birth order and relationships within the family, studies of overload as a particular form of role conflict, and studies which concentrate on the transition between work and nonwork roles. One of the latter category involves a longitudinal design in which 3000 adolescent boys are followed from the tenth grade through graduation or drop-out to work or unemployment. Another follows a panel of men through the threat and actuality of job loss, the individual and familial patterns of coping, and the eventual attainment of some new stability. The research on role overload utilizes diverse situations and populations, from National Aeronautics and Space Administration (NASA) staff to university professors. At the same time we are continuing attempts to understand stresses in the organizational environment by working backward from certain diseases to hypothetical contributory factors. Rheumatoid arthritis, peptic ulcer, and coronary heart disease are the major starting points for these researches.

The research aim of understanding the stressful characteristics of large-scale organizations is certainly grand but perhaps not grandiose. In any event the stakes are too high for researchers to refuse the game. Men will live increasingly in large organizations. Understanding them more fully is a prerequisite to making them more livable.

References

Boulding, K. *Conflict and defense.* New York: Harper & Row, 1962.

Cobb, S. Contained hostility in rheumatoid arthritis. *Arthritis and Rheumatism,* 1959, **2**, 419–425.

Cobb, S. The epidemiology of rheumatoid arthritis. *Academy of New Jersey Bulletin,* March 1963, **9**, 52–60.

Cobb, S., & Kasl, S. The epidemiology of rheumatoid arthritis. *American Journal of Public Health,* October 1966, **56**(10), 1657–1663.

Dublin, L. Cited in B. L. Wyatt, *Chronic arthritis and fibrositis.* Baltimore, Md.: William Wood, 1933.

Dunn, J. P., & Cobb, S. Frequency of peptic ulcer among executives, craftsmen, and foremen, *Journal of Occupational Medicine,* 1962, **4**, 343–348.

French, J. R. P., Jr. The social environment and mental health. *Journal of Social Issues,* 1963, **19**(4), 39–56. (Presidential address before the Society for the Psychological Study of Social Issues.)

French, J. R. P., Jr., & Kahn, R. L. A programmatic approach to studying the industrial environment and mental health. *Journal of Social Issues,* July 1962, **18**(3), 1–47.

French, J. R. P., Jr., & Raven, B. The bases of social power. In D. Cartwright & A. Zander (Eds.), *Group dynamics.* (3rd ed.) New York: Harper & Row, 1968. Also in D. Cartwright (Ed.), *Studies in social power.* Ann Arbor, Mich.: Institute for Social Research, University of Michigan, 1959.

Kahn, R. L., et al. *Organizational stress: Studies in role conflict and ambiguity.* New York: Wiley, 1964.

Kahn, R. L. The generation and resolution of organizational stress. A paper presented for the Institute of Management Sciences, October 1965.

Kasl, R. L., & French, J. R. P., Jr. The effects of occupational status and health. *Journal of Social Issues,* July 1962, **18**(3), 67–89.

King, S. H., & Cobb, S. Psychosocial factors in the epidemiology of rheumatoid arthritis. *Journal of Chronic Diseases,* 1958, **7**, 466.

King, S. H., & Cobb, S. Psychosocial studies in rheumatoid arthritis: Parental factors compared in cases and controls. *Arthritis and Rheumatism,* August 1959, **2,** 322–331.

Kraut, A. A study of role conflicts and their relationship to job satisfaction, tension, and performance. Unpublished Ph.D. thesis, University of Michigan, 1965.

Mott, P. E., et al. *Shift work: The social, psychological, and physical consequences.* Ann Arbor, Mich.: University of Michigan Press, 1965.

Sherwood, J. J. Self-identity and self-actualization: A theory and research. Unpublished Ph.D. thesis, University of Michigan, 1962. Also reported in Self-identity and referent others. *Sociometry,* 1965, **28**(1), 66–81.

Simmel, G. *The sociology of Georg Simmel.* Kurt H. Wolf (Transl.) New York: The Free Press, 1950.

Vertin, P. G. Bedrijfsgeneeskundige Aspecten van het Ulcus Pepticum (Occupational health aspects of the peptic ulcer). Thesis, Groningen, 1954.

15 community disaster and system stress: a sociological perspective

J. Eugene Haas
Thomas E. Drabek

In this paper we outline a sociological approach to the study of organizational stress. Following a brief review of the relevant literature, a conceptual framework is introduced and discussed at some length. Illustrations which point to the utility of the various concepts are drawn from the field and laboratory work conducted by the authors while on the staff of Ohio State University. Finally, some basic theoretical and methodological problems are discussed with possible solutions suggested.

ORGANIZATIONAL STRESS LITERATURE

In the attempt to develop a useful theoretical framework for both field and laboratory research on organizations under stress we reviewed a large body of stress literature and related studies of crises and disaster.

A brief summary of portions of this literature will be presented to provide background for the theoretical statement which follows.

It became clear that there was little consensus on the meaning of the concept *stress*. Two kinds of distinctions appeared necessary. First, we were interested in system stress, whatever that might be, and not individual stress. However, most of the literature dealt with personal or psychological stress.[1] Secondly, it was clear that stress as used in the literature referred to at least relatively distinct phenomena:

1. stimuli or stressors
2. a state or condition of a system
3. response or adaptation

These distinctions are illustrated in the summary that follows.

Research on "Extreme Situations"

Some authors have preferred to avoid the term stress and instead have focused on what they label extreme situations. Wallace (1956) viewed disaster as part of this larger category which he defined as follows:

> Situations involving the threat of, or experience of an interruption of normally effective procedures for reducing certain tensions, together with a drastic increase in tensions, to the point of causing death or major personal and social readjustment, may be called "extreme situation" [p. 1].

Bettleheim (1943) analyzed reactions of prisoners in Nazi concentration camps and attempted to describe certain characteristics of "extreme situations." He expands on this perspective in his more recent work (Bettleheim, 1960, p. 148).

At one point Torrance (1957) explicitly rejected the use of the term stress because of its many and confusing connotations and used instead the phrase "behavior in emergencies and extreme conditions [pp. 7–8]." Later (Torrance, 1965), however, he used the term and suggested that "the distinctive element in group stress is lack of structure or loss of anchor in reality experienced as a result of the stressful conditions [p. 140]." Thus, while food deprivation, extreme cold, or prolonged isolation

---

[1] A rather sizable volume of literature exists on personal or psychological stress. Among the better reviews are: Basowitz, H., et al. *Anxiety and stress*. New York: McGraw-Hill, 1955. Chiles, W. D. *Psychological stress as a theoretical concept*. July 1957, Dayton, Ohio, Wright-Patterson AFB, Wright Air Development Center. Harris, W., Machie, R., & Wilson, C. L. *Performance under stress: A review and critique of recent studies*. Los Angeles: Human Factors Research, 1956. Janis, I. L. *Psychological stress*. New York: Wiley, 1958. Selye, H. *The stresses of life*. New York: McGraw-Hill, 1956. Lazarus, R. S. *Psychological stress and the coping process*. New York: McGraw-Hill, 1966.

might be elements which partially characterize an "extreme situation," Torrance placed major emphasis on the loss of structure. This has its parallel in Bettleheim's description of deprivation which produces inability to predict outcomes of day to day events. We found this to be a central idea in related literature, for example, in the study of crises.

Crisis Research

Crisis, like the term stress, has been defined in a variety of ways. The early work of W. I. Thomas (1909) has been influential and many of his formulations remain current.[2] Thomas (1909) defined a crisis as "simply a disturbance of habit [p. 18]." He emphasized that crises precipitate change in societies and that specialized occupations are developed by societies to deal with crises, for example, medicine men, priests, and judges.

Interest in crises is found in many substantive areas. For example, Straus (1964) has reported on recent experiments in which families were subjected to a simulated crisis which was created through modification of procedures first developed by Swanson and later modified by Hamblin.

> Each family was directed to figure out the rules of a game and their scores were compared to those of a hypothetical "average family." After four periods of play those families selected as crisis families . . . receive penalty lights, and fail to keep up with the scores of the "average family." This is defined as a crisis because the previously successful mode of play suddenly becomes ineffective and the family fails to achieve its goals using these patterns [pp. 3–4].

The concept of crisis with implications for mental health was explored by Miller and Iscoe (1963) who concluded that the following criteria indicate when an emotional crisis is present: (1) the time factor (acute rather than chronic), (2) marked changes in behavior (less effective, attempts to discharge tensions), (3) subjective aspects (feelings of helplessness and ineffectiveness in the face of what appear to be insoluble problems), (4) relativistic aspects (what constitutes a crisis to one individual or group does not constitute it for another group), and (5) organismic tension (experienced in a variety of ways, may be temporary or long term) [p. 196].

A series of studies in decision making under crisis conditions were completed at Northwestern University. Efforts were made to identify

---

[2] For example, see Nall, E. W. The influence of crisis in the modification of social organization. Unpublished Master's thesis, Department of Sociology, Michigan State University, 1956, pp. 10–11. (A crisis is "a destruction of the social system resulting from any cause.")

basic characteristics of a crisis. Robinson (1962) concluded that "a situation of the greatest severity (the most crisis-like) would be one in which the occasion for decision arose from without the decisional unit, required a prompt decision, and involved very high stakes [p. 8]."

While working on the same project, Hermann (1963) suggested that an organizational crisis could be conceptualized along three dimensions. "An organizational crisis (1) threatens high priority values of the organization, (2) presents a restricted amount of time in which a response can be made, and (3) is unexpected or unanticipated by the organization [p. 64]."[3] It is important to note that Hermann utilized the concept of *crisis stimulus* and referred to the organization as responding to such a stimulus. However, "crisis stimulus" and "crisis response" or "reaction" were used by Hermann "to separate aspects of the same concept [p. 65]."

Form and Nosow (1958) used the concept of crisis to conceptualize individual, group, and organizational behavior following a community disaster. Note how the concepts of disaster and crisis are related; that is, the disaster creates a crisis:

> The concept "disaster" is generally applied to the condition of a community at a particular point in time. From the point of view of its residents, the disaster creates crisis. Crisis may be considered as a breakdown of the social relations and social systems in a community that are of greatest significance to the individual or particular organization involved. In another sense, crisis may be thought of as a destruction of the stable relationships that are necessary for the person. Crisis emerges when these relationships are perceived as being destroyed or in process of destruction [p. 12].

In summary, two important ideas should be noted. A crisis situation is defined as one where previous modes of behavior are applicable no longer. Secondly, crisis might be conceptualized as a continuous rather than a discrete variable such that the intensity of the crisis might be measured by several indicators, for example, priority of values threatened, amount of available response time, and so on.

Disaster Research

Natural disasters have long been a topic of interest of social scientists. While responses to numerous disasters have been "analyzed," most re-

---

[3] C. F. Hermann. Some consequences of crisis which limit the viability of organizations. *Administrative Science Quarterly*, June 1963, VIII, 64. A similar discussion was presented by C. F. Hermann et al., Memorandum No. 1 for Project Michelson: Some relations of crisis to selected decision process and outcome variables. Unpublished research report for the Studies in Crisis Decision-Making Project, pp. 3–6. Evanston, Ill.: Northwestern University, 1964.

ports have been descriptive and journalistic rather than theoretically oriented.[4]

Recently, Barton (1963) reviewed several classic disaster studies and attempted to develop a theoretical model. He conceptualized disaster as part of a larger category—collective stress—which was defined as "a large unfavorable change in the inputs of some social system [p. 3]." By inputs he referred to the physical environment, external economic relationships, external power relationships, and sources of personnel. Barton was able to weave previous disaster studies into this input-output model where social systems were viewed as existing not in a vacuum, but rather a dynamic, ever-changing environment. A disaster may result in changes in the input variables, which, in turn, may cause change in the social system.

From a different perspective, Bates and his associates (1963) analyzed portions of their data from the response to Hurricane Audrey in terms of various types of "role stresses." The hurricane was conceived as an external cause which created various types of stress, for example, loss of a family member, neighbor, or friend; loss of property; disruption of businesses and occupations; and the general disruption of the community social organization. The impact of these events on individuals was analyzed in terms of role stresses of which four types were formulated: (1) role conflict—conflict between the roles an individual plays; (2) role frustration—playing of normal roles may not be possible for some time

---

[4] Over 300 reports on natural disasters have been located and analyzed by the Disaster Research Center staff. Among the more theoretically oriented works are: Baker, G. W., & Chapman, D. W. *Man and society in disaster*. New York: McGraw-Hill, 1955. Barton (1963). Bates, (1963). Clifford, R. A. *The Rio Grande flood: A comparative study of border communities in disaster*. Washington, D. C.: National Academy of Sciences—National Research Council, 1956. Crane, B. G. Intergovernmental relations in disaster relief in Texas. Unpublished Ph.D. dissertation, Department of Sociology, University of Texas, 1960. Crawford, F. R. Patterns of family readjustment to tornadic disasters: A sociological case study. Unpublished Ph.D. dissertation, Department of Sociology, University of Texas, 1957. Fogleman, C. W. Family and community in disaster: A socio-psychological study of the effects of a major disaster upon individuals and groups within the impact area. Unpublished Ph.D. dissertation, Department of Sociology, Louisiana State University, 1958. Form & Nosow (1958). Fritz, C. E., & Mathewson, J. H. *Convergence behavior in disasters*. Washington, D. C.: National Academy of Sciences—National Research Council, 1957. Moore, H. E., et al. *Before the wind: A study of the response to hurricane Carla*. Washington, D. C.: National Academy of Sciences—National Research Council, 1963. Rosow, I. L. Conflict of authority in natural disaster. Ph.D. dissertation, Department of Sociology, Harvard University, 1955. Schatzman, L. A sequence pattern of disaster and its consequences for community. Ph.D. dissertation, Department of Sociology, Indiana University, 1960. Stoddard, E. R. Catastrophe and crisis in a flooded border community: An analytical approach to disaster emergence. Ph.D. dissertation, Department of Sociology, Michigan State University, 1961. Williams, H. B. Communication in community disasters. Ph.D. dissertation, Department of Sociology, University of North Carolina, 1956.

after the disaster; (3) role inadequacy—inability of the individual to play the role he is expected to play because of personal inadequacy; and (4) role saturation—overloading the individual with role expectations or not expecting enough of him [pp. 53–60].

Of major importance, however, is the idea that disasters may be viewed as external events which precipitate a variety of environmental changes within which individuals, groups, and organizations function. As they attempt to cope with the changed environment we might refer to them as being under stress.

Research on Complex Organizations

Many sociologists have used the concept of stress in the "natural system" organizational model.[5] With this model, organizations are viewed as complex systems which strive for survival through continuous adaptation. Merton (1957), for example, suggested that "strain" might serve as the key concept to avoid static functional analysis.

The key concept bridging the gap between statics and dynamics in functional theory is that of strain, tension, contradiction, or discrepancy between the component elements of social and cultural structure. Such strains may be dysfunctional for the social system in its then existing form; they may also be instrumental in leading to changes in that system. In any case, they exert pressure for change. When social mechanisms for controlling them are operating effectively, these strains are kept within such bounds as to limit change of the social structure [p. 122].

Similarly, Parsons (1962) utilized the concept of strain to inject a dynamic quality into social system analysis. He defined strain as "a condition in the *relation* between two or more structured units (i.e., subsystems of the system) that constitutes a tendency or pressure toward changing that relation to one incompatible with the equilibrium of the relevant part of the system [p. 71]." In his discussion of structural change, the concept of strain is crucial. Hence: "Structural change is possible only when a certain level of strain on institutionalized structure is reached [p. 75]."

In his paper, "A Theory of Role Strain," Goode (1960) re-echoed the view that structural inconsistencies exist in society. He made an initial effort to list the types or sources of role strain (difficulty in meeting given

---

[5] The term is from Gouldner in which he makes a distinction between the "natural system" and "rational" models for the analysis of complex organizations. See Gouldner, A. W. Organizational analysis. In Merton, R. K., et al. (Eds.), *Sociology today.* New York: Basic Books, 1959, pp. 400–428. See also Thompson, J. D. *Organizations in action.* New York: McGraw-Hill, 1967.

role demands) and suggested that because individuals cannot fully satisfy all demands, they must move through a continuous sequence of role decisions and bargains by which they attempt to adjust the demands. Society imposes limits on behavior as well as provides certain mechanisms for the reduction of strain. The degree of societal integration, determined by the amount and type of strain, is thus reflected by the sum of role decisions made by actors as they endeavor to reduce strain.

This idea is very similar to Guest's (1962) interpretation of the changes in "plant Y" which was "acutely ill" and became "extremely healthy" over a three-year period. Guest concluded that the organization became better integrated, that is, that consensus increased on role expectations held by various position incumbents. Lack of such consensus "determines the degree of tension and stress likely to be found in the organization [p. 144]." Similarly, Stogdill (1959) defined group integration as "the extent to which structure and operations are capable of being maintained under stress [p. 178]."

Using the terms somewhat differently, Bertrand (1963) suggested a similar analysis. He defined stress as "a force exerted between contiguous portions of a structural whole" and strain as "relating to the degree with which a given actor is able to manage his tensions." Thus, for Bertrand the difference is that "conceptually, strain may be distinguished as a functional (or dysfunctional) process, whereas stress is a structural element [p. 4]." He illustrated the distinction with the following example: "In a given factory system, stress will be inherent in the fact that the inept boss' son is selected to fill an important executive position. Strain associated with this stress will be manifest in the behavior of those persons who must put up with this 'actor,' even though his ineptness is a source of frustration for them."

Previous simulation research emphasized an additional basic notion. During the early 1950s, Kennedy, Chapman, Biel, and Newell conducted four experiments in the Air Defense Direction Center (Chapman & Kennedy, 1960). Teams of airmen worked together to "defend" an area of roughly 100,000 square miles by tracking all simulated air traffic. As the number of tracks increased and saturation of the group seemed imminent, the experimenters observed changes in group performance. These changes led Kennedy and Chapman to conclude: "These empirical results seem to indicate that an organization will look for new patterns of behavior when it needs them—when it is under stress [p. 144]."

More detailed analysis revealed that as the total number of tracks increased, the total team effort increased only slightly. However, there was severe reduction in attention to lower priority tracks as the airmen increasingly discriminated between threatening and nonthreatening flights. As task inputs were altered, they modified their model of organization (Chapman & Kennedy, 1960, p. 143). Thus the organization changed under stress, that is, when there was an increase in demands on the system.

Stress and strain are concepts which are used in the literature on complex organizations. Precise definitions usually are not offered; indeed, there appears to be little consensus as to whether they are interchangeable terms. However, the literature suggests clearly that structural inconsistency or strain is a necessary variable in understanding organizational change. Also, the degree of integration or lack of strain appears to be a key variable in predicting the amount of stress a social unit might tolerate. Finally, there is some evidence that as the demands on an organization increase new modes of response will develop, and that then there will be structural change.

A CONCEPTUAL FRAMEWORK FOR THE ANALYSIS OF ORGANIZATIONAL STRESS IN DISASTER

Firsthand observation by Disaster Research Center field teams in forty disasters over a three-and-a-half-year period indicates rather clearly that the organizations and groups which participate in disaster related activities following a community disaster are not of a single type. At the one extreme are organizations such as the police which routinely handle emergencies varying in scope and severity, and at the other are emergent units such as new coordinating bodies and rescue teams. We have identified four relatively discrete types of such organized units: established, expanding, extending, and emerging units. The conceptual framework to be presented here applies at a very general level to the first three types but in only a limited fashion to the fourth, the emerging groups. It was developed primarily in reference to what we call established organizations and seems to have its greatest utility in conducting research on them.

An organization is a relatively permanent and relatively complex discernible interaction system.[6] This definition emphasizes three major elements. First, the organization is conceived of as an interaction *system* and hence has the characteristics commonly associated with a social system, for example, interdependence of parts and some type of boundary. This interaction system is relatively complex, both horizontally and vertically. It is relatively permanent in that it exists over a period of time.

When organizational incumbents are observed over a prolonged period of time, certain patterns or similarities in activity and interaction

---

[6] Much of the basic framework outlined here was initially formulated by Haas. See Haas, J. E. Role, position and social organization: A conceptual formulation. *Midwest Sociologist*, December 1956, **XIX**, 33–37. Haas, J. E. *Role conception and group consensus*. Columbus, Ohio: Ohio State University Bureau of Business Research, 1964, pp. 25–31.

sequence can be noted.[7] These various interaction patterns, among members, as well as between incumbents and nonmembers, are summarized under the heading *performance structure* of the organization. There are, of course, many types of patterned interaction but we have chosen to focus initially on those dealing with (1) organizational tasks, (2) decision making, (3) enactment of authority and influence, and (4) communication.

As sociologists often point out, much of the patterning which occurs in human interaction flows from a framework of social norms. The patterned interaction and activity of an organization is produced in large measure by a host of social norms which come from the general culture as well as from within the organizational system itself. The *normative structure* of an organization is composed of social norms which specify required and permissible interaction and activity. Social norms are ideas about how classes or categories of persons ought to act and interact in specified situations. They are not descriptions of behavior but specifications for behavior. Norms are clustered into roles and positions; thus, any position incumbent is expected to (should) behave in accordance with an entire set of norms which specify the reciprocal behaviors which are to occur between a person in his position and those in a series of other positions.[8] Since norms are both official and unofficial in origin and source of sanctioning we make a conceptual distinction between the official normative structure and the unofficial normative structure. The stability of patterned interaction over time, even where member turnover is considerable, suggests that the normative structure has a persistence that goes beyond the participation of any particular combination of persons as members.

The *interpersonal structure* consists of relatively stable sets of person-to-person orientations and understandings that develop over time among the specific organizational members. In contrast to norms which are categorical in nature, these understandings emerge as persons respond

---

[7] This perspective, with its focus on analysis of interaction patterns has evolved from traditional small group research. See Whyte, W. F. *Street corner society: The social structure of an Italian slum.* Chicago: University of Chicago Press, 1943. Newcomb, T. M. *The acquaintance process.* New York: Holt, Rinehart and Winston, 1961. Sherif, M., & Sherif, C. W. *Reference groups: Exploration into conformity and deviation of adolescents.* New York: Harper & Row, 1964. Bales, R. F. The equilibrium problems in small groups. In A. P. Hare, E. F. Borgatta, & R. F. Bales (Eds.), *Small groups: Studies in social interaction.* New York: Alfred A. Knopf, 1961. Homans, G. C., *The Human Group.* New York: Harcourt, Brace & World, 1950. Mills, T. M. *Group transformation: An analysis of a learning group.* Englewood Cliffs, N. J.: Prentice Hall, 1964.

[8] Our usage of the concepts norm, role, and position are similar to Haas's original formulation. See Haas, J. E. Role, position and social organization. Gross et al. (1958), pp. 3–69. Merton, R. K. *Social theory and social structure.* (Rev. ed.) New York: The Free Press, 1957, pp. 368–384. Merton, R. K. The role set: Problems in sociological theory. *British Journal of Sociology,* June 1957, **VIII**, 106–120.

to each other as unique individuals. Note, however, that we are not referring to individual characteristics as such, but rather to types of relationships which emerge and exist between particular organizational members, independent of the positions they enact.

The internal and external resources of an organization also have a shaping and constraining influence on the patterned interaction and activity which can be observed. The ecological distribution of offices and equipment is but one example. Such resources are of three general types: (1) equipment, materials, and buildings, (2) information and records, and (3) personnel.[9] This notion includes physical objects, their location in space and perhaps most significantly sets of ideas about their appropriate and potential utilization. Also included would be the skills and organizational "know-how" of the members of the organization. To illustrate: After an earthquake, an organization legally responsible for coordinating the efforts of at least a dozen other organizations was housed in a building with grossly inadequate space, especially for a staff swollen to many times its normal size. Clearly these internal resources shaped and constrained the actions and patterned interaction which occurred. But just as obviously the performance structure was affected by external resources. The telephone system for the entire city had become almost totally inoperative but several nearby organizations had mobile radio units which could be utilized immediately and partial communication was quickly restored with those organizations whose efforts were to be coordinated.

But organizations are not static systems. After a disaster the dynamic quality is more readily observed. It should be noted that on any given "typical" day organizational incumbents engage in a large number of patterned actions which, when viewed collectively, constitute the performance structure of the organization. It is also clear that in addition to the current performance structure, an organization could be engaged in a variety of other actions. That is, given its normative structure, interpersonal structure, and resources, it is capable of carrying out what is already being done, and many other things as well. Thus, *organizational capability* is defined as the range of possible organizational actions which an organization could perform if appropriate decisions to do so were made.

Organizational demands may emanate from a variety of sources. They may come from individual citizens, another organization such as city or state governmental units, or any other organization with which the focal organization has a relationship. Often demands are self-imposed

---

[9] E. W. Bakke, Concept of the social organization. In M. Haire (Ed.), *Modern organizational theory.* New York: Wiley, 1959, pp. 16–75. Bakke made a similar distinction between ideational resources, human resources, material resources, and so forth, pp. 40–43.

by organizational members who, after receiving cues from the environment, proceed to act without waiting for a specific request from a nonmember. The normative structure of an organization will usually include a series of "if-then" specifications. For example, if a certain external change occurs (for example, a tornado which would probably knock down power lines), then a certain set of prescribed actions should take place. The broad concept, organizational demands, may thus be thought of as requests or commands for organizational action which are either received directly by some member of the organization or result from knowledge of demand-relevant cues. A distinction is made between potential demands and legitimate demands, the latter being those which are defined by organizational incumbents as falling within the areas of responsibility of the organization.

Demands on an organization may vary somewhat from day to day and in some organizations vary considerably from season to season. Such variation may be both quantitative and/or qualitative. For example, when the state fair is in session the police may have to cope with a sharp increase in traffic congestion. A highway department may be faced with a qualitative change when a freak snowstorm hits an area which seldom has significant snowfall.

In addition to quantitative or qualitative fluctuations in demands, variations as to priorities may also occur. Certain demands, if not fulfilled, have more serious consequences, that is, some are more important than others, for either the welfare of the organization or the total community. High priority values of the organization are threatened by some demands. Hence, a decision required by the mayor's office to order, or not to order, evacuation of a city in light of an approaching hurricane may be the most important decision the mayor might make while in his term of office. Closely related to the degree of seriousness attached to the demand is the variable of time, that is, how much time is available before organizational action is required. These two variables, considered jointly, determine the priority of the demand. Thus, organizational demands may vary along three separate axes: quantity of demands, actual qualitative changes in demands, and priorities attached to demands.

The interrelations among the variables discussed so far are crucial. Let us summarize briefly the framework thus far presented. An organization is a complex interaction system. Empirical referents which can be directly observed are the patterned interaction sequences which collectively make up the performance structure. As is illustrated in Figure 15–1, several concepts are used to explain why performance structures assume particular patterns. Much observed behavior of groups can be understood by the normative structure when such concepts as positions, roles, official and unofficial normative structures are used. However, certain activity will appear that will remain unexplainable unless analysts are aware of interpersonal relationships, idiosyncratic to the particular set of incumbents. Considered jointly, these two concepts explain much interaction. However, five groups may have very similar normative and interpersonal structures but exhibit different interaction patterns largely because of the physical design of work areas. Thus, such internal resources as ecological placement of desks or offices must be taken into account. Finally, differences in organizational behavior may result because of variation in external resources. These four concepts, viewed as highly interrelated, can account for all patterned interaction at any given point in time. It should be clear that the concepts are empirically overlapping—interaction is guided by all four factors simultaneously. Conceptually, however, they are four distinct analytical tools.

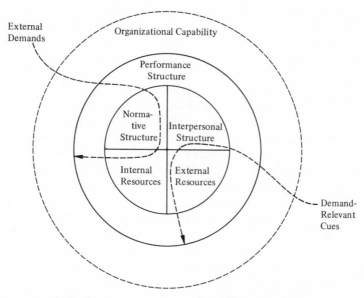

FIGURE 15–1. Interrelationships of basic concepts.

The paths of the arrows through the four elements are drawn for illustrative purposes only; no theoretical route is intended to be implied other than to point out that all of the four elements play a part in determining the effect of a demand on the performance structure.

These four elements are also related to the concepts of organizational demands and capability. The normative structure, which suggests how and when internal and external resources ought to be utilized, appears to occupy a central position in limiting organizational capability. Organizational demands are viewed as constantly entering an organization at a variety of points. Certain demand-relevant cues from outside the organization may also enter the system through the performance structure. However, response to such cues, as well as specific external demands, cannot be anticipated except through an awareness of the four basic elements, as the very acceptance or rejection of potential demands is determined by a composite of the four elements. Thus, a demand may enter an organization through an incumbent who may evaluate it not to be a legitimate concern of the organization on the basis of the normative structure, that is, the demand is not something the organization ought to fulfill. Such demands may be returned to the sender or just ignored.

Usually demands enter organizations at normatively prescribed entry points and are processed through similarly prescribed channels. It is obvious, however, that demands are not processed only on the basis of the normative structure, as frequently a demand will be rerouted so as to arrive at a position incumbent not prescribed by the normative structure. Such an incumbent may have been selected because of his perceived competence for dealing with this particular demand or because the sender just happened to like or dislike him. At any rate, the demand did not follow the channel prescribed by the normative structure, and explanations for such deviations may be found in the interpersonal structure. Similarly, assignment of priorities to demands determines how fast each will be acted upon. The four basic elements—normative and interpersonal structures and internal and external resources—can again be used to explain this process. Determination of the legitimacy of demands and assignment of priorities to demands is crucial in understanding organizational behavior as frequently there is dissensus among organizational incumbents concerning the legitimacy and/or priorities of demands. This brings us to the next basic concept, that of organizational strain.

Organizational strain is defined as inconsistencies or discrepancies between structural elements of an organization. Strain at the lowest structural level has been labeled *role conflict*; it occurs when various role requirements are of such a nature that individuals are faced with conflicting specifications (Gross et al., 1958). Evidence that role conflict exists in most organizations was best supported by the impressive study of Kahn, Wolfe, Quinn, and Snoek (1964). Strain at the dyadic level may involve role conflict in which specifications are inconsistent or excessive, or role ambiguity in which they are poorly defined.

At another level, inconsistencies may exist between official and unofficial structures. Similarly, normative dissensus may be focalized between two structural units of an organization (for example, departments). Among the several dimensions about which dissensus may exist are the legitimacy and priority of demands. For example, following an earthquake, first-aid units attached to a fire department may want to render all the help they can in searching for victims, even to the point of utilizing additional men from other units, for instance, those with a pumper. However, if there is danger of numerous fires developing (which frequently occurs after earthquakes because of the movement of underground gas pipes), fire officials may choose to place highest priority on maintaining a "state of readiness" for fire suppression.

Although such structural inconsistencies are probably found in varying degrees in all organizations and simply exist as part of the ongoing structure, they may result in serious organizational problems in times of disaster. Knowledge of such organizational strain is essential in predicting organizational reaction to stress situations since we would hypothesize that it is precisely at these points that one might anticipate "breakdown" or emergent problems.

It is assumed that organizational capability and demand represent a dynamic equilibrium, where under normal conditions a relatively stable relationship exists with capability exceeding demands. Organizational stress is not viewed as a set of external conditions, but rather is a term used to refer to the state of an organization when certain conditions are present. Thus, *organizational stress* is defined as the organizational state or condition when organizational demands exceed organizational capability.[10] Organizational stress is not a discrete variable but, rather, constitutes a continuum. The degree of stress is determined by the disparity between two variables: (1) level of organizational demands and (2) level of capability. Upon analysis, the complexity of this relationship becomes apparent. To simplify as much as possible let us examine the characteristics of a maximum stress situation such as might be produced initially by a natural disaster. Note that it is not the disaster per se that is the source of the stress, but rather the change in demands and capability.

A. Change in demands made on the organization
   1. Quantity
      a. Sharp increase.
      b. Increase is unanticipated.
   2. Priority
      a. Consequences of organizational action threaten central values

---

[10] Argyris has defined organizational stress as "a state that exists when the actual giving and receiving loads of the parts are forced to go beyond their 'threshold' so that there is a disequilibrium in the relationship among the parts."—Argyris, C. *Integrating the individual and the organization.* New York: Wiley, 1964, p. 128. Although somewhat similar to our conceptualization, the specific elements which should be measured to determine the presence or degree of stress remain vague. Note that Argyris refers to "an organizational state" rather than only a set of external conditions. For a somewhat similar analysis see R. L. Meier, Information input overload: Features of growth in communications-oriented institutions. In F. Massarik & P. Ratoosh (Eds.), *Mathematical explorations in behavioral science.* Homewood, Ill.: Richard D. Irwin, 1965, pp. 235–273.

of organization or society, that is, organizational actions are
viewed with increased seriousness.

    b. Immediate organizational action is required.

  3. Qualitative changes

    a. Demands previously met but not currently being met are made
on the organization.

    b. New demands not previously made on the organization are
made and temporarily accepted by the organization.

B. Change in capability of the organization[11]

  1. Intraorganizational

    a. Absence of personnel, especially key personnel.

    b. Absence of important equipment, material, or buildings.

    c. Absence of crucial information or records.

  2. Extraorganizational

    a. Absence of personnel, especially key personnel.

    b. Absence of important equipment, material, or buildings.

    c. Absence of crucial information or records.

Some of these factors may be illustrated in the following way by
examples drawn from the field work of the Disaster Research Center.

After the October 1963 Coliseum explosion in Indianapolis, one
hospital had 120 injured persons enter its emergency room within a
one-hour period. (A.1a.)

In the 1964 Anchorage, Alaska, earthquake, there was neither warning nor a previous event of a similar nature. The unexpectedness of
demands is perhaps best illustrated by the fact that no organization, with
the exception of the public utilities, had any plans for dealing with
peacetime disasters. (A.1b.)

Because of the high value placed on life within American culture,
the police at the Indianapolis Coliseum explosion initially focused much
of their effort on transporting the injured to hospitals instead of on
controlling traffic and securing the area. (A.2a.)

In Crescent City, California, following the March 27, 1964, Alaska
earthquake, the fire department, while assisting the police in security
and rescue activities, was suddenly faced, right after the fourth seismic

---

[11] The term "absence" is used in a broad sense here, for example, a key official
may have been killed or injured in the disaster or may have been out of town at
the time he was needed; similarly equipment, material, and information may have
been damaged, or have been taken elsewhere before the disaster. At any rate, they
were unavailable when needed. Key personnel from the viewpoint of the focal
organization, for example, a liaison person may be more important than a vice president
to an outside organization depending on the type of relationship with the focal
organization. Similarly in a nuclear accident, loss of members of a civil defense
radiological team may leave civil defense without anyone who can precisely measure
the level of radioactivity. This would be crucial to the police department and other
organizations even though top civil defense administrative officers may be present.

sea-wave hit, with a number of small fires over a twenty-nine block area as well as a major fire at an oil and gasoline facility. (A.2b.)

In floods, in Montana, in early June 1964, a city engineering department was called upon to direct rescue and evacuation operations and to help in traffic control and security in addition to its normal engineering functions. (A.3b.)

In the Niigata earthquake in Japan, some organizations had as many as half of their personnel absent for extended periods of time because their families had been affected by the earthquake itself or by resulting fires and floods. (B.1a.)

After Hurricane Betsy in New Orleans, both the police and fire departments lost vehicles when they were swamped by the rapidly rising water. (B.1b.)

Vital records which could have been of invaluable aid in identifying the thousands of dead were buried under tons of debris at the Vaiont Dam disaster in Italy, November 1963. (B.1c.)

SOME BASIC PROBLEMS

Measurement of Demand Level and Capability

It is clear then, that a condition of stress in an organization may be produced by a change in capability, by a change in demands, or some combination of both. The general hypothesis which emerges is that there will be a change in the organizational performance structure when the legitimate demands placed on the organization are greater than its capability. At this point a basic methodological problem must be treated. If one is interested in understanding and predicting the various consequences of organizational stress he must be able to determine if it is present and the degree to which it is present. This requires a valid measure of demand level and level of organizational capability. Further, the two measures must be in some type of commensurate units or at least translatable into some common unit of comparison so that it can be determined whether or not at a given point in time the total demand on the organization is in fact greater than its capability, that is, whether or not a condition of stress actually exists. As will be pointed out later, this measurement problem apparently can be handled satisfactorily for certain organizations but for many it still appears to be problematic—or at least not readily feasible.

Let us be more specific about these measurement problems. Even the problem of measuring demand level is not an uncomplicated one. Look at the hospital as an example. We may wish to count the number of patients entering the hospital as a crude indicator of demand level. But note that of those entering via the emergency room some are "treated and released," some are "held for observation" ranging from a few hours to several days, some are "critical" cases requiring immediate and intensive care, some require many hours of surgery while others only minor medical treatment. Clearly, each patient is not the same "demand unit" as every other patient. The same may be said for patients entering via the regular admitting office.

Quite apart from the time involved for diagnosis and treatment the various patients may represent different kinds of demand. Given the norms of the hospital, ten cases of food poisoning represent a different demand than ten patients with multiple fractures and massive hemorrhaging. This suggests the necessity for classifying the various types of demand and their concomitant capability requirements. A 30-quart supply of whole blood may be more than an adequate resource for accident victims but it is largely irrelevant for patients with food poisoning.

It is also clear from our research thus far that at a given point in time the demand level may vary considerably from one segment of the organization to the next. For an electric company, after a tornado the demand level for the maintenance and repair department may be very high while there may be no increase at all in the demand for meter reading and billing.

To summarize, then, it should be remembered that measurement of demand level in an organization must take the following, at least, into account.

1. Demand units may vary as to the total amount of effort required.
2. The total amount of time necessary for an acceptable response may also vary.
3. Speed or urgency will be critical in some cases but not in others.
4. Demand units will vary as to the kind of response required.
5. At any given point in time the demand level may vary among segments of the organization.

Now we need to note some of the problems involved in measuring organizational capability. In every organization there is undoubtedly some "interchangeability of parts," but in most modern organizations this possibility is relatively limited. Clearly, female clerks in an electric company contribute very little to the organization's capability to repair downed electric lines. A laboratory technician cannot be substituted for a surgeon. For most organizations, then, the total number of personnel is not a useful indicator of capability level. This would suggest that a useful measure of capability needs to include an assessment of the various capabilities of the various segments of the organization. In short, it requires a *profile* of capabilities which is relevant for the kinds of demands which do or could develop.

Capability does not refer to what has been accomplished but to what could be accomplished. Even though department X has never processed more than N units in any previous 24-hour period, it may actually have a capability of $N + 10$. Our observations indicate that when a disaster strikes a community the productivity of many organizations increases remarkably which suggests that predisaster estimates of capability would have been too low in many cases. Well-planned field exercises and laboratory simulations may provide reasonable estimates in some cases but the general problem is a difficult one.

The time factor is another crucial element in estimating capability. If given an indefinite amount of time even a small, "ill-equipped" organization can accomplish wonders. In most organizations, however, there are norms which specify what is an acceptable as contrasted to an intolerable time lag in the accomplishment of various tasks. The police may be able to disperse a crowd of 1000 in three hours but not in 10 minutes. Shall we say that the demand was greater than their capability from the very instant that the crowd formed or only after some reasonable length of time (for example, 45 minutes) has elapsed? Clearly some time parameter must be incorporated into measures of capability.

It should also be noted that capability is not a statistic variable. The personnel capability of an organization may triple when all of the off-duty members finally report for work. Furthermore, an organization will have some external resources which, when mobilized, may increase its capability sharply. Later, withdrawal of some of these resources can reduce the over-all capability. Injuries, illness, and equipment breakdown may also produce a reduction in capability level. Just as the demands on an organization may fluctuate over a period of time so too may the capability level. Any very useful research on organizational stress will need to include data on variation over time for both of these basic variables.

The discussion of these measurement problems is by no means complete, but from what has been presented it is probably safe to say that the *direct* measurement of organizational stress as conceptualized here will probably not be feasible for most research efforts in the near future. What then are the available alternatives?

Suppose that we view stress in the way that a physician thinks of illness. Illness refers to the state or condition of an organism and is said to exist when certain indicators or symptoms are present. Thus, when changes in normal functioning of the organism occur, as indicated by the presence of a fever, for example, illness is said to be present. The word *ill* is used as a descriptive adjective, that is, it describes the general state of the organism. The existence of this condition may be known only by certain observable indicators, and no direct measure of the condition may be available. It is possible then that we may be able to ascertain the existence of the stress condition by noting certain standardized symptoms as indicators. Further, we may discover that the symptoms of mild stress differ significantly from those of acute stress. In short, we may be able to get satisfactory but indirect measures of organizational stress. Such an approach has many precedents in sociological and psychological research.

The Search for Stress Indicators

How might social scientists proceed in an effort to locate valid indicators of organizational stress? What kinds of indicators should be seriously examined? We might start by looking for any significant changes in the performance structure of an organization which follow a large-scale alteration of the environment such as occurs in a natural disaster. But we have learned that some of these observable changes are planned and programed in advance. This is obvious when a hospital rehearses its "disaster plan." Such contingency plans will often produce an oversupply of personnel and significant modifications in procedures, interaction, and activity patterns. These changes can and do occur in the absence of any significant change in demand level as when a hospital is warned that mass casualties will soon arrive and they never materialize. Such planned changes may occur in the absence of stress.

But suppose we look at "unplanned" changes—those which occur with little or no consultation and overt decision making involved. On the face of it, one could anticipate that when demand exceeds capability the most obvious change would be either disorganization and irrelevant activity or a changed mode of organization which appears to be both relevant and somewhat effective. We have seen very little evidence of the former but a good deal of the latter. In short, it is our impression that when an organization or part thereof appears to be clearly overloaded (in a state of stress), a variety of unplanned changes in the performance structure occur most of which appear to be adaptive rather than maladaptive in relation to the immediate demand level. Among the unplanned changes which occur there ought to be certain kinds which reoccur in many organizations which appear to be under stress and, over a period of time, it ought to be possible to isolate some of the more valid ones to use as standard indicators of organizational stress.

The search for these stress indicators could proceed on two fronts. First, there should be field studies of organizations in disaster or other unusual settings where there appears to be a disparity in the demand-capability ratio. At a minimum, it should be possible to locate organizations or parts of organizations where the evidence clearly suggests that they are under stress even though exact measures of demand and capability are not readily available. For example, in the blizzard of

1967, the Chicago Transit Authority lost almost all of its bus transportation capability at a time when there was a sharp increase in demand. In cases like this a careful examination of the unplanned changes in the organizational performance structure, when compared to the normal patterns and contingency plans, should yield a variety of stress indicators. In other disasters, for example, where one hospital was clearly overloaded while others in the same community were not, the latter could be used for control purposes to be certain that some apparent indicators were not just artifacts of the altering and warning processes. During a widespread electric power blackout it is likely that many organizations would be under stress primarily through a drastic reduction in capability. It was a qualitative change in demands that probably put the Dallas police force under stress following the assassination of President Kennedy.

A second approach to the search for stress indicators can be conducted through laboratory simulation where small organizations or segments of larger organizations can be brought to the laboratory and realistic simulations of both normal and stress periods can be conducted.[12] The problems of observing and recording unplanned changes are considerably less than in field studies, but it must be recognized that it simply is not feasible to bring some organizations or segments of organizations into a laboratory, for example, the emergency room of a hospital, if the intent is to analyze such units under realistic conditions. But having stated this reservation, it should be made clear that realistic laboratory simulation in the social sciences has scarcely gotten under way. Practitioners of the "hard sciences" with all of their mathematical models and exotic instrumentation have nevertheless spent billions of dollars conducting research through the use of simulators of one kind or another. It would appear that social scientists have been both timid and lacking in imagination when it comes to attempting realistic simulation of social systems. If the study of system stress is a justifiable objective, then serious attention ought to be given to realistic simulation as one method to be used.

Whether in the laboratory or the field, what kinds of stress indicators might we hope to isolate? In any research effort what is observed and recorded flows from the theoretical framework being utilized. Since a number of theoretical perspectives dealing with system stress will undoubtedly emerge, it is almost certain that the stress indicators "found"

---

[12] T. E. Drabek, *Laboratory simulation of a police communication system under stress*. Columbus, Ohio: Ohio State University, College of Commerce, Division of Research, in press. See also Drabek, T. E., & Haas, J. E. Realism in laboratory simulation: Myth or method? *Social Forces*, March 1967, 337–346; and by the same authors, Organizational simulation: A study in method. Paper presented at the meeting of the Midwest Sociological Society, Madison, Wis., April 21–23, 1966.

to be the most significant will vary among researchers with different theoretical orientations, at least for a time.

Since we have begun work in this area and have attempted to outline a theoretical framework for the study of system stress, we will conclude by listing some of the ideas about stress indicators which appear to be potentially fruitful:

1. Drastic curtailment or complete cessation of certain ongoing activities of the organization.

The specific kind of activity may vary depending on the type of organization being observed. It could be record-keeping in some cases and sales or recruitment activity in another.

2. Change in the hierarchial level where "important" organizational decisions are made.

Evidence to date suggests that for some organizations critical decisions are made with greater frequency at lower levels of the organization during the stress period. It is possible that in other organizations the reverse trend may be in evidence.

3. Reduction in number of persons conferred with before certain types of decisions are reached.

This may apply to only certain types of decisions. Routine decisions may well be an exception.

4. Change in the pattern and utilization of standard channels of communication.

Since the actual communication channels normally used seldom are a carbon copy of the officially prescribed channels it will be necessary to use as a base line the network as it operates on a day-to-day basis prior to the stress period. It is anticipated that the changes would assume at least two forms: (a) reduction in the frequency and thoroughness of reporting upward in the organization, and (b) short-circuiting in both upward and downward communication.

5. Modes of communication shift to maximize speed even at the expense of established standards of thoroughness and accuracy.

Here we would anticipate a proportional increase in telephone and face-to-face communication as compared to written communication.

6. An increase in short-circuiting the lines of authority.

The sending of orders or requests is, of course, a special form of communication and some short-circuiting of official lines probably occurs almost daily. We would anticipate a significant increase in this phenomenon during the stress period.

Of course, the search for valid, standard stress indicators should not be viewed as an end in itself. It may well be true that some of the indicators will have relatively little theoretical import when viewed individually. The social scientist's ultimate interest here is in the processes and structural changes which make up the entire gestalt of organizational adaptation and response to overload. Nevertheless, the search for stress indicators appears to be a necessary step to both theoretical and methodological advances in the study of social systems under stress.

References

Barton, A. H. *Social organization under stress: A sociological review of disaster studies.* Washington, D. C.: National Academy of Sciences—National Research Council, 1963.

Bates, F. L., et al. *The social and psychological consequences of a natural disaster. A longitudinal study of hurricane Audrey.* Washington, D. C.: National Academy of Sciences—National Research Council, 1963.

Bertrand, A. L. The stress-strain element of social systems: A micro-theory of conflict and change, *Social Forces,* October 1963, **XLII.**

Bettelheim, B. Individual and mass behavior in extreme situations. *Journal of Abnormal and Social Psychology,* October 1943, **XXXVIII,** 417–452.

Bettelheim, B. *The informed heart.* New York: The Free Press, 1960.

Chapman, R. L., & Kennedy, J. L. The background and implications of the RAND corporation systems research laboratory studies. In A. H. Rubenstein & J. H. Chadwick (Eds.), *Some theories of organization.* Homewood, Ill.: Dorsey Press, 1960, pp. 139–146.

Form, W. H., & Nosow, S. *Community in disaster.* New York: Harper & Row, 1958.

Goode, W. J. A theory of role strain. *American Sociological Review,* August 1960, **XXV,** 483–496.

Gross, N., et al. *Explorations in role analysis.* New York: Wiley, 1958.

Guest, R. H. *Organizational change: The effect of successful leadership.* Homewood, Ill.: Dorsey Press, 1962.

Hermann, C. F. Some consequences of crisis which limit the viability of organizations. *Administrative Science Quarterly,* June 1963, **VIII,** 64.

Kahn, R. L., et al. *Organizational stress: Studies in role conflict and ambiguity.* New York: Wiley, 1964.

Merton, R. K. Social theory and social structure. (rev. ed.) New York: The Free Press, 1957.

Miller, K., & Iscoe, I. The concept of crisis: Current status and mental health implications. *Human Organization,* Fall 1963, **XXII,** 195–201.

Parsons, T., et al. *Theories of society.* New York: The Free Press, 1962.

Robinson, J. A. The concept of crisis in decision-making. *Series Studies in Social and Economic Sciences, Symposia Studies,* June 1962, No. 11. Washington, D. C.: The National Institute of Social and Behavioral Sciences.

Stogdill, R. M. *Individual behavior and group achievement.* New York: Oxford University Press, 1959.

Straus, M. A. Communication, creativity and social class difference in family response to an experimentally simulated crisis. Unpublished research report on Project 2027. Minneapolis: University of Minnesota, 1964.

Thomas, W. I. *Source book for social origins.* Boston: Gorham Press, 1909.

Torrance, E. P. Behaviorism emergencies and extreme situations. Unpublished final report, 1957, Lackland Air Force Base, Texas, Air Force Personnel and Training Research Center.

Torrance, E. P. *Constructive behavior: Stress, personality and mental health.* Belmont, Calif.: Wadsworth, 1965.

Wallace, A. F. C. *Human behavior in extreme situations: A survey of the literature and suggestions for further research.* Washington, D. C.: National Academy of Sciences—National Research Council, 1956.

16

the "ess" in stress: some conceptual and methodological problems[1]

Karl E. Weick

        Suppose someone asked you to list all the words you could think of that end in the letters *ess*. The word stress probably would be near the top of the list simply because of its salience in the context. But even more interesting is the fact that most of the *other* words on your list would be relevant to issues involving stress. At the risk of appearing trite, I have taken this correspondence seriously and will discuss several issues in stress research using labels that end in *ess*. Whether this exercise is merely cute, or acute in the sense of intensifying some signs that show promise of resolving problems (Webster's Third, 1966, p. 23), remains to be seen.

[1] Preparation of this paper was supported in part by the National Science Foundation through grant GS–1042.

CONCEPTUAL ISSUES

The Press of Stress: The Variable of Stimulus Intensity

It is certainly not a novel observation that the area of stress research has definitional problems. Because stress is so pervasive in human affairs, investigators have been tempted to use expansive definitions that incorporate stimuli, responses, and mediating processes. Unfortunately, efforts to be inclusive sometimes produce neglect of definitional components. In this section I intend to look closely at the stimulus side of stress, and specifically at the dimension of stimulus magnitude. We will try to see how much clarity is gained if we think seriously about the variable of stimulus intensity as a component of a stressful situation.

A sample definition of stress that incorporates the idea of stimulus intensity has been proposed by Harris, Mackie, and Wilson (1956): "stress will be thought of as operationally defined in terms of the stimulus conditions (which will) include those of sufficient intensity to have an eventual adverse effect upon the response of at least some of the people who have been exposed to them."

The view that stimulus intensity may be important in stress is rather widespread and crops up in areas as divergent as psychoanalysis and computer simulation. Freud (1936), discussing the concept of anxiety, proposed that excess stimulus intensity, or "overstimulation," was the prototypic origin of distress. Furthermore, the first occasion of overstimulation was the birth process. Although some ideas about the consequences of "birth trauma" seem ludicrous because of obvious implausibilities, the original Freudian analysis had a decidedly more plausible flavor. Freud argued that at birth, the infant was exposed to a dramatic change of environment which produced a sudden "flooding" of the immature nervous system with sensory excitation. This flooding was accompanied by a considerable amount of motor discharge, such as rapid breathing and heart beat, which served to rid the body of toxic products. Given this view of the birth process, it is not unreasonable to argue that over time, this pattern of responding becomes conditioned to cues that signify an imminent change or intensification of stimulus inputs. The fact that stress is often reflected in terms of increases in heart and respiration rates lends credence to this possibility.

It is interesting to note that Greenacre (1941) found some evidence supporting the Freudian position. If we assume that children born prematurely have less well-developed nervous systems than do infants born at full term, then we would expect premature infants to experience more "flooding" than do full-term infants. Their nervous systems would be less able to cope with the marked changes in stimulation. Consistent with this prediction, Greenacre found that premature children seem to maintain a generalized hypersensitivity to sensory stimulation, even after normal developmental processes have occurred, and that they have more generalized anxiety than do full-term infants. The important point for the moment is simply that psychoanalytic theory—despite its many complexities—makes the important and relatively straightforward point that overstimulation is one of the first experiences to which reactions that we now label as signs of stress can become conditioned. Thus, there is some reason to suspect that magnitude of stimulation may play an important role in the genesis of stress.

Equally interesting is the fact that some analyses of behavior made at one of the more austere levels of analysis—computer simulation—also use the dimension of stimulus intensity to account for the presence of emotionality and distress. One of the properties of computer simulation models is that they reduce complex behavior to a limited number of binary choices and decision rules. A common criticism of such models is that they are overly rational and fail to include motivation and emotion. Simon (1967) has recently taken such objections seriously and has attempted to incorporate these neglected processes into his model of behavior. The relevance of Simon's effort to the present discussion is that he has been able to accomplish this by means of an "interrupt" program, which is responsive to stimuli that are intense and unexpected. For example, he posits that ongoing behavior will be interrupted by the following events:

1. Needs arising from uncertain environmental events—"loud" stimuli, auditory, visual, or others that warn of danger.
2. Physiological needs—internal stimuli, usually warning of the impending exhaustion of a physiological inventory.
3. Cognitive associations—loud stimuli evoked not by sensory events, but by associations in memory, for example, anxiety arousal [p. 35].

Our argument so far can be summarized as follows. Any agreement among investigators that a given situation is potentially stressful occurs in part because they concur that the person is confronted with stimuli of an intensity which exceeds that to which he is accustomed. Furthermore, stimulus intensity has an effect *regardless* of the way in which the person appraises the stimuli. Investigators would probably also agree that their judgment that the person is engaged in coping, assumes that the person has attended to the stimulus situation sufficiently so that he knows something must be done. It is not too sizable an inductive leap to argue that intense stimuli are noticed more readily than are weak stimuli. Assuming that intense stimuli, over time, become paired with responses that differ along some dimensions from responses made to weaker stimuli, then it is conceivable that we could make sense out of the stress literature if we paid more attention to stimulus properties.

But this last statement, as it stands, is rather shallow. We need to look more closely at what would happen if we took the parameter of stimulus intensity more seriously in stress research. What would be accomplished? There seem to be at least four ways in which an analysis of intensity would be helpful.

The matching principle.   The first concerns an unusually simple yet provocative generalization that has been proposed by Buss (1967) and which he calls the *matching principle*. This principle states that "there is a tendency to make a strong response to stimuli of high magnitude and a weak response to stimuli of low magnitude [p. 40]." The features of this principle that keep it from being a restatement of the commonplace are that it applies to voluntary responses rather than to involuntary responses, it is assumed to be a learned rather than innate tendency, and it holds only when a person has a choice of response amplitude. The principle has been tested across several sets of stimuli, using a generalization paradigm. The subject is reinforced either for shouting highly aggressive words (high matching) or minimally aggressive words (low matching) or for whispering highly aggressive words (low matching) or minimally aggressive words (high matching). The central question is: What will happen to the generalization gradients for the reinforced responses of shouting or whispering? Findings show that when a *mismatched* stimulus and response are reinforced, there is more generalization than when a matched stimulus and response are reinforced. This result comes about for the following reason. When a mismatched pair has been reinforced, stimuli close in value to the training stimuli evoke the response that was reinforced, a standard finding in generalization research. For example, if a person is reinforced for shouting words of minimal aggressive content (for example, "contest," which has a scale value of 1.9), then he will also tend to shout when a new word of similar value (for example, "blunt," which is scaled at 3.0) is presented. However, as the values of the testing stimuli become farther removed from the training stimuli, there should be a lessened tendency to emit the reinforced response, namely shouting. But this is where the matching principle comes in. As we move up the scale from words of low aggressive content to words which are more and more aggressive (for instance, "annihilation," which has a scale value of 8.6), generalization should decrease; but according to the matching principle there should be an opposing tendency, generated by the amplitude of the stimuli themselves, to respond with an action of similar amplitude, namely shouting. Thus, contrary to predictions from theories of generalization, stimuli farther removed from the reinforced stimulus may evoke the reinforced response, *if* they are of a magnitude that matches the amplitude of that response. This relationship has been shown to exist for several kinds of stimuli (aggressive words, mood words, animal size, length of lines, and so forth), and with both vocal responses (shout-whisper) and skeletal responses (hard pulling on a handbrake versus light pulling on a handbrake).

Although this set of findings lends some support to the idea that stimulus intensity makes a difference, one may reasonably ask what does this have to do with stress? It could be argued that when we try to train people to cope with stress, we actually may have a much more difficult task than we realize. One of the things that may make training difficult is that we are working against a strongly embedded and learned tendency, namely the matching principle. If we look closely at the content of training which is supposed to facilitate coping, what such programs often try to do is reinforce people for *mismatching* stimuli and response amplitude. The person may be trained to give a "big" response to a "small" stimulus as when he is supposed to take protective cover and camouflage himself during combat at the mere rustle of leaves ahead of him. Or the person may be trained to give a "small" response to a "big" cue. For example, a person is most likely to avoid injury and death in a tornado if, when winds are whistling and trees crashing, he sits down next to the south wall of a basement. Thus, coping with stress is not just a matter of threat appraisal and a choice of viable strategies. It may consist, in addition, of overcoming strong tendencies to respond in ways that may be destructive.

This analysis takes on even more importance because of the well-documented finding that, as the magnitude of the stressor increases, persons are apt to respond with increasingly primitive responses (see, for example, Lazarus, 1966, p. 163). The argument here is that the matching principle constitutes one of the more basic and overlearned response tendencies which may be activated in stressful situations. Given this possibility, several specific problems within stress research take on added importance. One of the most important problems is: What training methods are most effective to override the matching principle? Perhaps, training should involve more overlearning of *mismatched* responses.

This suggests further that it is crucial to analyze more carefully so-called simulations of stress to determine just what types of reinforcement are occurring. Some persons argue that simulations are minimally involving and that people typically detach themselves from such a setting. Others argue that simulations are highly involving and produce vivid stimuli. Notice that, in the present context, this issue is much more than just an academic argument. It involves the question: Are participants being reinforced for mismatching (the simulation is seen as a vivid, realistic, intense stimulus situation to which persons are responding with low-amplitude actions)? Or are participants unwittingly being reinforced for matching (simulation is actually of low stimulus intensity and people are being reinforced for giving low-amplitude responses)?

If the simulation is of low intensity and minimally involving, then reinforcement of matching means that there will be *less* generalization of low-amplitude, calm responses when stimuli become more intense than would have been the case if a mismatch had been reinforced.

The present analysis also argues that attempts to train people to cope with stress will have to pay more attention to generalization phenomena. Stimuli outside the training session, as well as those within, may have to be manipulated. Training and generalization may have to be intermixed more than they are now.

In this latter regard, it is interesting to speculate concerning Latane and Wheeler's (1966) study in which several naval recruits had the incredibly grim task of finding and tagging the remains of human beings following an airplane crash. The predictable response of most of these men to the task followed closely what would be expected from the matching principle. Our question is, how might this experience interact with stress training in ways which would prove adaptive or nonadaptive? It is common for military units to assist local workers at times of disaster. Does the interspersing of these experiences with training serve to extinguish or reinforce the matching principle? It seems clear that trainers and experimenters alike should pay greater attention to the interplay between "classroom" and natural adaptations to stress.

Intensity and duration. The notion of stimulus intensity is important also from a second perspective, seemingly quite removed from the world of stress. This perspective involves the formula for visual photochemical processes that is known as the Bunson-Roscoe Law ($I \times t = K$). The meaning of this law is conveyed by Dember's (1960) description:

> The longer the duration of a visual stimulus, the greater the total amount of luminous energy that reaches the eye. There is, in fact, a critical duration below which the light entering the eye completely summates in its effect. It does not matter how this light is distributed over time within that interval. Thus, if within the interval a target having an intensity I were presented for a duration x, it would have the same visual effect as a target having an intensity of ½ I and a duration of $2x$. Below the critical duration, time and intensity are reciprocal [pp. 122–123].

This basic relationship takes on considerably more value for our purposes because Gampel (1966) has recently shown that this reciprocity function is *not* unique to visual processes. The interaction between intensity and duration seem to hold also for such processes as the punishment effects of electric shock, shock used as a reflex eliciting stimulus, and shock-induced fighting. The fact that these two parameters apparently transcend differences in sensory modalities and response measures has some important implications.

These two parameters, stimulus intensity and duration, are present in most studies of stress. Since they seem to transcend behavioral systems, they could be a means to compare stress reactions in different systems. Consider the following relationship. Kahneman and Norman (1964) in a study of visual perception found that the value of critical duration below which the $I \times t = K$ relationship holds *increases* as judgment tasks become more complex. At one level, this finding suggests that we should pay closer attention to the interactive effects of intensity and duration. Coping involves complex judgments. Therefore, the intensity-duration constant should affect that process considerably. However, we are interested in this relationship for another reason as well. It opens a number of questions relevant to stress research, such as: What are the reciprocity limits within a given behavioral system? How do reciprocity limits differ between behavioral systems when a stimulus is used to elicit action and when it is used to reinforce action? In asking these questions we are looking for functional similarities between stimuli in two different roles and for similarities of impact on different systems (for example, perception, learning, conditioning, sensory processes). Notice also that these manipulable parameters (perhaps "probes" is a better term) should help us to establish the degree of similarity and difference that obtain between psychological and physiological responses to stress, a problem that Lazarus correctly notes as being rather poorly articulated (1966, pp. 392–401).

This discussion makes at least two points. One, it shows from a different set of data that the variable of stimulus intensity is important not only in the determination of responses, but also that it is important to take account of stimulus duration. These two variables are manipulable variables and permit comparisons across behavioral systems. It seems that when people discuss the stimulus side of stressful situations, they often simply assume that the stimuli are "very intense" and let it go at that. This treatment seems to be oversimplified. Undoubtedly, there are discriminable gradations within the range of stimuli even when they are intense (Buss's generalization findings support this) and for this reason, subtle differences in intensity may make sizable differences.

But the second emphasis of this discussion of reciprocity should be given equal attention. It is clear that advances in stress research demand that we have some way to categorize and assess the state of knowledge we have about the field. McGrath and Altman (1966) have shown that classification (of small group research findings) in terms of shared operational properties of independent and dependent variables is both feasible and has a surprising amount of predictive power. I am suggesting that Gampel's (1966) attempt to demonstrate parallels across behavioral systems supplies additional evidence that this method of classification is useful.

Intensity and ongoing behavior.   Two final points should be made about the importance of stimulus intensity as a dimension in stress research. The first concerns a theme that will appear throughout this paper, namely, that any theory of stress must incorporate the fact that we are making predictions about the behavior of an *ongoing* organism. The human organism is active, constantly doing things, and at any point in time carries with it some residual amount of stress. It is not true, contrary to the implicit assumptions in some theories of stress, that any stimulus portending stress strikes an organism at rest. Stress always interrupts some form of ongoing behavior, and unless the fact of activity in progress is taken into account, the theory will have limited predictive power. I mention this theme now (and will elaborate on it later) because it suggests an obvious reason why stimulus intensity is an important variable. In order to incorporate the fact that stress is imposed on activity in progress, then we must begin to spell out conditions under which ongoing activity is abandoned. One of the most obvious occasions for interruption is when an intense stimulus compels attention.

Stimulus intensity and development.   To elaborate briefly on the presumed developmental significance of stimulus intensity, even if one does not buy the Freudian interpretation of birth as the initial occasion where overstimulation is paired with feelings of distress, it is still possible to argue that differences in intensity are one of the earliest discriminations made by infants. Given that this is one of the earliest ways in which the world is ordered, it is possible to go one step farther and argue that intensity is a dimension of stimuli that is potentially available as a basis for response associations throughout a sizable portion of life. Even though stimulus dimensions other than intensity may contribute more and more to associations as development proceeds, at the base of many of these associations will be differences in sheer magnitude of stimulation. Assuming that intense threat produces increasingly primitive responding, then the basic relationship between stimulus intensity and response amplitude is apt to assume more and more importance in the control of action.

I am not arguing that intensity is the only or even the most important component of events labeled as stress. Instead, I am arguing that intensity is a convenient wedge into the stimulus side of stress. Stimulus intensity is a parameter which has developmental significance, and which may have implications for coping responses via the matching principle and extensions of the Bunson-Roscoe Law.

The Recess in Stress: Stress and Ongoing Behavior

Even the most cursory reading of studies involving stress leaves the reader with the impression that stressful situations are rather dramatic, whether they occur naturally or in the laboratory. Most of these studies suggest that there is a rather explicit point at which the stressful sequence begins. As I have indicated, this is an inaccurate way to conceptualize stress. A more realistic (and undoubtedly more difficult) view is that a person experiences more or less stress, not presence or absence of stress. It is for this reason that this section has been labeled the recess of stress. It seems probable that we will gain a better understanding of stress if we view it as a process that recedes and increases.

A similar point is made by Weitz (Chapter 8). He notes that there is surprisingly little research on the effect of superimposing short-term stress on long-term existing stress. The importance of this issue is demonstrated by the research of Friedman, Mason, and Hamburg (1963) involving husbands and wives whose children were stricken with incurable cancer. This important study shows that the over-all level of stress felt by parents during the period of hospitalization was considerably less than one might expect (successful defenses were possible given the chronic nature of the background stress), but marked increments in stress occurred when the parent did not have the time or ability to mobilize for an unexpected event. In addition, events occurred during hospitalization which an outside observer might argue should have produced stress reactions (a rise in hydrocortisone levels in urinary excretions) but which did not. This can be explained in part because of the level of stress to which the parents had become accustomed.

Given the increasing emphasis in behavioral theory on *organized* units of behavior (for example, Locke & Bryan, 1967, on intentions; Mandler, 1964, on response sequences; Newell, Shaw, & Simon, 1958, on programs; Miller, Galanter, & Pribram, 1960, on plans), it seems clear that stress research must pay closer attention to inertial tendencies in behavior. As Atkinson and Cartwright (1964) note, "response to a stimulus is an incident in a larger unit, the goal-directed trend of the behavior at the time [p. 581]."

Fortunately, persons who are interested in stress do not have to start from scratch in their search for models which take more explicit account of ongoing activity. Some interesting leads are suggested in recent attempts by Atkinson and Cartwright (1964) to update Lewin's (1936) notion of substitution and to embed it more explicitly in expectancy $\times$ value theory. Their starting point is similar to that of Lewin, namely, the assumption that goal-directed tendencies, once aroused, persist until they are satisfied or dissipated. Thus, when an individual is engaged in one activity and we ask under what conditions will he lay aside pursuit of this goal in favor of an alternative activity, part of the answer lies in the assessment of inertial tendencies associated with the ongoing activity and substitute activity.

Atkinson and Cartwright develop a complex formula (p. 588) which specifies the conditions under which a substitute activity, B, will in fact be substituted for an ongoing activity, A. For our purposes, this formulation is important because it not only deals with the relative potencies of the two substitutes (in terms of expectancy × incentive value), but it does so in relation to two other sets of factors: (1) the inertial tendency to engage in ongoing activity A, and any existing inertial tendency to engage in the not-yet-ongoing substitute activity, B; and (2) the strength of motive forces relating to activity A and to activity B, respectively. The addition of these factors emphasizes the point that both aroused and latent personality characteristics interact with the environmental stimulus to determine whether the person will continue with his original activity or will adopt a particular alternative activity.

This model permits Atkinson and Cartwright to take more explicit account of the fact that persistent, unsatisfied goals exist at any point in time, and that this persistent tendency is added to any subsequently aroused tendency to perform any response which is expected to have, as its consequence, success. In other words, the immediate stimulus situation does not elicit certain tendencies from a state of rest, but "selectively strengthens or enhances already active tendencies to respond in certain ways [p. 585]."

The reasonable question at this point is: How does this help us make sense out of the fact that stressful events are imposed on various existing levels of stress? Perhaps the best way to answer this question is to look at three stages of a situation—prestress, within stress, and poststress—in terms of this model.

Suppose we have a man who manages a large corporation and has a high need for power; he is just about to begin a lengthy phone conversation in an attempt to win control of a competing firm when a siren blares, warning of an imminent tornado. The question is, under what conditions will the manager abandon the phone conversation and take steps to protect himself? If we assume that completion of the phone call is the initial activity and that taking cover is the alternate activity, this situation could be represented in a manner similar to the Atkinson and Cartwright (1964) formulation:

The person will quit phoning and take shelter when:

(Expectancy of gaining security × Incentive value of security) >

$$\left[\left(\begin{array}{c} N_{power} \times \begin{array}{c}\text{Expectancy} \\ \text{of success}\end{array} \times \begin{array}{c}\text{Incentive} \\ \text{of success}\end{array}\end{array}\right) + \begin{array}{c}\text{Inertial} \\ \text{power} \\ \text{tendencies}\end{array}\right] - \begin{array}{c}\text{Inertial} \\ \text{security} \\ \text{tendencies}\end{array}$$

$$N_{security}$$

Given this representation, what are some of the features we are alerted to in predicting his response to stress? The phone call should be continued if (1) he expects that it will be easy to get to the shelter and/or if the value of taking shelter is low; (2) if he has experienced a series of rebuffs to his assertion of power in the recent past; (3) if his persistent disposition toward security is low; and/or (4) if the need for security has been satisfied recently so that there is little inertial tendency associated with this motive. (The diagram shows the set of conditions *opposite to* those discussed in this paragraph.) Obviously there are additional properties that argue for his continuing the phone conversation. Our intent is simply to illustrate that unless we take account of ongoing activities, and the effects of both situational and personality variables, we cannot have a very clear idea of how the manager will respond to a potentially stressful stimulus. Although we are clearly asking whether he will appraise this situation as threatening, we are trying to answer this question in terms of what he is presently doing and the ratio of the forces favoring continuation of the activity over those favoring abandonment. In this example, we find reason to suspect that the person might not respond to the stimulus of the siren even though he might well appraise it as a threat.

Suppose we turn to the situation that occurs once the person feels threatened. Again, we need to take account of ongoing activity in order to understand what he will do. This situation can be exemplified if we use Janis's (1967) concept of "reflective fear." Janis assumes that the degree of "arousal of reflective fear is roughly proportional both to the perceived probability of the dangerous event materializing and to the anticipated magnitude of the damage, if it does materialize, that could be inflicted on himself, his family, and other significant persons or groups with whom he is identified [p. 7]." The important part of this concept for our present purposes concerns two potentially incompatible response tendencies that are generated by reflective fear. One tendency is *vigilance*, "which takes the form of increased attention to threat-relevant events, scanning for new signs of danger, attending to information about the nature of threat, and thinking about alternative courses of action for dealing with emergency contingencies [p. 8]." Reflective fear, however, also generates the need to *seek reassurance* by such means as "selective attention to complacent assertions that alleviate fear by minimizing the danger, and acquisition of new attitudes that alleviate fear by bolstering the person's confidence in his ability to cope with the danger [p. 9]." Given these two components of reflective fear (for the moment we will ignore the third consequence labeled the *compromise attitude*), let us try to predict what will happen when the person is engaged in vigilance. The question is: Under what conditions will he abandon (or reduce) vigilance, and devote more attention and effort to seeking reassurance? Suppose we assume that vigilance partially involves achievement needs

(the person wants to demonstrate competence in and mastery over the stressful situation) and that seeking reassurance depends in part on the person's need for affiliation. The situation could be represented as follows:
The person will shift from vigilance to reassurance seeking when:

(Expectancy of affiliation × Incentive of affiliation) >

$$\left[\left(\begin{array}{ccc} N_{achievement} & \times & \begin{array}{c}\text{Expectancy} \\ \text{of success}\end{array} & \times & \begin{array}{c}\text{Incentive} \\ \text{of success}\end{array}\end{array}\right) + \begin{array}{c}\text{Inertial} \\ \text{achievement} \\ \text{tendencies}\end{array}\right] - \begin{array}{c}\text{Inertial} \\ \text{affiliation} \\ \text{tendencies}\end{array}$$

$$N_{affiliation}$$

Our predictions about moving from vigilance to seeking of reassurance follow the same lines as before. The person will be expected to shift from vigilance when: (1) availability of reassurance is high; (2) the persistent level of unsatisfied achievement motivation is low; (3) the magnitude of persistent unsatisfied affiliation needs is high, and/or (4) the latent personality disposition of need for affiliation is intense.

Finally we come to one of the most interesting and most neglected questions in stress research: Under what conditions does the person presume that the stress situation is *over* and resume his previous activities? This is not as trite a question as it may appear. It is very possible that many of the observed failures to cope with stress come about either because the person concluded his coping efforts prematurely or because he maintained these coping responses too long and, in doing so, created new instances of stress. Let us continue with the example of the manager trying to acquire a competing company. Assume that he reluctantly took shelter when warned of an imminent tornado. The question, now, is: What are the conditions under which he will leave the shelter and resume the uncompleted activity of trying to acquire a competitor? The labels used in the earlier diagram apply here also. The only difference is that the direction of the relationships are changed. Given the earlier assumptions we made about this person, it seems clear that he will resume his telephone call at the earliest possible instance. His response to stress will be highly abbreviated.

Now notice how this urgency to resume the interrupted activity may *increase* stress. It is not unrealistic to imagine that the manager finds: (1) phone lines to the competitor are now inoperative or available only for emergency calls; (2) the competitor's establishment received some damage which changes its value; (3) the manager's own assets and those of his company may have changed; (4) it may be impossible to gather a sufficient staff of people to consummate the deal; (5) power needs may be further thwarted when employees are more responsive to family demands and directives of Civil Defense personnel than to his own.

These conditions in the immediate environment *add* to the prevailing level of motivation generated when the original activity of power asser- tions was interrupted. Thus the manager probably will experience stress in even greater magnitude than he did before. As a consequence, he may take actions which serve to raise the stress levels of other persons around him.

This hypothesized sequence of events is not as far-fetched as it might appear. Lazarus (1966, p. 402) cites an analysis made by Barton (1963) which exemplifies both the resumption of "unfinished business" in the poststress period and also hints at the additional stress which may be produced by such resumption:

> These difficulties (in the reconstruction period) seem to involve a feel- ing of relative deprivation, especially among members of the upper groups at seeing goods distributed on an equalitarian basis, and seeing income differentials reduced by the disaster work pay rates. The potentials for conflict of an equalitarian norm of "each according to his need" introduced into a stratified society are clearly indicated in this example. The solidarity of the emergency period when human life was at stake, the time horizon of people limited to the next few hours, and their aspiration-levels limited to bare necessity, had disappeared with the flood waters. For the upper classes, "restoration" meant restoration of inequality sanctioned by tradi- tion, and the temporary maintenance of equality appeared an offense against justice [p. 181].

I have spent some time with the issue of the recess of stress because I share with other investigators the feeling that this is a gap in current thinking about stress, and also because I wanted to show one way in which such information does make a difference. I am not advocating that the Atkinson and Cartwright model necessarily be adopted. I have used it to portray what happens when we take account of ongoing activity, because it includes both personality and situational determinants, and because it lends some order to our thinking about ongoing activities.

The Digress of Stress: Stress as Interruption

So far it has been suggested that stressful situations contain elements of high stimulus intensity which are imposed on ongoing activities. Hinted at in the previous remarks was the fact that interruption is also a component of stress. It is to the issue of interruption (a digression from ongoing activities) that we now turn our attention.

An appropriate point at which to start this discussion is a neglected finding in Brady's (1966) experiments with "executive" monkeys. In these avoidance conditioning situations, one monkey controls whether both he and another will receive an electric shock. It will be recalled that in the experimental runs, the monkeys spend 6 hours "on shock" followed by 6 hours of rest followed by 6 hours of shock avoidance, and so on. Further it will be recalled that all but one of the executive monkeys expired during the experiment from stomach ulcers.

A surprising finding in this research is what happened when the investigators changed to other schedules of shock and rest. When the monkeys were on shock for 18 hours and off for 6 hours, or when they were on the shock for 30 minutes and off for 30 minutes (with a shock occurring every 2 seconds during the shock period), *none* of the executive monkeys developed ulcers. In analyzing the curves for increases in stomach acidity, Brady found that the acidity did not start to increase until the *end* of the avoidance session, and the level of acidity reached its peak during the *resting* period. Although these data are preliminary, they seem to show that intermittent stress is more capable of creating ulcers than chronic stress. When the animal is exposed to continuous stress, some type of stable adjustment seems to occur.

It seems clear, both from Brady's findings and from other findings noted in this paper, that interruption does affect behavior. Since stressors typically interrupt activity in progress, we may be able to learn more about stress if we pay more attention to the psychology of interruption. This section of the paper attempts to pool some ideas about interruption that may be useful in stress research.

Interruption and reactance.   Brehm (& Sensenig 1966) has recently developed an engaging theory of psychological processes which he labels reactance. The concept is described as follows:

> When a person feels free to engage in a given behavior, then an elimination or threat of elimination of that freedom will arouse "psychological reactance" in him. Psychological reactance is defined as a motivational state directed toward the reestablishment of whatever freedom has been threatened or eliminated. Where there is a *threat* to a freedom, as distinct from an unequivocal elimination, it is possible for the individual to reestablish the freedom by actually engaging in the behavior that was threatened [p. 703].

Our interest in this theory centers on the idea of organized behavioral sequences (for instance, the making of a choice) that are interrupted when a choice is usurped. The question is: What does the person experience when an organized behavioral sequence is interrupted and how does he cope with the interruption? Brehm's data suggest that when a person faces a situation involving choice and one or more of the *perceived* alternatives are eliminated, the attractiveness of these eliminated alternatives increases relative to available alternatives. This increase in attractiveness occurs whether the elimination is caused by the actions of a social agent or an impersonal set of events. These data suggest that when we try to determine the effects of stress and predict how the person will respond, we need to inquire about potential threats to freedom. Some may argue that stressful situations are largely coercive and that choice is rare in such settings. Much of what we have said so far suggests that this is not true. Even though the person may be swamped by stimuli, this does not mean that his powers of discrimination drop to zero. Threats to freedom, a seemingly involved, complicated, and perhaps subtle, assessment may still absorb a sizable portion of the person's attention, regardless of the source or type of stress.

One implication of Brehm's analysis is that if a communicator tries to tell the person what kind of protective action he should take in the face of an impending disaster, and if the person saw more than one alternative form of protective action available, the person might well perceive the communicator's suggestion as a usurpation of freedom and show an increased tendency to do something other than what the communicator suggested. If we assume that the communicator actually proposed a viable solution, then what has happened is that the person ignored the suggestion, not because he assessed it as bad, but because he saw it as a threat to his freedom. In an effort to regain this freedom, he takes some other action which may objectively increase his chances of injury.

Resumption of interrupted activities.   Actually, interest in the concept of interruption is not new. Current research represents a more concerted effort to use a provocative set of ideas found in Lewin (1936) concerning substitution. It will be recalled that the basic paradigm for substitution studies was as follows: The subjects work on several tasks. They are interrupted midway through some of these tasks. Some substitute activity is performed. The question is: Will the person resume the interrupted activity after having completed the substitute activity? In many ways this is one of the most important problems within social psychology and it is disheartening that it has not received more attention. (See Deutsch, 1954, for a succinct summary of findings regarding substitution.)

It seems possible that the adequacy and success of a person's response to stress may in large part be determined by the extent to which his accomplishment of the adaptation task *substitutes for* the ongoing activity which was interrupted when the stress occurred. Stated in a different way, if the response to stress serves as a substitute source of satisfaction for the interrupted activity, then the substitute activity will be performed with greater intensity and adequacy than if the substitute activity is irrelevant to the interrupted activity. Given this proposal, it becomes crucial to designate variables that control whether substitution will be successful or not. It must be remembered that conclusions about substitution are based on a very small number of studies, and therefore these findings are largely suggestive. However, their substance is of sufficient value that were they to be replicated and refined, it seems clear that we would know more about the execution of coping behaviors.

Substitute activities (read here, "attempts to cope with stress when an ongoing activity has been interrupted") have a higher probability of reducing tension generated by an incomplete task to the extent that they are: (1) similar in degree of difficulty; (2) have high contiguity to the ongoing event; (3) have high intrinsic attractiveness; (4) are "connected" with the goal of the interrupted activity (that is, they match it in activities such as thinking, doing, telling); (5) have the same level of reality as the interrupted activity (for example, if interrupted activity involved actual performance of a task, wishful thinking or fantasy about the completion of the interrupted task will not serve as an adequate substitute); and (6) serve the same goal toward which the interrupted activity was directed. Given this rather imposing set of conditions (all of them do not necessarily have to obtain for substitution to be successful), one might well ask whether any kind of coping response could possibly match an ongoing activity. It should be remembered that the reason we even worry about this question is the hypothesis that the adequacy with which a coping response will be carried out is a direct function of the strength of the tendency to perform it. I am arguing that this tendency to perform the coping response is a function of the degree to which it serves as a substitute for the activity that was interrupted. In other words, the more a coping response substitutes for an interrupted activity, the greater the likelihood that the coping response will be performed successfully.

Interrupted activity and choice of coping response.   There is an additional proposition that is of considerable interest. It would be useful to pursue the possibility that the choice of a coping response is in part controlled by the nature of the activity that is interrupted. We have been assuming that persons are bothered by interruptions and that there are tendencies to complete goal-oriented activities. It seems reasonable that, given a choice among several coping activities, the person experiencing threat would choose that coping response which has the highest probability of furnishing satisfactions *equivalent* to those which were being pursued in the ongoing activity. Certainly, the person may make a "bad" choice in the sense that he chooses a coping response that is a poor substitute. All I am positing is that the nature of the interrupted event may exert more control over the choice of a coping response than we realize.

From this perspective, it should at least be clear that we need to pay more attention to ongoing activities and to the ways in which coping responses accomplish some of the same ends.

To make concrete what has been said, let us construct and analyze an example. Although the example is gross, what we will try to do is show how the three general coping patterns—attack, avoidance, defense —outline by Lazarus (1966) might afford greater or lesser degrees of substitutability for an ongoing activity.

Suppose that a college professor is totally absorbed day and night in writing a book which he feels will be an important contribution to this field. He is sufficiently far along with the project for him to have some reason to conclude that the book can be finished and that it will be a distinct contribution. One night while he is working on the book, his wife enters his study and says in a very deliberate manner: "You have been neglecting me for too long. I'm leaving tonight. There's no hope for us. I want a divorce." Assuming that the professor loves his wife and that this is a distinct threat, it seems clear that he will interrupt his writing of the book. The question is, to what extent are the various forms of coping response mentioned substitutable for the interrupted activity?

TABLE 16–1 Estimates of Degree of Substitutability of Three Modes of Coping for the Interrupted Activity of Book Writing

Dimension affecting substitutability	Attack	Avoidance	Defense
1. Difficulty	high (3)	medium (2)	medium (2)
2. Contiguity	high (3)	medium (2)	high (3)
3. Attractiveness	low (1)	high (3)	high (3)
4. Goal connected (doing, not thinking)	high (3)	low (1)	low (1)
5. Reality	high (3)	low (1)	low (1)
6. Serves same goal	low (1)	low (1)	low (1)
TOTALS	14	10	11

To give a crude format for considering this question, six potential determinants of substitutability have been listed in Table 16–1. The entries represent highly subjective estimates of the degree to which performance of the coping activity listed at the top of the column matches the interrupted activity of the book writing on each of the six dimensions of substitutability listed at the left-hand side of the table. For example,

consider the determinant "difficulty." It will be recalled that substitutability is more likely as the similarity between the substitute activity and
the ongoing activity is greater. If we assume that book writing is very
difficult, and if we further assume as Lazarus does that coping is partly
a function of judged comparative power of the target (the wife),
situational constraints, and internalized values (p. 299), then it is possible
to estimate the degree to which each mode of coping matches the
interrupted activity of book writing solely on the dimension of difficulty.
In this particular instance we have judged attack to be more difficult
than either avoidance or defense on the following assumptions: (1) the
wife is judged to have relatively high comparative power because she
controls important outcomes of divorce proceedings such as handling of
children, amount of alimony, and so forth; (2) the situational constraints
(against attack), even though the discussion occurs in the home, may be
sizable because of such factors as neighbors or children overhearing
angry remarks, the visibility of marks of physical combat the next day,
and so on; and (3) that the internalized values of the professor favor
deliberation, nonimpulsivity, reason, rather than attack. Taken together
these three components of attack suggest that actually engaging in this
activity will be more difficult than is true of the other two coping responses. Notice the unusual position in which we now find ourselves. If
we look only at the strength of inhibitions toward coping by means of
attack, each of the three elements listed above argues that the professor is
very *unlikely* to attack. But, if we ask the question, to what degree would
attack match the activity of book writing on the dimension of difficulty,
we come to the conclusion that attack has a potentially higher substitute
value for the interrupted activity than do either of the other two coping
responses. If persons choose among potential coping responses partly
in terms of their substitute value, then (considering the dimension of
difficulty alone) we would predict that attack would be preferred over
avoidance or defense.

Similar estimates have been made for the remaining five dimensions
of substitutability, and these estimates are entered in Table 16–1. In the
case of each entry, certain assumptions have been made about the
character of the professor and his wife. It should be possible for the
reader to reinstate the assumptions made, or, if this is not possible, to
substitute his own values.

Now suppose we attach numbers to each of the labels, assigning 3 to
every item where there is a high match between the coping response and
the interrupted activity, 2 where there is a moderate match, and 1 where
there is a low match. The totals of the sum of these values are listed at
the bottom of each column. If we now look back at our original questions,
the present analysis provides some crude answers.

One question was that of resumption. Once an activity has been interrupted, what is the likelihood that the activity will be resumed? It was argued that the greater the substitutability of the alternative action, the less the likelihood that the interrupted activity will be resumed. The estimates in Table 16–1 suggest that the book is more likely to be resumed if the professor responds with defense or avoidance than if he attacks. Notice that these are relative differences. In this example 18 points would be required before total substitutability along the six dimensions would occur, and the response of attack is four short of this total.

If we switch to the question, which coping response will be chosen, some possibilities are suggested. Assuming equal availability of the three general patterns of response (a rather drastic assumption to say the least), then if the professor chooses attack he will choose the response which is most like his ongoing activity. If we make the moderate assumption that people wish to continue with activities in which they are engaged, then it is not unreasonable to suggest that coping responses are chosen in terms of their similarity to the interrupted activity.

Concerning the intensity of the coping response, the example summarized in Table 16–1 implies that if attack were actually chosen as the mode of coping, it would be performed with greater vigor and possibly for a longer period of time than if either of the other two responses were adopted. The rationale for this prediction is that the tendency to engage in attack per se is increased when persistent forces associated with the interrupted activity are added to it.

Several other points could be made using this example, but we should not get distracted from the main issue. I am trying to make a rather simple point, that the majority of stressful situations involve interruptions of ongoing activity. What has been added here is the suggestion that the response to stress bears some formal resemblance to the interrupted activity. From existing research on substitution it is known that the likelihood that interrupted activities will be resumed, as well as the choice of alternate activity once an interruption has occurred, seem to follow orderly patterns. If we regard any type of response to stress as a substitute for some ongoing activity, then it is possible that we can learn more about the choice of a coping response as well as the intensity with which the response will be executed.

Inhibition of stress.   There are two issues concerning interruption that seem relevant to the topic of stress. Kesson and Mandler's (1961) discussion of the inhibition of stress makes the interesting point that there seems to be a specific class of actions (for example, sucking, rhythmic periodicity such as rocking) which serves as *general* inhibitors of feelings of distress regardless of the origin of the stress. These inhibitors take on considerable importance in their two-factor model of distress. Kessen and Mandler argue that when feelings of distress are evoked by a particular stimulus complex, the effects of the distress tend to ramify and are not dissipated immediately when the evoking situation is changed. In other words, stress bears only an indirect relation to a specific antecedent. Specific events do not terminate all discomfort immediately. There is some residual.

Given evidence suggesting that specific inhibitors do exist, Kessen and Mandler suggest that whenever a person experiences distress two types of action are needed: There is a need for specific inhibitors that reduce over-all feelings of distress but have little effect on the evoking situation; and there is a need for specific actions that change the evoking situation. From this background, let us look at the issue of interruption and stress.

Kessen and Mandler assume that distress is common in everyday life and that periods of greater or lesser distress occur because of the temporary loss of inhibitors, especially in the case of children. With infants, the presence of the mother serves to inhibit feelings of distress, and when the mother leaves, even momentarily, an inhibitor is removed and feelings of distress are released or reinstated. If these ideas are taken at face value, they suggest some of the psychological dynamics of interruption. Interruption, at least in the early stages of life, tends to be associated with the loss of an inhibitor and with the consequent arousal of distress. The child learns to detect cues that signal the imminence of disinhibition and, in the presence of these cues, experiences feelings of distress. Through processes of stimulus generalization, interruption (regardless of its genesis) may be the occasion for at least incipient feelings of distress. From this vantage point, it is reasonable to argue that persons would make sizable efforts to maintain *uninterrupted* behavioral sequences (for example, Mandler, 1964) in order to avoid feelings of distress. This analysis supplements in several ways the points developed in this section.

By now the reader may have concluded that I am rather obsessed with illustrations and concepts involving task performance, needs for achievement, and so forth. Much of this emphasis has been intentional. If we take seriously the idea that activity is ongoing, and that persons strive to complete behavioral sequences which they have initiated, then this suggests that it may be harder than we have imagined to get people to take stress seriously. They have interests in doing things other than the work necessary to handle stress.

Perhaps even more important, the tenacity with which people pursue activities leading to goal accomplishment may represent efforts to forestall interruption. Thus it may be that stress researchers should take more seriously research on need achievement (Atkinson, 1964), and competence (White, 1959), not just because these are interesting motives, but rather because they represent methods by which people try to reduce their chances of experiencing stress. A person who is highly involved in a task, and expends considerable effort to see it through to completion, may represent a person who is making a concerted effort to avoid interruption and distress.

The Kessen and Mandler analysis also suggests that one way to train persons to cope with stress would be to extinguish the association between interruption and distress. If interruption has rewarding consequences, or if the person becomes adapted to interruption, then it is possible he would be more willing to notice cues that signal threat and danger. This assumes of course that persistence in the face of cues signaling disaster would be less functional than taking some protective action. The Kessen and Mandler analysis is of most help because it adds information about the genesis and psychological properties of interruption. Their ideas also support our earlier hunch that it may be more difficult to break through defenses against stress and to train people in adaptive action than we imagine.

Interruption and psychotherapy. As a final point, many of the ideas concerning interruption and substitution which we have mentioned here have been taken as basic assumptions by a little known but unusually provocative form of psychotherapy called gestalt therapy (Perls, Hefferline, & Goodman, 1965). It is impossible to characterize this form of therapy in a few sentences; it is exceedingly complex as well as imaginative in its procedures. Suffice it to say that it is a form of therapy which is derived from basic principles of gestalt psychology, is concerned in large part with the psychology of "unfinished situations" (that is, situations which at one time the individual undertook but never completed and which have interfered with subsequent activities and evaluations), and relies heavily on tasks which the patient himself performs. The interesting point is that most of these therapeutic tasks are designed so that, if the person has certain difficulties, he *cannot* accomplish them successfully. The exercises, in other words, serve to "surface" the difficulties of the patient because both patient and therapist pay closer attention to the possible factors that interfere with successful completion of the task.

This resource is mentioned simply because it is an intriguing and offbeat source to learn more about the dynamics of interruption, completion, and substitution. Incidentally, it should be mentioned that the use of unfinished situations as a cornerstone of psychotherapy is by no means unique with the gestalt therapy group. The basic point behind Freud's analysis of dreams was that dreaming served as a means to express aroused but unfulfilled wishes, a viewpoint that has gained considerable support from the fascinating research by Demen (1960, 1965) on the effects of dream deprivation (which is discussed later in this chapter).

The Undress of Stress: Causal Attribution in Stress

The title of this section may not communicate it exactly, but the intention of this section is to gather some observations concerning an important topic, namely the ways in which persons uncover the origins of a stressful stimulus. In the parlance of social psychology, we are concerned here with the issue of causal attribution (Heider, 1958; Jones & Davis, 1965).

Let us start with an example which seems to capture some elements of causal attribution under stress. Suppose you are the director of a ten-member vocal group. You are having the final rehearsal for a public performance the next afternoon, and the rehearsal is going badly because one of the singers is uncooperative, tense, and is making it difficult for the other singers to perform and for you to conduct. On the music stand in front of you is a small box containing one tranquilizer. Now the problem is, given the increasing level of tension at the rehearsal, do you give the pill to the errant singer or take it yourself?

Actually this problem is quite complex. What is accomplished if you give the pill to the singer? Presumably his behavior would become more quiescent and the rehearsal would proceed more smoothly. But notice what you have assumed. The "agent of harm" has been located outside yourself and, in fact, the singer may not be disrupting the rehearsal. It may be your increased edginess that has placed all the singers under duress, and the errant singer is only the first of many who will behave similarly during the rehearsal.

Suppose, instead, that you as conductor took the pill. This might occur if you thought your tension was "contagious" and was affecting the other performers (cause of the stress is located internally) or if you felt more capable of handling the errant singer if that person did not bother you so much.

Locating the agent of harm.   Now let us look more closely at some properties of this example. Several persons experience stress because they perceive that the progress of the rehearsal is a distinct threat to giving an accomplished performance the next day. Given the emergence of threat, there is the problem of locating the "agent responsible for the threat" and taking corrective action. This is the problem of causal attribution. And in this instance we have operationalized the actual attribution in terms of what is done with the tranquilizer.

Notice that, in this example, the problem of locating the agent of harm is not a single decision; it involves at least two steps. First, the director asks the question, "What caused it?"; second, he seems to ask the question, "What are the implications if that assessment is true?" Sometimes, in discussing causal attribution and stress, we seem to ignore this latter question. It seems possible that if the person decides that the consequences of the attribution are favorable, he will retain the attribution; but if the consequences promise to be unfavorable, he will abandon the initial attribution and look for another explanation. In short, we are suggesting that the favorability of a given attribution (from the point of view of the aims of the attributor) may retrospectively control the attribution which the person finally settles on.

Attribution and control.   It seems probable that when persons can explain the origin of stress in several ways, attribution operates in the service of control. Persons tend to make that attribution which enables them to retain the greatest amount of control over the situation. Having asserted this, the problem shifts to the equally elusive question, just what is it that the person wants to control? And here there are no easy answers.

In many stress situations, a person may feel powerless, in which case he may assign responsibility to those factors which enable him to control at least his own feelings of helplessness and/or anger that result because there is little he can do. In part, this analysis leads us to somewhat the same position as that mentioned by Lazarus (1966, p. 174), namely, that persons are often better able to cope with threat if they locate the agent of harm outside themselves (which permits projection, scapegoating, and so forth). Our hesitance at fully accepting this view arises because externalization is a rather specious mode of control. True, it handles immediately pressing unease, but it gives the person little assurance that he will be able to handle future situations of stress in a more effective way. His immediate efforts to handle stress produce scant re-evaluation and modification of his own resources for combating future stress. When we say that causal attribution operates in the service of control, it is important to note that control is defined in terms of relatively longer or shorter periods of time. Locating the agent of harm within oneself (internal attribution) may produce such consequences as guilt, depression, and defensiveness (Lazarus, 1966, p. 174), but internal attributions can also hasten efforts to reduce the frequency and intensity of future occasions of stress. It is interesting in this regard to reflect on the finding reported by Drabek and Quarantelli (1967, p. 12) that if persons exposed to disaster blame another person for its origin, constructive changes involving social structure are less likely to occur. If a person blames himself, there may be a greater chance that changes will be effected. Even if social agencies rather than individual people are blamed there should be a higher probability that corrective action will be taken, because the person *does* have some relationship to such agencies. In other words, when some segment of society rather than a specific individual is blamed, the person is actually making an attribution which is at least partly internal; he has partial membership in the society that is blamed for the disaster.

To conclude this discussion of control, it is helpful to review the finding of an interesting experiment by Champion (1950). Subjects were exposed to electric shock under one of three experimental conditions: (1) they were told to keep their bodies perfectly still during the administration of shock; (2) they were told to clench their fists whenever the shock was delivered; or (3) they were told to clench their fists in order to "turn off" the shock. Measures of skin conductance revealed that the subjects in the third condition recovered from the immediate effects of shock significantly faster than did either of the other two groups, and they apparently were unaware of this effect. These data are interesting because they are at least consistent with the view that as the person feels in more control of the situation there is a greater likelihood that he will adapt to the situation more readily. He will either feel less stress or recover from its effects more rapidly.

Criterion for attribution.   Another feature of causal attribution is suggested by the example, and this concerns the question: How does a person know that he has made a satisfactory attribution? What criteria does he use to judge when his explanation is adequate? In the earlier suggestion, that consequences of an attribution retrospectively control the attribution, I hedged somewhat on the issue I am now raising. In that discussion, there emerged the general model of a person who continues his search for an explanation until he finds one that is maximally satisfying. This view gets us uncomfortably close to the assumption that, when persons attribute causes under conditions of stress, they hold out for optimal solutions. Given the repeated finding that primitization is common in appraisal and responding, an optimizing model seems quite out of character. We are apt to formulate a more accurate picture of attribution processes if we adopt a satisficing rather than an optimizing model. Pat as this solution sounds it creates problems, because satisficing models of causal attribution have not been very fully developed. Discussions of satisficing behavior do contain suggestions of simple decision rules that persons use (for example, search in the vicinity of the problem), but these do not translate easily into specific predictions about the conditions under which a person will make internal or external attributions, and the amount of data he will require before he becomes committed to an explanation.

Self-fulfilling prophecies.   An interesting property of the example of the rehearsal is that one suspects that whatever attribution the conductor makes, his subsequent actions will confirm the attribution. Causal attribution, in other words, is ripe for self-fulfilling prophecies (Merton,

1957). The data of Drabek and Quarantelli (1967) suggest that such a process operates; and it seems clear that once an attribution is made, people are reluctant to entertain other possibilities. Even more important is the fact that, having made an attribution, people do not remain passive. They take actions which tend to confirm their conclusions.

This suggests a range of problems within the area of causal attribution which need close attention. For example, we need to know the conditions under which it is actually possible to engage in behavior that validates "prophecies," in particular those prophecies that have a sizable amount of "error" in them. Investigators who use the concept of self-fulfilling prophecies sometimes seem to assume that people can make "occur" anything they want to have occur. They write as if once committed to an explanation, people can make even the most unlikely events materialize. In actuality, this view is probably wrong. Undoubtedly there are conditions that limit the amount of "validation" that is possible, and it would seem vital to learn precisely what these conditions are. This information is important because it would tell us when it is difficult or impossible for a person to generate data supporting an attribution which is detrimental to adaptive responding.

Actually, answers to this question need not be phrased in such negative terms. If we knew what blocked, as well as what enhanced, the phenomenon of the self-fulfilling prophecy, then it might be possible to commit persons to an attribution that would portend adaptation and then establish conditions which would *facilitate* their validation of this attribution.

Attribution and ambiguity.   A final property of the example concerns the variable of ambiguity. Even though there seemed to be an obvious source of the problem—the uncooperative singer—it will be recalled that the situation was not that simple. There was considerable ambiguity. Ambiguity undoubtedly surrounds most occasions of stress and, therefore, must be incorporated into any formulation concerning causal attribution.

To begin our inquiry into ambiguity it is helpful to extract two propositions discussed by Lazarus (1966). One of these concerns the interaction between personality and ambiguity. This relationship is phrased as follows: "ambiguity permits maximum latitude for idiosyncratic interpretations of situations, based on the individual's psychological structure [p. 118]." The second proposition concerns the relationship between ambiguity and threat. Ambiguity seems to intensify threat because it limits the sense of control and increases the sense of helplessness [p. 117].

Taken together these two propositions have some interesting implications. The latter proposition concerning the relationship between ambiguity and threat argues strongly that causal attribution under stress should operate in the service of control. Since ambiguity increases the sense of helplessness, and since helplessness is generally an aversive state, persons should respond to the stressful situations in ways that help them arrest the impression of helplessness.

But we need to look more closely at what it means to be confronted with ambiguity at the same time that we look for a cause. One implication of Lazarus' propositions is that ambiguity increases threat because the person is unable to locate a specific agent of harm. However, it also seems possible that a situation of high ambiguity would permit maximum latitude to identify any agent the person wanted to as the source of threat. It is true that there are few specific clues that point to a specific agent, but this same datum can be turned around so that we can argue that there are few cues which prevent a person from blaming whatever agent he prefers to blame. If idiosyncratic psychological structure emerges under ambiguity, then it seems even more likely that persons will size up situations in their most preferred ways. I would argue, then, that they would apply those explanations which are of greatest functional value (for instance, Katz & Stotland, 1959). In other words, if the person has few constraints (in terms of caused information) on the attribution process (ambiguity is high), and if under conditions of high ambiguity he responds in ways that are most characteristic of his psychological structure, then he will explain the situation in the way that is most compatible with his own need satisfaction. If some process like this unfolds, then it might not be true that ambiguity intensifies threat. Quite to the contrary. It might well intensify comfort, the reason being that the person is able to apply that explanation which is most appropriate and most compelling within his own psychological structure. He tailors the explanation to his own interests.

This point of view also is relevant to the earlier point about self-fulfilling prophecies. If attributions are made under conditions of high ambiguity, and if they consist of explanations that are highly relevant to individuals, then this argues that persons will have a sizable stake in confirming these attributions. Should the attribution be disconfirmed, then not only is the person left without an explanation of why stress occurred, but even more important, a portion of his self-concept has been disconfirmed. If more of his unique structure emerges under ambiguity, then there is a more significant portion of him available for disconfirmation. This argues that the tenacity with which attributions will be maintained should always be considerable, but especially when the attributions are made under conditions of high ambiguity. It is important that we take this possibility seriously because it is easy to presume that if a situation is blurred and unclear, any explanation will be highly tentative and easily abandoned. Typically, this is probably true. But if ambiguity is associated with stress, and if ambiguity enhances the assertion of psychological structure, then whatever explanation the person arrives at may be anything but tentative.

The Dress of Stress: Scenic Trappings und Stress

The main point to be made in this section is a simple one. It concerns the obvious fact that the trappings of any stressful situation have a sizable influence over the person's definition of the situation and over his choice of coping response. This point is brought home forcibly by a recent study by Ball (1967) entitled "An Abortion Clinic Ethnography."

The situation of an abortion clinic has several features which by themselves, should interest stress researchers. Not only does the abortion clinic engage in activities that are legally defined as deviant, but the people who make use of the clinic's services are also engaged in "deviant" activity involving considerable threat and stress. Ball's analysis depicts several ways in which the setting, appearance, and manner of the clinic are "managed" in order to reduce both the deviant and stressful aspects of getting an abortion. Ball labels the use of props to reduce threat as the "rhetoric of legitimization," an unusually accurate phrase summarizing his findings.

Ball describes several ways in which the clinic attempts to convey the impression that it is a legitimate, professional enterprise. The practitioners are clothed in tunics, don surgical gloves, and display an impressive array of tools and medicines in full view of the patient prior to the operation. This all looks very impressive. Perhaps most interesting are the features that *contradict* this impression, features which are seldom noticed by the patient who also has a stake in accepting the definition of legitimacy that is being fostered. They are conveyed by the following excerpt from Ball.

> It should be pointed out that, aseptically, tunics are no substitute for full surgical gowns, that full precautionary tactics would also include items such as face masks, caps, etc.; and that it is highly irregular for an operating room to lack an autoclave (for the sterilization of instruments) and changeable covering for the table, and for surgical instruments to stand on display, exposed to air for long periods of time. Additionally, it may be noted that the portion of preoperative medical history which is taken by the senior practitioner is recorded by him after his elaborate display of putting on the surgical gloves—a less than ideal practice for sterility [p. 299].

In concluding the discussion of the clinic, Ball gives a succinct summary of what the construct "rhetoric of legitimacy" means: "a set of presentational strategies which allows the clinic to minimize problems inherent in typically anxious and fearful patrons, and thus to function more effectively; and in addition to generate the reputation necessary for an establishment of its kind, dependent upon referrals from physicians [p. 301]."

This example points out rather forcefully the extent to which situational props and mannerisms can affect feelings of stress. Notice that in this setting the patrons are quite threatened when they arrive for the operation. What seems to happen is that the setting of the clinic aids the person to "defensively reappraise" the activity of getting an abortion. Although in this instance there is considerable effort by the clinic staff to enhance defensive reappraisal, it seems likely that in most other settings there also are properties that foster reappraisal. These props might involve something like the specific inhibitors discussed by Kessen and Mandler (1961); they might consist of props that a person associates with situations of minimal duress; they could involve props that are incongruent with the feeling of threat, for example, someone who expresses calm and confidence (see Kelley, Condry, Dhalke, & Hill, 1965). Since we have only the most elementary formats to conceptualize the effects of setting variables, it is difficult to give a detailed picture of the form or effects of such properties. The study of the abortion clinic shows that such props do exist, that they do have an impact on the participants, and therefore that it would be fruitful to look for functionally similar props in other settings.

The importance of discovering situational properties that aid redefinition is underscored by the well-known research of Schachter and Singer (1962), which showed that persons confronted with heightened states of arousal which they are unable to label are quite influencible. Under these conditions, situational properties have a decided influence on definitions. Although we can always argue that, at times of stress, the prominent situational cues involve terror and panic, we may have underestimated the potential for "safe" properties of the setting to reduce the level of tension.

Perhaps the most concrete suggestion that can be gleaned from this is that we should pay serious attention to the rhetoric of stress. The words and symbols commonly associated with stress are often quite compelling and persuasive and may account for a sizable portion of the observed consequences. The idea of rhetoric seems to have more value as an explanatory device than we may have imagined. This is shown perhaps most clearly in recent attempts by Brown (1965) and Kelley and Thibaut (1968) to explain the "risky shift" observed in problem solving groups. Having analyzed the several studies that demonstrate this phenomenon, Kelley and Thibaut are led to the conclusion that much of the data can be explained by the idea of the "rhetoric of risk" (Brown, 1965, p. 688). For one thing, the language associated with risky positions is apt to be more colorful, dramatic, and rich in imagery than is language associated with cautious positions. For this reason alone, arguments favoring risky actions may be listened to more intently and taken more seriously than arguments favoring caution. The language is more potent.

If rhetoric does have an effect on stress, then we need to learn about ways to neutralize the symbols that lead persons to adopt excessively fearful definitions of situations and to enhance the potency of the "rhetoric of deliberation." In short, how do we get people enthused about caution?

Almost any investigator could at least approach the problem of props, regardless of the setting in which he works, by simply taking time to find out what in the setting bothered and comforted the person. He could have the person recall what happened and note which items are listed, in what order and with what omissions. He might give the person several verbal or photographic descriptions of the stressful setting, varying the properties of these photos in a systematic way, and ask the person simply to indicate which setting he was in, which he would most like to have been in and which he would least like to have been in. Even though stressful situations are sometimes exceedingly complex—lots of things happen at several different locations—we can be certain that not everything is noticed. Some properties are apt to be more controlling than others; and, for this reason, it seems mandatory to attend to, and vary in a systematic manner, the "dress" of stress.

The Egress of Stress: Undermanned Settings

As was true in the previous section, I intend here to make a simple point. I make this point mostly to balance a direction in which at least some thinking in stress theory is moving, namely toward the study of territoriality (Hall, 1966) and overcrowding (for example, Calhoun, 1962) as occasions for stress. The bulk of these studies demonstrate convincingly that, as physical distances among persons are reduced beyond a critical point, feelings of threat increase. Evidence shows this to be an extremely promising direction in which to move. Our only point here is to urge that investigators pay some attention to the problems of the opposite sort: What happens when settings are *undercrowded?*

The psychology of the undermanned setting seems important because, just as people are sometimes thrown into unusual proximity during stress, they may also have to cope with stress when there is an insufficient number of persons available. A growing body of evidence compiled by Barker (1960) and Barker and Gump (1964) shows that when activities are undertaken in settings with an insufficient number of people, there are far-reaching effects on the participants. The consequences of undermanning as described by Barker (1960) include the following. When a setting is undermanned, the strength of obligations and opportunities increase for the remaining persons. This means that they are pressured more intensively in a greater number of directions. Their tasks become more varied, more difficult and more important, with the result that fatigue and inadequate skills lower the over-all level of performance. Each person does more things, but he does them less well. Because each remaining person is crucial for the maintenance of the setting, persons become more tolerant and less evaluative of one another. In addition, each remaining person feels more responsibility for the outcome, more insecurity because there are few reserves if he fails his task, and instances of both success and failure are more frequent. Finally, persons in under-manned settings are evaluated more in terms of what they can do and less in terms of the kind of persons they are (that is, attractive, person-able, and so forth). Barker and Gump (1964) found that the predicted consequences of undermanning held true when students in small schools were compared with those in large, consolidated schools. Large schools contain more overmanned settings and, as a consequence, students excel in a relatively small number of activities. In the smaller schools children demonstrate average competence at a considerably wider range of activities.

Davis' (1966) recent study of the campus as frog pond (is it better to be a big frog in a small pond or a small frog in a big pond) suggests that students in smaller schools tend to elect careers that are more ambi-tious than do students in more prestigious institutions. The rationale is that, comparatively, students in the smaller school have experienced more successes in class; and this experience exerts a strong influence on career choices. These findings seem consistent with those of Barker and suggest that the number of personnel in a setting (relative to the demands in a setting) makes a difference, whether there are too many or too few.

It is also interesting that the data on undermanning begin to show some of the benefits that can be gained from stress. The undermanned setting produces people who have had a wider range of experiences, even though all of these experiences are by no means successful. Participants seem to emerge with greater confidence in their abilities to handle a variety of situations. It is interesting to note the similarity between this finding and that reported by Law (1960), who found that men subjected to extreme isolation in Antarctica for a period of a year emerged from this experience with considerably more confidence in themselves than they had before. Law also notes that one of the strong contributors to this enhanced confidence was the fact that during the period of isolated duty persons were evaluated on the basis of what they could do, not on the basis of particular idiosyncracies.

One implication of Barker's results is that persons in undermanned settings may cope with immediate stress less efficiently than would be true in an overmanned setting, where tasks can be specialized and where "backup" personnel are available. On the other hand, if we consider the long-term consequences of coping with stress, it may be that persons trained to cope with stress in undermanned settings will show greater adaptability in meeting future stressful occasions. When persons perform a rather small task and are given more than enough time to complete it, they may redefine the task as one which actually requires the excessive amount of time they have spent on it (Aronson & Gerard, 1966). If this finding in support of "Parkinson's Law" were to replicate and generalize, it would indicate that in the overpopulated setting where persons do relatively small tasks they may invest these tasks with value in excess of their actual importance. Having done so, if the person is then exposed to stress in a setting where there are insufficient people, he may be even less able to cope with stress than if he had never been exposed to ("trained in") the overmanned setting.

In conclusion, it seems clear that population density, both too many or too few, is a potential antecedent of stress, and also that it affects modes of coping with stress.

METHODOLOGICAL CONSIDERATIONS

Most of the preceding conceptual suggestions are of virtually no value unless we test them to see if they make any sense. Stress research presents some knotty problems of methodology, but many of these problems are not as intense as they appear. The purpose of this section is to discuss briefly some ways in which the methodology in stress studies could be improved.

The Express of Stress: Nonsubjective Dependent Variables

Despite the fact that stress seems to have a marked effect on behavior, stress researchers have been content to use a surprisingly narrow set of dependent measures. The nature of this difficulty becomes apparent in Lazarus' (1966) useful effort to integrate work in the area of stress. At several points in this book, there are scholarly attempts to approach studies of stress involving both physiological and psychological measures. The objection we have is that most of the psychological measures that are used consist of self-reports. At several points, Lazarus argues that before we can make definitive statements about the relationships between psychological and physiological stress, we must improve self-reports, and get subjects to be more candid. This aim is laudable but it is only a partial solution. There exist a host of behaviors other than self-reports which are available for observation. Here we have in mind motor-behavioral indicators of stress. The fact that these indicators have not been given much attention by stress researchers is exemplified by the fact that Lazarus's discussion of these measures (pp. 341–349) is brief and rather uninformative.

Perhaps we can make this point more clearly with an example. Several persons, including Lazarus (for example, Lazarus, Speisman, Mordkoff, & Davison, 1962) have had considerable success producing stress by means of vicarious threats generated through dramatic motion picture films. The dependent measures commonly used in these studies include physiological measures and self-reports. However, there is a wide range of motor-behavioral responses to these films which have not yet been tapped and these should provide valuable supplementary data.

Suppose, for example, that researchers using stress films took pictures of eye movements made by subjects watching the films. One could then count actions such as squinting, eye closure, excessive rate of blinking (Ponder & Kennedy, 1927) as indicators of psychological stress. Perhaps they could give the subject a device which controls the intensity of the lamp within the projector, and notice at which points in the film he brightens or darkens the picture. These data should give important supplementary information about vigilance processes in stress. Instead of permitting the subject to control light intensity, the experimenter could outfit each subject with a set of opaque goggles, which he could make more or less transparent; this would permit group administration of the film. Valuable data might also emerge if the subject were permitted to repeat any portions of the film that he wanted to, or if he had to "brief" the next subject on the content of the film. To extend the latter idea, rather than having S control the light intensity of the projector it might be possible to give him a device which could let him control the speed at which the film ran through the projector. This might be highly revealing, because it would give the subject a chance to manipulate temporal dimensions of the stress event. For example, in the vivid film portraying mill accidents (Lazarus, Opton, Nomikos, & Rankin, 1965) there are sizable portions of the film during which the viewer can anticipate the actual gruesome accidents. A subject who could control the speed of the projector might slow it down in order to prolong the anticipatory phase, and then speed it up considerably when the actual accident occurs, so much so in fact that the accident would appear unreal and even whimsical with a "keystone cop" quality. It should be noted that if we did find that persons prolong the anticipatory phase, these data would directly contradict research involving shock (for example, Cook & Barnes, 1964), which shows that when people have the opportunity to delay the onset of shock, they prefer *minimal* delays. Subjects less sensitive to anticipation (that is, experiencing less threat) might make very few adjustments of speed.

Perhaps even a more subtle measure of stress would involve what the subject does if he has control of the over-all illumination in the viewing room. When the film starts, the room could be brightly lit making it difficult to see the picture. The subject could then manipulate a rheostat in order to dim the illumination. Three central questions would be: At what point is the illumination dimmed, for how long, and how do these changes in illumination coincide with differences in the initial scenes and in the soundtrack?

In some studies with stressful films (for example, Speisman, Lazarus, Mordkoff, & Davison, 1964) the content of the soundtrack has been varied (denial, intellectualization, trauma). It is presumed that all persons "hear" the sound track and that their physiological reactions indicate their response. It would be interesting to see what happens were the subject to hear various soundtracks, and to be able to control their volume, or actually select among the several soundtracks. It might also be possible to embed considerable static in the soundtrack and give the subject a device which can be used to clear up the static. The dependent variables would involve how often he uses this device and at what points.

Suppose that portions of the film were damaged and the film had to be rethreaded by the subject midway through the exercise. Measures of latency with which rethreading occurs should give valuable information about the impact of the film at the time of the interruption.

Persons who watch films of the types used by Lazarus and his associates probably do a lot of squirming and as Webb, Campbell, Schwartz, and Sechrest (1966) note, squirming is a relatively easy behavior to quantify. Recent attempts to record gestures in darkened rooms by means of infrared films (for example, Haworth, 1965) have been rather successful, and might furnish a means to learn more about the behavioral correlates of stress. Since infrared films can be shot in totally darkened rooms, the subject would not be aware that his reactions were being recorded. He probably would be more guarded when the room is illuminated than when it is not. (Notice that the use of infrared films does not involve deception, or at least does so less than other techniques. The subject comes to the experiment knowing that he will be observed, and this is just what is happening. The only difference is that he is being observed in a way that he had not expected.)

Other suggestions could be offered, but the preceding should be sufficient to exemplify the point being made. The stress researcher is not confined just to measures involving physiological responses or self-reports. There are a sizable number of intermediate indicators which are less subject to distortion, often more reliable, and can supplement other forms of data. Even highly cognitive models of the intervening processes in stress should reckon with behavioral correlates, so an interest in cognition need not rule out behavioral measures. If stress researchers pay attention to a wider range of behaviors and to task variables, they should gain greater insight into additional indicators that will help them assess stress.

The preceding discussion of behavioral measures in film experiments contains a rather subtle point which I would like to emphasize. In almost all of the measures that were mentioned, the subject was given distinct opportunities to *avoid* some of the more traumatic portions of the stress film. Most laboratory studies of stress make it difficult for the subject to employ flight, avoidance, or defense as means to cope with stress. Laboratory settings tend to be quite confrontative, and it is difficult for the subject to avoid the stressful situation. As a result, findings from the laboratory are somewhat unrepresentative of coping in real life, where avoidance is more available as an alternative. It is generally easier for subjects to attack, show aggression, or get angry. Each measure mentioned above serves the important function of making avoidance a more viable alternative, one which the subject may use with greater frequency.

The Access to Stress: Natural Outcroppings of Stress

In the face of growing concern about deception in experiments (for example, Kelman, 1967) and the issue of "permanent harm" to subjects, it seems probable that stress researchers will have to become more resourceful in locating natural settings where they can study stress. Movement to field settings by no means implies that the researcher must necessarily surrender control over his observations (see Weick, 1967). Any person who is at all observant can think of several natural settings where there are "outcroppings" of stress. Therefore, we do not mean to imply that settings mentioned in this discussion are unique or even particularly good. We intend simply to point out by example that natural instances of stresslike situations are available and can be used to answer many questions which are increasingly difficult to study in the laboratory.

Use of selected populations. Several stress studies employ selected populations, the members of which are exposed to a common stressor. For example, Bluestone and McGahee (1962) held extensive interviews with prisoners in Sing Sing who were awaiting execution. Even though their study itself is not particularly informative, the population is of obvious relevance in stress research. For example, Lazarus (1966, p. 116) makes the prediction that the greater the imminence of a confrontation, the greater the perceived threat. Although there are almost no experimental tests of this proposition, the prisoner population awaiting execution should provide some data on this issue. Not all prisoners will be executed on the same date, and the prediction would be that the more distant the date of execution the less the perceived threat. It would also be interesting to study causal attribution in this population. Who does the prisoner blame for his situation; the warden, arresting officer, courts, society, witnesses, himself because he was caught? It would then be interesting to see if the imminence of threat exerts any systematic effect on where the prisoner places responsibility for his plight.

Victims of disasters are valuable informants about the nature of stress, but they are seldom used to answer specific questions. Instead, investigators typically gather general impressions from them. Some idea of the way in which such populations could be used to learn about specific issues can be seen if we look at the interesting topic of the "near-miss phenomenon" (Lazarus, 1966, p. 42). Persons who are exposed to a disaster but escape unharmed may reflect on this experience in drastically different ways. Some may conclude that their escape confirms their belief that they are invulnerable, while others may reflect on the same events and conclude that the near-miss relates their feeling of invulnerability. Such widely differing reactions need to be explained. A rather simple-minded prediction is that persons more distant from the actual point where the disaster struck would utter more themes of continued invulnerability than would those closer to the disaster. This prediction would be easy to quantify and would require minimal imposition on victims in order to get their judgments. It would be even more interesting to test this hypothesis under conditions where the disaster had a predictable versus unpredictable course. Tornados are notorious for their capricious paths of destruction, whereas fires or explosions have a more predictable and circumscribed locus of damage. Given this difference, it is possible that the distance-vulnerability prediction would hold more for persons confronted by a localized disaster which takes a predictable course than it would for those who had escaped a disaster which involved a less predictable course.

As a final example of interesting "stress" populations, the careful work of Ilfeld and Lauer (1964) suggests nudists as a population experiencing considerable stress. Beyond the obvious point that when a person first disrobes and walks into a nudist camp he may experience to a considerable extent feelings of threat, the analysis by Ilfeld and Lauer suggests that there is considerable background tension generated by the mixture of rebellion and conformity expressed in nudism. They phrase the issue this way:

> Stress may occur for potential nudists because socially defined roles do not satisfy their personal motives or desires. . . . Both rebellion and conformity are in fact found in nudism. Rebellion occurs in the sense that the institutionalized norm of wearing clothes is broken. Conformity is present in that all other commonly observed American norms are retained, and many of them, primarily those relating to sexual behavior, are strengthened [p. 186].

It is clear from the data presented that observation of norms regarding sexual behavior at times imposes considerably more strain than "official" nudist literature would suggest, although overt actions to remedy this strain are exceedingly rare. This argues that nudist populations should provide an unusually appropriate population in which to study modes of coping that involve nonovert actions (for example, defensive reappraisal). It would also be interesting to see under what conditions, these covert methods of coping break down (for example, divorce rates and wife swapping are quite high among nudists). It is probably true that study of nudists would occasion more stress for the stress researcher than he could ever hope to see in others, so it is not worth belaboring this example. The value of this illustration is that it suggests a population, and there are probably many others, which at first glance may seem irrelevant to stress research but which, in fact, is quite relevant.

Use and modification of selected natural situations.   Several investigators (for example, Beam, 1955; Mechanic, 1962; Osler, 1954) seem to have had unusual success in studying stress by strategically locating their measurements around academic examination periods. There is little doubt that course examinations produce sizable stress and controlled measurements (generally using S as his own control) around these events seem to be quite useful. The use of natural testing situations may make even more sense because many critics of current laboratory practice argue that the most prominent feature of any laboratory study is that the person is being examined and he knows it (for example, Riecken, 1962; Rosenberg, 1965). This "evaluation apprehension" is assumed to be sufficiently strong that it over-rides everything else that happens. Undoubtedly there is some truth to this. This view would suggest, in the case of stress research, that we might continue to run laboratory studies and conceptualize them in terms of stress produced by assessment, or else we might move outside the laboratory and make use of natural situations involving assessment.

As everyone knows, there are numerous everyday harassments which threaten people and which can afford valuable access to stress. Consider the situation of a person who is stopped by a patrolman for speeding. The amount of threat here probably is greater when the arresting officer blows his siren and flashes his red light, than when he merely flashes his light. The offense is more visible to bystanders when a siren is used. If predictions are made concerning the effect of magnitude of threat on location of harmful agent, these predictions should reveal differences between the siren plus light condition and the light only condition. But we need not stop here. Having stopped the driver, the officer then is free to issue either a warning or a ticket. These actions should have different effects on the aroused threat and on the choice of coping response. To determine whether or not this is true, we might follow the driver once he is released by the officer and record the caution or abandon that characterizes his subsequent driving behavior. Essentially, what we are suggesting is that there are groups of people whose work leads them repeatedly to generate situations of stress for other persons. It may be possible to systematize their handling of the stimulus situation in ways that are meaningful for stress theory. In the example here used, the officer is free to execute his job, but he is asked to execute his job in ways that are consistent with parameters in the experimental design.

A similar controlled situation of stress could occur in a restaurant where the waiter either imposes greater or less stress by the ways in which he takes orders, his speed or lack of same in delivering orders, and the degree to which he gives people either the correct or incorrect dishes. Giving separate checks or a single check to a group of unrelated diners seems to produce an uncommon amount of threat. If we then measured dependent variables such as (1) size of tip to hatcheck girl, (2) latency in leaving after check is brought to table, (3) behavior of group when it leaves the restaurant, (4) interactions with doorman and taxi drivers, and the like it should be possible to learn about the effects of different stress parameters on the choice of a coping strategy.

In both of these examples, what essentially happens is that natural occasions of distress have been made more orderly by having one person in the situation systematically play the role required for experimental purposes. The situation is natural, the person encounters a particular set of behaviors by the attendant which he has every reason to expect might occur anyway, and thus little deception is involved. A commonplace event is rearranged in such a way that meaningful data are generated. This general format for experimentation is shown perhaps most elegantly in studies conducted by Garfinkel (1964) and by Sommer (for example, Felipe & Sommer, 1966). Felipe and Sommer set out to see what happens when a student invades the personal space of another student in a library. The experimenter located a girl sitting alone at a large table in a library, and then took a position at various distances from the isolated student (for example, constant distance between the experimenter's and the girl's shoulders of no more than 12 inches, distance of 2 feet between shoulders, 3½ feet between shoulders, 5 feet between shoulders, or across the table from the subject). It is important to remember that the subject is sitting alone when the experimenter arrives and that there are a host of locations available *other than* those adjacent to the student. The dependent variable is the number of persons who change their seats in each condition, and the speed with which they do so. The main finding of that study was that significantly more students changed seats in the

12-inch conditions than in any of the other four conditions (there were no differences among the other four conditions).

Again in this example, we see an instance where the principal mode of coping appears to be avoidance rather than attack. It would be interesting to change parameters in this situation to see under what conditions attack or confrontation would be produced rather than avoidance. Evidence in this same article, gained from a study in a mental hospital, indicates that there are occasions (for example, strictly enforced territory) where an impingement on space does not produce flight. Careful study of these situations would not just tell us what happens when people sit close to one another, but rather might give us general leads as to crucial factors that control the choice between attack and flight, leads which could then be tested in other settings.

Use of special props.   As a final point in this discussion, we should mention that control can be gained not only by systematizing the people and their actions in the setting, but also by judicious choice and embedding of props. This principle is perhaps best exemplified in the highly realistic simulations staged by Berkun, Bialek, Kern, and Yagi (1962). They wanted to learn about the effects of stress on performance and their performance measures were extremely well embedded. For example, when recruits were aboard a plane which suddenly lost an engine (by design) and was preparing to ditch, they were asked to fill out forms telling how their last effects should be disposed of, these forms to be jettisoned before the crash. The forms were written in such a way that they were difficult to comprehend, and the dependent variable was the accuracy with which the form was completed. In other settings used by those same investigators, the dependent measures were how quickly and accurately the person exposed to stress could rewire a malfunctioning radio in order to summon help. In both of these cases, the props were quite plausible components in the setting; they were in no way reactive (Campbell, 1957); and for this reason they constitute important ways to lend order to data collection.

It seems clear that investigators can gain access to stress in natural settings without waiting for large-scale disasters to occur. Small-scale disasters are commonplace, they permit data collection without the necessity for major deceptions, they often permit some rearrangement in the interests of control and manipulation, and, therefore, they should be examined more carefully as possible sites for data collection.

The Finesse of Stress: Promising Laboratory Techniques

The preceding discussion should not be read as a fatalistic statement regarding the demise of the laboratory. We hope to show, both in this section, and the next one, that there is a decided reason for optimism about the future of laboratory studies of stress. This section contains several examples of different strategies which seem to capture stress in the laboratory. The section has been labeled "the finesse of stress" because the emphasis is on subtlety of manipulations and on deception-free strategies.

Example of a nonreactive, nondeceptive stress experiment.   Suppose we were interested in testing Lazarus' (1966) proposition that "threat is less in the presence of effective counterharm resources than it is without them [p. 106]." Conceivably all we might need to test this proposition is a cap pistol, some caps, and several balloons. To produce two values of perceived counterharm resources, we would have half of the subjects fire the cap pistol twenty times without any caps in it, and the other half fire the pistol twenty times with extremely loud-report caps loaded in it. The intent here is simply to accustom the subjects differentially to the sound of loud noises. Following the firing of cap guns, we simply ask each subject to blow up a balloon until it breaks. Throughout the experiment measures are taken of GSR. The interesting features of blowing up a balloon until it breaks are: (1) there is considerable uncertainty in the task; (2) there is a sizable period of anticipation as the balloon grows larger and larger; (3) when the balloon bursts it makes a sudden, loud noise which can unsettle even the most complacent person; and (4) if the experimenter had made some offhand comment to the effect that "It's a good thing to be able to take unexpected events in stride," then the stage would be set for the production of stress in a controlled microcosm. In this case, we would predict that subjects exposed to loud cap guns (high effective counterharm resources) would blow up and burst the balloon significantly faster than would the quiet cap gun group (low counterharm resources). The rationale would be that the quiet group would draw out the period prior to the bursting of the balloon because they feel more threatened by the imminent burst. They have fewer resources to combat the unsettling experience of a sudden loud noise. This dependent measure could be further quantified if we had measures of breathing. The quiet group should take more breaths and expel less wind in each breath than is true for the loud group.

Although I certainly would not consider this simple exercise as any kind of earth-shaking stress study, it does seem to capture some elementary points that I hope to make about laboratory studies. First, it is possible to translate many relevant parameters of real-life stress (for example, counterharm resources) into plausible laboratory analogues. Second, these translations need not require deception. Third, the manipulations can be chosen so that there is almost no lingering unease for the subject when he leaves the laboratory. Fourth, the events need not be highly dramatic and contain all of the trappings commonly associated with natural instances of stress. Fifth, the experiments do not have to be of long duration in order to produce the desired effects. Sixth, it is possible to learn about important relationships from relatively slight events. Seventh, subject involvement is not necessarily a function of the drama or trappings in the laboratory. It can be produced, perhaps even more convincingly, in the simple exercises which the subject is "certain" he can master. Many laboratory exercises are so complex that the subject correctly perceives that he will not be able to master them in the time allotted. One consequence of this is that he may take the exercise less seriously. A simple task like the balloon task may tempt the subject much more than other, more formidable tasks.

Some further nondeceptive, nonreactive laboratory paradigms.   In the following examples, we have tried to gather some laboratory technologies which fit most of the requirements listed above. There are several innocuous events which, when brought into the laboratory, might serve to be rather unsettling to the subject even though they involve no deception. Three examples of such events are sleep deprivation, boredom, and being watched.

Although several investigators have produced stress simply by having subjects report to the laboratory at midnight and remain awake all night (for example, Gifford & Murewski, 1964), there is additional variation of this procedure used by Dement (1960) which seems even more productive. He had subjects sleep in the laboratory for several nights. During the first portion of the experiment, subjects slept undisturbed during the night so that baseline measures of several physiological responses could be obtained. For the next five nights, subjects were awakened whenever there was a physiological indication that they were beginning to dream. Subjects, in other words, were never allowed to have a dream. Following this period, they were allowed five "recovery" nights in which they slept undisturbed and the number of dreams was recorded. Finally, subjects were awakened for five nights in a row whenever they had *completed* a dream and then were allowed five additional recovery nights. While the results of this study are more detailed than we can summarize here, the findings show that a phenomenon resembling dream deprivation seems to exist. During the five nights when all dreams were interrupted, the number of interruptions (that is, incipient dreams) increased substantially from the first to the fifth night. In other words, the investigator had to awaken the subjects more times as the deprivation series continued. Second, during the first recovery period, the number of dreams was far in excess of the number obtained during the baseline period, and it took exactly as many days for the subjects to recover from the deprivation as they had been deprived, that is, five. Finally, interruptions whenever a dream had been completed did not lead to an increase in dreaming during the final recovery period. While it is unfortunate that Dement did not run subjects in the opposite sequence of events (interrupt completed dreams then interrupt dreams at their onset), it seems clear that this problem area might be a fruitful means to create stress in the laboratory.

Geiwitz's (1966) complex but informative studies of the structure of boredom suggest that subjects become quite unsettled and experience considerable threat when they do simple repetitive tasks for extended periods of time. These data are consistent with those obtained by investigators who have studied the reactions of persons assigned to isolated military outposts for considerable periods of time (for example, Gross & Miller, 1960; Rohrer, 1959).

Finally there is evidence in the studies of Wapner and Alper (1952) and Bernal (1966) that a present but unseen audience causes considerable distress for persons working on tasks, especially tasks with personal significance. The interesting twist in the Bernal study is that she had subjects, whose backs were toward a one-way mirror, estimate the amount of time that E was looking at them. These estimates were obtained when S was answering neutral questions in a personality inventory and when she was answering questions of a highly personal nature about which she might feel considerably guilty.

Some standardized laboratory technologies for stress.   Stress in the laboratory can take other forms. Investigators using delayed auditory and visual feedback (for example, Pronko & Leith, 1956) seem to be quite successful in producing stress. Here again, the subject has considerable opportunity to manage the threat which the situation produces. He has a concrete apparatus which he can blame for his poor performance and thus is unlikely to leave the laboratory in an agitated state. Even with these safeguards, it is still true that the delayed auditory feedback produces considerable unease and has marked effects on performance. This seemingly innocuous procedure generates sizable threat to feeling of competency, but because of the uniqueness of the procedure and the fact that the subject is unlikely to confront it again, it is relatively easy for him to compartmentalize this experience and not be bothered by it when he leaves the laboratory. Nevertheless, at the time he is actually trying to perform tasks while reading instructions aloud, sizable threat is produced, especially when the experimenter stipulates that failure to execute the instructions within three seconds will result in the subject's receiving a shock (for example, Pronko & Leith, 1956).

One of the virtues of stress films used in laboratory studies is that they comprise a standardized stimulus situation which can be kept relatively intact across several different kinds of manipulations. This increases greatly the comparability of studies and would seem to be a good model for stress researchers to keep in mind. The efforts by Kelley et al. (1965) to standardize the Mintz (1951) experiment involving "mobs" is another example of a standardized situation which fosters cumulative knowledge. One-shot experiments, in which a host of parameters vary, considerably retard the emergence of any kind of cumulative body of knowledge.

A final example of a standardized stress situation, and one that seems to deserve more attention than it has received, is the complication apparatus designed by Freeman (1945). This apparatus requires the subject to perform, simultaneously, two distinct discrimination problems which vary considerably in their requirements (for example, one requires gross movements, the other fine movements; one requires adjustment by the hands, the other by the feet, and so on). Although at first glance this apparatus may seem to be nothing but a complex test of motor skills, the task is designed so that the subject typically perceives it as a threat to his sense of competence and mastery. The task appears to be quite simple, thereby engaging the subject's interest. As he soon discovers, the task is quite difficult, and it is at this point that feelings of stress and threat increase substantially. If stress researchers pay more attention to task variables, as Hackman (Chapter 13) has argued forcibly in his paper, then it seems clear that tasks such as the complication apparatus will take on considerably more meaning and value.

Hypnosis provides a technology that may deserve closer attention from stress researchers. Some indication of its fruitfulness is found in an interesting experiment by Mendelsohn (1962) concerning the degree to which various affective states are complementary or antagonistic in their effects. Under hypnosis, Mendelsohn paired different affective states with different letters of the alphabet. For example, the subject was told that whenever he saw the letter *H* he would feel anxious, whenever he saw the letter *N* he would feel neutral. Letters were also paired with the affective states of contentment, depression, and delight. Once these suggestions were implanted the subject was then awakened. During the post-hypnotic period, letters, both singly and in combination were shown to the subject, and GSR measures were taken of his reactions. This methodology is of interest because of the degree of control that it affords, because it is free of deception, and because once the experimental inductions are removed, the subject remains largely unaware of what happened during the experiment.

Undoubtedly the most venerable stress induction used in the laboratory is electric shock. Some of the most interesting uses of this manipulation have been in studies where persons are given choices concerning when the shock will be applied (for example, Cook & Barnes, 1964;

D'Amato & Gumenik, 1960; Pervin, 1963). The general procedure is that the subject gets some indication that he is going to receive a shock, but he is given the choice of whether he will receive it immediately, at some specified future time (for instance, 8 seconds from now), or at some indefinite future time. As noted earlier, the general direction of these findings is that unpredictable punishment seems to be more aversive than predictable punishment, and short delays are preferred over longer delays. These findings are interesting because cognitive models of stress may be hard-pressed to explain how appraisal processes can function in such short periods of time. It seems clear that time is required for "cognitive work" to proceed (for example, Miller, 1967; Walster & Berscheid, 1967), and the results with the shock studies suggest that subjects take very little time to make their decisions.

Manipulation of temperature. It is tempting (at least to someone trying to "appreciate" Minnesota climates) to speculate on possible ways in which the simple act of raising or lowering the temperature in an experimental room might serve to produce stress. Suppose for example, that several groups of three persons were told that, as part of their course grade, they were to spend an hour "brainstorming" all possible uses they could think of for a burned out light bulb, and that members of the best group would have their grades raised a full letter. Now suppose we put one set of groups in a room with the temperature set at 70°, another in a room with the temperature set at 100°, and the third in a room where the temperature is 40°. It is probably safe to assume that, in the extreme temperature groups, the subjects are not thinking just about the task; they are distracted by the uncomfortable conditions. Threat should be heightened for these subjects because they are not able to direct their full attention to the task, and consequently they may lose a chance to raise their grades. In other words, the uncomfortable temperature is a threat in the sense that their attention becomes self-centered at a time when they need to direct all of their thoughts to the problem. The distracting quality imposed by self-centeredness might be even more pronounced if subjects were told to spend an hour simply talking to a stranger, and to be as spontaneous and natural with this person as possible. Undoubtedly, temperature extremes would distract the person considerably from appearing relaxed, and if the stranger showed no apparent discomfort, the subject might experience considerable threat.

Other offbeat possibilities could be suggested. Suppose that art students were induced to produce pieces of sculpture to be judged by the art school faculty, but that they had to sculpt either butter or ice in a room with the temperature set at 90°.

Perhaps more subtle would be the following exercise. Suppose that four subjects were assembled and told to spend 30 minutes discussing any topic because the investigators "wanted to get some recordings of conversation against which they could try out several coding schemes." Suppose that one of the four persons is instructed to snap a Polaroid picture of the group every 30 seconds to enable the investigators to coordinate verbal remarks with facial expressions. The problem for the photographer would be considerable if the temperature in the discussion room was around 45°. Polaroid film is quite sensitive to temperature differences, and the lower the temperature, the longer it takes to develop the picture. The well-known 10-second developing time for this type of film holds only under conditions of normal room temperature. If the apprentice photographer tried to get one picture every thirty seconds as the experimenter stated, none of his pictures would turn out. They would all be underdeveloped. This should prove especially bothersome if he had been given a thorough indoctrination period and if the experimenter had stressed the importance of the photographs.

In each of these temperature experiments there is a premium on the person acting in a composed manner and accomplishing a task which, under ordinary conditions, would not cause much hardship. The problem for the subject is that the climatic conditions distract or render more difficult his completion of the task and, as performance falters, it is presumed that the person will be threatened. These situations get even more interesting because it is difficult to locate a "specific agent of harm." While it is a partial explanation to say that the working conditions are not ideal, this explanation does not constitute a clear attribution. Moreover, the person may well feel that temperature should not make that much difference.

Although the reader may consider this discussion of climate largely a digression, it does not seem too outlandish to suggest that manipulation of this variable might produce some of the phenomena in which we are interested.

Use of learning paradigms.   A particularly elegant example of a sensitive measure of stress embedded in an unfortunately confounded setting, is a study by Barthol and Ku (1959). They were interested in the question, does regression under stress consist of the primitization of a response or historical regression (reverting to a formerly acquired response)? To answer this question, they had subjects learn to tie a bowline knot in two different ways. One group of subjects first learned to tie the knot in a simple way, and then in a much more elegant and complex manner. The other group of subjects were exposed to the opposite sequence; they learned the elegant solution first and then learned the simple solution. After the learning task, all subjects were exposed to a "massive" induction of stress which included taking a three-and-a-half hour intelligence test, late at night, with no-smoking rules strictly enforced, and so forth. Following completion of this test, subjects were asked to tie a bowline knot, and it was found that sixteen of the eighteen subjects used the method that they had learned *first*. While the complexity of the stress situation makes it virtually impossible to know to what this effect should be attributed, the basic approach to this important question seems to be a good one, and, given some refinements, the technique seems an elegantly simple way to answer a crucial question.

Stress and the seated subject.   One limitation which laboratory experimenters have imposed on themselves unnecessarily is that subjects remain seated during the experiment. There is very little movement during a laboratory study (see Swanson, 1953, for a refreshing exception to this general practice) and it may be that these constraints on mobility have some effect on the generality of laboratory findings. Many occasions of stress in everyday life involve massive motor actions, movements, milling and other forms of physical activity, which may influence both the intensity of the perceived stress and the choice of a coping activity. Freedom of movement, for example, may give a person greater feelings of control over the stressful circumstances.

Some clues about ways in which movement could be preserved in the laboratory are found in the method of stimulus presentation used by Capretta and Berkun (1962). Although this method was used in a field experiment, it seems adaptable to the laboratory. These investigators outfitted army recruits with headsets and microphones, after which the recruits were to run across a rope bridge which was suspended either 50 feet above a rocky gorge or (for a control condition) 1 foot above the ground. At two points during the crossing (either beginning and middle, or middle and end) a list of digits was read to the recruit and he was to repeat the list backwards. Analysis of error scores revealed that there were no differences among conditions.

Although this study is interesting because of the unique method of stimulus presentation involved, it is also a good example of a study using an *impoverished* set of measures. These investigators clearly underexploited the data that were potentially available to them. For example, they made no observation of the performance of the recruit at the time the stimulus materials were presented. There is no indication of whether he stopped mid-bridge when the materials were presented, whether he continued without any deviation in his pace, whether his speed of transit decreased or increased after the digit-span test, what the latency was between the time the list was read to him and the time he started to repeat it, or how long it took him to repeat it. These "absent data" primarily underscore the point made earlier that sometimes stress researchers are not very observant. Data such as those just mentioned could have been recorded at only a moderate increase in effort and would have been quite relevant for the concepts of interruption and inertial tendencies.

But the useful point in the Capretta and Berkun (1962) example is that it is possible to present stimulus materials to subjects at times other than when they are seated. It should be possible for experimenters to devise stress situations in the laboratory which would take advantage of this added flexibility.

Use of photographic evidence.   Recent work on nonverbal behavior by Ekman (1965) suggests again that investigators can be poor observers of people undergoing stress. Part of Ekman's procedure is to take still pictures of patients at various stages during psychotherapy, and then have judges either match the photos with statements actually uttered by the patient or match the photos with different stages in the person's progression through psychotherapy. Then Ekman attempts to analyze what bodily cues the judges used in order to make these judgments. Even though this is a very incomplete summary of the extensive program currently being conducted by Ekman and his associates, it does suggest an approach that might prove fruitful for stress researchers.

Suppose that we took several still photos of individual subjects who are observing stress films such as those of subincision rites or mill accidents. Judges are then asked to match the photos with the sequences in the films. Assuming that the judges have some success at this task, we could then look for the cues that the judges used in order to make these categorizations. Having identified these cues, we could then shift to a highly speculative but potentially lucrative level of analysis.

Given information about nonverbal behaviors that distinguish between periods of high and low stress, we might assume the position of a radical behaviorist, as Bem (1967) has done recently in re-evaluating studies of cognitive dissonance. Bem's argument goes something like this. The major way that people learn to attach labels to their internal, private states is through interpretations provided by other people (the verbal community). The major data that the community has access to, in socializing the person, are his observable responses. Having observed a particular response, the community suggests an interpretation to the person about the way he "feels." As socialization progresses, the person begins to make more and more of these judgments for himself, still relying largely on the same *overt* indices used by the verbal community. The point of all this for the stress photos is that the cues which judges pick up in other people as signs of stress or relief may be the same signs they process to determine whether they, themselves, are experiencing stress. The point we are making is that photos concerning overt stress reactions may portray cues that each person uses to make his own judgments about the degree of stress that he is experiencing. Thus, the photos are valuable not just as interesting supplementary data, but because they suggest one way of interpreting the origin of stress reactions.

Although the preceding discussion has ranged over an unusually wide variety of manipulations, the important point which should emerge is that there is considerable flexibility within the laboratory to capture crucial problems in stress. There are more opportunities to study stress in this setting than have been realized. But perhaps the most important point is that it is possible to create the necessary conditions without resorting to deception and without leaving the subject in a shambles after the experiment has taken place.

The Redress of Stress: Debriefing and "Permanent Damage"

Stress research, no matter what form it takes, can be taxing on the investigator who is basically human and gets no thrill from intentionally hurting people. Many investigators shy away from stress research because they are squeamish about exposing people to conditions that make their lives even more difficult. But if we are going to study stress, we have to learn about it somehow. It makes no sense to abandon this area simply because it involves "making trouble" for subjects, but neither do we have to legitimize psychopathy on the part of investigators. Instead, the solution seems to be twofold. Part of it has been sketched in the preceding section, namely the use of nondeceptive modes of stress induction. This strategy is valuable because it does not violate the "contract of trust" between the experimenter and the subject; the subject is given a more substantial rationale for his poor performance, and the debriefing period does not have to be a time of major revelations about gullibility. Instead, the postexperimental period can be spent discussing more subtle issues and questions which the experiment raised for the subject. The purpose of the present section is to look at the second portion of this solution. We want to know in what ways debriefing periods might be handled differently to increase the chances that when subjects leave the laboratory they are in no worse shape than when they came in (see Kelman, 1967).

At the outset we might as well admit one point concerning the redress of stress: at this stage of our knowledge it *will* be difficult to debrief subjects. The reason is simple; we don't know a great deal about stress or how to reduce its effects. That's the problem we are trying to study. If we knew enough to know how to conduct an adequate debriefing of subjects in stress experiments, there probably would be no need to run the experiment; we would already have the important information. Critics of laboratory methodology sometimes forget that, in the early stages of research when investigators are identifying the parameters of a phenomenon, they do not intentionally abuse their subjects by conducting incomplete debriefings. Rather, they do not know enough about the phenomenon to be certain of how to reduce its impact or hasten recovery. As knowledge accumulates, however, there is every reason to expect investigators to apply the knowledge they have learned and to preserve the integrity of subjects. As we learn more about variables that aid recovery from stress, these findings can be put into immediate use in helping the subject consolidate his experiences after the experiment. And, as more is learned about stress, the magnitude and intensity of stress used in experiments is apt to decline considerably.

Incidentally, a comment should be made to arrest any notions that field research is more "sanitary" because issues of deception, trust, permanent damage, and the like do not arise. Field research has just as many problems of redress as are found in the laboratory. To interview a person shortly after he has experienced a sizable loss in a disaster when he is in a highly agitated state is certainly no more humane than it is to invade the privacy of a subject via the laboratory. Furthermore, since the disaster victim responds to the interview questions at a time when he may not be thinking clearly, there is every chance that he may later reflect and be horrified at what he has said and the kind of person it shows him to be. The problem is that there is no one around to ease him through this period of reflection and "second thoughts." In many ways this is more inconsiderate than working carefully to identify all of the problems a person feels shortly after he has responded in a potentially "dangerous" way in a laboratory setting.

Legitimate as these points may be, they certainly do not excuse the investigator from doing everything he can to insure the safety of the subject. He cannot hide behind incomplete knowledge as an excuse for careless debriefing, and there do seem to be more effective ways in which subjects' unease could be handled. The problem of debriefing is a crucial one, but it profits little from a harangue which points to the problems but gives no help with the solution. While many of the suggestions that follow may sound bizarre (and probably are), I have detailed them simply in the hope that they will trigger associations in other persons which could lead to more productive solutions.

Debriefing and substitution.   Actually this entire paper had its origin in the central issue of this section. I began this project with a concern for a specific question: What *could* you do, with subjects exposed to Milgram's (1965) obedience study, to insure that they would not leave the laboratory discomforted? One of the first ideas that came to mind was the idea of substitution. You have already seen where that took us in terms of substantive issues. But let us revisit the idea of substitution and see what it suggests about debriefing.

At the end of a Milgram experiment, the subject is faced with the troublesome thought that he can be coerced to inflict sizable damages on someone else. The experimenter's assurance that the other person was not actually hurt has very little relevance to the subject's problem. At the time of the experiment, he did *not know* that the victim felt nothing.

Let us assume that the main unfinished business for Milgram's subject is a need to reassert his independence of authority and his consideration toward other people. Satisfaction of these motives has been jarringly interrupted by the experimental participation. The question, then, is: What could we have the subject do in the debriefing period that would increase his feelings of independence and humanity? One thing is certain: talking about the procedures probably does not help much. Perhaps, if the subject were given a chance to criticize the experiment, this would help him to feel somewhat that he is not obedient to all authorities; but this is unlikely to occur or to be effective because the experimenter probably does know more about the experiment than the subject does.

To gain effective substitution, the experimenter has to provide opportunities during the debriefing period for the subject to resist his suggestions successfully. For example, the experimenter might say that he is the campus chairman for the Red Cross drive and that he would like the subject to donate $1.00 (the subject has just been paid $4.00 for his participation). If the subject then refuses to donate any money he would be resisting the experimenter successfully; but note that if he gives more than the experimenter suggests, this makes it possible for him to view himself as a considerate, thoughtful person. As another example, the experimenter might tell the subject that although he normally pays his assistant $2.00 an hour, the subject can decide what the accomplice will be paid. Here, again, the subject has the opportunity to resist what the experimenter has said, and also to demonstrate some considerateness for a fellow student who has a difficult job.

Several other strategies for debriefing might work. Subjects often are angered after an experiment is explained because they feel gullible. To combat this impression, experimenters usually emphasize the great effort it took to fool the subject. This probably does not help much, because all the experimenter is really saying is that, having tried very hard, he *did* find a way to fool the subject. Perhaps more convincing would be efforts by the experimenter to divorce feelings of gullibility from judgments of intelligence. Part of the subject's discomfort may arise because he equates gullibility with stupidity; hence not only has he been shown to be gullible, but also stupid. The experimenter might supplement this disengagement with information that what the subject actually demonstrated was that he was sensitive to events around him and that he is capable of trust, both of which are admirable attributes. The same datum—namely, being taken in by the experiment—can be interpreted as a sign of weakness or as a sign of strength; and it seems possible that experimenters may have paid less attention to the latter possibility.

A successful form of debriefing might consist of satiation (Lewin, 1935). To make the experimental task and the attendant trappings seem less offensive, the experimenter might simply have the subject repeat the experimental task several times until he no longer finds it interesting or unique. The same procedure might be used to neutralize the Milgram experiment. The experimenter could replay several items, portions of a tape in which the subject hears himself being urged to give increasingly strong levels of shock. This procedure might serve to desensitize the subject to some of the more troublesome portions of the experiment and thus leave him considerably less bothered afterwards.

Part of the problem in debriefing subjects is that they are angered because someone has invaded their privacy. If this bothers subjects, it might be possible for the experimenter to effect some kind of "privacy trade-off." For example, the experimenter might comment that he has taken some privacy away from the subject and would like to repay him by giving increased privacy in another area. He might then volunteer to provide quiet study space for the subject, or try to obtain increased privacy for the subject in some area that he values.

As a variation of this procedure, the experimenter might say something like, "I've found out information about you, now it's only fair that you have equal opportunity to find out about me. What would you like to know?" Here the investigator both acknowledges that he did learn something about the subject, and makes it a more equitable exchange by allowing the subject similar access to him. Needless to say, the experimenter would have to give honest answers to the subject's questions. It is doubtful that many investigators would be comfortable with this inversion of roles; but, at least in the abstract, this example does suggest one model that might be used to increase the relevance and value of debriefing.

Relaxation and arousal.   It is conceivable that in very intense manipulations, drugs might be used to facilitate debriefing, although additional problems might be produced by doing so. A tranquilizer given immediately after the experiment should aid the subject to become less concerned about what happened and to have fewer residual effects from the experiment. Ironically, a stimulant such as epinephrine might have the same effect. One of the reasons that debriefing sessions may be so ineffective is that when the subject finally participates in them he is fatigued because of the tension generated by the experiment, he is mulling over the previous events, and he may only partly hear what the experimenter says. Regardless of how much care the experimenter takes to tell the subject everything, little of this information may sink in. The purpose of a drug that heightens arousal would be to increase the impact of the words that the experimenter says during the debriefing period. This might increase the chances that the subject will listen closely to what he says and ask whatever questions seriously bother him. There may be drugless devices such as drawings, patterns of lights, soundtracks, and the like that would have many of the same effects as the drugs. Perhaps these might afford a way to increase either the impact or the relaxation possible during debriefing.

The "terrycloth letter."   Some assistance in debriefing might occur if the experimenter made use of a device which we will label the "terrycloth letter" (after Harlow's infamous terrycloth mothers). At the beginning of the experiment, the subject is handed a sealed envelope and is told that the envelope contains a sheet of paper which tells in great detail what the experiment is about, what its value is to science, and which explains all deceptions involved *if* there are any. He is also told that the letter is his property and that if, at any time during the experiment, he feels sufficiently uncomfortable that he does not want to continue, he is free to halt the experiment and to read the letter, after which the experimenter will answer any questions he might have. This device could serve several purposes. First, the experiment has been described in detail so the subject does not have to worry that he will be given a hasty, uninformative brush-off by the experimenter. Second, the experimenter has immediately expressed some trust in the subject by his statement that the letter is the permanent property of the subject. Even though the subject might show the letter around campus, the experimenter has entrusted him with this information. Third, the letter is written and therefore the subject does not have to listen to the "frightening" experimenter talk about the study, and he is not as open to the experimenter's anger should he decide to stop midway through the experiment. He will get the same description regardless of when he stops. Fourth, if the subject has a class the next hour, he still is comforted that he will get a thorough explanation of the experiment. Fifth, the letter would serve as a reminder that if he had second thoughts about his participation and started to worry about it several days later, all he would need to do is reread the letter and his memory would be refreshed concerning the *actual* purpose of the experiment.

Use of humor.   Even though stress researchers are often charming and extremely witty when interacting with their colleagues, they unfortunately are often boorish when debriefing subjects. This observation should not be taken lightly or defensively. We probably have missed a major avenue for easing subject discomfort by not injecting more humor into the post-experimental period. This suggestion gains considerable plausibility from the recent brilliant essay by Lorenz (1963) noting the unusual facility that humor has for channeling feelings of aggression, increasing honesty, and strengthening ties among people. As he notes, "we do not as yet take humor seriously enough [p. 293]." A flavor of Lorenz's analysis can be gained from the following excerpt:

> Nowadays we are all radically intolerant of pompous or sanctimonious people, because we expect a certain amount of self-ridicule in every intelligent human being. Indeed, we feel that a man who takes himself absolutely seriously is not quite human. . . . The best definition of man is that he is the one creature capable of reflection, of seeing himself in the frame of reference of the surrounding universe. Pride is one of the chief obstacles to seeing ourselves as we really are and self-deceit is the obliging servant of pride. It is my firm belief that a man sufficiently gifted with humor is in small danger of succumbing to flattering delusions about himself because he cannot help perceiving what a pompous ass he would become if he did [pp. 295–296].

To appreciate what Lorenz is saying one need only reflect on feelings experienced when reading commentaries on psychology found in the "Worm Runner's Digest," *Games People Play* (Berne, 1965), and so forth.

The point is that although *we* know that there is a certain amount of levity in what we do, our subjects do not. There is no good reason why we should prevent them from coming "backstage." After all, it is partly their capricious acts which force us toward levity. But how, concretely, might this be accomplished? While the subject is waiting for the debriefing session, the experimenter might let him leaf through a scrapbook which contains some of the more pithy graphic cartoons that pertain to experimentation. The subject might listen to a humorous recording spoofing an experimenter who is trying to conduct an experiment with an overly cooperative student. Humor unrelated to the experimental setting might also be effective.

The use of humor would not have to be this blatant. Having concluded the major experiment, the subject could be given a stack of pertinent cartoons and told to rate how funny each one is. Or the subject might be given a humorous essay and told to underline every phrase which he found amusing. Undoubtedly there are better devices than these. The important point is that we should not take ourselves or the experiment too seriously. We can relax considerably without any great risk that we or the subject will feel it is all worthless. There is a close tie between humor and honesty; the investigator ought to try to be honest, and the suggestion here is that humor may aid him significantly in doing so.

It probably will take a considerable amount of original thinking before we can decide on some reasonable solutions. One thing seems clear: talking about procedures, rationale, and hypotheses is probably a waste of time. Such intellectualization of an emotionally charged setting probably is of little value to the subject. What I have tried to suggest are topics that may deal more directly with what the subject is worrying about.

The Less of Stress: Stress Studies with Small Ns

Is there any reason why stress experiments require large populations? Not really. Given that most stress manipulations do have a sizable impact on subjects, and that this makes it even more crucial to debrief adequately, then it makes sense that stress researchers should consider the value of studies with relatively small samples. The use of small samples would help insure that intense manipulations would not produce widespread "damage," that more extensive sets of measures could be obtained and analyzed, and that debriefing could be made more effective.

There is considerable precedent in current thinking for re-examination of the entire issue of sample size and the meaning of significance tests (for example, Bakan, 1966; Lykken, 1966; Shapiro, 1961; Skipper, Guenther, & Nass, 1967). One of the main themes in these discussions is that investigators are not sufficiently flexible in their choice of significance levels for different types of problems, nor are they necessarily warranted in making strong assertions about results when significance is obtained. Solely on statistical grounds, then, there is reason to question whether a large sample is quite as crucial as is generally assumed.

Rethinking the issue of sample size should also include careful review of the recent discussion by Dukes (1965) of situations where it is appropriate to draw conclusions from $N = 1$. Having reviewed several examples of important principles that were derived from studies of one person, Dukes states that studies with small Ns may be appropriate in the following circumstances: (1) when uniqueness is involved, that is, when a sample of one exhausts the population; (2) when between-individual variability for the function under investigation is negligible; (3) when the investigator wishes to preserve unity of the organism and dramatize a point; (4) when a single finding would serve to reject an assumed or asserted universal relationship; and (5) when there is limited opportunity to observe the phenomenon.

There are some precedents within the stress area for studies with extremely small Ns. Bixenstine (1955) obtained daily palmar sweat measures from a graduate student and his wife over a period of six months which spanned the student's taking of doctoral qualifying examinations. Peaks and valleys in the stress measures were closely associated with dramatic and bland events in the lives of these two people. In terms of the list proposed by Dukes, the Bixenstine study seems to be most consistent with points 3 and 5.

The Chess of Stress: Grand Strategies

Recently there have emerged formal descriptions of three research strategies which, until now, have been described mostly in informal ways. Each of these involve naturalistic strategies. Our intent is to alert stress researchers to the existence of these statements so that they can peruse them for possible relevance to their own interests.

Bruyn (1966) has presented a highly articulate and scholarly analysis of the assumptions and methodological prescriptions involved in participant observation. Until now this methodology has been communicated largely through informal field notes and research apprenticeships. Bruyn has made this methodology considerably more accessible to researchers and has developed a sound rationale for the methodological prescripts.

Argyris (1966), in a paper which is bound to be controversial, develops the argument that experimenter-subject relationships in experiments resemble closely superior-subordinate relationships found in many organizations. Given this similarity, one might expect to find in experiments many of the same unexpected consequences that are observed in organizations (for example, sabotage, apathy). Argyris notes there are definite signs that subjects behave much like subordinates.

Having expressed dissatisfaction with the state of affairs in experiments, Argyris then proceeds to discuss field observation and ways to categorize natural events. It is here where his ideas become most relevant to our present concern. He notes that "redundancy and over-determination are . . . basic properties of human behavior. . . . Human beings build their interpersonal relationships with the use of many imprecise and overlapping units [p. 29]." Given the assertion that human beings satisfice rather than optimize, Argyris concludes that in order to comprehend everyday behavior, the categories which are used should reflect properties associated with human problem solving. A category system which he has used to describe interpersonal confrontations in organizations consists of several categories having the properties of redundancy, overlap, and overdetermination. It is argued that such properties are more similar to the way in which behavior actually unfolds and can be readily applied by observers because they are developed in ways that coincide with individual perceptual tendencies. This point of view is summarized in Argyris's final remarks: "Perhaps what social science methodology needs to do is take on more of the characteristics of human problem solving. It would then enter a realm of overlapping, redundant, over-determined models and thus be able to operate and predict in the world in which we live even though it is full of noise [p. 30]."

It would seem reasonable to suggest that persons in stress research might at least try category systems built along the lines mentioned by Argyris to see if they help. This seems even more important because the canons of category construction that we typically espouse are markedly opposed to those mentioned here.

There is an incidental finding in Argyris' paper which has some intriguing implications for observation of stress. Argyris found that persons who were low in interpersonal competence had great difficulty using the category system, and never were able to obtain acceptable levels of inter-rater reliability when working with other judges. Apparently the person has to be experienced with the phenomenon he is judging for his judgments to be of any value. It is interesting that this notion coincides with Allport's (1961) suggestion that "as a rule people cannot comprehend others who are more subtle and complex than they are. The single-track mind has little feeling for the conflicts of the versatile mind. People who prefer simplicity of design and have no taste for the complex in their esthetic judgments are not as good judges as those with a more complex cognitive style and tastes [p. 508]."

If we take seriously the points mentioned by Argyris and Allport, they argue that the best observers of stress will be those persons who have experienced stress. This has an even more fascinating twist. Most of the prominent names in stress theory at the present time are persons who have had first hand experience with such stressful situations as the depression, World War II, and the Korean War. However, many of the younger investigators, born in the late 1930s and early 1940s, have been exposed mostly to secondhand stress, (via newspapers, radio, television, books) and have not had experiences that are equivalent to those found in the former group. If the analysis by Allport and Argyris is correct, then it argues that the younger group of stress researchers may need to be careful of a tendency to develop oversimplified models of stress. Unless researchers are aware of this possibility, stress research may find itself in the unfortunate position of generating its own "generation gap."

The final strategy which we should note has been mentioned at different points in this paper and has been labeled "tempered naturalness" (Weick, 1967). It is built on the premise that it is possible to make subtle alterations in natural situations without altering the ways in which behaviors unfold. These alterations are made to improve visibility of phenomena, lend more order to behavior, and assure greater equivalence between groups.

It should at least be clear that stress researchers have an abundance of tools available. At a time when we are taking stock of what we know about stress, it might be worthwhile for each investigator to review his own research strategies also, to see if they still constitute the best means for him to answer the questions he wants to answer.

References

Allport, G. W. *Pattern and growth in personality.* New York: Holt, Rinehart and Winston, 1961.

Argyris, C. Some unintended consequences of rigorous research. *Psychological Bulletin,* 1968, **70** (3), 185–197.

Aronson, E., & Gerárd, E. Beyond Parkinson's law. *Journal of Abnormal and Social Psychology,* 1966, **3**, 336–339.

Atkinson, J. W. *An introduction to motivation.* Princeton, N. J.: Van Nostrand, 1964.

Atkinson, J. W., & Cartwright, D. Some neglected variables in contemporary conceptions of decision and performance. *Psychological Reports,* 1964, **14**, 575–590.

Bakan, D. The test of significance in psychological research. *Psychological Bulletin,* 1966, **66**, 423–437.

Ball, D. W. An abortion clinic ethnography. *Social Problems,* 1967, **14**, 293–301.

Barker, R. G. Ecology and motivation. In M. R. Jones (Ed.), *Nebraska symposium on motivation.* Lincoln, Neb.: University of Nebraska, 1960, pp. 1–49.

Barker, R. G., & Gump, P. V. *Big school, small school.* Stanford, Calif.: Stanford University Press, 1964.

Barthol, R. P., & Ku, N. D. Regression under stress to first learned behavior. *Journal of Abnormal and Social Psychology,* 1959, **59**, 134–136.

Barton, A. H. *Social organization under stress: A sociological review of disaster studies.* Disaster Research Study No. 17. Washington, D. C.: National Academy of Sciences, 1963.

Beam, J. C. Serial learning and conditioning under real-life stress. *Journal of Abnormal and Social Psychology,* 1955, **51**, 543–552.

Bem, D. J. Self-perception: An alternative interpretation of cognitive dissonance phenomena. *Psychological Review,* 1967, **74** (3), 188–200.

Berkun, M. M., Bialek, H. M., Kern, R. P., & Yagi, K. Experimental studies of psychological stress in man. *Psychological Monographs,* 1962, **76** (Whole No. 534).

Bernal, M. E. The report of being watched as a measure of guilty behavior. In R. N. Haber (Ed.), *Current research in motivation.* New York: Holt, Rinehart and Winston, 1966, pp. 619–625.

Berne, E. *Games people play.* New York: Grove, 1964.

Bixenstine, V. E. A case study of the use of palmar sweating as a measure of psychological tension. *Journal of Abnormal and Social Psychology,* 1955, **50**, 138–143.

Bluestone, H., & McGahee, C. L. Reaction to extreme stress: Impending death by execution. *The American Journal of Psychiatry,* 1962, **119**, 393–396.

Brady, J. V. Ulcers in "executive" monkeys. In R. N. Haber (Ed.), *Current research in motivation*. New York: Holt, Rinehart and Winston, 1966, pp. 242–248.

Brehm, J. W. *A theory of psychological reactance*. New York: Academic, 1966.

Brehm, J. W., & Sensenig, J. Social influence as a function of attempted and implied usurpation of choice. *Journal of Personality and Social Psychology*, 1966, **4**, 703–707.

Brown, R. *Social psychology*. New York: Free Press, 1965.

Bruyn, S. T. *The human perspective in sociology: the methodology of participant observation*. Englewood Cliffs, N. J.: Prentice-Hall, 1966.

Buss, A. H. Stimulus generalization and the matching principle. *Psychological Review*, 1967, **74**, 40–50.

Calhoun, J. B. Population density and social pathology. *Scientific American*, 1962, **206**, 139–148.

Campbell, D. T. Factors relevant to the validity of experiments in social settings. *Psychological Bulletin*, 1957, **55**, 297–312.

Capretta, P. J., & Berkun, M. M. Validity and reliability of certain measures of psychological stress. *Psychological Reports*, 1962, **10**, 875–876.

Champion, R. A. Studies of experimentally induced disturbance. *Australian Journal of Psychology*, 1950, **2**, 90–99.

Cook, J. O., & Barnes, L. W. Choice of delay of inevitable shock. *Journal of Abnormal and Social Psychology*, 1964, **68**, 669–672.

D'Amato, M. E., & Gumenik, W. E. Some effects of immediate versus randomly delayed shock on an instrumental response and cognitive processes. *Journal of Abnormal and Social Psychology*, 1960, **60**, 64–67.

Davis, J. A. The campus as a frog pond: An application of the theory of relative deprivation to career decisions of college men. *American Journal of Sociology*, 1966, **72**, 17–31.

Dember, W. N. *The psychology of perception*. New York: Holt, Rinehart and Winston, 1960.

Dement, W. The effect of dream deprivation. *Science*, 1960, **131**, 1705–1708.

Dement, W. An essay on dreams. In F. Barron, W. Dement, W. Edwards, H. Lindman, L. D. Phillips, J. Olds, & M. Olds (Eds.), *New directions in psychology*. Vol. II. New York: Holt, Rinehart and Winston, 1965, pp. 136–257.

Deutsch, M. Field theory in social psychology. In G. Lindzey (Ed.), *Handbook of social psychology*. Vol. 1. Reading, Mass.: Addison-Wesley, 1954, pp. 181–222.

Drabek, T. E., & Quarantelli, E. L. Scapegoats, villains, and disasters, *Transaction*, 1967, **4**(4), 12–17.

Dukes, W. F. N = 1. *Psychological Bulletin*, 1965, **64**, 74–79.

Ekman, P. Communication through nonverbal behavior: A source of information about an interpersonal relationship. In S. S. Tomkins & C. E. Izard (Eds.), *Affect, cognition, and personality*. New York: Springer, 1965, pp. 390–442.

Felipe, N. J., & Sommer, R. Invasions of personal space. *Social Problems*, 1966, **14**, 206–214.

Freeman, G. L. Suggestions for a standardized "stress" test. *Journal of General Psychology*, 1945, **32**, 3–11.

Freud, S. *The problem of anxiety.* H. A. Bunker (Transl.) New York: Norton, 1936.

Friedman, S. B., Mason, J. W., & Hamburg, D. A. Urinary 17-hydroxy-corticosteroid levels in parents of children with neoplastic disease: A study of chronic psychological stress. *Psychosomatic Medicine,* 1963, **25,** 364–376.

Gampel, D. H. Data parallels across behavioral systems. *Psychological Bulletin,* 1966, **66,** 499–510.

Garfinkel, H. Studies of the routine grounds of everyday activities. *Social Problems,* 1964, **11,** 225–250.

Geiwitz, P. J. Structure of boredom. *Journal of Personality and Social Psychology,* 1966, **3,** 592–600.

Gifford, S., & Murewski, B. Minimal sleep deprivation alone and in small groups: Effects on ego-functioning and 24 hour body temperature and adrenocortical patterns. *Symposium on medical aspects of stress in the military climate.* Washington, D. C.: Walter Reed Army Medical Center, 1964.

Greenacre, P. The predisposition to anxiety. *Psychoanalytic Quarterly,* 1941, **10,** 66–94.

Gross, E., & Miller, C. The impact of isolation on worker adjustment in military installations of the United States and Japan. Unpublished manuscript. Maxwell Air Force Base, Texas, 1960.

Hall, E. T. *The hidden dimension.* New York: Doubleday, 1966.

Harris, W., Mackie, R., & Wilson, C. *Research on the development of performance criteria.* No. VI. *Performance under stress: a review and critique of recent studies.* Los Angeles, Calif.: Human Factors Research Inc., 1956.

Haworth, M. R. An exploratory study to determine the effectiveness of a filmed puppet show as a group projective technique for use with children. Unpublished doctoral dissertation, Pennsylvania State University, 1956.

Heider, F. *The psychology of interpersonal relations.* New York: Wiley, 1958.

Ilfeld, F., & Lauer, R. *Social nudism in America.* New Haven, Conn.: College and University Press, 1964.

Janis, I. L. Effects of fear arousal on attitude change: Recent developments in theory and experimental research. In L. Berkowitz (Ed.), *Advances in experimental social psychology.* Vol. 3. New York: Academic, 1967, pp. 167–224.

Jones, E. E., & Davis, K. E. From acts to dispositions: The attribution process in person perception. In L. Berkowitz (Ed.), *Advances in experimental social psychology.* Vol. 2. New York: Academic, 1965, pp. 219–266.

Kahneman, D., & Norman, J. The time-intensity relation in visual perception as a function of the observer's task. *Journal of Experimental Psychology,* 1964, **68,** 215–220.

Katz, D., & Stotland, E. A preliminary statement to a theory of attitude structure and change. In S. Koch (Ed.), *Psychology: A study of a science.* Vol. 3. New York: McGraw-Hill, 1959, pp. 423–475.

Kelley, H. H., Condry, J. C., Dahlke, A. E., & Hill, A. H. Collective behavior in a simulated panic situation. *Journal of Experimental Social Psychology,* 1965, **1,** 20–54.

The "Ess" in Stress: Some Conceptual and Methodological Problems   345

Kelley, H. H., & Thibaut, J. W. Group problem solving. In G. Lindzey & E. Aronson (Eds.), *Handbook of social psychology.* (Rev. ed.) Reading, Mass.: Addison-Wesley, 1968.

Kelman, H. C. Human use of human subjects: The problem of deception in social psychological experiments. *Psychological Bulletin,* 1967, **67,** 1–11.

Kessen, W., & Mandler, G. Anxiety, pain, and the inhibition of stress. *Psychological Review,* 1961, **68,** 396–404.

Latané, B., & Wheeler, L. Emotionality and reactions to disaster. *Journal of Experimental Social Psychology,* 1966, Supplement 1, 95–102.

Law, P. Personality problems in Antarctica. *Medical Journal of Australia,* February 20, 1960, 273–282.

Lazarus, R. S. *Psychological stress and the coping process.* New York: McGraw-Hill, 1966.

Lazarus, R. S., Opton, E. M., Nomikos, M. S., & Rankin, N. O. The principle of short-circuiting of threat: Further evidence. *Journal of Personality,* 1965, **33,** 622–635.

Lazarus, R. S., Speisman, J. C., Mordkoff, A. M., & Davison, L. A. A laboratory study of psychological stress produced by a motion picture film. *Psychological Monographs,* 1962, **76**(34, Whole No. 553).

Lewin, K. *A dynamic theory of personality.* New York: McGraw-Hill, 1935.

Locke, E. A., & Bryan, J. F. *Goals and intensions as determinants of performance level, task choice, and attitudes.* Washington, D. C.: American Institute for Research, 1967.

Lorenz, K. *On aggression.* New York: Harcourt, Brace & World, 1963.

Lykken, D. T. Statistical significance in clinical research. Unpublished manuscript, University of Minnesota, 1966.

Mandler, G. The interruption of behavior. In D. Levine (Ed.), *Nebraska symposium on motivation.* Lincoln, Neb.: University of Nebraska, 1964, pp. 163–219.

McGrath, J., & Altman, I. *Small group research.* New York: Holt, Rinehart and Winston, 1966.

Mechanic, D. *Students under stress.* New York: Free Press, 1962.

Mendelsohn, G. A. The competition of affective responses in human subjects. *Journal of Abnormal and Social Psychology,* 1962, **65,** 26–31.

Merton, R. K. *Social theory and social structure.* New York: Free Press, 1957.

Milgram, S. Liberating effects of group pressure. *Journal of Personality and Social Psychology,* 1965, **1,** 127–134.

Miller, G. A., Galanter, E. H., & Pribram, K. *Plans and the structure of behavior.* New York: Holt, Rinehart and Winston, 1960.

Miller, N. As time goes by. In R. Abelson, E. Aronson, W. McGuire, T. Newcomb, M. J. Rosenberg, & P. Tannenbaum (Eds.), *Sourcebook on cognitive consistency.* Skokie, Ill.: Rand McNally, 1967.

Mintz, A. Non-adaptive group behavior. *Journal of Abnormal and Social Psychology,* 1951, **46,** 150–159.

Murray, E. N., & Buss, A. H. Mediated stimulus generalization and words connoting mood. *Journal of Abnormal and Social Psychology,* 1963, **67,** 586–593.

Newell, A., Shaw, J. C., & Simon, H. A. Elements of a theory of human problem solving. *Psychological Review*, 1958, **65**, 151–166.

Osler, S. F. Intellectual performance as a function of two types of psychological stress. *Journal of Experimental Psychology*, 1954, **47**, 115–121.

Perls, F., Hefferline, R. E., & Goodman, P. *Gestalt therapy*. New York: Dell, 1965.

Pervin, L. A. The need to predict and control under conditions of threat. *Journal of Personality*, 1963, **31**, 570–587.

Ponder, E., & Kennedy, W. P. On the act of blinking. *Quarterly Journal of Experimental Physiology*, 1927, **18**, 89–110.

Pronko, N. E., & Leith, W. R. Behavior under stress: A study of its disintegration. *Psychological Reports*, 1956, **2**, 205–222.

Riecken, H. A program for research on experiments in social psychology. In N. F. Washburne (Ed.), *Decisions, values, and groups*. Vol. 2. New York: Pergamon, 1962, pp. 25–41.

Rohrer, J. H. Studies of human adjustment to polar isolation and implications of those studies for living in fallout shelters. Washington, D. C.: Disaster Research Group, National Academy of Sciences, 1959.

Rosenberg, M. J. When dissonance fails: On eliminating evaluation apprehension from attitude measurement. *Journal of Personality and Social Psychology*, 1965, **1**, 28–42.

Schachter, S., & Singer, J. E. Cognitive, social, and physiological determinants of emotional state. *Psychological Review*, 1962, **69**, 379–399.

Shapiro, M. B. The single case in fundamental psychological research. *British Journal of Medical Psychology*, 1961, **34**, 255–262.

Simon, H. A. Motivational and emotional controls of cognition. *Psychological Review*, 1967, **74**, 29–39.

Skipper, J. K., Guenther, A. L., & Nass, G. The sacredness of .05: A note concerning the uses of statistical levels of significance in social science. *The American Sociologist*, 1967, **2**(1), 16–18.

Speisman, J. C., Lazarus, R. S., Mordkoff, A. M., & Davison, L. A. The experimental reduction of stress based on ego-defense theory. *Journal of Abnormal and Social Psychology*, 1964, **68**, 367–380.

Swanson, G. E. A preliminary laboratory study of the acting crowd. *American Sociological Review*, 1953, **18**, 522–533.

Walster, E., & Berscheid, E. The effects of time on cognitive consistency. In R. Abelson, E. Aronson, W. McGuire, T. Newcomb, M. J. Rosenberg, & P. Tannenbaum (Eds.), *Sourcebook of cognitive consistency*. Skokie, Ill.: Rand McNally, 1967.

Wapner, S., & Alper, T. G. The effect of an audience on behavior in a choice situation. *Journal of Abnormal and Social Psychology*, 1952, **47**, 222–229.

Webb, E. J., Campbell, D. T., Schwartz, R. D., & Sechrest, L. *Unobtrusive measures: A survey of non-reactive research in social science*. Skokie, Ill.: Rand McNally, 1966.

Webster's Third New International Dictionary of the English Language: Unabridged. Springfield, Mass.: G. & C. Merriam, 1966.

Weick, K. E. Systematic observational methods. In G. Lindzey & E. Aronson (Eds.), *Handbook of social psychology*. (Rev. ed.) Reading, Mass.: Addison-Wesley, 1967.

White, R. W. Motivation reconsidered: The concept of competence. *Psychological Review*, 1959, **66**, 297–333.

17 some strategic considerations for future research on social-psychological stress

Joseph E. McGrath

One important aim of the conference which this book reports, and of its accompanying research effort, was to identify issues crucial for future research on human stress and to articulate, in so far as possible, systematic programs for long-range research on those issues.

There are, of course, countless worthwhile research topics pertinent to investigation of human stress. Many are mentioned in earlier chapters. They could not begin to be listed here, nor would such a list be profitable. This chapter will attempt to recapitulate certain strategic themes which have already been noted, so as to give them special emphasis.

The first of these strategic themes is the need to approach the problem of stress systematically, with a set of concepts that encompasses the full sequence of events (objective demand, subjective demand, response, and consequences) and with an approach aimed at seeking the linkages among the parts of this sequence.

There is a need, also, for stress research that uses multiple levels or degrees of potentially stressful conditions rather than just stress versus nonstress. Such research would permit exploration of a number of key issues. It would permit a critical test of the hypothesis that there is a U-shaped relationship between level of demand and stress effects— or of alternative hypotheses about the shape of that relationship. Furthermore, use of multilevel stressor conditions would permit us to explore the relation between stress effects produced by overload and underload, in order to determine whether these are similar or comparable phenomena. Moreover, we could at the same time investigate the comparability of stress effects produced by shifts in demand and those produced by shifts in capability. Finally, such multilevel stressor studies would give us the opportunity to calibrate "degrees of demand" and "degrees of stress," and ultimately, to build commensurate measures.

Another apparent need is for stress research that uses multiple stress conditions *and* multiple measures of stress effects. Such studies also open the door for investigation of several key issues. First, they would permit us to search for convergences and divergences—in the sense of the multitrait multimethod paradigm—among different measures of stress effects. Such studies would also permit us to utilize the ipsative strategy, or alternatives to it, in a search for personal correlates of sensitivity to particular kinds of stress conditions. Multistressor, multimeasure studies would also make it possible to examine divergent patterns of stress response to search for personal correlates of those coping patterns. In this way, we may come to understand better the complexities of human coping responses.

The problem of external validity—generalizability—is critical for stress research. In that light, certain features of the strategies and settings of stress research are important. We need stress research which permits subjects to choose among the complete range of potential alternative responses to stress, including ignoring or escaping the situation or otherwise preventing the occurrences of stress and its consequences. We need stress research in settings where responses are perceived by the subject as having important consequences for him. We need stress research which encompasses relatively long segments of the subject's life, and which deals with stress or conditions indigenous to that life. And we need procedures and measures which are unobtrusive or nonreactive, that is, which do not themselves change the phenomena to be measured.

Temporal parameters are also crucial in stress research. We need studies which explore the temporal dynamics of stress: temporal aspects of demand; temporal variations in capabilities; temporal requirements for response; temporal artifacts of our measures; and, above all, crucial temporal features of the coping process.

Related to the temporal problem is that of setting, especially microsettings. We need stress research which deals, simultaneously, with physical, social, and temporal aspects of microsettings, and does so in ways that permit us to learn about their joint or interactive effects within the stress sequence.

And we badly need research that studies the coping process itself. Such studies need a broad conception of coping. That conception must take into account preventive or anticipatory coping as well as adjustive coping. It must look at the consequences of flexible coping styles as well as the consequences of consistent use of various single coping strategies. It must recognize the cognitive or skill components, as well as the psychodynamic components, of adaptation to stress. It must recognize that much human coping behavior is a temporally extended and continuous process, rather than an instantaneous, one-shot resolution to stress.

Over-all, then, we need stress research which deals—simultaneously and strategically—with four main axes of variation within the stress problem: stressor situations (that is, settings, tasks, stimuli, and so forth); stress responses (that is, coping behaviors); time; and individual differences. We need to apply some multivariate rationale (such as the new three-mode factor analysis) to investigate the interplay of these four sets of factors. Within that rationale, we could seek the answers to a number of pressing questions in the stress area, such as:

1. Are there "types" of persons, in regard to: (a) which stressor conditions they are sensitive to; (b) which coping patterns they are apt to use; and (c) which stressor-coping combinations are typical for them?

2. If so, are there measurable correlates of these person types—personality, ability, role occupancy, or other person properties?

3. Are there convergent subsets of stressor conditions, each specifying a "type" of stressor, and each cluster differentiated or diverging from other stressor types?

4. Are there convergent subsets of stress responses, each cluster specifying a response pattern or coping pattern, and divergences between different coping patterns?

5. Are there systematic effects through time, and can we identify temporal patterns of (a) stress effects or (b) stress response? If so, are these temporal patterns systematically related to "types" of stressors, coping behaviors, or person types?

These brief indications of some strategic research needs, of course, point to studies which will be tremendously complex and difficult to implement. But we may well be past the time—if there ever was a time—when it was meaningful to do simple or easy studies in the stress area. Any one isolated stress study will probably not advance our cumulative knowledge about human stress to a degree commensurate with its cost, however clever or well gimmicked it may be, if it is: (1) badly designed; (2) uses single stressor conditions or single measures; (3)

uses inadequate sampling; or (4) tries to infer change from cross-sectional comparisons.

There is a strong emphasis here, on method and measurement, and particularly on developing methods and measures which can be applied over a wide range of specific settings. With such methods and measures, then successive studies can be more comparable, and thus can potentially contribute to a truly cumulative body of knowledge about human stress. Without generalizable methods and measures, the stress research literature will surely fractionate still further—leading to more and more concentration of effort within narrower enclaves, each bounded by a single method, setting, or measure, and unrelated to one another.

Good long-range research planning must make a substantial commitment to the need for improvements in method. Adequate methods are the *sine qua non* for effective research in any field. New methods, in any field, can identify new issues not previously visible and can make old issues amenable to research. They can also indicate that certain issues previously considered vital are really unimportant artifacts of earlier methods.

But too often, in program planning, development of methods is presumed to be a natural and more or less routine part of the process of doing studies. Hence, resources devoted to development of tools all too often must be "bootlegged" out of resources planned for study of substantive issues. They are seldom adequate to the task.

Part of the reason for the lack of commitment of resources to methodology lies in the support and reinforcement systems of American behavioral science. Methodological studies—one is tempted to say *mere* methodological studies—are less glamorous, more pedestrian, than studies of exciting substantive issues. Research to develop methods has a built-in instrumental quality; methods are means not ends. Better methods only open possibilities and raise questions; they never "solve" any substantive problems.

For these and other reasons, method-oriented research often seems to be less highly valued, both by those who support behavioral science research and by the scientific community to whom investigators look for evaluations of their work, than research aimed at direct test of hypotheses or direction solution of pressing problems. It seems clear though, from the material in this book as well as from the other recent integrative efforts in this area, that much basic groundwork in the development of methods is needed before the many exciting theoretical and practical issues about social-psychological stress can really be attacked effectively.

We have tried, throughout the book, to pose and explore some of those issues, and to point up some of the methodological problems that accompany them. We can perhaps best close this book by presenting a plea for a more balanced allocation of resources and efforts in future research on stress, so that the underlying methodological needs can receive more attention than they have. This probably implies the need for more long-term programs, rather than short "projects," so that investigators can afford to invest time and effort in development of adequate tools. It also implies the need for broader programs—in the sense that investigators develop and test their hypotheses, and their methods, in multiple settings and under a range of conditions.

There are many interesting and important substantive issues within the stress area and no one study or program can tackle them all. And there are many useful approaches, not just one, for research on any one of the issues. But in whatever subject area and with whatever research approach, the clear and central need is that future research on stress be *systematic* not superficial, *comprehensive* not casual, *programmatic* not piecemeal.